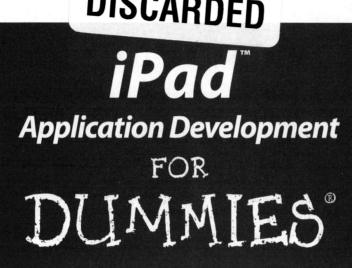

iPad™
Application Development
FOR
DUMMIES®

by Neal Goldstein and Tony Bove

Wiley Publishing, Inc.

iPad™ Application Development For Dummies®

Published by
Wiley Publishing, Inc.
111 River Street
Hoboken, NJ 07030-5774

www.wiley.com

Copyright © 2010 by Wiley Publishing, Inc., Indianapolis, Indiana

Published by Wiley Publishing, Inc., Indianapolis, Indiana

Published simultaneously in Canada

For general information on our other products and services, please contact our Customer Care Department within the U.S. at 877-762-2974, outside the U.S. at 317-572-3993, or fax 317-572-4002.

For technical support, please visit www.wiley.com/techsupport.

Wiley also publishes its books in a variety of electronic formats. Some content that appears in print may not be available in electronic books.

Library of Congress Control Number: 2010925696

ISBN: 978-0-470-58447-7

Manufactured in the United States of America

10 9 8 7 6 5 4 3 2 1

WILEY

About the Authors

Neal Goldstein is a recognized leader in making state-of-the-art and cutting-edge technologies practical for commercial and enterprise development. He was one of the first technologists to work with commercial developers at firms such as Apple Computer, Lucasfilm, and Microsoft to develop commercial applications using object-based programming technologies. He was a pioneer in moving that approach into the corporate world for developers at Liberty Mutual Insurance, USWest (now Verizon), National Car Rental, EDS, and Continental Airlines, showing them how object-oriented programming could solve enterprise-wide problems. His book (with Jeff Alger) on object-oriented development, *Developing Object-Oriented Software for the Macintosh* (Addison Wesley, 1992), introduced the idea of scenarios and patterns to developers.

Neal was an early advocate of the Microsoft .NET framework and successfully introduced it into many enterprises, including Charles Schwab. He was one of the earliest developers of Service Oriented Architecture (SOA), and as Senior Vice President of Advanced Technology and the Chief Architect at Charles Schwab, he built an integrated SOA solution that spanned the enterprise, from desktop PCs to servers to complex network mainframes. (He holds three patents as a result.) As one of IBM's largest customers, he introduced them to SOA at the enterprise level and encouraged them to head in that direction.

He is currently a principal in mobilefortytwo with four applications (and many more to come, so check regularly) in the App Store — *Photographing San Francisco Digital Field Guide, Photographing Yosemite Digital Field Guide, Photographing New York Digital Field Guide,* and *Photographing Washington Digital Field Guide.* These apps take the information and tools needed to take postcard perfect pictures and turn them into something that a photographer can use and apply in the field.

He started his writing career with *Developing Object-Oriented Software for the Macintosh: Analysis, Design, and Programming* (Addison-Wesley). He is currently passionate about the real value that mobile devices can provide and has written several books on iPhone programming, including *iPhone Application Development For Dummies,* both editions, *Objective-C For Dummies*, and he coauthored (with Tony) *iPhone Application Development For Dummies* (all from Wiley).

Tony Bove is crazy about the iPad, iPod, and iPhone, and not only provides free tips on his Web site (www.tonybove.com) but also developed an iPhone application (Tony's Tips for iPhone Users) and is fast developing an iPad app. Tony has written more than two dozen books on computing, desktop publishing, and multimedia, including *iPod & iTunes For Dummies* (Wiley), *Just Say No to Microsoft* (No Starch Press), *The Art of Desktop Publishing* (Bantam), and a series of books about Macromedia Director, Adobe Illustrator, and PageMaker, and he coauthored (with Neal) *iPhone Application Development For Dummies* (Wiley). Tony founded Desktop *Publishing/Publish* magazine and the *Inside Report on New Media* newsletter, and wrote the weekly Macintosh column for *Computer Currents* for over a decade, as well as articles for *NeXTWORLD,* the *Chicago Tribune* Sunday Technology Section, and *NewMedia* for over two decades.

Tracing the personal computer revolution back to the 1960s counterculture, Tony produced a CD-ROM interactive documentary in 1996, *Haight-Ashbury in the Sixties* (featuring music from the Grateful Dead, Janis Joplin, and Jefferson Airplane). He also developed the Rockument music site, www.rockument. com, with commentary and podcasts focused on rock music history. As a founding member of the Flying Other Brothers, which toured professionally and released three commercial CDs, Tony performed with Hall of Fame rock musicians. Tony has also worked as a director of enterprise marketing for leading-edge software companies, as a marketing messaging consultant, and as a communications director and technical publications manager.

Dedication

Neal Goldstein: To my children, Sarah and Evan, and all of my personal and artist friends who have kept me centered on the (real) world outside of writing and technology. But most of all to my wife Linda who is everything that I ever hoped for and more than I deserve. Yes Sam . . . the light at the end of the tunnel is not a freight train.

Tony Bove: I dedicate this book to my mother, my brothers, and my sons, nieces, nephews, their cousins, and all their children . . . the iPad generation.

Authors' Acknowledgments

Neal Goldstein: Thanks to my business partners Jeff Enderwick and Jeff Elias in mobilefortytwo and for their support and picking up the slack while I was engaged in finishing this book. Maggie Canon for putting Tony and I together. Carole Jelen, for her continued work and support in putting this project together.

Acquisitions Editor Kyle Looper for keeping us on track and doing whatever he needed to do to allow us to stay focused on the writing. The Project Editor's Project Editor Paul Levesque who has been known to do even more than six impossible things before breakfast. Copy Editor Virginia Sanders did another great job in helping us make things clearer. Technical reviewer Jesse Fuller added a great second pair of eyes.

Tony Bove: I owe thanks and a happy hour or two to Carole Jelen at Waterside for agenting, to Maggie Canon for putting the authors together, and to Kathy Pennington for support.

Publisher's Acknowledgments

We're proud of this book; please send us your comments at http://dummies.custhelp.com. For other comments, please contact our Customer Care Department within the U.S. at 877-762-2974, outside the U.S. at 317-572-3993, or fax 317-572-4002.

Some of the people who helped bring this book to market include the following:

Acquisitions, Editorial, and Media Development

Senior Project Editor: Paul Levesque

Acquisitions Editor: Kyle Looper

Copy Editor: Virginia Sanders

Technical Editor: Jesse Feiler

Editorial Manager: Leah Cameron

Media Development Project Manager: Laura Moss-Hollister

Media Development Assistant Project Manager: Jenny Swisher

Media Development Associate Producers: Josh Frank, Marilyn Hummel, Douglas Kuhn, and Shawn Patrick

Editorial Assistant: Amanda Graham

Sr. Editorial Assistant: Cherie Case

Cartoons: Rich Tennant (www.the5thwave.com)

Composition Services

Project Coordinator: Kristie Rees

Layout and Graphics: Timothy C. Detrick, Joyce Haughey, Nikki Gately

Proofreaders: Laura Albert, Sossity R. Smith

Indexer: BIM Indexing & Proofreading Services

Publishing and Editorial for Technology Dummies

    Richard Swadley, Vice President and Executive Group Publisher

    Andy Cummings, Vice President and Publisher

    Mary Bednarek, Executive Acquisitions Director

    Mary C. Corder, Editorial Director

Publishing for Consumer Dummies

    Diane Graves Steele, Vice President and Publisher

Composition Services

    Debbie Stailey, Director of Composition Services

Contents at a Glance

Table of Contents

iPad Application Development For Dummies

Chapter 2: Creating a Compelling User Experience 29
Deep Thoughts on the User Experience 30
Creating Compelling Content...32
Focusing on the task at hand 33
Maintaining consistency with the user's world 34
Modeling apps on real-world metaphors.........................35
Engaging the user..35
Making it obvious..36
Using stunning graphics with aesthetic integrity...........37
Designing the User Experience 38
Understanding the real-world context 38
Doing it better on the iPad..39
Playing to the iPad's Strengths 40
Sensing multifinger gestures 41
Tracking orientation and motion....................................41
Displaying stunning graphics and images 42
Playing and recording content..42
Knowing the location of the device 42
Accessing the Internet...43
Avoiding Practices that Get Apps Rejected 43

Chapter 3: The App Store Is Not Enough 45
Why People Buy Apps from the App Store 46
Finding out how to reach your potential customers.......47
Marketing 101: Pricing your app.....................................49
Knowing Your Customers..50
Tracking downloads 51
Adding analytical code to your app 53
Putting ads in your app..54
Deploying the In App Purchase Feature 54
Links Are Not Enough 57
Using iTunes affiliate links 58
Making use of user reviews 58
Going social 59
Updating your app for attention 60
Buying advertising and publicity....................................60

Part II: Becoming a Real Developer 63

Chapter 4: Enlisting in the Developer Corps 65
Becoming a Registered Developer 66
Joining the Developer Program 70
Exploring the iPhone Dev Center 74
Looking forward to using the SDK 76
Resources in the Dev Center 77
Downloading the SDK...78
Getting Yourself Ready for the SDK 80

Introduction

The world stood on its toes as Steve Jobs announced the iPad in January 2010, as "our most advanced technology in a magical and revolutionary device at an unbelievable price."

Do you believe in magic? The iPad has that magical quality of disappearing into your hands as you explore content with it. You have to hold one and use it to understand that feeling of the hardware disappearing — you have the software application itself in your hands, with no extraneous buttons and controls in the way of your experience with the content. And yes, the music is groovy — it's based on the iPod and iPhone.

But the iPad is more than groovy: It's a game changer for the Internet as a publishing medium, for the software industry with regard to applications, and for the mobile device industry with regard to the overall digital media experience. The form factor, portability, swift performance and software experience changes the game with all devices that access the Internet. And I'm tickled pink to be writing about developing software for it at this early stage of its evolution, because I know the iPad will in fact revolutionize portable computing and Internet access.

Due to the success of the iPhone and iPod touch, the App Store has grown to become the repository of over 140,000 applications, which collectively are driving innovation beyond the reach of other mobile devices — and all these apps already run on the iPad. Opportunities are wide open for inventions that build on all the strengths of iPhone apps, but take advantage of the iPad's larger display.

As I continue to explore the iPad as a new platform, I keep finding more possibilities for applications that never existed before. The iPad is truly a mobile computer with a decent display. Its hardware and software make it possible to wander the world, or your own neighborhood, and stay connected to whomever and whatever you want to. It enables a new class of here-and-now applications that enable you to access content-rich services and view information about what's going on around you and where you are, and you can interact with those services or with others on the Internet.

One of the hallmarks of a great iPad application is that it leverages the iPad's unique hardware and operating system (iPhone OS). The iPhone SDK, which you use to develop iPad applications, includes tools such as MapKit, which makes it much easier to use the location-based features of the iPad in an application. MapKit makes it possible for even a beginning developer to take full advantage of knowing the location of the device, and we've included the code for an example app (called iPadTravel411) to show you how. And the frameworks supplied in the SDK are especially rich and mature. All you really have to do is add your application's user interface and functionality to the framework, and then *poof . . .* an instant application.

If you're familiar with older versions of the SDK, you're in for a pleasant surprise: SDK version 3.2, which includes Xcode 3.2.2, is a lot, lot better and easier to use. This new edition is based on iPhone OS 3.2 (the latest version of the iPhone operating system) and Xcode 3.2.2.

If this seems too good to be true, well, okay, it *is,* sort of. What's really hard, after you've learned the language and framework, is how to create a structure for the iPad application's data, and models for the logic of how the application should work. Although there are lots of resources, the problem is exactly that: There are *lots* of resources — as in *thousands* of pages of documentation! You may get through a small fraction of the documentation before you just can't take it anymore and plunge right into coding. Naturally enough, there will be a few false starts and blind alleys until you find your way, but I predict that after reading this book, it'll be (pretty much) smooth sailing.

Editor's note: Both authors (Tony and Neal) have previously published applications for the iPhone — you can find several of Neal's apps, including ReturnMeTo, *in the App Store, along with Tony's app,* Tony's Tips for iPhone Users.

About This Book

iPad Application Development For Dummies is a beginner's guide to developing applications for the iPad, which runs the iPhone OS. And not only do you *not* need any iPad (or iPhone) development experience to get started, you don't need any Macintosh development experience either. I expect you to come as a blank slate, ready to be filled with useful information and new ways to do things.

Because of the nature of the iPad, you can create content-rich, truly immersive applications that can be really powerful (as well as amazing to look at). And because you can also start small and create real applications that do something important for a user, it's relatively easy to transform yourself from "I know nothing" into a developer who, though not (yet) a superstar, can still crank out quite a respectable application.

The iPad can be home to some pretty fancy software as well — so I take you on a journey through building not just a simple app but also an industrial-strength app, so that you know the ropes for developing your own app.

This book distills the hundreds (or even thousands) of pages of Apple documentation, not to mention my own development experiences, into only what's necessary to start you developing real applications. But this is no recipe book that leaves it up to you to put it all together; rather, it takes you through the frameworks and iPad architecture in a way that gives you a solid foundation in how applications really work on the iPad. This book acts as a roadmap to expand your knowledge as you need to.

It's a multiple-course banquet, intended to make you feel satisfied (and really full) at the end.

Conventions Used in This Book

This book guides you through the process of building iPad applications. Throughout, you use the provided iPhone OS framework classes for the iPad (and create new ones, of course) and code them using the Objective-C programming language.

Code examples in this book appear in a monospaced font so they stand out a bit better. That means the code you'll see will look like this:

```
#import <UIKit/ UIKit.h>
```

Objective-C is based on C, which (I want to remind you) *is* case-sensitive, so please enter the code that appears in this book *exactly* as it appears in the text. This book also uses the standard Objective-C naming conventions — for example, class names always start with a capital letter, and the names of methods and instance variables always start with a lowercase letter.

All URLs in this book appear in a monospaced font as well:

```
www.nealgoldstein.com
www.tonybove.com
```

If you're ever uncertain about anything in the code, you can always look at the source code on Neal's Web site at www.nealgoldstein.com. (You can grab the same material from the *For Dummies* Web site at www.dummies.com/go/ipaddevfd.) From time to time, he provides updates for the code there and posts other things you might find useful. Tony offers tips about everything from developing apps and marketing them to using the iPad, iPhone, and iTunes, all at www.tonybove.com.

Foolish Assumptions

To begin programming your iPad applications, you need an Intel-based Macintosh computer with the latest version of the Mac OS on it. (No, you can't program iPad applications on the iPad.) You also need to download the iPhone Software Development Kit (SDK) — which is free — but you do have to become a registered iPhone developer before you can do that. (Don't worry; I show you how in Chapter 4.) And, oh yeah, you need an iPad. You won't start running your application on it right away — you'll use the Simulator that Apple provides with the iPhone SDK during the initial stages of development — but at some point, you'll want to test your application on a real, live iPad.

This book assumes that you have some programming knowledge and that you have at least a passing acquaintance with object-oriented programming, using some variant of the C language (such as C++, C#, or maybe even Objective-C). If not, we point out some resources that can help you get up to speed. The examples in this book are focused on the frameworks that come with the SDK; the code is pretty simple (usually) and straightforward. (We won't use this book as a platform to dazzle you with fancy coding techniques.)

This book also assumes that you're familiar with the iPad itself, and that you've at least explored Apple's included applications to get a good working sense of the iPad look and feel. It would also help if you browse the App Store to see the kinds of applications available there, and maybe even download a few free ones (as if I could stop you).

How This Book Is Organized

iPad Application Development For Dummies has five main parts.

Part 1: Creating the Killer App

Part I introduces you to the iPad world. You find out what makes a great iPad application and how to exploit the iPad's best features to create a compelling user experience. You also discover the marketing secrets for getting the most out of the Apple App Store and distributing your app to more customers.

Part II: Becoming a Real Developer

In this part, you find out how to become an "official" developer and what you need to do to in order to be able to distribute your iPad applications through the Apple App Store. You go through the process of registering as a developer and downloading the Software Development Kit (SDK) — and then you unpack all the goodies contained therein, including Xcode (the Apple development environment for the OS X operating system) and Interface Builder. Chapter 6 spells out the details of obtaining the proper certificates and submitting your app to the App Store — and the dire consequences of not following the rules.

Part III: Understanding Apps

Part III is deceptively short but intensely illuminating. These two chapters explain the frameworks that form the raw material of your iPad app (which you then refine with your code and user interface objects), and they reveal the design patterns that you should adopt to make use of these frameworks. Part III also describes in detail the lifecycle of an iPad app from launch to termination. When you finish this part, you should have enough information to get started coding your application.

Part IV: Building DeepThoughts

With the basics behind you and a good understanding of the application architecture under your belt, it's finally time to have some fun doing something useful. In this part, I show you how to create an application that is simple enough to understand, and yet demonstrates enough of the building blocks for creating a sophisticated app. I show you how an app fits into the frameworks that do all of the user interface heavy lifting on the iPad. And because you design the app the right way from the start, you can plug in user interface elements with minimal effort using Interface Builder (part of the SDK). No sweat, no bother. Putting this handy little app together will give you some practice at creating a useful iPad program that presents a view of content, responds to simple gestures, and lets users change preference settings. It's a great application to learn about iPad development — it has enough features to be useful as an example, but it's simple enough not to make your head explode.

Part V: Building an Industrial-Strength Application

Part V shows you how to create an application that contains major functionality — I take an idea that was developed for the iPhone and expand it to take advantage of the iPad's capabilities. The app (iPadTravel411) makes it easier to travel by reducing all those hassles of getting to and from a strange airport, getting around a city, getting the best exchange rate, and knowing how much you should tip in a restaurant — that sort of thing. I don't go slogging through every detail, but I demonstrate almost all the technology you need to master if you're going to create a compelling iPad application on your own.

Part VI: The Part of Tens

Part VI consists of some tips to help you avoid having to learn everything the hard way. It talks about approaching application development in an "adult" way right from the beginning (without taking the fun out of it, I assure you).

Icons Used in This Book

This icon indicates a useful pointer that you shouldn't skip.

This icon represents a friendly reminder. It describes a vital point that you should keep in mind while proceeding through a particular section of the chapter.

This icon signifies that the accompanying explanation may be informative (dare I say, interesting?), but it isn't essential to understanding iPad application development. Feel free to skip past these tidbits if you'd like (though skipping while leaning may be tricky).

This icon alerts you to potential problems that you may encounter along the way. Read and obey these blurbs to avoid trouble.

Where to Go from Here

It's time to explore the iPad! If you're nervous, take heart: The iPad is so new, and such rich territory for developers to mine, that no company or individual has a lock on innovating with it. Your idea just might be the killer app everyone's waiting for.

So get ready to have some fun.

Part I
Creating the
Killer App

The 5th Wave   By Rich Tennant

"I build bookshelves and Bernice buys an iPad."

In this part . . .

Υου say you want a revolution? Well, here's the plan: This part lays out what you need to know to get started on the Great iPad Development Trek. After reading this part, you can evaluate your idea for an iPad application, see how it stacks up, and maybe figure out what you have to do to transform it into something that knocks your users' socks off.

- ✔ Chapter 1 describes the features of the iPad and the elements that make a great iPad application. You find out how to exploit the platform's features and embrace its limitations. You also discover how to design with Apple's expectations in mind.

- ✔ Chapter 2 goes into more detail about how to create a compelling user experience with your iPad app. You find out how to design for the iPad and its entirely new set of user interaction features.

- ✔ Chapter 3 explains what motivates your potential customers to download apps, how to reach these customers and learn from them, what marketing methods you can use to drum up interest, and how to determine the right price for your app.

Chapter 1

What Makes a Killer iPad App

Douglas Adams, in the bestseller *The Hitchhiker's Guide to the Galaxy* (conceived in 1971 and published in 1979), introduced the idea of a handy travel guide that looked "rather like a largish electronic calculator," with a hundred tiny flat press buttons and a screen "on which any one of a million 'pages' could be summoned at a moment's notice. It looked insanely complicated, and this is one of the reasons why the snug plastic cover it fitted into had the words DON'T PANIC printed on it in large friendly letters." According to Adams, this guide was published in this form because "if it were printed in normal book form, an interstellar hitchhiker would require several inconveniently large buildings to carry it around in."

The iPad is a hitchhiker's dream come true, and its users don't even have any reason to panic. The only "insanely complicated" part of the iPad experience may be trying to develop a killer app that best exemplifies the iPad's features, but that's why I think this book should have DON'T PANIC printed on its cover — it takes you through the entire process of imagining, creating, developing, testing, and distributing your iPad app. And in this chapter, I talk about what would make that app a killer app.

As you already know, the iPad is a new category of device — located somewhere between a Mac laptop and an iPod touch or iPhone in terms of its capabilities — that evolved from the iPhone design and uses the iPhone Operating System (OS).

The iPad already runs the 140,000+ iPhone apps in the Apple App Store with either pixel-for-pixel accuracy in a black box in the center of the display, or scaled up to full screen (which is done on the fly by doubling the pixels). The

App Store is loaded with travel and digital media apps, so you know already that the iPad as a "Hitchhiker's Guide" is not a fantasy. You may think it a fantasy that you could develop an iPad app in less than two months, starting from where you are now, with no iPad programming experience. But you *can* — the only question is whether you can make a *great* app, or even a *killer* app. To do that, you need to look at what it takes for an iPad app to be truly great.

Figuring Out What Makes a Great iPad Application

You use the same iPhone developer kit, and much of the same code, to develop iPad applications, and the iPad runs the same operating system as the iPhone, but the iPad is a bigger device with more horsepower and a larger display, as shown in Figure 1-1.

For many iPhone app developers, the iPad's larger display alone changes everything. Apple demonstrated exactly how *far* things have changed when the company demonstrated the iWork suite of productivity tools (Keynote for presentations, Numbers for spreadsheets, and Pages for word processing and page formatting) on the iPad, which would be unthinkable for today's iPhone.

Figure 1-1:
The iPad runs the iPhone OS (left) and offers a larger display to show content such as a newspaper (right).

The biggest challenge in making a killer app for the iPad is to design for the iPad *experience,* and one reason why the iPad offers such a better experience than any Windows netbook or tablet computer is its sex appeal (which for many apps can mean *more excellent content* and *finer style*). For example, according to Douglas Adams, the Encyclopedia Galactica describes *alcohol* as "a colorless volatile liquid formed by the fermentation of sugars" and also notes "its intoxicating effect on certain carbon-based life forms." On the other hand, The Hitchhiker's Guide to the Galaxy not only tells you what *alcohol* is, it says "the best drink in existence is the Pan Galactic Gargle Blaster," describes its effect as "like having your brains smashed out by a slice of lemon wrapped round a large gold brick," tells you which planets have bars that offer it and at what prices, and then shows you how to mix one yourself. As Adams points out, "The Hitchhiker's Guide to the Galaxy *sells rather better* than the Encyclopedia Galactica."

If the explosion of new iPhone apps over the last year is any indication, you will want to take advantage of the iPad's sexiness, and that means leveraging its fabulous touch-sensitive interface and other features. Because the iPad evolved from the iPhone design, the iPad has design advantages that make netbooks and laptops feel like the dull Encyclopedia Galactica. Most iPhone apps are designed to take advantage of the iPhone's Multi-Touch display; accelerometer (which detects acceleration, rotation, motion gestures, and tilt); or location services for detecting its physical location — or all three.

But you can create iPad apps that are not just a little bit better than their iPhone counterparts, but a *lot* better (and an order of magnitude more powerful), with an interface that's simpler to use than a Mac.

Providing an immersive experience

An iPad app can offer a more immersive experience compared with an iPhone app by adding *more content* — full pages from the Internet or in memory, maps you can zoom into, full-screen videos and slideshows with music, and so on. People can enjoy this content while away from their desks — on living room couches, in coffee shops, on the train, in outer space — and more easily share it with others, far more easily than they can with an iPhone or iPod touch.

Whenever possible, add a realistic, physical dimension to your application. *The New York Times,* for example, designed an iPad app (refer to Figure 1-1, right side) that offers an immersive experience with the newspaper that includes truly embedded, fully functional videos (not just videos that appear in a separate window), and lets you tap the page to change the layout of columns, resize the text with a pinch, or show pop-up menus for more stories.

Electronic Arts created a version of its popular game Need for Speed for the iPad that feels like you're driving the display with your hands as you steer the car using the iPad like a steering wheel. The high-definition screen is just inches from your face — the field of view and the sensation of speed you get is incredible. The full-screen display is also fully touch sensitive — you can tap on a car and see inside it, flick a lifelike gear shifter to shift gears, and tap the rear-view mirror to look behind you.

Even utility apps can be rethought to be a better experience. On the iPhone, the Contacts app is a streamlined list, but on the iPad, Contacts is an address book with a beautifully tangible look and feel. The more true to life your application looks and behaves, the easier it is for people to understand how it works and the more they enjoy using it.

Making content relevant

An iPad app can present information relevant to where you are, what time it is, what your next activity might be, and how you're holding the device (in portrait or landscape view, tilting and shaking it, and so on), just like an iPhone or iPod touch app.

For example, the version of Google Maps for the iPad displays a full-screen map that can show your location and immediately find commercial establishments nearby. (For example, you can search for "sushi" to find sushi restaurants.)

The iPad platform offers a strong foundation for pinpointing the device's current location on a map, controlling views, managing data, playing multimedia content, switching display orientations, and processing gestures. Because the iPad platform can do all that, an app can know your current location, the hotels or campgrounds you're going to stay at, and the planets you're planning to visit. It can even show videos and play the music of the stars all at the same time. Rather than orbiting some moon while searching maps and brochures, you can know at a glance where you are, how to get to your destination, and what the weather's like so that you know what to wear.

Designing for the touch-display experience

The important design decision to make, whether you're starting from scratch with a new iPad app or evolving one from an iPhone app, is to use the large iPad screen and the new user interface elements to give people access to more information in one place. Although you don't want to pack too much information into one screen, you also want to prevent people from feeling that they must visit many different screens to find what they want. An iPad app can offer the primary content on the Main view and provide additional information or tools in an auxiliary view (such as a *popover* that appears semi-transparently above the Main view) to give users access to functions without requiring them to leave the context of the Main view.

The large iPad screen also gives you a lot more room for multifinger gestures, including gestures made by more than one person. An iPad app can react to gestures and offer touch controls and pop-up settings that are relevant to what you're actually doing in the app and where you place your fingers. With a display the size of a netbook, you have a lot more screen real estate to allow dragging and two-finger gestures with graphics and images, and depending on what you're doing, a tap or gesture on a particular part of the screen can have a particular function. For example, in the Gameloft version of the first-person shooter called *Nova* (as adapted to the iPad), the display size gives you more flexibility than the iPhone version, with more controls and objects such as mini-maps, and you can slide two fingers across the screen to throw grenades.

With all this in mind, there are at least two things that you need to consider — besides functionality, of course — when it comes to creating a great iPad app:

✔ Exploiting the platform and ecosystem

✔ Creating a compelling user experience

The rest of this chapter and Chapter 2 dig more into this Two-Part Rule of Great iPad Applications.

Exploiting the Platform

Okay, enough talk about the iPad's unique experience. Just what exactly is the iPad platform, and what are its features?

The iPad runs iPhone OS 3.2 as its operating system, and iPad apps use many of the same views and controls you used if you already developed an iPhone app. But the design similarities end there. The iPad's *hardware* is ground zero for conceiving the design of an iPad app — it's the place to start dreaming of what kind of experience to provide:

✔ A touch-sensitive display size of 1,024 x 768 pixels that supports multifinger gestures.

✔ The connection features of the iPhone (except phone calls): Wi-Fi and optional 3G Internet access; a compass; location services (although a hardware GPS isn't included in the first version of the iPad, so it isn't as accurate); and the ability to play audio and video with ease.

✔ Flexible orientation — users can tilt it, rotate it, and turn it upside down.

✔ The capability to plug in an external keyboard and use it in place of the onscreen keyboard for extended typing.

✔ The ability for users to dock the iPad and share files with a computer or other iPad users.

Exploiting advantages of the system

One of the keys to creating a great app is taking advantage of what the device offers. In the case of a new platform with new possibilities, such as the iPad, exploiting advantages is especially important. The combination of hardware and system software open up design advantages that depart from the typical design approach for desktop and laptop applications.

For example:

✔ **Multifinger gestures:** Applications respond to multifinger gestures, not mouse clicks. If you design an app that simply uses a single finger tap as if it were a mouse click, you may be missing an opportunity to design a better user experience.

✔ **Movement and orientation:** The iPad includes an accelerometer just like an iPhone and iPod touch, so you can also design apps that detect accelerated movement, as well as change the display for different orientations.

✔ **Split views and unique keyboards:** You can use a Split view to display more than one view onscreen at a time. You can also bring up a special keyboard unique to the task, such as the numbers-and-formulas keyboard that appears in the Numbers app for the iPad.

✔ **Internet access:** Users can send and receive e-mail and browse the Web, as well as sync contacts, calendars, and notes over the Internet, and download content from Apple stores, just like an iPhone or iPod touch.

✔ **Computer sync over USB connection or local area network:** Users can sync their photos, contacts, calendars, music, video, and other content from their computers (again, just like an iPhone or iPod touch), and with some apps (such as Bento from FileMaker), you can sync data over a local area network.

✔ **Television or projection system connection:** Users can connect the iPad to an HDTV or projection system in order to show content to larger audiences.

✓ **Consistent system environment:** The Home button quits your app, and the volume controls take care of audio, just like you'd expect them to. User preference settings can be made available in the Settings application (to avoid cluttering up your app's user interface) and your iPad and iPhone/iPod touch apps can coexist on an iPad with Web services and apps created in HTML5.

✓ **Breathtaking imagery:** Photos and video already look fantastic on this display, but the artwork you create yourself for your app should be set to 24 bits (8 bits each for red, green, and blue), plus an 8-bit alpha channel to specify how a pixel's color should be merged with another pixel when the two are overlaid one on top of the other. In general, the PNG format is recommended for graphics and artwork.

In the following sections, you get to dive into some of the major features, grouped into the following major areas:

✓ Accessing the Internet

✓ Tracking location

✓ Tracking motion

✓ Supporting multifinger gestures and touches,

✓ Playing content

✓ Accessing the content of Apple's supplied apps (such as Contacts and Photos)

✓ Taking advantage of the iPad display.

Accessing the Internet

An iPad can access Web sites and servers on the Internet through Wi-Fi or optional 3G services. This Internet access gives you the ability to create apps that can provide real-time information. An app can tell a user, for example, that the next tour at the Tate Modern in London is at 3 p.m.

This kind of access also allows you, as the developer, to go beyond the limited memory and processing power of the device and access large amounts of data stored on servers, or even offload the processing. You don't need all the information for every city in the world stored on your iPad. You can send the request to a server for all that information, especially information that changes often.

This technique is called *client-server computing* — a well-established software architecture where the client provides a way to make requests to a server on a network that's just waiting for the opportunity to do something. A Web browser is an example of a client accessing information from other Web sites that act as servers.

Knowing the location of the user

You can create an app that can determine the device's current location or even be notified when that location changes, using the iPad's location services. As people move, it may make sense for your app to tailor itself to where the user is, moment by moment.

Many iPad and iPhone apps use location information to tell you where the nearest coffee house is or even where your friends are. The iPadTravel411 sample application described in Part V uses this information to tell you where *you* are and give you directions to your hotel.

When you know the user's location, you can even put it on a map, along with other places he or she may be interested in. You find out how easy it is to add a map to your app in Chapter 14.

Tracking orientation and motion

The iPad contains three *accelerometers* — devices that detect changes in movement. Each device measures change along one of the primary axes in three-dimensional space. An app can, for example, know when the user has turned the device from vertical to horizontal, and it can change the view from portrait to landscape if doing so makes for a better user experience.

You can also determine other types of motion such as a sudden start or stop in movement (think of a car accident or fall) or the user shaking the device back and forth. It makes some way-cool features easy to implement — for example, the Etch-A-Sketch metaphor of shaking the iPad to undo an operation. You can even control a game by moving the iPad like a controller — such as the aforementioned Need for Speed game for the iPad (Electronic Arts), in which you drive the car by using the iPad like a steering wheel.

Tracking user's fingers on the screen

People use their fingers to select and manipulate objects on the iPad screen. The moves that do the work, called *gestures,* give the user a heightened sense of control and intimacy with the device. Several standard gestures — tap, double-tap, pinch-close, pinch-open, flick, and drag — are used in the applications supplied with the iPad.

You may want to stick with the standard gestures in your app, just because folks are already aware of (and comfortable with) the current pool, but the iPad's multifinger gesture support lets you go beyond standard gestures when appropriate. Because you can monitor the movement of each finger to detect gestures, you can create your own.

Playing content

Your iPad app can easily play audio and video. You can play sound effects or take advantage of the multichannel audio and mixing capabilities available to you. You can also play back many standard movie file formats, configure the aspect ratio, and specify whether controls are displayed. You can put up pages that look like Web pages or book pages if you want, and you can easily mix content for an immersive experience.

Accessing information from Apple's apps

Your app can access the user's information in the Contacts app on the iPad and display that information in a different way or use it as information in your application.

Your app can also access the Photo library in the iPad Photos app, not only to display them, but also to use (or even modify) them. For example, the Photos app lets you add a photo to a contact, and several applications enable you to edit your photos on the iPad itself.

Living large on the big screen

The iPad display offers enough space to show a laptop application (which is one reason why Web pages look so great). You can organize your app with a master and detailed list, or a source list layout (with a view) similar to the Mac OS X versions of iTunes and iPhoto and exemplified by the Photos, Contacts, and Keynote apps on the iPad.

If you're familiar with iPhone apps and Mac OS X applications, think somewhere in-between. With the iPad touch-sensitive display, you no longer have to create different screens of menus (as you might for an iPhone app) or deploy drop-down menus and toolbars (as you might for an Mac OS X app) to offer many functions.

For example, to crop and mask out parts of an image in Apple's Keynote app for the iPad (which lets you create slideshows), you don't have to select a photo and then hunt for the cropping tool or select a menu item — just double-tap the image, and a mask slider appears. In Apple's Numbers app for the iPad, if you double-tap a numeric formula, the app displays a special numeric and function keyboard rather than a full text keyboard — and the app can recognize what you're doing and finish the function (such as a Sum function) for you.

These are examples of redesigning a known type of application to get rid of (or at least minimize) that modal experience of using a smartphone app — in which you have only one path of communication to perform a task or supply a response. iPad applications should allow people to interact with them in nonlinear ways. Modality prevents this freedom by interrupting a user's workflow and forcing the user to choose a particular path.

Lists are a common way to efficiently display large amounts of information in iPhone apps. Lists are very useful in iPad apps, too, but you should take this opportunity to investigate whether you can present the same information in a richer way on the larger display.

Embracing the iPad's Limitations

Along with all those features, however, the iPad has some limitations. The key to successful app development — and to not making yourself too crazy — is to understand those limitations, live and program within them, and even learn to love them. (It can be done. Honest.) These constraints help you understand the kinds of applications that are right for this device.

Often, it's likely that if you *can't* do something (easily, anyway) because of the iPad's limitations, then maybe you shouldn't.

The iPad evolved from the iPhone and iPod touch, and there are related limitations you need to consider, as well as a few things left out. So learn to live with and embrace some facts of iPad life:

- ✔ Users have fat fingers. That may be easy to deal with, but keep in mind that you may want to design a multiuser app for the iPad that takes into account multiple fingers. (Anyone for a nice game of air hockey?)

- ✔ Memory and battery power are limited, just like an iPhone or iPod touch. This limitation may or may not be a decisive factor, depending on what kind of app you want to create, but smaller apps generally perform better.

- ✔ Users can run only one application at a time — again, just like an iPhone or iPod touch. Although this limitation may change in the future, you need to keep this in mind before designing an app that relies on another app (such as one that offers links that can open the Safari browser).

- ✔ A camera isn't included in the first version of the iPad, but your iPad app can access the synced Photo library as well as synced contacts.

The next sections help get you closer to a state of iPad enlightenment.

Designing for fingers

Although the Multi-Touch interface is a feature of both the iPad and the iPhone/iPod touch, it brings with it some limitations — although not as many as with the smaller iPhone/iPod touch displays.

First of all, fingers aren't as precise as a mouse pointer, which makes some operations even more difficult on an iPhone or iPod touch than on an iPad (text selection, for example). Still, due to fat fingers, user-interface elements need to be large enough and spaced far enough apart so that users' fingers can find their way around the interface comfortably. Apple recommends that anything a user has to select or manipulate with a finger be a minimum of 44 x 44 pixels in size.

Because it's so much easier to make a mistake using fingers, you also need to ensure that you implement a robust — yet unobtrusive — Undo mechanism. You don't want to have your users confirm every action (it makes using the app tedious), but on the other hand, you don't want your app to let anybody mistakenly delete a page without asking, "Are you *sure* this is what you *really* want to do?" Lost work is worse than tedious. Fortunately, the iPad supports the same shake-to-undo feature as the iPhone.

Balancing memory and battery life

As an app designer for the iPad, you have several balancing acts to keep in mind:

- ✔ Although significant by the original Macintosh's standards, the computer power and amount of memory on the iPad are limited.

- ✔ Although access to the Internet can mitigate the power and memory limitations by storing data and (sometimes) offloading processing to a server, those Internet operations eat up the battery faster.

- ✔ Although the iPad power-management system conserves power by shutting down any hardware features that are not currently being used, a developer must manage the trade-off between all those busy features and shorter battery life. Any app that takes advantage of Internet access, core location, and a couple of accelerometers is going to eat up the batteries.

The iPad is particularly unforgiving when it comes to memory usage. If you run out of memory, in order to prevent corruption of other apps and memory the system will simply *shut down your app* (unfortunately not to the tune of "Shut Down" by the Beach Boys).

This just goes to show that not *all* limitations can be exploited as "features."

Why Develop iPad Applications?

Because you can. Because it's fun. And because the time has come (today!). Developing iPad apps can be the most fun you've had in years, with very little investment of time and money (compared with developing for platforms like Windows). Here's why:

- ✔ **iPad apps are usually bite-sized, which means they're small enough to get your head around.** A single developer — or one with a partner and maybe some graphics support — can do them. You don't need a 20-person project with endless procedures and processes and meetings to create something valuable.

- ✔ **The apps use the most innovative platform available for mobile computing.** The iPad is a game-changer. It's completely changing the Internet as a publishing medium, the software industry with regard to applications, and the mobile device industry with regard to the overall digital media experience.

- ✔ **The free Software Development Kit (SDK) makes development as easy as possible.** This book reveals the SDK in all its splendor and glory. If you can't stand waiting, you *could* go on to Chapter 4, register as an iPhone/iPad developer, and download the SDK . . . but (fair warning) jumping the gun leads to extra hassle. It's worth getting a handle on the ins and outs of iPad app development beforehand.

The iPad has three other advantages that are important to you as a developer:

- ✔ **You can distribute your app through the App Store.** Apple will list your app in the App Store in the category you specify, and the store takes care of credit-card processing (if you charge for your app), hosting, downloading, notifying users of updates, and all those things that most developers hate doing. Developers name their own prices for their creations or distribute them free; Apple gets 30 percent of the sales price of commercial apps, with the developer getting the rest. However, keep in mind that Apple must approve your app before it appears in the App Store — see Chapter 6 for details on submitting your app and jumping through the hoops to get it approved.

- ✔ **Apple has a developer program.** To get your app into the store, you have to pay $99 to join the iPhone Developer Program (which includes iPad development support). (An enterprise pays $299 to join up.) But that's it. There are none of the infamous hidden charges that you often encounter, especially when dealing with credit-card companies. Go to the Apple iPhone Developer site (`http://developer.apple.com/iphone/program`) and click the Enroll Now button. Chapter 6 describes how to work with the App Store to get your apps published.

✔ **It's a business tool.** The iPad has become an acceptable business tool, in part because it has tight security as well as support for Microsoft Exchange and Office. This happy state of affairs expands the possible audience for your application.

Developing with Apple's Expectations in Mind

Just as the iPad can extend the reach of the user, the device possibilities and the development environment can extend your reach as a developer. It helps to understand Apple's perspective on what iPad apps should be — the company clearly has done some serious thinking about it, far longer than anybody else out there, having taken years to bring the iPad to market under a veil of secrecy.

So what does Apple think? Spokespeople often talk about three different application styles:

✔ **Productivity applications use and manipulate information.** The iPadTravel411 sample app that I show in this book is an example, and so are Bento (FileMaker), and Apple's iWork apps — Keynote, Pages, and Numbers. Common to all these apps is the use and manipulation of multiple types of information. (I'm not talking about the Productivity category in the App Store — that's a marketing designation.)

✔ **Utility applications perform simple, highly defined tasks.** The preinstalled Weather app is an example — it deals only with the weather data. The Brushes app for painting (Steve Sprang) is considered a utility, as it performs a simple, highly defined task. (Again, I'm not talking about the Utilities category in the App Store, although many of those apps are considered utility apps because they perform simple, highly defined tasks.)

✔ **Immersive applications are focused on delivering — and having the user interact with — content in a visually rich environment.** A game is a typical example of an immersive application.

Although these categories help you understand how Apple thinks about iPad apps (at least publicly), don't let them get in the way of your creativity. You've probably heard *ad nauseam* about stepping outside the box. But hold on to your lunch; the iPad "box" isn't even a box yet. So here's a more extreme metaphor: Try diving into the abyss and coming up with something really new.

An Overview of the Development Cycle

To keep from drowning in that abyss, you need a plan to guide you through it. Socrates anticipated software development when he said that there's nothing stable in human affairs. Tacitus, with more data in hand 450 years later, saw that in all things there is a law of cycles. By the late 1960s, the Jefferson Airplane singers were singing, "go with the natural flow, like water off a spinning ball."

In plain words, your software development plan is a cycle; perhaps a vicious cycle, but it can be a cycle through the park. You may repeat procedures within the cycle iteratively until you get it right, but the key to understanding the cycle is the recognition that once you spin off version 1 of your app, you start all over again to develop an update.

In general terms, the software development cycle is the process of creating or altering a software product or service. Theorists have created models and methodologies for defining this cycle. Although there are at least half a dozen models (Neal's a recovering software development methodologist), the one I go through here is pretty simple and is well suited for the iPad to boot. Here goes:

1. Defining the problems

2. Designing the user experience

    a. Understanding the real-world context

    b. Understanding the device context

    c. Categorizing the problems and defining the solutions

3. Creating the program architecture

    a. A Main view

    b. Content views

    c. View controllers

    d. Models

4. Writing the code

5. Doing it until you get it right

Of course, the actual analysis, design, and programming (not to mention testing) process has a bit more to it than this — and the specification and design definitely involve more than what you see in this book. But from a process perspective, it's pretty close to the real thing. It does give you an idea of the questions you need to ask — and have answered — in order to develop an effective iPad application.

A word of caution, though. Even though iPad apps are much easier to get your head around than, say, a full-blown enterprise service-oriented architecture, they come equipped with a unique set of challenges. Between the iPad platform limitations and the high expectation of all the new iPad users, you'll have your hands full.

The Sample Applications

It's hard enough to understand how to develop an app, and even harder if the first example you turn to is too complex to get your head around. The first sample app, DeepThoughts (shown in Figure 1-2), which you find out how to build in Part IV, is simple enough to understand, and yet it demonstrates enough of the building blocks for creating a sophisticated iPad app that you should have no trouble following along and building it. With a little more (although not much more) work, you can use the development environment to actually create something of value.

DeepThoughts displays whatever text you enter in a flowing animation that fills the display, supposedly suggesting a meditative state (as in "peace love groovy music"). You can speed up or slow down the animation by swiping left or right, so you find out how to deal with that simple gesture, as well as with tapping an Info button or the display to change the text and speed.

After you know a bit more about the application design cycle and what makes a good user interface, and even more (actually quite a bit more) about the iPad technologies that work behind the screen — such as frameworks, windows, views, and view controllers — and then just a few more details about getting your app ready for the App Store and the public, you're ready to do some real coding — the DeepThoughts app.

After that, you find out about the design of the iPadTravel411 app (shown in Figure 1-3), starting in Chapter 13. You find out how to use a Split view, present a map, work with Table views, add content, access data on the Web, include data with your app, and allow users to set preferences.

Figure 1-2:
This book
will provoke
Deep
Thoughts.

Figure 1-3:
This sample
app may
provoke
a trip to
London.

What's Next

You must be raring to go now and just can't wait to download the Software Development Kit (SDK). That's exactly what many new developers do — and later are sorry that they didn't spend more time upfront understanding the iPad user experience, how applications work in the iPad environment, and the guidelines that Apple enforces for apps to be approved for the App Store.

So be patient. The Hitchhiker's Guide to the Galaxy, that wonderful fantasy of an iPad from 1979, suggests that since space is "big, really big . . . you just won't believe how vastly hugely mind-bogglingly big it is," and suggests that you bring a towel. The guide says a towel "is about the most massively useful thing an interstellar hitchhiker can have." (Again with Douglas Adams? But I promise not to get into the meaning of life, the universe, and everything, or the ultimate question — for which the answer is 42.) This book is your towel for the journey. The following chapters cover all the aspects of development you need to know before you spend time coding. Then, I promise, it's off to the stars.

Chapter 2

Creating a Compelling User Experience

*W*hen you have a handle on the possibilities and limitations of the iPad, your imagination is free to soar to create a compelling user experience. But what is a "compelling user experience," really?

For openers, a compelling user experience has to result from the interaction of several factors:

✔ Interesting, useful, and plentiful content that fills the display in an immersive experience

✔ Content relevant to what you're doing, where you are, what your next activity might be, and how you're holding the device

✔ An intuitive, well-designed user interface designed for a full touch-sensitive display that supports multifinger gestures

The iPad allows both immediacy and intimacy as it blends mobility and the power of the desktop to create a new kind of freedom. I like to use the term *user experience* because it implies more than a pretty user interface and nice graphics. A *compelling* user experience enables users to do what they need to do with a minimum of fuss and bother. It includes meeting the expectations of the user based on the *context* — all the stuff going on around a user — in which they're using the app. A guidebook app may have a great user interface, for example, but it may not give me the most up-to-date information or let me know a tour of the Houses of Parliament is leaving in five minutes from the main entrance. Without those added touches, I don't consider an app compelling.

If you've developed applications for a desktop or laptop, or even for an iPhone or iPod touch, you have to rethink your design for any new app you create for the iPad, because the iPad is a singular game-changer that introduces an entirely new set of user interaction features. Albert Einstein once said that technological change is like an axe in the hands of a pathological criminal. If you've developed user interfaces before, you may want to adopt this attitude — grab an axe to chop through your previous design ideas and take a hard look at the newest apps that are just now arriving on the iPad (especially the ones from Apple), and remember Pablo Picasso's immortal words: "Bad artists copy. Good artists steal."

Apple goes out of its way to provide sample code for many of the neater tricks and features out there, all in hopes of demystifying how they work. Apple's supplied apps, including Contacts, Photos, and Calendar, are already on your iPad and ready to be examined for user interface ideas. In addition, Apple's iWork set of apps for the iPad — Keynote for slide presentations, Numbers for spreadsheets, and Pages for word processing and page formatting — are excellent examples to crib from, especially for productivity apps.

This chapter gently urges you to reinvent the user experience for your app to match an iPad user's expectations, from the perspective of the content you provide and the app's functionality. But first, you need to envision the totality of what your app's user experience should be.

Deep Thoughts on the User Experience

Pun intended — creating DeepThoughts, the star of Part IV, is a fast way to get familiar with iPad software development. DeepThoughts was designed to do only one thing, so that it would be easy to understand and quick to create. Because it does only one thing, it is in some respects a utility app by Apple's perspective, similar to the Brushes app (because it does only the one thing), or to the Weather app (because it offers only one type of data for users to change — the city for the weather).

But DeepThoughts is also the skeleton of an immersive app. It's similar to any app that lets the user interact with content in a visually rich environment, except that it provides only a single view and a single piece of content. (I planned it that way so that it's easy to understand and quick to create.) With the DeepThoughts application under your belt, you'll have a much easier time understanding and using all the resources Apple provides to help you develop iPad apps.

iPadTravel411, the star of Part V, starts in many ways where DeepThoughts leaves off — by providing a more immersive experience in a *productivity* app — a kind of app that uses and manipulates different types of information. iPadTravel411 manipulates foreign currency rates, airport transportation routes, maps, your location, weather, events, and traveler's tasks.

Because of its ease of use and convenience, its awareness of your location, and its ability to connect seamlessly to the Internet from most places, the iPad lets you develop a totally new kind of application — one that integrates seamlessly with what the user is doing when he or she is living in the real world (what a concept). It frees the user to take advantage of technology away from the tether of the desk or coffee shop, and skips the hunt for a place to spread out the hardware. I refer to such applications as *here-and-now* apps that take advantage of technology to help you do a specific task with up-to-date information, wherever you are and whenever you'd like.

Although iPhone apps share some of these characteristics, iPad apps can offer wildly better experiences due to the larger display, including the ability to provide well-organized content in a *Split view,* which displays more than one view onscreen at a time. Split view lets you present data in a master-detail or source list–style arrangement, as demonstrated by the App Store app on the iPad in Figure 2-1 (left side). The Split view is a common organizational element in iPad applications because it helps flatten the information hierarchy, and you find out how to take advantage of it in iPadTravel411 as described in Chapter 15.

Whenever possible, add a realistic, physical true-to-life dimension to the way your app looks and behaves, so that it is easier to understand and fun to use — such as the Need for Speed app in Figure 2-1 (right side). Remember that a great user interface follows design principles that are based on the way people think and work. A user interface that's unattractive, convoluted, or illogical can make even a great app seem like a chore to use. But a beautiful, intuitive, compelling experience inspires a positive emotional attachment in users, and that's a good thing for an app to do.

All the features inherent in iPad apps enable you to add a depth to the user's experience that you usually don't find in laptop- or desktop-based applications — in effect, a third dimension. Not only can the use of an iPad app be a part of what you're doing and where you are, but *what you're doing and where you are* can be part of the app itself. iPad developers can achieve a goal that's been elusive for years: the seamless integration of technology into everyday life.

The why-bother-since-I-have-my-laptop crowd still has to wrestle with this level of technology, especially those folks who haven't grown up with it. They look at an iPad as a poor substitute for a laptop or desktop — well, okay, for certain tasks, that's true. But an iPad app trumps the laptop or desktop big-time in two ways:

✔ The iPad's compact portability lets you do stuff not easily done on a laptop or desktop — on site and right now — as with the iPadTravel411 app you find out how to build in Part V.

✔ The iPad is integrated into the activity itself, creating a transparency that makes it as unobtrusive as possible. This advantage — even more important than portability — is the result of *context-driven design.*

Figure 2-1:
The App
Store app
shows a
split screen
(left) and
Need for
Speed feels
like driving a
car (right).

The key to designing a killer iPad application is to understand that the iPad is *not* a bigger iPod touch, nor is it a more portable version of a laptop computer. It's another animal altogether, as I describe in Chapter 1, and is therefore used entirely differently. With maps you can zoom into, full-screen videos and slideshows with music you can play, and so on, you can provide content in your app that people can enjoy anywhere and more easily share with others, far more than they can with a laptop or an iPod touch. So get ready to take a closer look at how to create compelling content.

Creating Compelling Content

It's a powerful experience to hold full pages of content (from the Internet or in memory) in your hands in a device that weighs little more than a thick magazine. But keep in mind that the iPad has no default orientation — people don't pay much attention to the minimal device frame, and they're uncon-cerned with the location of the Home button. They can rotate from portrait to landscape with ease, and your app should encourage people to interact with iPad from any side by providing a great experience in all orientations. You can see how the iPadTravel411 looks in Figure 2-2, which shows a full-screen map in portrait orientation, and a split-screen map in landscape orientation.

Figure 2-2:
iPadTravel
411 in
portrait
orientation
(left) and
landscape
(right).

The large iPad display offers many ways to give people access to information all in one place, without having to switch screens (as in an iPhone) or open separate windows and modal dialogs (as in desktop applications). If your app currently provides information in a hierarchy (such as a sequence of iPhone screens), I strongly consider that you flatten the hierarchy to present more information in one place. Your app's content can appear in the Main view, and if you need to provide additional information or tools in an auxiliary view, you can employ a popover (a view that appears semi-transparently above the Main view) so that users don't have to leave the context of the main task.

Focusing on the task at hand

What most of the really good iPad apps have in common is *focus:* They address a well-defined task. The best iPad apps give people innovative ways to interact with content while they perform a clearly defined, finite task. You should resist the temptation to fill the display with features that aren't directly related to the main task. Concentrate instead on ways to amplify the user experience, without diluting the main task with extraneous features.

For example, a book-reader app that also allows people to keep track of reading lists shouldn't make people leave the book page to go to another screen to manage their reading lists — rather, the app should put the list in a translucent popover that appears above the page, and allow people to copy favorite passages into it. In a football game app, users should be able to see information about characters without leaving the field view.

The content itself then, especially for here-and-now apps, must be stream-lined and focused on the fundamental pieces of the task. Although you *can* provide a near-infinity of detail just to get a single task done, here's a word to the wise: Don't. You need to extract the essence of each task; focus on the details that really make a difference.

When you're using a good app, every piece of the app is not merely impor-tant to the task, but also important to *where you are in the task.* For example, if you're trying to decide how to get to central London from Heathrow, the app shouldn't offer detailed information about the Tube until you need it.

Maintaining consistency with the user's world

Great apps are based on the way people — users — think and work. When you make your app a natural extension of the user's world, it makes the app much easier and more pleasant to use and to learn.

Your users already have a mental model that describes the task your soft-ware is enabling. The users also have their own mental models of how the device works. At the levels of both content and user interface, your app must be consistent with these models if you want to create a superb user experi-ence (which in turn creates loyalty to your app).

The user interface in iPadTravel411 was based on how people divide the tasks they need to do when traveling, especially when arriving at an airport such as London's Heathrow. Here are typical categories:

- ✔ **See a map of the territory.** You'd want to see a map right away that shows your current location and lets you pin other locations on it (such as your hotel) so you can find them quickly.

- ✔ **Deal with foreign currency.** You need to know how much it really costs to convert money and buy things abroad.

- ✔ **Check the current weather and forecast.** You don't want to walk out-side the airport terminal into a driving rainstorm without your coat on, and you want to know what to expect over the next few days.

- ✔ **Look up events.** You may want to check any special events happening while you're in the city so that you can avoid traffic around them or find out the schedule for an event you're attending.

- ✔ **Find transportation.** You want to know how to get to and from the air-port with maximum efficiency and minimum hassle, as well as how to get around the city.

This is only a partial list, of course. Chapter 13 gets into the iPadTravel411 application design in more detail.

There are other ways to divide the tasks, but anything much different would be ignoring the user's mental model, which would mean the app wouldn't meet some of the user's expectations. It would be less pleasant to use because it would impose an unfamiliar way of looking at things instead of building on the knowledge and experiences those users already have. Basing your app on how the user interacts and thinks about the world makes designing a great user interface easier.

Modeling apps on real-world metaphors

When possible, model your application's objects and actions on objects and actions in the real world. For example, the Settings app displays on-off switches you can slide to turn things on or off. Many e-book readers let you flick the screen as if it were a paper page.

All these interface details are based on physical counterparts in the real world. You should help people focus on the content, and one way is to design your app as a subtle frame around the information they're interested in, like the App Store app does (refer to Figure 2-1, left side). In the App Store, the content (in this case, apps for download) appears in a carousel that reminds one of a diner jukebox at your table — and everyone who uses iTunes already knows how to navigate through the album cover art choices.

Consider creating custom controls that subtly integrate with your app's graphical style. In this way, controls are discoverable, but not too conspicuous. The car-driving metaphor in the Need for Speed app (refer to Figure 2-1, right side) is so right for a touch-sensitive display that it's sexy — you can shift gears with your finger and tap other controls that appear like they belong on the dashboard while you cruise.

Engaging the user

While I'm on the subject of shifting gears, here are two more important aspects of a compelling application: direct manipulation and immediate feedback. Here's what's so great about them:

✔ **Direct manipulation makes people feel more in control.** On the desktop, it meant a keyboard and mouse; on the iPad, the Multi-Touch interface serves the same purpose. In fact, using fingers gives a user a more immediate sense of control; there's no intermediary (such as a mouse) between the user and the object onscreen. To make this effect happen in your app, one way is to keep your onscreen objects visible while the user manipulates them.

✔ **Immediate feedback keeps the users engaged.** Great apps respond to every user action with some visible feedback — such as highlighting list items briefly when users tap them.

Also, consider fading controls after people have stopped interacting with them for a little while, and redisplaying them when people tap the screen. This gives even more of the screen space to the content people want to see.

Because of the limitations imposed by using fingers, apps need to be very forgiving. For example, you don't want your app to pester the user to confirm every action, but you also don't want the app to let the user perform potentially destructive, nonrecoverable actions (such as deleting all contacts or restarting a game) without asking, "Are you sure?" It should also be obvious to users how to stop a task that's taking too long to complete.

Making it obvious

Although simplicity is a definite design principle, great apps are *also* easily understandable to the target user. If you're designing a travel app, it has to be simple enough for even an inexperienced traveler to use. But if you're designing an app for foreign exchange trading, you don't have to make it simple enough for someone with no trading experience to understand.

Keep these points in mind as you plan and create your app:

✔ The main function of a good application is immediately apparent and accessible to the users it's intended for.

✔ The standard interface components also give cues to the users. Users know, for example, to touch buttons and select items from popovers.

✔ You can't assume that users are so excited about your app that they're willing to invest lots of time in figuring it out.

Early Macintosh developers were aware of these principles. They knew that users expected that they could rip off the shrink-wrap, put a floppy disk in the machine (these were *really* early Macintosh developers), and do at least something productive immediately. The technology has changed since then; user attitudes, by and large, haven't.

Your application's text should be based on the target user. For example, if your user isn't steeped in technical jargon, avoid it in the user interface.

Avoiding jargon doesn't mean that you have to dumb down the app. Here are some guidelines:

✔ If you're targeting your app toward people who already use (and expect) a certain kind of specialized language, then sure, use the jargon in your app. Just do your homework first and make sure you use those terms *correctly*.

For example, if your app is targeted at high-powered foreign-exchange traders, it might use *pip* (price interest point — the smallest amount that a price can move, as when a stock price advances by one cent). In fact, a foreign-exchange trader expects to see price movement in pips, and not only *can* you, but you *should* use that term in your user interface.

✔ If your app requires that the user have a certain amount of specialized knowledge about a task in order to use your application, identify what that knowledge is upfront.

✔ If the user is an ordinary person with generalized knowledge, use ordinary language.

✔ Gear your app to your user's knowledge base. In effect, meet your users where they are; don't expect them to come to you.

Don't underestimate the effect of the user interface on the people who are trying to use it. A bad user interface can make even a great app painful to use. If users can't quickly figure out how to use your app or if the user interface is cluttered or obscure, they're likely to move on and probably complain loudly about the app to anyone who will listen — or worse, give your app a lousy review and a bad rating in the App Store.

Using stunning graphics with aesthetic integrity

Appearance has a strong impact on how people perceive your app's value. As mentioned previously, an app that appears cluttered or illogical is hard to understand and use. The high-resolution display supports rich, beautiful, engaging graphics that can draw people into an application and make the simplest task rewarding.

It's a pretty safe bet that part of the appeal of the iPad to many people — especially to nontechnical users — is aesthetic: The device is sleek, compact, and fun to use. But the aesthetics of an iPad app aren't just about how beautiful your app is onscreen. Aesthetic integrity is about how well your app's appearance integrates with its function, as in the appearance of car dashboard and windshield view in Need for Speed.

An immersive app like Need for Speed offers what users expect — a beautiful appearance that promises a thrilling experience — but more importantly, its appearance is integrated with the task of driving a car, and the user interface elements are designed carefully so that they provide an internally consistent experience.

On the other hand, for productivity apps you may want to keep decorative elements subtle while giving prominence to the main task. One of the early appeals of the prehistoric Macintosh and the recent iPhone was how similarly all the applications worked. Use the iPad standard behavior, gestures, and metaphors in standard ways. For example, users tap a button to make a selection and flick or drag to scroll a list. iPad users understand these gestures because the Apple-supplied apps utilize them *consistently*.

Fortunately, staying consistent is easy to do on the iPad; the frameworks at your disposal have that behavior built in. This is not to say that you should never extend the interface, especially if you're blazing new trails or creating a new game. For example, if you're creating a roulette wheel for the iPad, why not use a two-finger circular gesture to spin the wheel, even if it isn't a standard gesture?

Designing the User Experience

It's rare (except with sample apps) for an app's user experience to be simply a combination of some of the iPad's basic experiences. But DeepThoughts, which you build in Part IV, is simplicity itself. It displays whatever text the user enters, and the mechanism for changing the text is just like most other iPhone or iPod touch apps — touch the *i* (information) button or tap the display itself, and tap the text field to use the onscreen keyboard. As you build DeepThoughts, you discover how to use the basic building blocks of the iPad user experience.

The iPadTravel411 app in Part V presents a more complex set of problems. A traveler doesn't need a lot of information at any one time. In fact, the user wants as little info as possible (just the facts ma'am) but also as current as possible. It doesn't help to have last year's train schedule.

To get the design ball of your application rolling, start thinking about what your user will want from the application; not necessarily the features, but what the experience of using the application should be like.

Understanding the real-world context

You can reach the goal of seamlessness and transparency by following some very simple principles when you design the user experience — especially with respect to the user interface.

Become the champion of relevance

There are two aspects to this directive:

- ✔ Search and destroy anything that isn't relevant to what the user is doing while he or she is using a particular part of your application.

- ✔ Include — and make easily accessible — everything a user needs when doing something supported by a particular part of your application.

You want to avoid distracting the user from what he or she is doing. The application should be integrated into the task, a natural part of the flow, and not something that causes a detour. Your goal is to supply the user with only the information that's applicable to the task at hand. If your user just wants to get from an airport into a city, he or she couldn't care less that the city has a world-renowned underground or subway system if it doesn't come out to the airport.

Seconds count

At first, the "seconds count" admonition may appear to fall into the "blinding flash of the obvious" category — of *course* a user wants to accomplish a task as quickly as possible. If the user has to scroll through lots of menus or figure out how the app works, the app's value drops off exponentially with the amount of time it takes to get to where the user needs to be.

But there are also some subtleties to this issue. If the user can do things as quickly as possible, he or she is a lot less distracted from the task at hand — and *both* results are desirable. If your app's user switches to another app and then back to your app, your app should be in the same state it was in before the user quit — showing the same views and information (such as the map in iPadTravel411, which shows the same location you just viewed).

Combine these ideas and you get the principle of *simply connect:* You want to be able to connect easily whether that connection is to a network, to the information you need, or to the task you want to do. For example, a friend of mine was telling me he uses his iPad when watching TV so he can look up things in an online dictionary or Wikipedia. (He must watch a lot of Public TV.)

Doing it better on the iPad

What you get by using the application has to have more value than alternative ways of doing the same thing.

The quality of information has to be better than the alternative

You can find airport transportation in a guidebook, but it's not up-to-date. You can get foreign exchange information from a *bureau de change,* but unless you know the bank rate, you don't know whether you're being ripped off. You can get restaurant information from a newspaper, but you don't know whether the restaurant has subsequently changed hours or is closed for vacation. If the app can consistently provide better, more up-to-date information, it's the kind of app that's tailor-made for a context-driven design.

The app has to be worth the real cost

By *real cost,* I don't mean just the amount you actually pay out — you need to include the time and effort of using the app. The real cost includes both the cost of the application and any costs you might incur by *using* the application. This can be a real issue for an app that requires the Internet, because international roaming charges can be exorbitant for using data services to access the Internet. That's why the app must have the designed-in capability to download the information it provides and then to update the info when you find a wireless connection.

Keep things localized

With the world growing even flatter (from a communications perspective, anyway) and the iPad available in more than 80 countries, the potential market for an app is considerably larger than just the folks who happen to speak English. But having to use an app in a language you may not be comfortable with doesn't make for transparency. This means that applications have to be *localized* — that is, all the information, the content, and even the text in dialogs need to be in the user's language of choice.

Playing to the iPad's Strengths

Key to creating applications that go beyond the desktop and that take advantage of context-based design are several important features of the iPad and its operating system:

- ✔ Sensing multiple fingers and multifinger gestures
- ✔ Tracking orientation and motion
- ✔ Displaying stunning graphics and images (which you can even show on a connected TV or projection system)
- ✔ Knowing the location of the device and displaying a compass

  ✔ Playing digital content and recording sound (and, of course, syncing with a computer for the content)

  ✔ Accessing the Internet via Wi-Fi or optional 3G service

There are others, of course, but you can expect to find many of these features in an iPad app.

Sensing multifinger gestures

The large iPad display gives you lots of room for multifinger gestures, including gestures made by more than one person. You can offer the standard swipe, pinch, and rotation gestures, among others, and use other gestures to trigger additional behavior, such as triple-tap, and touch-and-hold (also called long press). If your app offers an important task that users perform frequently and want to complete quickly, you should probably use only standard gestures, but if you're designing an app that can measure up to some of the iPad games, with realistic controls, multiplayer support, or an environment for exploring, you should think about using custom or multifinger gestures.

However, to maintain consistency with other iPad apps, use standard gestures for standard behaviors. For instance, pinching gesture should scale a view, zooming it in and out; it should not be interpreted as, say, a selection request, for which a tap is more appropriate. Stick with real-world models, and in this case stick with the metaphors that have already appeared on the iPhone: tapping iPod playback controls, sliding on-off switches, and flicking through the data shown on picker wheels.

There are some limitations you need to be aware of. Fingers aren't as precise as a mouse pointer, and user interface elements need to be large enough and spaced far enough apart so that the user's fingers can find their way around the interface comfortably. If you design interface elements to be integrated with your graphics and images, be sure to make them large enough.

Tracking orientation and motion

When you rotate the iPad from a vertical view (portrait) to a horizontal view (landscape), the accelerometer detects the movement and changes the display accordingly. The iPad can also sense motion using its built-in accelerometer. Even in its simplest form, motion is useful: When entering text or using the copy and paste functions, you can just shake the iPad to undo the action.

Motion detection happens so quickly that you can control a game with these movements. Although the accelerometer is used extensively in games, it also has other uses, such as enabling a user to erase a picture or make a random song selection by shaking the device (not to mention undoing the recent action).

Displaying stunning graphics and images

To rise above the inevitable swarm of new iPad apps, you'll want to offer graphics and images that truly take advantage of the display. The iPad displays 1,024 x 768 pixels, with up to 24 bits per pixel (8 bits each for red, green, and blue), plus an 8-bit alpha channel — which specifies how the pixel's colors should be merged with another pixel when the two are overlaid one on top of the other.

In most cases, you wouldn't set the alpha channel on a pixel-by-pixel basis in a drawing or painting program, but rather on an object-by-object basis, so that different parts of the object would have different levels of transparency depending on how much you wanted the background to show through. With an alpha channel, you can create rectangular objects that appear as if they are irregular in shape — you define the rectangular edges as transparent so that the background shows through.

Always create your artwork in a larger multiple of the pixel dimensions you need, so that you can add depth and details before scaling it down accurately to the iPad display size. That way your graphics and images crackle and snap with clarity and color.

Playing and recording content

The iPad evolved from the iPod, in which content is king. Not only can your app play music and videos, but it can also record voice-quality (actually telephone-quality) sound with its built-in microphone, or higher quality through external microphones. A number of audio-mixing apps have already made their debut in the App Store. The iPad can sync images from your computer's Photo library, send and receive images and video clips by e-mail and share multimedia content through the MobileMe service.

Knowing the location of the device

Because the device knows its own location (and hence, the user's location), you can further refine the context by including the actual physical location and adding that to the relevance filter. If you're in Rome, the application can ask the user whether he or she wants to use Rome as a filter for relevant information (so that when in Rome . . .).

Because the iPad knows where it is, apps can make use of this information to present content that is closer to the user. The feature isn't just for travel — apps that have nothing to do with travel, such as an app that shows you the movies playing in your area, may still use location to improve the user experience.

Accessing the Internet

Accessing the Internet allows you to provide real-time, up-to-date information. In addition, it enables you to transcend the CPU and memory limitations of the iPad by offloading processing and data storage out to a server in the clouds.

Of course, there's always a possibility that the user may be out of range, or on a plane, or has decided not to pay exorbitant roaming fees for 3G and isn't close enough to a Wi-Fi hotspot. You need to account for that possibility in your application and preserve as much functionality as possible. This usually means allowing the user to download and use the current real-time information, where applicable.

Avoiding Practices that Get Apps Rejected

Apple exerts control over the app-development and App Store ecosystem, and if you want to play ball in Apple's ballpark, you have to, well, play ball. No matter how many developers complain about Apple's rejection policies, there will always be more developers willing to follow the guidelines. All you need to do is read the documentation, steer away from the Apple trademarks and images, and stay away from content that's questionable in any legal sense. By keeping those things in mind, you can make design decisions about your app now, before developing the app, which can save you time and money later.

Some people believe Apple has not only a right, but also an obligation, to police the App Store and reject questionable apps, if only to build trust with consumers. Anacharsis, one of Greek mythology's Seven Wise Men, warned people that the market is "the place set apart where men may deceive each other." Given the way the iPad can be integrated into your everyday life and communications, a malicious app could do considerably more damage than a similar one on a desktop computer.

But Apple also wants the user experience to be a rewarding one, as well as one that's consistent with the way Apple designed its own apps and OS. And that makes perfect sense for a company that wants to expand its ecosystem and users so that it can continue to invest in research and keep innovation on the front burner.

So what kinds of things will get your app bounced before it ever has a chance to shine in the App Store? Here are just a few:

- ✔ **Linking to private frameworks:** Apple rejects apps that call external frameworks or libraries that contain non-Apple code. In addition, you can't download interpreted code to use in an app except for code that is interpreted and run by Apple's published APIs and built-in interpreters. Private frameworks and interpreted code may hide functions that Apple would want to know about. (Some private frameworks have been found to mine personal information from iPhone users without their knowledge.) Apple already knows about most of the private frameworks, so don't bother with them.

- ✔ **Straying too far from Apple's guidelines:** When I submitted my iPhone app (Tony's Tips for iPhone Users), it was initially rejected because the app used highlighting in a menu in a way that did not conform to Apple's guidelines. Be sure to follow these guidelines, which are published in the iPhone Developer Center (which you find out how to access in Chapter 4).

- ✔ **Copying existing functionality:** Although you should use the functionality provided for developers, you shouldn't simply copy something that Apple already does. Mini Web browsers — apps that essentially show Web pages and do little else — are particularly vulnerable. For example, a simple iPhone app that duplicated the functionality of Safari's bookmark button was rejected.

- ✔ **Using an inappropriate keyboard type:** If your app needs a phone number or other numeral-only input, and it presents a keyboard that also includes the possibility of entering standard alphanumeric input, it will most likely be rejected.

- ✔ **Being oblivious about whether your user lost connection:** The iPad is all about using the Internet. If your app uses a network connection, it is *your app's responsibility* to tell the user if and when his or her iPad loses its network connection while using your app.

Now that you have some idea about what Apple expects of you — in terms of designing and developing your app — it's time for you to find out what to expect of Apple in terms of supporting your development efforts. Next, you should find out the marketing challenges for apps in the App Store and even more practices that could either enhance or inhibit your ability to effectively distribute your apps. So, onward to the next chapter, where you find out all about the App Store and your chances of success with it.

Chapter 3

The App Store Is Not Enough

*P*eter Drucker, known as the father of modern management, is also known for pointing out that business has only two functions: innovation and marketing. Because most of this book is about innovation, I need to spend at least one chapter explaining why so many developers don't make enough money from iPad, iPod touch, and iPhone apps, and what you can do to mitigate the complex issues surrounding the marketing of these apps.

Apple will list your application along with 150,000+ apps already listed in the App Store — remember that an iPad can run all iPhone and iPod touch apps as well. Yes, it's wonderful that Apple takes only 30 percent of the sales price and takes care of hosting, downloading, credit card processing, and notifying users of updates. And if you remember the early days of developing for game machines, you may appreciate the fact that Apple lets you name your own price for your app. You can even distribute an app for free. What you can't do, and perhaps this is a good thing, is pay for preferential treatment. And as of this writing, Apple doesn't accept advertising within the store.

The App Store *does* offer lists of the top paid and free apps in each category, and it lists the newest apps by release date, but unless your app is already successful and in the top paid or top free lists, your app's fleeting appearance in the list sorted by release date may provide only a short spike in sales — unless you prepare yourself to take advantage of it by applying some of the methods in this chapter.

The trouble with using any kind of technology to reach customers is the same, old or new: measuring the results. "Half the money I spend on advertising is wasted; the trouble is, I don't know which half," said John Wanamaker, founder of the first department store in Philadelphia (one of the first department stores in the United States) in 1861.

Why People Buy Apps from the App Store

If you think the reason people buy apps is "because it's there" (that is, the App Store is right in your iPad, iPod touch, or iPhone), you're only partly right. According to AdMob (www.admob.com), more than 90 percent of iPhone and iPod touch users browse and search for apps directly on their mobile device instead of their computer, and as of this writing, it's too early for statistics to be meaningful for the iPad.

But that doesn't explain why people are attracted to buying apps on the iPad and flocked to the App Store on the iPhone and iPod touch in the first place — and continue to do so. Besides the fact that Apple has created an ecosystem and the iPhone OS platform for true innovation, the company has wasted no time using traditional advertising to lure people into buying things they didn't know they needed, with the well-known tagline "There's an app for that."

A major factor in the App Store's appeal is its equal treatment of all customers. This equal treatment is a fact of life today in all but the most posh stores, but it was an innovation in John Wanamaker's store in 1861. Wanamaker created the price tag because he believed that if everyone was equal before God, then everyone should be equal before price. (He also invented the cash refund and guaranteed the quality of his merchandise in print.) Apple has also established trust with its customers by screening apps before listing them and enforcing guidelines among app developers for a "quality experience" for consumers. And, of course, the price tag is right up front.

Speaking of a quality experience, people are attracted to new technologies *just for* the experience. Wanamaker embraced innovation as early as possible to attract customers with a new experience — his was the first department store with electrical illumination (1878), the first with a telephone (1879), and the first to install pneumatic tubes to transport cash and documents (1880). Today, people are attracted to the App Store's use of technology, its ease of use, and this highly innovative form of shopping-on-demand right from your mobile device.

There is no substitute for combination of trust, equal treatment, and a high-quality experience. The App Store is *the* place to list your iPad, iPhone, and iPod touch apps. Marketing them, however, is entirely up to you.

Finding out how to reach your potential customers

The App Store is right at your iPad customers' fingertips. Tap the Featured button long the bottom row of buttons, and the Featured screen appears with a *cover flow* browser (familiar to all iPod and iTunes users) showing apps under the In the Spotlight heading, as shown in Figure 3-1. More apps appear under the New and Noteworthy heading. Featured, Genius Categories, Top Charts, and Updates buttons appear along the bottom, ready to entice potential customers.

The Featured screen also includes the What's Hot button at the top, showing the most popular apps based on downloads. The Featured screen's New and Noteworthy list, and the What's Hot list, are where early adopter customers go to buy on impulse. Your app may make a brief appearance in the New and Noteworthy list when you release it, only to be crowded out almost immediately by more new apps. There are, by my rough estimates as of this writing, about nine iPhone and iPod touch apps born in the App Store every hour of every day, and the developers are just getting started with iPad apps, which double or triple this rate.

But if you've properly categorized your app, it should appear in the list of apps on the screen devoted to that category. Attaching your app to the appropriate category, as I describe in Chapter 6, is extremely important. Customers looking for a social networking app tap the Social Networking category to find the apps they're looking for.

The Top Charts screen is for those customers who need to catch up to the early adopters and only have time to look at the most popular apps of all time. Your app will not reach these lists unless you've engaged in a successful marketing strategy.

Some customers will take the time to tap the Search entry field in the upper right corner (refer to Figure 3-1) to bring up the onscreen keyboard and search the store. As they type a keyword you assigned to your new app, or something close to its name, your app should pop up right away as a suggestion. It is therefore extremely important to use an appropriate name for your app (with terms that people might search for) and to assign appropriate keywords, as shown in Chapter 6.

Figure 3-1:
The App
Store app's
Featured
screen with
cover flow
browser.

Many developers choose to develop a free, or *lite* version, of an app to draw attention to the paid version. Free apps are more likely to be downloaded because, well, they're free. And according to AdMob, upgrading from the lite version was the top reason given when iPhone and iPod touch users were asked what drives them to purchase a paid app.

Note, however, that the free lite version of your paid app must be a fully functional app and can't reference features that are not implemented or point users directly to the full paid version. What this means is that, although you can publish a free lite app with fewer features than the paid version, the free version must be a complete app in its own right, and you can't badger the free app's users with reminders to upgrade to the paid version, nor can you use placeholders in your app's interface for missing functionality that, when tapped, points users to the paid version. Tricks like these will get your free lite app rejected.

Developers also have the In App Purchase feature at their disposal to offer their app users the opportunity to buy other apps, merchandise, game levels, premium features, e-books, and so on. (See the "Deploying the In App Purchase Feature" section, later in this chapter, for more.) You may also want to consider offering your customers an incentive, such as free deals through the In App Purchase feature, if they tell their friends about your app. Anyone browsing the App Store can choose Tell a Friend from the Buy App pop-up on the app's information screen in the store, to send the app information in an e-mail.

Besides getting your app listed in the App Store's lists, there's no way through Apple to reach potential customers. You need to consider all methods of reaching customers, and you need to price your app according to what your target customer expects, which is a primary topic of Marketing 101.

Marketing 101: Pricing your app

The literature about marketing could probably fill all the Trump Towers in the world, but if you want to learn about marketing quickly, there are at least two iPhone apps for that. Marketing Master and MarketingProfs, both free in the App Store, walk you through the basic concepts, and even though you certainly could do better by enrolling at Wharton (where the first Marketing 101 course was taught in 1909), it's a place to start.

Marketing is setting up a strong bait attraction system that generates leads, sorts those leads into qualified prospects, and then turns those prospects into customers. Besides fishing for the right prospects, you have to convince them to buy your app — in other words, "ABC, *always be closing*" (as Alec Baldwin so succinctly put it in the movie *Glengarry Glen Ross*).

One of the biggest lessons of Marketing 101 is to determine your target audience for your product. Assemble as much information about your target customer as possible — demographics, education, income level, and so on — because this information will influence all your marketing decisions, from the text you write in your descriptions and ads to the channels you use to distribute your message.

Another big lesson is to determine the cost of acquiring new customers. The simple math here is to divide all the dollars you spend in marketing per month by all the new dollars you receive each month in sales. When you know this, it begs the question of how much you *should* be spending. To figure that out, you need to know how much your customers are worth to you — the *lifetime value* of your customer. The secret to increasing the lifetime value of your customer is to increase the quality of the customer experience, thereby encouraging repeat business. You're not in the app game to do just one app for the iPad; you need to develop more apps for the iPad (and possibly apps for the iPhone and iPod touch) and build a customer base that will be happy to buy them.

Although it is too early to predict iPad customer behavior, keep in mind that iPhone users download approximately ten new apps a month, according to AdMob, and those who regularly download paid apps spend approximately $9 on an average of five paid downloads per month. You need to attract the right people, not just anyone — potential customers are those who will understand the value of your app (also known as the *value proposition,* otherwise known as "what's in it for me?").

But at what price? Much has been written about iPhone and iPod touch app pricing strategies, and these theories haven't changed much with the iPad. At the beginning of the iPhone gold rush, pricing an app at $0.99 helped to get the app into the Top 100. But now, with over 150,000 iPhone apps that already run on the iPad, and iPhone developers scrambling to design iPad versions, that's no longer true. All good marketers know that price is never a good selling point; anyone can come along and be cheaper. A better approach is to determine the true value of the app. People will pay for quality — and as more business apps become available, their prices will likely reflect their value.

The best approach is to check out similar apps, especially competing ones (if any). Remember how costly it is to acquire customers. Starting at a higher price gives you some room to offer discounted prices at different times, such as the Black Friday and Cyber Monday that follow Thanksgiving, or the start of the annual Apple Developer Conference.

Knowing Your Customers

One of the biggest problems facing the iPad, iPod touch, and iPhone app marketer is that the App Store doesn't tell you *who* your customers are. Sure, you know how many customers you have, and you also know from which countries, and how many of them have updated your app (if you provided an update). You even know how much they spent. What you don't know, however, can hurt you. How can you possibly build relationships with customers you don't know?

The vast majority of iPhone and iPod touch apps downloaded from the App Store are in use by less than 5 percent of users a month after downloading, according to Pinch Media. Just 20 percent of users return to run a free application one day after downloading. As time goes by, that decline in usage continues, eventually settling below 5 percent after one month and nearing 0 percent after three months.

Category matters, too — games are used for longer periods than any other genre. Pinch Media found the long-term audience for the average app is just one percent of the total number of downloads.

So customer loyalty is hard to build. It's difficult to determine whether a user's positive experience with your app will translate into sales of your next app or your more expensive desktop app. There are no guarantees. You need to get as much data about your customers as you can find.

You may want to add a link to a Web page that offers an optional customer registration process. You could then ask questions during this process to get more information about your customer. You probably need to offer some kind of incentive to get your customers to register, such as credit toward an in-app purchase, or an exclusive service — for example, in my app Tony's Tips for iPhone Users, I offer registered customers access to a support forum in which they can ask me specific questions about using the iPhone.

Tracking downloads

You use iTunes Connect, described in Chapter 6, to submit apps to the App Store and manage apps in the store. Apple releases daily sales reports in iTunes Connect, which you can view online or download, with the name of the app, how many were sold and in which country, and your profit. You can import these reports into any spreadsheet program, like Excel or iWork Numbers.

To find the reports, first follow the instructions in Chapter 4 to register as an Apple developer and join the iPhone Developer Program. Then log in to iTunes Connect (as shown in Chapter 6), and click the Sales/Trend Reports link, as shown in Figure 3-2.

Doing so gets you shunted to the Transaction Reports page, which should look a lot like what you see in Figure 3-3. Pick Summary in the Report Type pop-up menu and then click Daily or Weekly in the Report Period pop-up — you can't pick Monthly Free unless your app is free. After picking your report, click Download to download it or Preview to view it.

Figure 3-2:
Visit iTunes
Connect
and click
Sales/Trend
Reports.

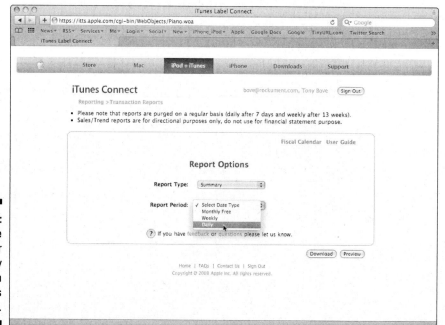

Figure 3-3:
Pick the
Daily or
Weekly
report in
iTunes
Connect.

Some savvy developers out there have come up with a number of desktop applications that have been designed to download and graph the iTunes Connect sales data for you. For example, AppViz (`www.ideaswarm.com/products/appviz`) is a Mac application that can import the reports from the Web or from a downloaded file, and it displays charts of your daily, weekly, and monthly sales. appFigures (`www.appfigures.com`) is a Web-based solution for tracking app sales that can download and graph your reports from iTunes Connect.

Adding analytical code to your app

There are several analytics options for iPad, iPod touch, and iPhone apps if you're willing to compile the necessary code into your app.

For example, Pinch Analytics from Pinch Media (`http://pinchmedia.com`), shown in Figure 3-4, is used in thousands of popular apps because it can track any action anywhere in your app. Armed with this information, you can fine-tune the user experience in your updates and offer new features to try to catch usage drop-off as early as possible and retain more customers. You can also measure all types of revenue, from paid downloads and subscriptions to advertising and in-app purchases.

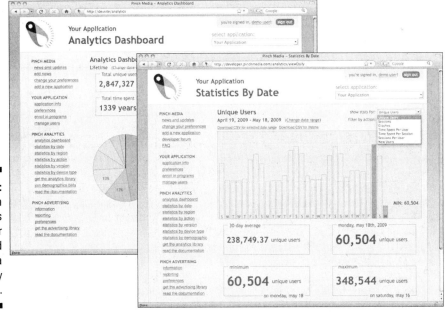

Figure 3-4: Pinch Analytics tracks user actions and reports on a wide variety of metrics.

AdMob, recently acquired by Google, offers AdMob Analytics (`http://analytics.admob.com`), a service that works with your Web site to track customers that access pages on the site through your app. All you have to do is install a code snippet onto each page you want to analyze, and AdMob does the rest. When your app requests a page from your site, your server passes analytics-related data to AdMob, which processes your data and makes it available on `http://analytics.admob.com`. It can track the number of unique visitors and pages consumed on your site, and it can monitor user engagement metrics such as the length and depth of each visit.

Putting ads in your app

Free apps can still generate revenue. To put your free app to work, you need to *monetize* the app with advertisements. Just as you can add Google AdSense ads to your Web pages, you can put ads in your apps from AdMob (`www.admob.com`, now part of Google), Mobclix (`www.mobclix.com`), and Quattro Wireless (`www.quattrowireless.com`, now part of Apple).

These are *ad exchanges* (like Google AdSense, by the way) that act as online marketplaces for buying and selling advertising impressions. Developers can earn income by placing space in their apps (known as *inventory*) in an auction for advertisers, ad networks, and agencies. The latter can maximize their click-through rates by bidding on precisely targeted audience segments. Thus, the more you know about your own customers, the more ads you can get for your app that are precisely targeted for more clicks (and therefore, more income).

For details about advertising on these networks, see the "Buying advertising and publicity" section, later in this chapter.

Deploying the In App Purchase Feature

Apple offers the In App Purchase feature, which developers can use in their apps. When incorporated, this feature enables the app users to purchase virtual items directly from inside the app. If you're developing a game app with multiple levels or environments, or virtual property, consider adding the In App Purchase feature to your app to sell more levels, environments, or property — the Eliminate app from ngmoco:) (yes, that's the developer's username) is a good example of an iPhone app that does this.

If you're developing a specialized e-book reader, use In App Purchase to sell your specialized e-books. Even if you're developing a productivity or travel app, you can deploy In App Purchase to sell additional premium features — Magellan RoadMate for the iPhone, for example, offers spoken street names and directions.

It's important to note that In App Purchase collects only payment. It doesn't download the e-book, add the game level, or hand over the virtual property. You need to provide the additional functionality, including unlocking built-in features or downloading content from your servers.

You put the In App Purchase store directly in your app using the Store Kit framework. (For more about frameworks, see Chapter 7.) The Store Kit framework connects to the App Store on your app's behalf to securely process the user's payments — see the model in Figure 3-5.

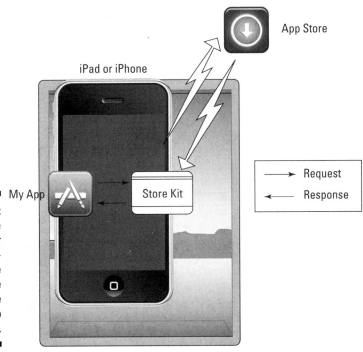

Figure 3-5: Use Store Kit in your app to communicate with the App Store for In App Purchase.

You use iTunes Connect to set up your products the same way you set up new apps. In App Purchase supports four types of products:

✔ **Content:** You can offer game levels, virtual property, and characters; digital books and magazines; photos and artwork; in short, any content that can be delivered within your app.

✔ **Functionality:** You can unlock or expand features you've already delivered in your app, such as a game that offers multiple smaller games for purchase.

✔ **Services:** You can charge users for a one-time service, such as voice transcription — each time the service is used, In App Purchase processes it as a separate purchase.

✔ **Subscriptions:** You can provide access to content or services on a subscription basis, such as a finance magazine or an online game portal. You're responsible for tracking subscription expirations and renewal billing — the App Store doesn't send out renewal notices for you.

Although the In App Purchase feature provides a general mechanism for creating products, everything else is up to you. You can't sell real-world goods and services, only digital content, functionality, services, or subscriptions that work within your app. No intermediary currency is allowed (such as a virtual world's currency), and you can't include real gambling (although simulated gambling is okay). And it goes without saying that pornography, hate speech, and defamation are not allowed.

In App Purchase divides the responsibilities of selling products between your app and the App Store, handling only the payment portion. Here's how it works (refer to Figure 3-6): Your app retrieves the list of product identifiers (set up with iTunes Connect) from its *bundle*. (You learn more about adding a bundle to your app in Chapter 16.) The app sends a request to the App Store for localized information about the products. Your app then displays this information in a store format, so that users can purchase items. When a user elects to purchase an item, your app calls Store Kit to collect payment. Store Kit prompts the user to authorize the payment and then notifies your app to provide the items the user purchased.

This process is spelled out (in more detail than I can go into here) in the In App Purchase Programming Guide, which you can find in the iPhone Dev Center — see Chapter 4 for instructions on registering as a developer and exploring the iPhone Dev Center.

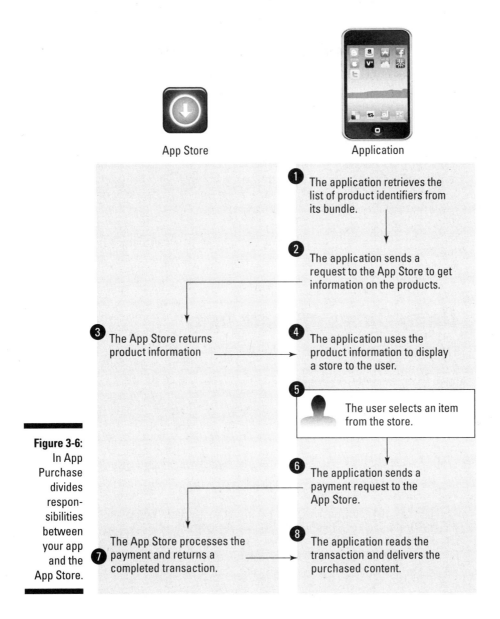

Figure 3-6:
In App
Purchase
divides
respon-
sibilities
between
your app
and the
App Store.

Links Are Not Enough

It goes without saying that you have a Web page (or an entire site) devoted to your app, and you've outfitted your site with keywords for search engine optimization so that searches in Google result in your Web page appearing on or near the first search page. You also use Google Analytics to measure traffic. Reams have been written on this topic. (See Pedro Sostre's and Jennifer

LeClaire's *Web Analytics For Dummies* for one particularly good use of such paper reams.)

When promoting an app, use well-written copy, good screen shots, quotes from user reviews, and third-party recommendations. If you have the skills or the budget, develop a quick video, upload it to YouTube, and put that on your page.

Don't forget to display prominently on your Web page the Apple-legal App Store button that links visitors to the App Store on iTunes. You can find the link to this button in the iPhone Developer Program Portal under App Store Resources — see Chapter 4 for instructions on registering as a developer and exploring the iPhone Developer Program Portal.

But Web page links are not enough. This ecosystem (of iTunes, the App Store, the iPad, the iPhone, and the iPod touch) offers more than a few methods of reaching potential customers, as discussed in the following sections.

Using iTunes affiliate links

Your App Store links should make you some spare change as well as tell you a few things about your customers. The iTunes affiliate program gives you links to put on your Web pages. When a visitor clicks this link and then buys something in the iTunes Store (including the App Store), you get 5 percent. Although that's not much, it doesn't hurt. You can add affiliate links to *any* apps (or songs or videos) in the store, not just your apps.

You can put an affiliate link on your blog, on your friends' Web pages, and even in the signature of your e-mails. Anywhere that you would normally link to your app in the App Store, replace it with your affiliate link.

Another good reason to do this is to obtain more data. You can find out how often visitors see your link, what percentage actually clicks on your link, and where they come from. Apple uses LinkShare (`www.linkshare.com`), a fairly popular affiliate manager. LinkShare also manages affiliate programs for AT&T, LEGO, Macys.com, TigerDirect.com, and hundreds of other companies.

Making use of user reviews

Users are your friends, even when they're bashing you in public.

The App Store customer review is one of the most valuable tools you have to convince potential customers to buy your app. Only people who have purchased your app can write a review. If you offer your users an optional registration on a Web site or by e-mail (using incentives such as insider news, discounts, or free stuff), you can use that opportunity to remind them to write a review of the app in the App Store.

Even harsh reviews can be helpful, pointing out bugs that you may have not previously uncovered, or offering ideas for additional features and functions you didn't think of. You should use this information to prioritize your development activities for future updates, and you can add information about fixed bugs in the app's description when you submit the update.

Going social

Social networking spreads the buzz about your app. One of the most popular techniques is to publicize your app on dozens of forums including the iPhone Blog Forum (`http://forum.theiphoneblog.com`), MacRumors Forums (`http://forums.macrumors.com`), or iPhone Fans (`www.iphonefans.com`), most of which cover iPad apps as well as iPhone and iPod touch apps. New ones are springing up every week.

Spreading buzz is a time-consuming job. Developers often turn to professional PR agencies that can put out press releases and work the blogs and forums for you. A good PR blast can drive thousands of sales within a few days. But beware: sales can fall off a cliff as new stories replace the old ones.

You should submit a press release about your app to the blogs and publications that directly serve your customers. You may not get attention for a paid app without also including a promotional code so that the reviewer can download the app for free. As of this writing, Apple gives you 50 promotional codes for each version of an app; use them wisely because there are far more than 50 general review blogs for iPad apps, and there may be thousands of other blogs that serve your potential customers, such as travel blogs for customers of a travel app.

Remember that each promotional code you request expires four weeks after you requested it, so request only the number of codes you need at the moment. After you've submitted your app's information and promotional code to a few blogs, go back and request more. These codes can be used only in the U.S. iTunes Store.

To get your promotional codes, visit iTunes Connect and click the Request Promotional Codes link. (Refer to Figure 3-2.) Then type the number of codes you need, as shown in Figure 3-7, and click Continue. iTunes Connect then provides the promotional codes to send in your e-mail or blog request. Reviewers already know how to enter promotional codes into the iTunes Store before buying an app.

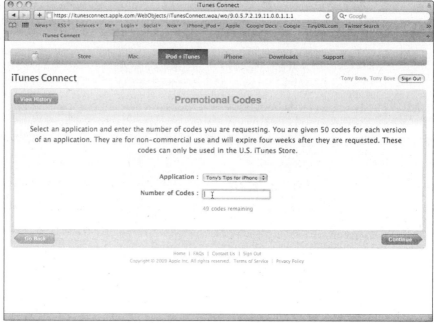

Figure 3-7:
Request
promotional
codes to
give your
app away to
reviewers.

Updating your app for attention

I dislike having to mention this cheap trick, but some developers are still trying to take advantage of it, even though Apple watches out for it. The Release Date lists in each App Store category lists major updates — and some developers believe that if you release updates often, these updates will be on that list more often, reaching more eyeballs.

The problem with this trick is that it's not true. Apple no longer lists updates on the Release Date lists. Besides, customers might be irritated by frequent updates.

Buying advertising and publicity

Generating buzz through advertising is a time-honored tradition in marketing dating back to ancient times when Egyptians used papyrus to make sales messages and wall posters, and Roman emperors advertised military victories and public works on coins.

The coins are a good example: They were mobile, the image appeared often (at every transaction) to establish the "brand" of the emperor, and they cross-promoted other victories and public works.

Branding is a topic covered in grandiose detail in enough books to fill at least one Trump Tower. (Yup, there's even a *Branding For Dummies.*) Companies with very recognizable brands tend to make free apps to promote the brand. You may want to consider creating a version of your app that you could license or sell to a client company that then puts its recognizable brand on it. Such an arrangement is called a *white label* deal because the client company supplies the brand on the label.

If you're publishing more than one paid app, the first place to advertise your newest app is in your older apps — add links to cross-promote your other paid app. It costs nothing and helps to build customer loyalty, just because the customer can see that you've developed other apps.

Consider *buying* ads on other mobile networks that offer ads in apps. AdMob and Mobclix (described in "Putting ads in your app" earlier in this chapter) target iPhone apps as of this writing, and offer different ways to precisely target your ads. AdMob, for example, offers a video ad unit that runs a dedicated video player inside the app. The app's users can engage with interactive campaigns without leaving the video player. As the advertiser, you can also set up action buttons that let the app's users share video content with friends and connect to social networking sites — again, without ever leaving the video player. As an advertiser, you have a choice of auto-play or click-to-play: The former plays your video ads as soon as the app loads, whereas the latter requires the app's users to tap your banner in order to engage with the campaign.

Another popular choice is Google AdWords. You can reach anyone that searches on Google or on partner networks using any browser. There are close to a google of books available on this topic. (Well, almost 100; try *AdWords For Dummies* by Howie Jacobson.)

Publicity offers the biggest payoff in the short term, and the best way to get it is to pay an excellent PR firm. Good publicity can create a spike in sales that could be misleading, but if you've implemented other marketing campaigns to take advantage of it, sales could level out at a much higher rate that before the publicity hit. The best of the PR firms can help you with your entire marketing strategy.

But if you can't afford that . . . Publicity stunts work well if received well by the public. Some of world's most beloved annual events began their existence as cheap publicity stunts. In 1903, publisher Henri Desgrange started a bicycle road race as a publicity stunt to promote his newspaper, never imagining that the *Tour de France* would be going strong more than 100 years later. The Rose Bowl grew out of an 1890 stunt designed to promote Pasadena, Calif., the Miss America pageant began in 1921 as a publicity stunt to lure tourists to Atlantic City after Labor Day, and the Academy Awards began in 1929 as a cheap publicity stunt for the movie industry. As Lenny Bruce put it, "Publicity is stronger than sanity: given the right PR, armpit hair on female singers could become a national fetish." (It did, about 15 years later.)

If you can generate publicity, be sure to have a demo on hand — something to titillate people whether they have their iPads in hand or not. Create a video on YouTube and link it to your press release. Offer a free lite version of your app, and one for the iPhone and iPod touch as well, and time their release to occur at the start of the publicity campaign. Leave no stone unturned when looking for promotional opportunities as part of the campaign. And make sure your demo works — a sacrifice to the demo gods can't hurt. Or just keep repeating the mantra from the patron prophet of demos, Demosthenes: "Small opportunities are often the beginning of great enterprises."

Part II
Becoming a Real Developer

The 5th Wave   By Rich Tennant

"Has the old media been delivered yet?"

In this part . . .

Yaou can work at home alone, but it takes a village to develop an iPad app — the Apple developer village.

You have to register as an Apple developer if you want to get the Software Development Kit (SDK) and all the other goodies that Apple provides for developers — and of course, that means agreeing to a confidentiality agreement. And if you actually want to run your application on a real iPad, you have to join the iPhone developer program. This part gets you through these processes and introduces you to the SDK.

✔ Chapter 4 gets you into the Apple developer village. You find out how to register as a developer, join the program, explore the developer center on the Web, and download the SDK.

✔ Chapter 5 goes into more detail about the SDK itself. You find out all about Xcode and Interface Builder, how to start a project from a template, how to build and run an iPad app in the Simulator, and how to customize Xcode to your liking.

✔ Chapter 6 guides you through the excruciating process of provisioning your iPad to run your app during development, and the even more inscrutable process of setting up your iPad app for development and for submission to the App Store. I put all this murky stuff into one chapter so that you don't have to hunt all over the developer center and portal looking for it.

Chapter 4

Enlisting in the Developer Corps

*B*enjamin Franklin's famous *Join, or Die* political cartoon of the 1760s could well be applied to Apple's role in today's mobile software industry. You can't gain independence on your own; you need the powerful movement of a large group. Apple needs developers, and developers need Apple.

For sure, you can develop your applications independently, and for other platforms (which is the topic of other books), but many of those platforms offer immature Software Development Kits and little or no support. What's more, you could develop for a number of platforms and then watch your product die in a diffused marketplace.

Apple is clearly on a mission with the iPad, iPhone, and App Store ecosystem to change the user experience, and you *have* to join (or die). No, you won't automatically turn into an Apple fanboy (but it doesn't hurt to be one, either). You *will* be supported with a robust Software Development Kit, comprehensive information, and reliable support.

Most importantly, you *must* join if you want to develop apps for the iPad, iPod touch, or iPhone (or any combination of these). You have to follow Apple's policies and procedures. Although the developer kit you use to develop apps for the iPad, iPod touch, and iPhone — the iPhone Software Development Kit (SDK) — is *free*, you have to register as an iPhone developer first. And don't forget — you need an Intel-based Mac running Mac OS X Snow Leopard version 10.6.2 or a newer version, in order to run the SDK.

Registering also gives you access to all the documentation and other resources found on the iPhone Developer Web site, which is where you find your iPad resources as well. This whole ritual transforms you into a *Registered iPhone Developer* capable of developing for the iPad, iPod touch, and iPhone.

You read that right: as of this writing, you use the *iPhone* developer kit, and you register as an *iPhone* developer, in order to develop for the *iPad*. You visit the *iPhone* Dev Center for resources, and use the *iPhone* OS Reference Library, and so on, for *iPad* developer information. By the time you read this, Apple may have changed the titles of all these things (my choice would be "Apple Mobile developer").

Becoming a registered developer is free, but there's a catch: If you actually want to run your application on a real iPad as opposed to only on the Simulator that comes with the SDK, you have to join the iPhone Developer Program. Fortunately, an individual membership costs only $99 as of this writing. (I should mention as well that an individual membership is required of anyone who wants to distribute his or her app using the App Store.)

Although you can register as a developer and join the iPhone Developer Program all in one step (as I show in "Joining the Developer Program" in this chapter), you may want to register as an Apple developer first. (After all, it's free.) Then, after you get your feet wet with the SDK, you can pay the fee and join the iPhone Developer Program. That's why I provide separate sections in this chapter for "Becoming a Registered Developer" and "Joining the Developer Program."

What you see when you go through this process yourself may be slightly different from what you see here. Don't panic. It's because Apple changes the site from time to time.

Becoming a Registered Developer

Although just having to register is annoying to some people, it doesn't help that the process itself can be a bit confusing. Fear not! Follow the steps, and you can safely reach the end of the road.

Your first stop is to become an Apple Registered Developer if you're not already registered, and obtain your Apple ID. If you don't want to join the iPhone Developer Program right away, you can register first for free, and then join later when you're ready to pay for the Program.

If you've already registered, you can skip to the next section to join the iPhone Developer Program with your registered developer Apple ID and password, or you can skip ahead to "Downloading the SDK" and join the iPhone Developer Program later. (You can develop software using the SDK without joining, but as you find out later, you can't run this software on your iPad until you join.)

So, without further ado, here's how to quickly become a Registered Developer:

1. **Go to the iPad section of Apple's Web site (`http://www.apple.com/ipad/`) and click the Learn More link in the SDK section in the lower-left corner, or just point your browser to `http://www.apple.com/ipad/sdk/`.**

   Doing so brings you to a page similar to the one shown in Figure 4-1, with the SDK globe logo. Apple does change this site occasionally, so when you get there, it may be a little different.

2. **Click the Download the iPhone SDK from the iPhone Dev Center link (refer to Figure 4-1).**

   The iPhone Dev Center main page appears, as shown in Figure 4-2. You may be tempted by some of the links, but they get you only so far until you log in as a registered developer. If you are registered already, click Log In and supply your Apple ID and password; you can then skip to the next section to join the iPhone Developer Program, or skip ahead to "Downloading the SDK" and join the iPhone Developer Program later.

Figure 4-1:
Start developing iPad apps here.

3. **Click the Register link in the top-right corner of the screen. (Refer to Figure 4-2.)**

   You see a page explaining why you should become a registered developer as well as what Apple has to offer registered developers, as shown in Figure 4-3.

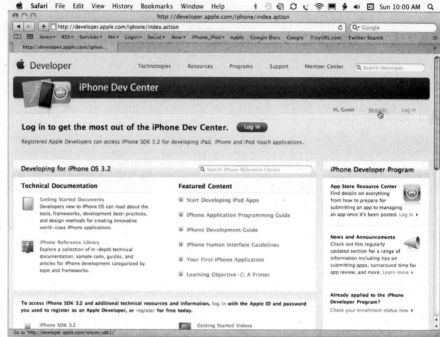

Figure 4-2:
The iPhone
Dev Center
for develop-
ing iPad
apps.

4. Click Get Started. (Refer to Figure 4-3.)

A new page appears, asking whether you want to create a new Apple ID or use an existing one.

You can use your current Apple ID (the same one you use for iTunes, MobileMe, or the Apple Store) or create a new Apple ID and then log in.

- *If you don't have an Apple ID,* select Create an Apple ID and click Continue. You find yourself at the Complete Your Personal Profile page, where you can enter your desired Apple ID and password, and proceed to Step 5.

- *If you already have an Apple ID,* select the Use an Existing Apple ID option and then click Continue. You're taken to a screen where you can log in with your Apple ID and password. That takes you to the Complete Your Personal Profile page, with some of your information already filled out.

Figure 4-3:
Register as
an Apple
Developer.

5. Continue filling out the personal profile form and then click Continue.

If you have an Apple ID, most of the form is already filled out.

You must fill in the country code in the phone number field. If you're living in the United States, the country code is 1.

6. Complete the next part of the form to finish your professional profile.

You're asked some basic business questions. After you've filled everything in and clicked the Continue button, you're taken to yet another new page, which asks you to agree to the Registered iPhone Developer Agreement.

7. Click I Agree.

Don't forget to select the confirmation check box that you have read and agree to be bound by the agreement and that you're of legal age.

If you just created your Apple ID, you're asked for the verification code sent to the e-mail address you supplied when you created your Apple ID. If you used your existing Apple ID, you'll be taken to Step 9.

8. Open the e-mail from Apple, enter the verification code, and click Continue.

Clicking Continue takes you to a thank-you page.

9. **On the thank-you page, click the Visit Phone Development Center button, and you're automatically logged in to the iPhone Dev center, which I describe in "Exploring the Dev Center" in this chapter.**

So, you're now an officially registered iPad, iPod touch, and iPhone developer, which enables you to explore the iPhone Dev Center and download the SDK (as I show in "Exploring the Dev Center" in this chapter — and you can jump to that section if you're not ready to join the iPhone Developer Program).

However, simply registering as a developer doesn't give you the status you need to actually run your app on your own (or anyone else's) iPad, iPod touch, or iPhone, or distribute your app through the App Store. The next section shows you how to get with the program — the iPhone Developer Program.

Joining the Developer Program

The Simulator application for the Mac that comes standard with the iPhone SDK is a great tool for learning to program the iPad, but it does have some limitations. It doesn't support some hardware-dependent features, and when it comes to testing, it can't really emulate such everyday iPad realities as CPU speed or memory throughput.

"Minor annoyances," you might say, and you might be right. But the real issue is that *just registering* as a developer doesn't get you two very important things — the ability to actually run your app on your own iPad, and to distribute your app through the App Store. (Remember that the App Store is the only way for commercial developers to distribute their apps — even free apps — to more than a few people.)

To run your app on a real iPad or get a chance to profile your app in the App store, you have to enroll in either the Standard or Enterprise version of the iPhone Developer Program.

It used to be that the membership approval process could take a while, and although the process does seem quicker these days, it's still true that you can't run your apps on your iPad until you're approved for the program (and of course you can't submit apps to the App Store until each app is approved, but I talk about that in Chapter 6). You should enroll as early as possible.

To join the iPhone Developer Program, follow these steps:

1. **Go to the iPad SDK section of Apple's Web site (**`http://www.apple.com/ipad/sdk`**) as shown in Figure 4-1, and scroll down to the "Test and Distribute Your iPad App" section near the bottom.**

2. **Click the Learn More button in the "Test and Distribute Your iPad App" section.**

   The iPhone Developer Program page appears, as shown in Figure 4-4.

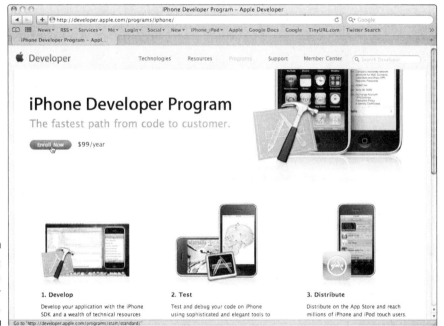

Figure 4-4:
The iPhone Developer Program.

3. **On the left side of the screen, click the Enroll Now button.**

   A new page appears with an overview of the process of joining the program, as shown in Figure 4-5.

4. **Click Continue to enroll.**

   After clicking Continue, a screen appears with the option to create a new Apple account (or use an existing one), as shown in Figure 4-6.

5. **Choose an option to create a new Apple account or use an existing one, and then click Continue.**

   Here's how to pick your option:

   • *If you already registered* (as I describe in the previous section), choose the "I'm registered as a developer with Apple…" option from the Existing Apple Developer options on the right. Choose the "I'm currently an ADC Select, Premier, or Student Member…" option if you are a student, ADC Select, or Premier member (for more information about these programs, see `http://developer.apple.com/programs/adcbenefits/`). If you already joined the Mac Developer Program, choose the "I'm currently enrolled…" option to add the iPhone Developer Program to your account.

Figure 4-5:
Overview of
the process
of joining
the program.

Figure 4-6:
Create
a new
account
or use an
existing one.

• *If you haven't registered yet,* choose one of the New Apple Developer options: if you have an Apple ID already (from iTunes Store or Apple Store purchases), choose the "I currently have an Apple ID..." option. If not, choose the "I need to create a new account..." option.

As of this writing, the Individual program costs $99 for developing for the iPad, iPhone, and iPod touch; the Company program costs $299 and is designed for companies developing proprietary in-house apps for the iPad, iPhone, and iPod touch. To be sure you're selecting the option that meets your needs, give the program details a once-over.

After clicking Continue, a screen appears asking if you are enrolling as an Individual or a Company, and providing information about the Individual and Company enrollment options.

6. **Click Individual to enroll as an Individual, or Company to enroll as a Company.**

   After clicking Individual or Company, the Apple Developer Program Enrollment Personal Profile page appears if you need to continue adding personal information for an Apple account and to register as a developer — follow the steps in the previous section to register and agree to the developer agreement, and you are taken to the page for entering payment information. If you are already registered and have already agreed to the developer agreement, you go directly to the payment page.

7. **Enter your payment information, and click Continue.**

   Depending on the option you selected, you're either given the opportunity to pay (if you selected Individual) or you're asked for some more company information and then given the ability to pay. (But pay you will.)

   Although joining as an Individual is easier than joining as a Company, there are clearly some advantages to enrolling as a Company. For example, you can add team members (which I discuss in connection with the developer portal in Chapter 6), and your Company name appears in your listing in the App Store.

When you join as an Individual, your real name shows up when the user buys (or downloads for free) your app in the App Store. If you're concerned about privacy, or if you want to seem "bigger," the extra work involved in signing up as a Company may be worthwhile for you.

8. **Continue through the process, and eventually you will be accepted in the Developer Program of your choice.**

After acceptance, you can log in to the iPhone Dev Center as an Official iPhone Developer and see the page shown in Figure 4-7.

If you click the iPhone Provisioning Portal link in the right column, as shown in Figure 4-7, you see all sorts of things you can do as a developer in the portal, which is shown in Figure 4-8.

You shouldn't linger too long in the iPhone Provisioning Portal, simply because it can be really confusing unless you understand the process. Click the Go To iPhone Dev Center link in the upper-right corner of the page (refer to Figure 4-8) to go back to the iPhone Dev Center. In Chapter 6, I explain the iPhone Provisioning Portal, which lets you provision your device, run your application on it, and prepare your creation for distribution to the App Store.

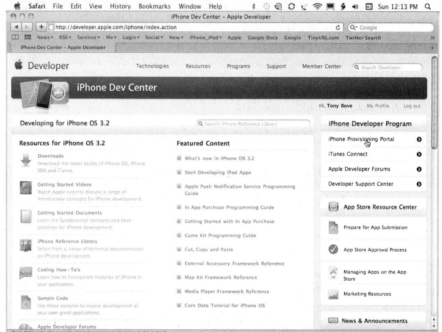

Figure 4-7:
The iPhone Dev Center with resources and downloads.

Exploring the iPhone Dev Center

You can find out more about the resources available to you in the iPhone Dev Center later in the section entitled "Resources in the Dev Center," but for the moment, I want you to get prepared for what you're *really* after — the iPhone SDK, which enables you to develop apps for the iPad.

The SDK offers tools for developing iPad, iPod touch, and iPhone apps. Here's a handy list of what's inside:

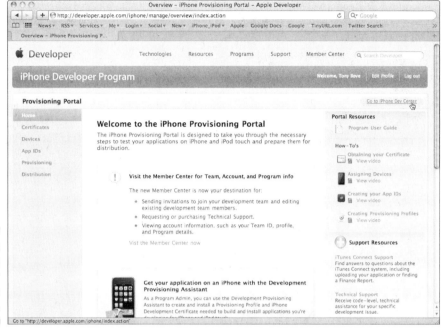

Figure 4-8:
The iPhone
Developer
Program
Portal.

✔ **Xcode:** This refers to Apple's complete development environment, which integrates all the SDK's features: the code editor, the build system, the graphical debugger, and project management. (I introduce you to the code editor's features in more detail in Chapter 5.)

✔ **Frameworks:** The SDK's multiple *frameworks* (code libraries that act a lot like prefab building blocks for building your app) help make it easy to develop apps for the Mac as well as for the iPad, iPhone, and iPod touch. Every iPad, iPhone, and iPod touch application is built using the UIKit framework and therefore has essentially the same core architecture; our sample app DeepThoughts in Part IV also uses the Foundation and CoreGraphics frameworks. Creating an app can be thought of as simply adding your application-specific behavior to the frameworks. The frameworks do all the rest. The frameworks provide fundamental code for building your iPad app: the required application behavior, classes for windows, views (including those that display text and Web content), controls, and view controllers. (I cover all these things in Chapter 7.) The UIKit framework even provides standard interfaces to core location data, the user's contacts and Photo library, and accelerometer data.

✔ **Interface Builder:** You find out about Interface Builder in Chapter 5, and use it to build the user interface for the DeepThoughts application in Part IV. But Interface Builder is more than your run-of-the-mill program that builds graphical user interfaces. In Chapter 11, you see how Xcode and Interface Builder work together to give you ways to build (and automatically create at runtime) the user interface — as well as helping to create the infrastructure for your application.

✔ **iPad/iPhone Simulator:** The Simulator enables you to debug your app and do some other testing on your Mac by simulating the iPad or iPhone. The Simulator runs most iPad and iPhone apps, but it doesn't support some hardware-dependent features. I give you a rundown on the Simulator in Chapter 5.

✔ **Instruments:** The Instruments application lets you measure how your app performs while it's running on an iPad. It gives you a number of performance metrics, including those for testing memory and network use. It also works (in a limited way) on the Simulator, and you can test some aspects of your design there.

The Simulator doesn't emulate such real-life iPad characteristics as CPU speed or memory throughput. If you want to understand how your app performs on the iPad from a user's perspective, you have to use the actual iPad and the Instruments application.

Looking forward to using the SDK

The tools in the SDK support a development process that most people find comfortable. They allow you to rapidly get a user interface up and running to see what it actually looks like. You can add code a little at a time and then run it after each new addition to see how it works. I take you through this incremental process as you develop the DeepThoughts app; for now, here's a bird's-eye view of iPad app development, one step at a time:

1. **Start with Xcode.**

   Xcode provides several project templates that you can use to get off to a fast start. (In Chapter 5, you do just that, and then you add code and more interface objects in Part IV.)

2. **Design and create the user interface.**

   Interface Builder has graphic-design tools you can use to create your app's user interface. These tools save you a great deal of time and effort. They also reduce the amount of code you have to write by creating resource files that your app can then upload automatically.

   If you don't want to use Interface Builder, you can always build your user interface from scratch, creating each individual piece and linking them all together within your app. Sometimes Interface Builder is the best way to create onscreen elements; sometimes the hands-on approach works better.

3. **Write the code.**

   The Xcode editor provides several features that help you write code. You can find out more about these features in Chapter 10.

4. **Build and run your app.**

   You build your app on your Mac and run it in the iPad/iPhone Simulator application or (provided you've joined the iPhone Development Program) on your iPad.

5. **Test your app.**

   You'll want to test the functionality of your app as well as response time.

6. **Measure and tune your app's performance.**

   After you have a running app, make sure that it makes optimal use of resources such as memory and CPU cycles.

7. **Do it all again until you're done.**

Resources in the Dev Center

You're not left on your own when it comes to the Seven-Step Plan for Creating Great iPad Apps in the preceding section. After all, you have this book to help you on the way — as well as a heap of information squirreled away in various corners of the iPhone Dev Center (refer to Figure 4-7). The following resources are especially helpful:

✔ **Getting Started Videos:** These videos are relatively light on content.

✔ **Getting Started Documents:** Think of them as an introduction to the materials in the iPhone Reference Library, which is the essential library for learning about developing for the iPad, iPod touch, and iPhone. These give you an overview of development and best practices. Included is "Learning Objective-C: A Primer," an overview of Objective-C — the programming language you'll use to code your apps. You can also find links to "Object-Oriented Programming with Objective-C" and "The Objective-C 2.0 Programming Language" (the definitive guide).

If you've never programmed in the Objective-C language, you should check out the basic information in the iPhone Reference Library. If you want to get a handle on Objective-C as quickly (and painlessly) as possible, go get yourself a copy of *Objective-C For Dummies* by coauthor Neal. (Neal does a great job explaining everything you need to know in order to program in Objective-C, and he assumes you have little or no knowledge of programming.)

✔ **The iPhone Reference Library:** This library includes all the documentation you could ever want for developing for the iPad, iPod touch, and iPhone (except, of course, the answer to that one question you really need answered at 3 a.m., but that's the way it goes). To be honest, most of this stuff only turns out to be really useful *after* you have a good handle on what you're doing. As you go through this book, however, you'll discover that an easier way to access some of this documentation will be through the Xcode Documentation window, described in Chapter 10.

✔ **Coding How-To's:** These tend to be a lot more valuable when you already have something of a knowledge base.

✔ **Sample Code:** On the one hand, sample code of any kind is always valuable. Most good developers look over sample apps before they get started building their own. They'll take something that closely approximates what they want to do, and they modify it until it does exactly what they want it to do. When I started iPad development, there were no books like this one; so much of what I learned came from looking at the samples and then making some changes to see how things worked. On the other hand, perusing the sample apps can give you hours of (misguided) pleasure and can be quite the time waster and task avoider.

✔ **Apple Developer Forums:** I'm not the first to say that developer forums can be very helpful, and I'm also not the first to admit that they're a great way to procrastinate. As you scroll through the questions people have, be careful about some of the answers you see. No one is validating the information people are giving out. But take heart: Pretty soon you'll be able to answer some of those questions better yourself.

Downloading the SDK

Enough prep work. Time to do some downloading.

As of this writing, Apple offers version 3.2 of the SDK for both iPad and iPhone development. You use SDK version 3.2 to develop apps that are compatible with iPhone OS 3.2 (the iPad's operating system).

To install the SDK, click the Downloads link near the top of the iPhone Dev Center page under "Resources for iPhone OS 3.2" (refer to Figure 4-7) to automatically jump down to the Downloads section at the bottom of the page, as shown in Figure 4-9 (or scroll down the page yourself until you find the Downloads section).

Version 3.2 requires an Intel-based Mac running Mac OS X Snow Leopard version 10.6.2 or a newer version.

By the time you read this book, it may no longer be version 3.2. You should download the latest SDK. That way, you'll get the most recent version to start with.

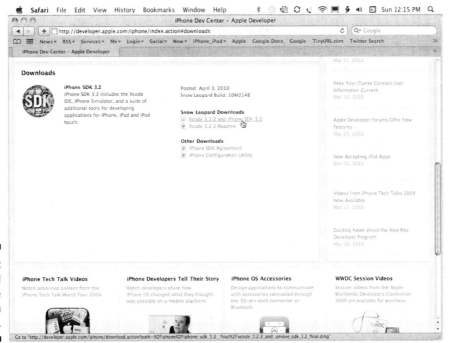

Figure 4-9:
Download
the iPhone
SDK version
3.2 beta.

In the Snow Leopard Downloads section, there is a link to a Read Me file (Xcode 3.2.2 Read Me). Click this link to read the file, which describes what Xcode can do (most of which I explain in Chapter 5).

After perusing the Read Me file, download the SDK by clicking the Xcode 3.2.2 and iPhone SDK 3.2 link in the Snow Leopard Downloads section, or just click the SDK globe logo.

You can watch the download in Safari's download window (which is only a little better than watching paint dry).

When it's done downloading, the iPhone SDK window appears onscreen, complete with an installer and various packages tied to the install process. All you then have to do is double-click the iPhone SDK installer and follow the (really simple) installation instructions. After you do all that, you have your very own iPhone Software Development Kit on your hard drive, ready to create iPad apps.

Getting Yourself Ready for the SDK

Don't despair. The preceding process was tedious, but as the song goes, "It's all over now." Going through the process of registering and joining the program is probably the *second* most annoying part of your journey toward developing software for the iPad. The most annoying part is figuring out what Apple calls *provisioning* your iPad — the hoops you have to jump through to actually run your app on a real, tangible, existing iPad. You go through the provisioning process in Chapter 6, and frankly, getting *that* process explained is worth the price of this book.

In the next chapter, you get started using the SDK you just downloaded, and you'll become intimately acquainted with the SDK during the course of your project. I assume that you have some programming knowledge and that you also have some acquaintance with object-oriented programming, with some variant of C, such as C++, C#, and maybe even with Objective-C. If those assumptions miss the mark, help me out, okay? Take another look at the "Resources in the Dev Center" section, earlier in this chapter, for an overview of some of the resources that can help you get up to speed on some programming basics. Or, better yet, get yourself a copy of *Objective-C For Dummies*.

I also assume that you're familiar with the iPad itself and that you've explored at least Apple's preinstalled apps to become familiar with the iPad's look and feel.

Chapter 5

Getting to Know the SDK

● ●

In This Chapter

▶ Getting a handle on the Xcode project

▶ Compiling an iPhone app

▶ Peeking inside the Simulator

▶ Checking out the Interface Builder

▶ Demystifying nib files

● ●

*A*rthur C. Clarke's Third Law is that any sufficiently advanced technology is indistinguishable from magic, and Steve Jobs echoed these words when he announced the iPad as "our most advanced technology in a magical and revolutionary device." To deploy this magic and practice the alchemy of application development, you need to learn how to use the development tools.

The collection of tools known as the iPhone Software Development Kit (SDK) is the crucible for grinding out an iPad app. You pick a template for the type of app; stir in the content, behavior, and user interface; and cast your spells with magical code. The SDK builds your final product. Sounds easy, and to be truthful, it's *relatively* easy.

In this chapter, I introduce you to the SDK. It's going to be a low-key, get-acquainted kind of affair. You get into the real nuts-and-bolts stuff in Parts IV and V, when you actually develop the two sample applications.

Developing Using the SDK

The Software Development Kit (SDK) gives you the opportunity to develop your apps without tying your brain up in knots. It includes Xcode, Apple's development environment that runs on the Mac OS X operating system. To develop an iPad app, you have to work within the context of an Xcode project. The SDK also includes Interface Builder, an application that runs on Mac

OS X, which you can use to quickly build your app's user interface. The idea here is to add your code incrementally — step by step — so that you can always step back and see how what you just did affects the Big Picture.

Starting an app from scratch

This chapter assumes that you are creating a new iPad app (in particular, the DeepThoughts sample app) from scratch, using the Xcode templates to get started — which is certainly the fastest way to get started. The Seven Development Steps to iPad App Heaven should look something like this:

1. Start with an Xcode template.

2. Design the user interface.

3. Write the code.

4. Build and run your app.

5. Test your app.

6. Measure and tune your app's performance.

7. Do it all again (or at least Steps 3–6) until you're done.

If you have an idea for a new iPad app, the decision to start from scratch should be obvious. But if you've already developed an iPhone/iPod touch app, you have choices in how you use Xcode to develop your iPad app.

Starting from an existing iPhone app

Besides the fact that iPhone apps already run on the iPad in "compatibility mode" (in a black box in the center of the display, or scaled up to full screen), you can also *port* the iPhone app — modify its code just a bit — to use iPad device resources. Xcode makes the porting process easier by automating much of the setup process for your project. The most noticeable difference between the iPad and iPhone, besides the absence of telephony, is the size of views you create to present your user interface.

Xcode simplifies the process of updating your existing iPhone project to include the necessary files to support the iPad. Essentially, you would be using a single Xcode project to create two separate apps: one for the iPhone (and iPod touch) and one for the iPad. After selecting the target in the Targets section of the Groups & Files list of the Xcode Project window (which I show in the next section of this chapter), you can choose Project⇨Upgrade Current Target for iPad, and then choose to either upgrade your iPhone target to a *universal* application that supports both iPhone and iPad, or create a *separate* iPad application target based on your iPhone target. Here are the differences to help you make that decision:

- ✔ A *universal* application is optimized for all device types. Although I don't cover creating a universal application in this chapter, creating a universal application allows you to sell one app that supports all device types. This choice makes the download experience simpler for users. (You can set one price, and users can use the same copy of the app on both their iPhone and iPad.)

- ✔ *Separate* application targets are designed specifically for the device — iPhone (and iPod touch) or iPad. Although I don't cover this method in this chapter, it gives you the advantage of reusing code from your existing iPhone app while also taking less development and testing time than developing a universal app.

You also have the choice of using *separate Xcode projects* to create separate apps for the iPad and iPhone. Essentially, this means starting from scratch. (See the earlier section "Starting an app from scratch.") If you have to rewrite large portions of your code anyway, then creating a separate Xcode project for the iPad is usually simpler. Creating a separate project gives you the freedom to tailor your code for the iPad without having to worry about whether that code runs on other devices. If your app's data objects are tightly integrated with the views that draw them, or if you just need the freedom to add more features to the iPad version, this is the way to go.

Whether you create separate application targets in one project, or create separate projects, you still end up with two separate apps to manage. The only way to have only one app to manage for both iPhone and iPad is to create a universal app.

In this chapter, you start at the very beginning, from scratch, with the very first step, which is Xcode. (Starting with Step 1? What a concept!) And the first step of the first step is to create your first project.

Creating Your Xcode Project

To develop an app, you work in what's called an *Xcode project*. So, time to fire one up. Here's how it's done:

1. **Launch Xcode.**

   After you've downloaded the SDK (painstakingly described in Chapter 4), it's a snap to launch Xcode. By default, it's downloaded to `/Developer/Applications`, where you can track it down to launch it.

Here are a couple of hints to make Xcode handier and more efficient:

- Drag the icon for the Xcode application all the way down to the Dock, so you can launch it from there. You'll be using it a lot, so it wouldn't hurt to be able to launch it from the Dock.

- When you first launch Xcode, you see the Welcome screen shown in Figure 5-1 (after using Xcode to create projects, your Welcome screen will list all of your most recent projects in the right column). It's chock-full of links to the Apple Developer Connection and Xcode documentation. (If you don't want to be bothered with the Welcome screen in the future, deselect the Show This Window When Xcode Launches check box. You can also just click Cancel to close the Welcome screen.)

Figure 5-1:
The Xcode
Welcome
screen.

2. **Choose Create a New Xcode Project from the Welcome screen (or choose File⊃New Project) to create a new project.**

   You can also just press Shift+⌘+N.

   No matter what you do to start a new project, you're greeted by the New Project window, as shown in Figure 5-2.

   The New Project window is where you get to choose the template you want for your new project. Note that the leftmost pane has two sections: one for the iPhone OS and the other for Mac OS X.

3. **In the upper-left corner of the New Project window, click Application under the iPhone OS heading if it isn't already selected.**

   With Application selected, the main pane of the New Project window shows several choices. (See Figure 5-2.) Each of these choices is actually a template that, when chosen, generates some code to get you started.

Figure 5-2:
The New
Project
window.

4. **Select View-based Application from the template choices displayed.**

   You'll use the Select View-based Application option to start the DeepThoughts app, the first sample app, which you develop in Part IV.

   Note that when you select a template, a brief description of the template is displayed underneath the main pane. (Again, refer to Figure 5-2 to see a description of the View-based Application template. In fact, click some of the other template choices just to see how they're described as well. Just be sure to click the View-based Application template again when you're done snooping around so you can follow along with developing the DeepThoughts app.)

5. **Select iPad from the Product pop-up menu, as shown in Figure 5-3, and then click Choose.**

   You must choose iPad (*not* iPhone) from the Product pop-up menu to start a new iPad project from scratch — this choice puts the standard iPad resources into your project. After clicking Choose, the Save As dialog appears.

6. **Enter a name for your new project in the Save As field, choose a Save location (the Desktop or any folder works just fine) and then click Save.**

   I named the first sample app project DeepThoughts. (You should do the same if you're following along with developing DeepThoughts.)

   After you click Save, Xcode creates the project and opens the Project window, which should look like what you see in Figure 5-4.

Figure 5-3:
Select
iPad in the
Product
pop-up.

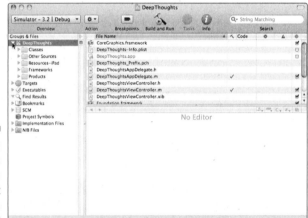

Figure 5-4:
The Deep
Thoughts
Project
window.

Exploring Your Project

It turns out that you do most of your work on projects using a Project window. If you have a nice, large monitor, expand the Project window so you can see everything in it as big as life. This is, in effect, Command Central for developing your iPad app; it displays and organizes your source files and the other resources needed to build your app.

You have control over Command Central — you can organize your source files and resources as you see fit. The Groups & Files list on the left is an outline view of all of your project's files — source code, frameworks, and graphics, as well as some settings files. You can move files and folders around and add new folders.

For example, back in Figure 5-4, you can see that I renamed the plain-vanilla Resources folder to Resources-iPad — I just clicked on the name of the folder, as you would in the Finder, and typed over the name with the new name.

You might want to rename Resources to Resources-iPad so that you can distinguish between iPad and iPhone resources, in case you use a single project to develop both iPad and iPhone apps. To learn more about using a single project for both types of apps, see "Starting from an existing iPhone app" in this chapter.

You may notice that some of the items in the Groups & Files list are folders, whereas others are just icons. Most items have a little triangle (the disclosure triangle) next to them. Clicking the little triangle to the left of a folder/icon expands the folder/icon to show what's in it. Click the triangle again to hide what it contains.

To see more of the code that's already provided with the View-based Application template, select Classes in the Groups & Files list on the left side of the Project window, as shown in Figure 5-5. The first file should already be selected in the Detail view of the Project window: `DeepThoughtsAppDelegate.h`. (Actually, you can select any file in the Detail view to see code.) The code appears in the Editor view.

Breakpoints button   Build and Run button

Toolbar   Action menu   Tasks button   Text editor navigation bar

Overview menu   Info button   Search   Detail view

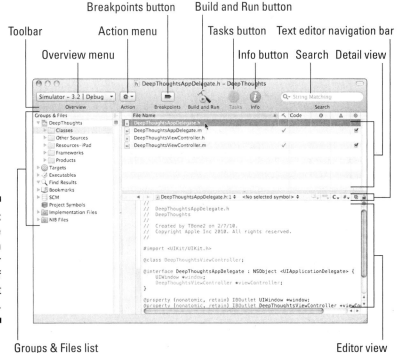

Figure 5-5: Code appears in the Editor view of the project window.

Groups & Files list   Editor view

Here's a summary of what you see in Figure 5-5:

- ✔ **The Groups & Files list:** As described above, the Groups & Files list provides an outline view of everything in your project. If you select an item in the Groups & Files list, the contents of the item are displayed in the topmost-pane to the right — otherwise known as the Detail view.

- ✔ **The Detail view:** Here you get detailed information about the item you selected in the Groups & Files list.

- ✔ **The Toolbar:** Here you can find quick access to the most common Xcode commands. You can customize the toolbar to your heart's content by right-clicking it and selecting Customize Toolbar from the contextual menu that appears. You can also choose View➪Customize Toolbar.

  - The Overview menu lets you specify the active SDK and active configuration, which I describe in "Building and Running Your Application" in this chapter.

  - The Action menu lets you perform common operations on the currently selected item in the project window. The actions change depending on what you've selected (the same actions are available in the context-sensitive shortcut menu that appears when you Control-click a selected item).

  - Pressing the Build and Run button compiles, links, and launches your app.

  - The Breakpoints button turns breakpoints on and off and toggles the Build and Run button to Build and Debug. (I explain breakpoints in Chapter 12.)

  - The Tasks button allows you to stop the execution of the app that you've built.

  - The Info button opens a window that displays information and settings for your project.

  - The Search field lets you search the items currently displayed in the Detail view. I show you how to search for items in Chapter 10.

  - The Show/hide Toolbar button shows or hides the entire Toolbar.

- ✔ **The status bar:** Look here for messages about your project. (There are none yet in Figure 5-5; for a peek at a status message, see Figure 5-7.) For example, when you're building your project, Xcode updates the status bar to show where you are in the process — and whether or not the process completed successfully.

- ✔ **The favorites bar:** Works like other favorites bars you're certainly familiar with; so you can bookmark places in your project. This bar isn't displayed by default (nor is it shown in Figure 5-5); to put it onscreen, choose View➪Layout➪Show Favorites Bar from the main menu.

✔ **The Text Editor navigation bar:** As shown in Figure 5-6, this navigation bar contains a number of shortcuts (I explain more about them as you use them):

- *Bookmarks menu:* You create a bookmark by choosing Edit⇨Add to Bookmarks.

- *Breakpoints menu:* Lists the breakpoints in the current file — I cover breakpoints in Chapter 12.

- *Class Hierarchy menu:* The superclass of this class, the superclass of that superclass (if any), and so on. In Objective-C, you can base a new class definition on a class already defined, so that the new class inherits the methods of the base class it is based on. The base class is called a superclass; the new class is its subclass, and the hierarchy defines the relationship between a superclass, its subclass, and sublcasses of the subclass (and so on). For a background in Objective-C, see *Objective-C For Dummies.*

- *Included Files menu:* Lists both the files included by the current file, as well as the files that include the current file.

- *Counterpart button:* Due to the natural split in the definition of an Objective-C class into interface and implementation, a class's code is often split into two files. The Counterpart button allows you to switch between the header (or interface) file, such as `DeepThoughtsAppDelegate.h`, and the implementation file, such as `DeepThoughtsAppDelegate .m`. The header files define the class's interface by specifying the class declaration (and what it inherits from); instance variables (a variable defined in a class — at runtime all objects have their own copy); and methods. The implementation file, on the other hand, contains the code for each method.

- *Lock button:* Indicates whether the selected file is unlocked for editing or locked (preventing changes). If it's locked, you can click the button to unlock the file (if you have permission).

Figure 5-6:
The Text Editor navigation bar.

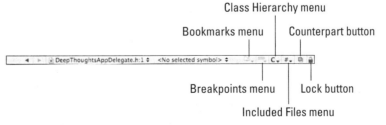

Class Hierarchy menu

Bookmarks menu   Counterpart button

Breakpoints menu   Lock button

Included Files menu

✔ **The Editor view:** Displays a file you've selected, in either the Groups & Files list or Detail view. You can also edit your files here — after all, that's what you'd expect from the Editor view — although some folks prefer to double-click a file in Groups & Files list or Detail view to open the file in a separate window.

To see how the Editor view works, refer to Figure 5-5, where I've clicked the Classes folder in the Groups & Files list, and the DeepThoughtsAppDelegate.h class in the Detail view. You can see the code for the class in the Editor view.

Right under the Lock button (refer to Figure 5-5) is a tiny window shade icon that lets you split the Editor view. Click it to look at the interface and implementation files at the same time, or even the code for two different methods in the same or different classes.

If you have any questions about what something does, just position the mouse pointer above the icon, and a tooltip explains it.

The first item in the Groups & Files list, as you can see back in Figure 5-5, is labeled DeepThoughts. This is the container that contains all the source elements for the project, including source code, resource files, graphics, and a number of other pieces that will remain unmentioned for now (but I get into those in due course). You can see that this project container has five distinct groups — Classes, Other Sources, Resources (now renamed to Resources-iPad), Frameworks, and Products. Here's what gets tossed into each group:

✔ **Classes** is the group in which Xcode places all of the template code for DeepThoughts, and you should also place new classes you create in the Classes group — although you are not obliged to. The Classes group has four distinct source-code files (which you can see in Figure 5-5):

  • DeepThoughtsAppDelegate.h

  • DeepThoughtsAppDelegate.m

  • DeepThoughtsViewController.h

  • DeepThoughtsViewController.m

✔ **Other Sources** is the group in which you typically would find the frameworks you are using — stuff like DeepThoughts_Prefix.pch as well as main.m, your application's main function, both of which are described in Chapter 8.

✔ The **Resources** group (renamed to Resources-iPad) contains, well, resources specifically for the iPad, such as .xib files (which you learn about in "Using Interface Builder" in this chapter), property lists (which you will encounter in Chapter 16), images, and other media files, and even some data files.

Whenever you choose the View-based Application template (refer to Figure 5-2), Xcode creates the following files for you:

- *YourProject*-Info.plist
- DeepThoughtsViewController.xib
- MainWindow.xib

I explain .xib files in excruciating detail in this chapter, and you get to play with them in Chapter 9 and the rest of Part IV. Soon you'll love .xib files as much as I do.

✔ **Frameworks** are code libraries that act a lot like prefab building blocks for your code edifice. (I talk a lot about frameworks in Chapter 7.) By choosing the View-based Application template, you let Xcode know that it should add the UIKit framework, Foundation.framework, and CoreGraphics.framework to your project, because it expects that you'll need them in an app based on the View-based Application template.

The DeepThoughts app is limited to just these three frameworks, but I show you how to add an additional framework to the iPadTravel411 sample app in Chapter 14.

✔ The **Products** group is a bit different from the previous three items in this list: It's not a source for your app, but rather *the compiled app itself.* In it, you find DeepThoughts.app. At the moment, this file is listed in red because the file can't be found (which makes sense because you haven't built the app yet).

A file's name appearing in red lets you know that Xcode can't find the underlying physical file.

If you happen to open the DeepThoughts folder on your Mac, you won't see the "folders" that appear in the Xcode window. That's because those folders are simply groupings that help organize and find what you're looking for; this list of files can grow to be pretty large, even in a moderate-size project.

When you have a lot files, you'll have better luck finding things if you create subgroups within the Classes, and/or Resources groups, or even whole new groups. You create subgroups (or even new groups) in the Groups & Files list by choosing New Project⇨New Group. You then can select a file and drag it to a new group or subgroup.

Building and Running Your Application

It's really a blast to see what you get when you build and run a project that you yourself created — even if all you did was choose a template from the Project window. Building and running a project is relatively simple:

1. **If it is not already chosen, choose Simulator - 3.2 | Debug from the Overview drop-down menu in the top-left corner of the project window to set the active SDK and Active Build Configuration.**

This combination (Simulator - 3.2 | Debug) may be already chosen, as you can see back in Figure 5-5. Here's what that means:

- When you download an SDK, you may actually download *multiple* SDKs — a Simulator SDK and a device SDK for each of the current iPhone OS releases.

- The one to use for iPad development is the *Simulator* SDK for iPhone OS *3.2.* Later, you can switch to the actual device SDK and download your app to a real-world iPad, as described in Chapter 6. But before you do that, there's just one catch. . . .

- You have to be in the iPhone Developer Program to run your app on a device, even on your very own iPad. Go to Chapter 4 and enlist in the program if you haven't done so already.

A *build configuration* tells Xcode the purpose of the built product. You can choose between Debug, which has features to help with debugging (there's a no-brainer for you); and Release, which results in smaller and faster binaries. You use Debug most of the time as you develop and app, and I use Debug for most of this book — so go with Debug for now. (Choose Simulator - 3.2 | Debug from the Overview drop-down menu.)

2. **Choose Build⇨Build and Run from the main menu to build and run the application.**

   You can also press ⌘+Return or click the Build and Run button in the Project Window toolbar. The status bar in the Project window tells you all about build progress, build errors such as compiler errors, or warnings — and (oh, yeah) whether the build was successful. Figure 5-7 shows that this was a successful build, (Check out the `Succeeded` message in the bottom-right corner of the window.)

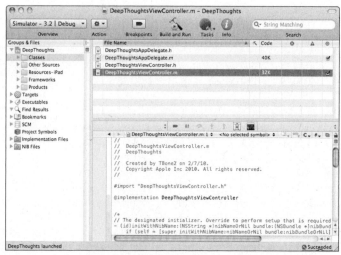

Figure 5-7:
A success-
ful build.

Because you selected Debug for the active build configuration (Simulator – 3.2 | Debug), the Debugger Console may launch for you, as shown in Figure 5-8, depending on your Xcode preferences (more about them in a second). If you don't see the console, choose Run➪Console to display it. You can also display the Build Results window, shown in Figure 5-9, by clicking the Succeeded message in the Status bar (You find out more about debugging and the Build Results window in Chapter 12.)

Figure 5-8:
The
Debugger
Console.

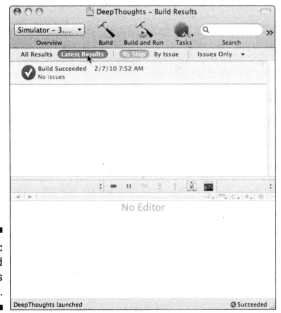

Figure 5-9:
The Build
Results
window.

After it's launched in the Simulator, your first app looks a lot like what you see in Figure 5-10. You should see the black status bar and a white window, and the simulated Home button on the bottom to quit your app, but that's it. You can also choose actions in the Hardware menu (shown in Figure 5-10), which I explain next.

Figure 5-10:
The Deep
Thoughts
app in the
Simulator.

The Simulator

When you run your app, Xcode installs it on the Simulator (or a real iPad if you specified the device as the active SDK, as shown in Chapter 6) and launches it. Using the Hardware menu and your keyboard and mouse, the Simulator mimics most of what a user can do on a real iPad, albeit with some limitations that I point out shortly.

Hardware interaction

You use the Simulator's Hardware menu (refer to Figure 5-10) when you want the Simulator to simulate the following:

- **Rotate left:** Choosing Hardware➪Rotate Left rotates the Simulator to the left. If the Simulator is in portrait view, it changes to landscape view; if the Simulator is already in landscape view, it changes to portrait view.

- **Rotate right:** Choosing Hardware➪Rotate Right rotates the Simulator to the right, with the same effect as choosing Hardware➪Rotate Left.

- **Use a shake gesture:** Choosing Hardware➪Shake Gesture simulates shaking the iPad.

- **Go to the Home screen:** Choosing Hardware➪Home does the expected — you go to the Home screen.

- **Lock the Simulator (device):** Choosing Hardware➪Lock locks the simulator.

- **Send the running app low-memory warnings:** Choosing Hardware➪ Simulate Memory Warning fakes out your app by sending it a (fake) low-memory warning. I don't cover this in this book, but it's a great feature for seeing how your app may function out there in the real world.

- **Toggle the status bar between its Normal state and its In Call state:** Choose Hardware➪Toggle In-Call Status Bar to check out how your app functions when the device is not answering a call (Normal state) and when it supposedly *is* answering a call (In Call state) — these choices apply only to the iPhone as of this writing.

- **Simulate the hardware keyboard:** Choose Hardware➪Simulate Hardware Keyboard to check out how your app functions when the iPad is connected to the optional physical keyboard dock.

Gestures

On the real device, a gesture is something you do with your fingers to make something happen in the device, like a tap, or a drag, and so on. Table 5-1 shows you how to simulate gestures using your mouse and keyboard.

Table 5-1	Gestures in the Simulator
Gesture	*iPad Action*
Tap	Click the mouse.
Touch and hold	Hold down the mouse button.
Double tap	Double-click the mouse.
Swipe	1. Click where you want to start and hold the mouse button down.
	2. Move the mouse slowly in the direction of the swipe and then release the mouse button.
Flick	1. Click where you want to start and hold the mouse button down.
	2. Move the mouse quickly in the direction of the flick and then release the mouse button.
Drag	1. Click where you want to start and hold the mouse button down.
	2. Move the mouse slowly in the drag direction.
Pinch	1. Move the mouse pointer over the place where you want to start.
	2. Hold down the Option key, which makes two circles appear that stand in for your fingers.
	3. Hold down the mouse button and move the circles in or out.

Uninstalling apps and resetting your device

You uninstall applications on the Simulator the same way you'd do it on the iPad, except you use your mouse instead of your finger.

1. **On the Home screen, place the pointer over the icon of the app you want to uninstall and hold down the mouse button until all of the app icons start to wiggle.**

2. **Click the app icon's Close button — the little *x* that appears in the upper-left corner of the icon — to make the app disappear.**

3. **Click the Home button — the one with a little square in it, centered below the screen — to stop the other app icon's wiggling and finish the uninstallation.**

You can also move an app's icon around by clicking and dragging with the mouse.

To reset the Simulator to the original factory settings — which also removes all the apps you've installed — choose iPhone Simulator⇨Reset Content and Settings.

Limitations

Keep in mind that running apps in the Simulator isn't the same thing as running them in the iPad. Here's why:

- ✔ **Different frameworks:** The Simulator uses Mac OS X versions of the low-level system frameworks, instead of the actual frameworks that run on the device.

- ✔ **Different hardware and memory:** The Simulator uses the Mac hardware and memory. To really determine how your app is going to perform on an honest-to-goodness iPad, you're going to have to run it on a real iPad. (Lucky for you, I show you how to do that in Chapter 6.)

- ✔ **Different installation procedure:** Xcode installs *your* app in the Simulator automatically when you build the app using the Simulator SDK. All fine and dandy, but there's no way to get Xcode to install *other* apps from the App Store in the Simulator.

- ✔ **Lack of GPS:** You can't fake the Simulator into thinking it's lying on the beach at Waikiki. The location reported by the CoreLocation framework in the Simulator is fixed at

    - Latitude: 37.3317 North

    - Longitude: 122.0307 West

    Which just so happens to be 1 Infinite Loop, Cupertino, CA 95014, and guess who "lives" there?

- ✔ **Two-finger limit:** You can simulate a maximum of two fingers. If your application's user interface can respond to touch events involving more than two fingers, you'll need to test that on an actual iPad. The motion of the two fingers is limited in the Simulator — you can't do two-figure swipes or drags.

- ✔ **Accelerometer differences:** You can access your computer's accelerometer (if it has one) through the UIKit framework. Its reading, however, will differ from the accelerometer readings on an iPad (for some technical reasons I don't get into).

✔ **Differences in rendering:** OpenGL ES (OpenGL for Embedded Systems), one of the 3D graphics libraries that works with the iPhone SDK, uses renderers on devices that are slightly different from those it uses in Simulator. As a result, a scene on the Simulator and the same scene on a device may not be identical at the pixel level.

Customizing Xcode to Your Liking

Xcode gives you options galore; I'm guessing you won't change any of them until you have a bit more programming experience under your belt, but a few options are actually worth thinking about now.

1. **With Xcode open, choose Xcode➪Preferences from the main menu.**

2. **Click the Debugging button on the toolbar to display the Debugging pane, as shown in Figure 5-11.**

   The Xcode Preferences window refreshes to show the Debugging pane.

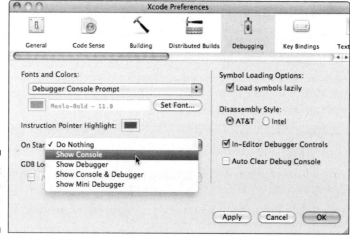

Figure 5-11: Show the console on startup.

3. **Open the On Start drop-down menu and choose Show Console (as shown in Figure 5-11). Then click Apply.**

   This step automatically opens the Console after you build your app, so you won't have to take the extra step of opening the Console to see your app's output.

4. Click the Building button in the toolbar to show the Building pane, as shown in Figure 5-12.

5. In the Build Results Window section of the Building pane, select the Open During Builds drop-down menu, and choose Always, as shown in Figure 5-12. Then click Apply.

The Always choice opens the Build Results window and keeps it open. You might not like this, but some people find that having the Build Results window onscreen all the time makes it easier to find and fix errors.

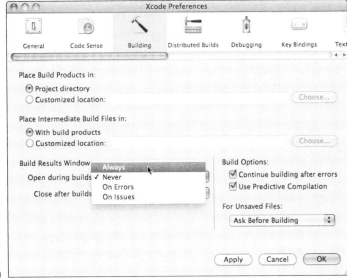

Figure 5-12:
Show
the Build
Results
window.

6. Click the Documentation button on the toolbar, as shown in Figure 5-13.

You may have to scroll the toolbar horizontally to access it.

7. Select the Check for and Install Updates Automatically check box (shown in Figure 5-13) and then click the Check and Install Now button.

This step ensures that the documentation remains up-to-date and also allows you to load and access other documentation.

8. Click OK to close the Xcode Preferences window.

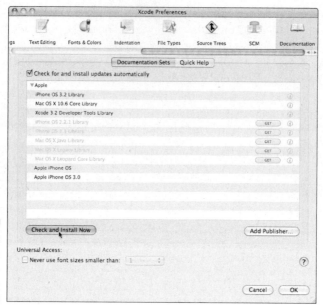

Figure 5-13:
Accessing
the docu-
mentation.

Set the tab width and other formatting options in the Indentation pane of the
Preferences window.

You can also have the Editor show line numbers. If you click Text Editing in
the Xcode Preferences toolbar to show the Text Editing pane, you can select
the Show Line Numbers check box under Display Options.

Using Interface Builder

Interface Builder is a great tool for graphically laying out your user interface.
You can use it to design your app's user interface and then save what you've
done as a resource file, which is then loaded into your app at runtime. This
resource file is then used to automatically create the single window, as well
as all your views and controls, and some of your app's other objects — view
controllers, for example. (For more on view controllers and other application
objects, check out Chapter 7.)

TIP

If you don't want to use Interface Builder, you can also create your objects programmatically — creating views and view controllers and even things like buttons and labels using your very own application code. Often Interface Builder makes things easier, but sometimes just coding it is the best way.

Here's how Interface Builder works:

1. **In your Project window's Groups & Files list, select the Resources group (renamed Resources-iPad for this example).**

   The Detail view shows the files in the Resources-iPad group, as shown in Figure 5-14.

2. **Double-click the `DeepThoughtsViewController.xib` file in the Detail view. (See Figure 5-14.)**

REMEMBER

Note that `DeepThoughtsViewController.m` is still in the Editor window; that's okay because you're set to open its associated `DeepThoughtsViewController.xib` file in the Interface Builder, not in the Editor window. That's because double-clicking always opens a file in a new window — this time, the Interface Builder window.

What you see after double-clicking are the windows as they were the last time you left them. If this is the first time you've opened Interface Builder, you see windows that look something like those in Figure 5-15.

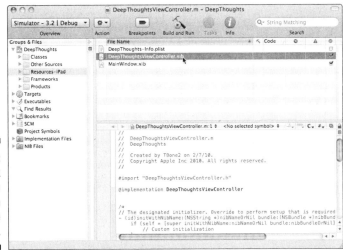

Figure 5-14:
Double-click the .xib file to launch Interface Builder.

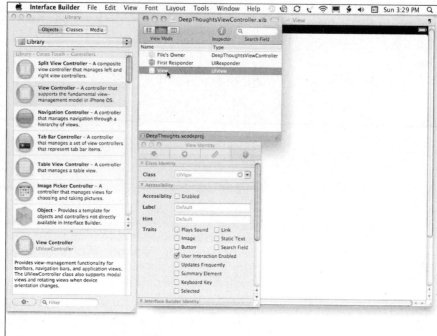

Figure 5-15:
The .xib file
in Interface
Builder.

Interface Builder supports two file types: an older format that uses the extension `.nib` and a newer format that utilizes the extension `.xib`. The iPad project templates all use `.xib` files. Although the file extension is `.xib`, everyone still calls them *nib files*. The term *nib* and the corresponding file extension `.xib` are acronyms for NeXT Interface Builder. The Interface Builder application was originally developed at NeXT Computer, whose OPENSTEP operating system was used as the basis for creating Mac OS X.

The window labeled `DeepThoughtsViewController.xib` (the top center window in Figure 5-15) is the nib's main window. It acts as a table of contents for the nib file. With the exception of the first two icons (File's Owner and First Responder), every icon in this window (in this case, there's only one, View, but you'll find more as you get into nib files) represents a single instance of an Objective-C class that will be created automatically for you when this nib file is loaded, as I describe in Chapter 8.

Interface Builder doesn't generate any code that you have to modify or even look at. Instead, it creates the ingredients for "instant" Objective-C objects that the nib loading code combines and turns into real objects at runtime.

If you were to take a closer look at the three objects in the
DeepThoughtsViewController.xib file window (refer to Figure 5-15) —
and if you had a pal who knew the iPad backwards and forwards — you'd find
out the following about each object:

✔ **The File's Owner proxy object:** This is the controller object that's
responsible for the contents of the nib file. In this case, the File's Owner
object is actually the DeepThoughtsViewController that was created by Xcode. The File's Owner object is not created from the nib file.
It's created in one of two ways: either from another (previous) nib file or
by a programmer who codes it manually.

✔ **First Responder proxy object:** This object is the first entry in an app's
dynamically constructed responder chain (a term I explain in Chapter
8) and is the object with which the user is currently interacting. If,
for example, the user taps a text field to enter some data, the First
Responder would then become the Text Field object.

Although you might use the First Responder mechanism quite a bit in
your apps, there's actually nothing you have to do to manage it. It's
automatically set and maintained by the UIKit framework.

✔ **View object:** The View icon represents an instance of the UIView class
of objects. A UIView class of object is an area (in this case, the view)
that a user can see and interact with.

If you take another look at Figure 5-15, you notice three other windows open
besides the main window. Look at the View window (the one with "View" in
the window's title, which appears on the right side partially hidden by the
other windows). In the far-right corner of the top of the View window, you see
the battery icon for the iPad in the black simulated status bar. That window
is the graphical representation of the View icon in your app — how your new
app appears on the iPad display.

If you close the View window and then double-click the View icon in the
DeepThoughtsViewController.xib window, this View window opens
again.

Not surprisingly (because you haven't added any data or unique code to
your app yet), the View window shows the same view — a white screen with
the black status bar and battery icon — as the Simulator shows when it runs
your bare-bones template-based app. (Refer to Figure 5-10.) This window is
your canvas for creating your user interface: It's where you drag user-interface elements such as buttons and text fields.

These buttons, text fields, and other objects come from the Library window (the leftmost window in Figure 5-15). If the Library window isn't open, select Tools➪Library to open it. The Library window contains all the stock Cocoa Touch objects that Interface Builder supports. (Cocoa Touch is an application-programming interface for building apps to run on the iPad, iPhone, or iPod touch.) Dragging an item from the Library to the View window adds an object of that type to the View. You start adding objects to the DeepThoughts view in Chapter 9.

If you happen to close the Library window, whether by accident or by design, you can get it to reappear by choosing Tools➪Library.

It's Time to Get Real

Well, you still have quite a bit more to explore. But before you look behind the curtain of the iPad screen to see how iPad apps *really* run (and there's no fake Wizard of Oz back there, as I explain in Part III), and certainly before you start adding code to your first sample app in Part IV, it helps to know more about the app publishing process, how to provision your app for development, and the App Store do's and don'ts (discussed in Chapter 6).

When you've had a stroll through those adventures, you'll know everything you need to know about provisioning your app for the App Store, and designing an app that customers might actually want. (How's that for a plan?)

Chapter 6

Death, Taxes, and iPad Provisioning

In This Chapter

▶ Running your application on the iPad

▶ Getting the app ready for distribution

▶ Taking the app to market — that is, the App Store

*B*enjamin Franklin once said, "In this world nothing can be said to be certain, except death and taxes." Here's another certainty in this earthly vale of tears: Everybody has the same hoops to jump through to get an app onto an iPad and then into the App Store — and nobody much likes jumping through hoops, but there they are.

So you're working on your app, running it in the Simulator, as happy as a virtual clam, and all of a sudden you get this urge to see what your creation will look like on the iPad itself. Assuming that you've joined the requisite developer program (see Chapter 4), what do you have to do to get it to run on the iPad?

For most developers, getting their apps to run on the iPad during development can be one of the most frustrating things about developing software for the iPad. The sticking point has to do with a technical concept called *code signing,* a rather complicated process designed to ensure the integrity of the code and positively identify the code's originator. Apple requires all iPad (and iPhone and iPod touch) apps to be digitally signed with a signing certificate — one issued by Apple to a registered developer — before the apps can be run on a development system and before they're submitted to the App Store for distribution. This signature authenticates the identity of the developer of the app and ensures that there have been no changes to the app after it was signed.

As to why this is a big deal, here's the short and sweet (and, to my ears, convincing) answer: Code signing is your way of guaranteeing that no bad guys have done anything to your code that can harm the innocent user.

Okay, so nobody really likes the process, but it's doable, and it's certainly worth the trouble. In this chapter, I give you an overview of how it all works by jumping right to that point where you're getting your app ready to be uploaded to the App Store and then distributed. I'm starting at the end of the process, which for all practical purposes begins with getting your app to run on an iPad during development. I'm doing the overview in this order because the hoops you have to jump through are a direct consequence of code signing, and of how Apple manages it through the App Store and on the device.

After the overview, which will give you some context for the whole process, I revert back to the natural order of things and start with getting your app to run on your iPad during development.

How the Process Works

It's very important to keep clear that you have to go through *two* processes: One for development, and one for distribution. Both produce different (but similarly named) certificates and profiles, and you'll need to pay attention to keep them straight. This section starts with the *distribution* process — how you get your app to run on *other people's* iPads. Next up is the *development* process — how to get your app running on *your* iPad during development.

The distribution process

Before you can build a version of your app that will actually run on your users' iPads, Apple insists that you have the following:

- ✔ **A Distribution Certificate:** An electronic document that associates a *digital identity* (which it creates) with other information that you have provided that identifies you, including a name, e-mail address, or business. The Distribution Certificate is placed on your *keychain* — that place on your Mac that securely stores passwords, keys, certificates, and notes for users.

- ✔ **A Distribution Provisioning Profile:** These profiles are code elements that Xcode builds into your application, creating a kind of "code fingerprint" that acts as a unique *digital signature*.

After you've built your app for distribution, you then send it to Apple for approval and distribution. Apple verifies the signature to be sure that the code came from a registered developer (you) and has not been corrupted. Apple then adds its own digital signature to your signed app. The iPhone OS on the iPad runs only apps that have a digital signature from Apple. Doing it this way ensures iPad owners that the apps they download from the App Store have been written by registered developers and have not been altered since they were created.

To install your distribution-ready app on a device, you can also create an *Ad Hoc Provisioning Profile,* which enables you to distribute your app on up to 100 devices.

Although the system for getting apps on other people's iPads works pretty well, leaving aside the fact that Apple essentially has veto rights on every app that comes its way, there are some significant consequences for developers. In this system, there really is no mechanism for testing your app on the device it's going to run on:

- ✔ You can't run your app on an actual device until it's been code-signed by Apple, *but* Apple is hardly going to code-sign something that may not be working correctly.

- ✔ Even if Apple *did* sign an app that hadn't yet run on an iPad, that would mean an additional hassle: Every time you recompiled, you'd have to upload the app to the App Store again — *and* have it code-signed again because you had changed it, *and* then download it to your device.

A bit of *Catch-22* here. (Milo Minderbinder would be proud.)

The development process

To deal with this problem, Apple has developed a process for creating a *Development Certificate* (as opposed to the Distribution Certificate discussed in the preceding section) and a *Development Provisioning Profile* (as opposed to the Distribution Provisioning Profile). It's easy to get these confused — the key words are Distribution and Development. With these items in hand, you can run your application on a *specific* device.

This process is required only because of the code-signing requirements of the distribution process.

The Development Provisioning Profile is a collection of your App ID, Apple device UDID (a unique identifier for each iPad), and Development Certificate (belonging to a specific developer). This Profile must be installed on each device on which you want to run your application code. (You see how that's done in the section "Creating your Development Provisioning Profile and Development Certificate" in this chapter.) Devices specified within the Development Provisioning Profile can be used for testing only by developers whose Development Certificates are included in the Provisioning Profile. A single device can contain multiple provisioning profiles.

It's important to realize that a Development Provisioning Profile (as opposed to a distribution one) *is tied to a device and a developer.*

Even with your Provisioning Profile(s) in place, when you compile your program, Xcode will build and sign (create the required signature for) your app *only* if it finds one of those Development Certificates in your Keychain. Then, when you install a signed app on your provisioned iPad, the iPhone OS verifies the signature to make sure that (a) the app was signed and (b) the app has not been altered since it was signed. If the signature is not valid or if you didn't sign the code, the iPhone OS on the iPad won't let the app run.

This means that each Development Provisioning Profile is also tied to a particular Development Certificate.

And to make sure the message has really gotten across:

> A Development Provisioning Profile is tied to a *specific device* and a *specific Development Certificate.*
>
> Your app, during development, must be tied to a specific *Development Provisioning Profile* (which is easily changeable).

The process you're about to go through is akin to filling out taxes: You have to follow the rules, or there can be some dire consequences. But if you *do* follow the rules, everything works out, and you don't have to worry about it again. (Until it's time to develop the next app, of course.) Although this process is definitely not my favorite part of iPad software development, I've made peace with it, and so should you.

After developing your app, it's time for the next step: getting it ready for distribution. (This process is somewhat easier.) Finally, you definitely want to find out how to get your application into the App Store. After that, all you have to do is sit back and wait for fame and fortune to come your way — or read Chapter 3 again to discover why it hasn't yet.

What I describe on these pages is the way things looked when I wrote this book. What you see when you go through this process yourself may be slightly different from what you see here. Don't panic. It's because Apple changes things from time to time.

Provisioning Your Device for Development

Now I can go back to the natural order of things and start by explaining the process of getting your device ready for development. Although Apple documents the steps very well, do keep in mind that you really have to carry them out in exactly the way Apple tells you. There are no shortcuts! But if you do it the way it prescribes, you'll be up and running on a real device very quickly. Here's the drill:

1. **Go to the iPhone Dev Center Web site (which offers all of Apple's resources for iPad development) at**

   ```
   http://developer.apple.com/iphone
   ```

   If necessary, log in with your developer ID. The iPhone Dev Center appears, as shown in Figure 6-1. You can see the iPhone Provisioning Portal link, along with the iTunes Connect and the Developer Support Center links, in the iPhone Developer Program section on the right side of the Web page. (You can see those links if you're a registered developer. You did take care of that, right? If not, look back at Chapter 4 for more on how to register.)

2. **Click the iPhone Provisioning Portal link.**

   The iPhone Developer Program Portal screen appears, as shown in Figure 6-2.

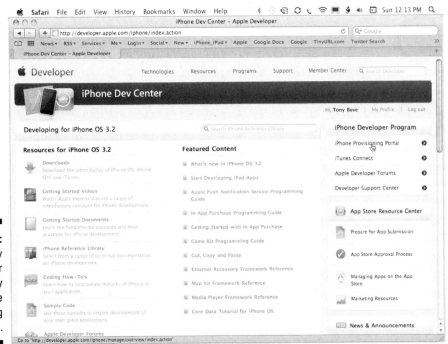

Figure 6-1: The Dev Center gateway to the Provisioning Portal.

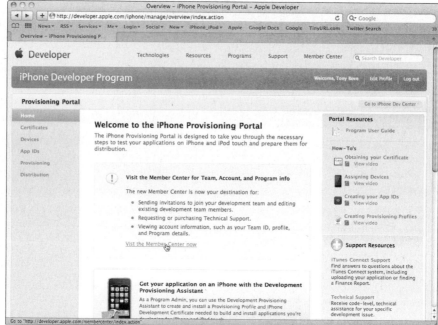

Figure 6-2:
Behold
the iPhone
Provisioning
Portal.

3. **Visit the Member Center for account, team, and program information, to edit team members, or to request support.**

   You should bookmark the Member Center, shown in Figure 6-3, so that you can return to it quickly. It's really a hub for everything you need as a registered developer and iPhone program member. To return to the portal, click the iPhone Provisioning Portal link or your browser's back button.

4. **Assuming you're either a Team Admin or Team Agent or are enrolled in the Developer Program as an individual, use the Development Provisioning Assistant to create and install a Provisioning Profile and Development Certificate, as shown in the next section.**

   You need these to build and install applications on the iPad. But you knew that.

You've already identified yourself to Apple as one of two types of developers:

✔ **If you're enrolled in the Developer Program as an individual,** you're considered a Team Agent with all the rights and responsibilities.

✔ **If you're part of a company,** you've set up a team already. If not, click the Setting Up a Team link on the right side of the iPhone Developer Program Portal page — right there under the Portal Resources heading — to get more info about setting up a team and who needs to do what when.

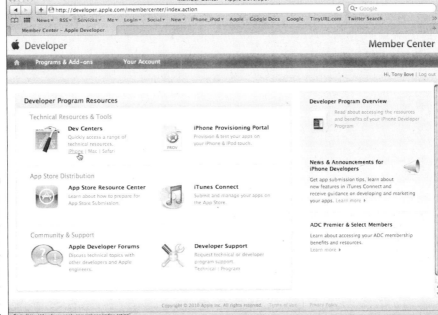

Figure 6-3:
The
Member
Center is a
hub for
managing
develop-
ment.

Creating Your Development Provisioning Profile and Development Certificate

When you've settled the matter of which kind of developer you are (for Apple's purposes), scroll the iPhone Provisioning Portal page to the Provisioning Assistant section, and click the Launch Assistant button. The Assistant launches with a diagram showing the three steps for provisioning: configuring your profile, downloading and installing the certificate, and building your app. Click Continue to start.

As I mention earlier in this chapter, to run the app on the iPad you must have a Provisioning Profile installed on the iPad, as well as a Development Certificate on your Mac. The whole point of the Development Provisioning Assistant is to guide you through the steps to create and install your Development Provisioning Profile and Development Certificate.

Development and Distribution stay off each other's turf. The Development Provisioning Assistant creates a *Development* Provisioning Profile, not a *Distribution* Provisioning Profile. You have to use the Provisioning section of the Program Portal, described later in this chapter, to create the Distribution Provisioning Profile required to distribute the app to customers through the App Store.

Here's what the Development Provisioning Assistant has you do:

1. **Choose an App ID.**

   An App ID is a unique identifier that is one part of your Development Provisioning Profile. The iPhone OS on the iPad uses it to allow your app to connect to the Apple Push Notification service (which I discuss momentarily), share keychain data between apps, and communicate with external hardware accessories that you want to pair your app with. But even if you don't want to do those things, you need to create an App ID anyway in order to install your app on an iPhone OS–based device such as an iPad.

   The App ID that the Assistant creates *can't be used* with the Apple Push Notification service. (This service lets your app keep its users up-to-date, offering the capability of sending a message that lets the user launch your app, or triggering audible alerts with your own custom sounds, or adding a numbered badge to your app icon — for details, see the App IDs section of the iPhone Developer Program Portal at `http://developer.apple.com/iphone/manage/bundles/index.action`). The App ID created by the Assistant *also can't be used* for In App Purchase. (See Chapter 3 for details on In App Purchase.) If you've previously created an App ID already that can be used with the Apple Push Notification service or for In App Purchase, you *can't* use the Assistant to create a Development Provisioning Profile. This isn't a big deal; you just have to follow the steps the Assistant follows on your own.

2. **Choose an Apple Device and connect your iPad.**

   Development provisioning is also about the device, so you have to specify which particular device you're going to use, and connect it. You do that by providing the Assistant with the device's Unique Device Identifier (UDID), which the Assistant shows you how to locate using Xcode. Connect your iPad with a USB cable to your computer, launch Xcode, and choose Window➪Organizer. The 40-character string in the Identifier field is the device's UDID.

3. **Provide your Development Certificate.**

   Your existing Development Certificate appears in the Assistant, and all you need to do is click Continue. All apps must be signed with a valid certificate before they can run on an Apple device, so you have to create one at this point if you don't already have one. You can do so by visiting the Certificates section of the iPhone Provisioning Portal (click the Certificates link in the left column of the portal's home page, which is shown in Figure 6-2), and following the instructions to request individual Development Certificates.

   For a Company (that is, a Team), each developer has to first create a Certificate Signing Request, which then has to be approved by your Program Admin or Team Agent. Visit the Certificates section of the iPhone Provisioning Portal for instructions.

4. **Name your Provisioning Profile.**

   You then give your Provisioning Profile a name and click Generate. The Provisioning Profile pulls together your App ID (Step 1), Apple device UDID (Step 2), and Development Certificate (Step 3). The Assistant then steps you through downloading the profile and handing it over to Xcode, which installs it on your device. You hand it over to Xcode by dragging it over the Xcode icon in the Mac OS X Dock or by dragging it directly to the Provisioning Profiles section of the Organizer window. (Choose Window⇨Organizer in Xcode to open the Organizer window.)

5. **Verify that the Provisioning Profile is installed.**

   In Xcode, choose Window⇨Organizer and click the device's name in the Devices section of the Projects and Sources pane of the Organizer window. The profile should appear in the Provisioning section of the Summary pane for the device.

At this point, you can switch from the Organizer window to the Xcode Project window, and choose iPhone Device 3.2 as the active SDK, as shown in Figure 6-4. (This means the device running iPhone 3.2 OS, which is your iPad.) You can then build your app and have it installed on the provisioned iPad.

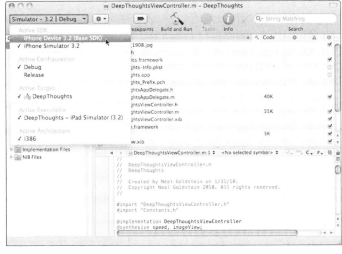

Figure 6-4: Choose iPhone Device 3.2 to install and run your app on the iPad.

Provisioning Your Application for the App Store

Although there's no dedicated assistant to help you provision your application for the App Store, that process is actually a little easier — which may be why there's no assistant for it.

You start at the Provisioning Portal (refer to Figure 6-2), but this time you click the Distribution link on the menu on the left side of the page. Doing so takes you to the Prepare App tab of the Distribution page, shown in Figure 6-5, where you can find an overview of the process, as well as links that take you where you need to go when you click them.

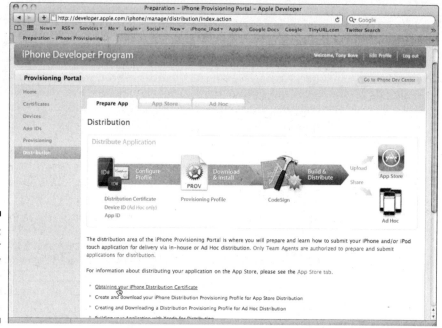

Figure 6-5:
Getting your app ready for distribution: You are here.

You actually jump through some of the very same hoops you did when you provisioned your device for development — except that this time, you're going after a *Distribution* Certificate.

Here's the step-by-step account:

1. **Obtain your Distribution Certificate.**

    To distribute your iPad app, you (as an Individual developer, or your Team Agent as a development team) create a Distribution Certificate. This works much like the Development Certificate, except that only the Team Agent (or whoever is enrolled as an Individual developer) can get one. Clicking the Obtaining Your iPhone Distribution Certificate link on the Prepare App page (shown at the bottom of Figure 6-5) leads you through the process.

2. **Create your Distribution Provisioning Profile for App Store Distribution.**

To build your app successfully with Xcode for distribution via the App Store, first you have to create and download an App Store Distribution Provisioning Profile, which is (lest you forget) *different* from the Development Provisioning Profiles described in the previous section.

Apple will accept an app only after it's built with an App Store Distribution Provisioning Profile.

3. **Click the Create and Download Your iPhone Distribution Provisioning Profile for App Store Distribution link.**

   Scroll the Prepare App tab of the Distribution page (refer to Figure 6-5) to click the link, which leads you through this process.

4. **When you're done creating the Distribution Provisioning Profile, download it and drag it over the Xcode icon in the Mac OS X Dock.**

   That loads your Distribution Profile into Xcode, and you're ready to build an app you can distribute for use on actual iPads.

5. **(Optional) You can also create and download a Distribution Provisioning Profile for Ad Hoc Distribution.**

   Going the Ad Hoc Distribution route enables you to distribute your application to up to 100 users without going through the App Store. Scroll the Prepare App page (refer to Figure 6-5) to click the Creating and Downloading a Distribution Provisioning Profile for Ad Hoc Distribution link, which leads you through the process. (Ad Hoc Distribution is beyond the scope of this book — the iPhone Developer Program Portal has more info about this option.)

6. **Build your app with Xcode for distribution.**

   After you download the distribution profile, you can build your app for distribution — rather than just building it for testing purposes, which is what you've been doing so far. It's a well-documented process that you start by scrolling the Prepare App tab of the Distribution page (refer to Figure 6-5) and clicking the Building Your Application with Xcode for Distribution link.

7. **Verify that it worked.**

   Scroll the Prepare App tab of the Distribution page (refer to Figure 6-5) and click the Verifying a Successful Distribution Build link to get the verification process started. In this case, there are some things missing in the heretofore well-explained step-by-step documentation — it tells you to open the Build Log detail view and confirm the presence of the `embedded.mobileprovision` file. In Chapter 5, I show you how to keep the Build Results window open in Xcode, but if you haven't been doing that, choose Build⇨Build Results.

   Depending on the way the Build Results window is configured, you may see a window showing only the end result of your build. To get the actual log of the process and confirm the presence of the `embedded.mobileprovision` file, you have to change Errors & Warnings Only in the drop-down menu in the scope bar to All Messages.

When you've done this elaborate (but necessary) song and dance, you're ready to rock 'n' roll. You can go to iTunes Connect, which is your entryway to the App store. This is where the *real* fun starts.

Using iTunes Connect to Manage Apps in the App Store

iTunes Connect is a group of Web-based tools that enables developers to submit apps to the App Store as well as manage those apps of theirs that have found a home there. It's actually the very same set of tools that the other content providers — the music and video types — use to get their content into iTunes.

In iTunes Connect, you can check on your contracts, manage users, and submit your app with all its supporting documentation — the *metadata,* as Apple calls it — to the App Store. iTunes Connect is also where you get financial reports and daily/weekly sales trend data, as I describe in Chapter 3.

Your first detour is the App Store Resource Center (shown in Figure 6-6). To get there, click the App Store Resource Center link in the Member Center (refer to Figure 6-3). Here you find information about how to submit your app, what to expect in the approval process, how to manage your apps in the store, and how to raise awareness and market your apps. You should read these sections carefully because Apple changes procedures and resources from time to time.

At some point, you should visit the Marketing Resources section of the App Store Resource Center to become an Authorized Licensee for marketing images. You can then use the App Store artwork and iPad images in your advertising, Web sites, and other marketing materials.

To go to iTunes Connect to add or manage apps in the store, click the iTunes Connect link in the Member Center (refer to Figure 6-3) to go to the login page. You need to use your Apple ID and password to log in. Before you can do anything, you're asked to review and accept the iTunes Distribution Terms & Conditions. After taking care of that chore, you land on the iTunes Connect page shown in Figure 6-7.

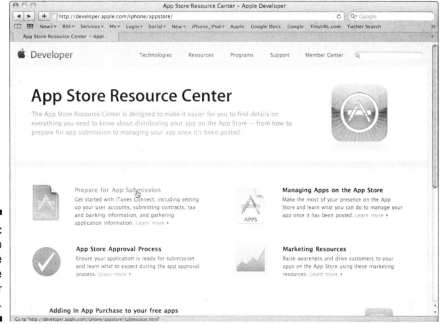

Figure 6-6:
The App
Store
Resource
Center
page.

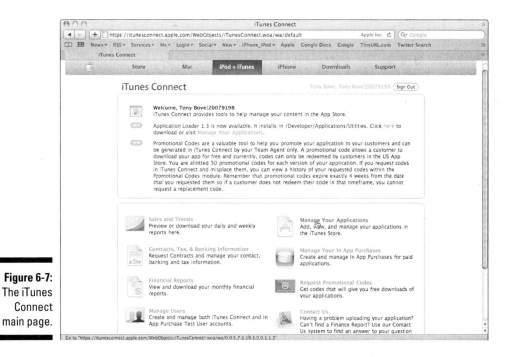

Figure 6-7:
The iTunes
Connect
main page.

When you want to add an application to the App Store or manage what you already have there, the iTunes Connect main page is your control panel for getting that done.

Supplying the Information Required for the App Store

Apple is very strict about the App Store.

For example, the first time co-author Neal submitted the ReturnMeTo iPhone app from his other book, *iPhone Application Development For Dummies,* he received a polite, but firm, e-mail rejecting the application because the app's icon used an iPhone image. You may not think this is such a big deal, but it certainly is with Apple. The artwork you use for the app icon is just one of many pieces of information that must be submitted in advance and is subject to Apple's approval.

So how do you get your app into the App Store? The Uploading Your Application to the App Store part is pretty easy. The hard part is collecting all the little bits of information you need to enter into all the text fields in the upload page.

Adding the metadata and artwork

Here's an overview of the kind of information you need (for more information, click the Prepare for App Submission link in the App Store Resource Center section of the iPhone Dev Center page shown earlier in Figure 6-1):

✓ **Metadata:** The ever-present data about data. Here's what Apple wants from you:

- *Application Name:* The name must conform to guidelines for using Apple trademarks and copyrights. Apple takes this very seriously, as evidenced by the company sending a cease-and-desist order to Neal's ISP when Neal tried (innocently) to use the word *iPhone* in his domain name. (A word to the wise: Don't mess with Apple.)

- *Application Description:* When you go through the process of uploading your data, the field you have to paste this into will say you're limited to 4,000 characters. Apple suggests no more than 700.

  This description is what users will see when they click on your app in the App Store or follow a link from another Web page to a browser page for the App Store, so it's important that this description is well written and points out all your app's key features.

Don't include HTML tags; they will be stripped out when the data is uploaded. Only line breaks are respected.

- *Device:* Choose iPad (as of this writing).

- *Primary Category:* A drop-down menu offers the primary category choices for your app — choose one. The App Store offers about 20 categories ranging from Reference to Games to Social Networking to Travel to Utility.

- *Secondary Category:* (Optional) You're offered the same categories that you see for the Primary Category.

- *Rating Information:* You're asked to provide additional information describing the content. This allows you to set your rating for your app for the purpose of parental controls on the App Store. You may see content types such as Cartoon or Fantasy Violence, Simulated Gambling, Mature/Suggestive Themes, and so on. For each type of content, you need to describe the level of frequency for that content — None, Infrequent/Mild, Frequent/Intense. Apple has strict rules stating that an app must not contain any obscene, pornographic, or offensive content. Oh and by the way, it's entirely up to Apple what is to be considered offensive or inappropriate.

- *Copyright:* Use a line such as:

  © Copyright *your name* 2010. All rights reserved.

  You can type the copyright symbol by pressing Option-G. If you have any questions about copyright registration, talk to your lawyer or check out www.copyright.gov.

- *Version Number:* People usually start with 1.0. Then, as you update the app to respond to suggestions and constructive criticism, you can move on to 1.1 and eventually version 2.0.

- *SKU Number:* The Stock Keeping Unit (SKU) number is any alphanumeric sequence of letters and numbers that uniquely identifies your app in the system. (Be warned — this is not editable after you submit it.)

- *Keywords:* Keywords describe your app. These are matched to App Store searches. Spend some time on this one. Keywords can be changed only when you submit a new version of your app or if the app status is Rejected.

- *Support URL and Company URL:* You need a support URL, which appears on the app product page at the App store — this is the link users will click on if they need technical support from you or have a question about your app. You also need a company URL, which also appears on the app product page and enables potential customers to find out more about you. After you've assigned these URLs, you want to keep them unchanged for as long as possible, even if you change the Web site's contents, because people bookmark them.

If you don't have a Web site yet and don't know how to build one, try using iWeb with MobileMe (if you already have the service) or with your friendly ISP. MobileMe offers automatic Web publishing to a reasonably unique domain name that can serve well enough for your URLs — to find out more, see my book *iLife For Dummies*. (That's me, Tony, talking.) If you use an ISP, obtain a domain name for your URLs that reflects your company or product name. You can also find out more about building a professional-looking site from David Crowder's book *Building a Web Site For Dummies,* 3rd Edition.

- *Support E-mail Address:* (For use by Apple only, not visible to end users of your app.) This address will likely be the one you used when you registered for the developer program.

- *Demo Account — Full Access:* This is a test account that the App Store *reviewers* can use to test your app. Include usernames, passwords, access codes, demo data, and so on. You should include any messages to the Apple app reviewers, in case they might incorrectly reject something — for example, lack of permission to use a piece of music in the app that it is in the public domain. Make sure the demo account works correctly. You'd hate to have your app rejected because you didn't pay attention to setting up a demo account correctly.

- *End User License Agreement:* (Optional) If you don't know what this is, don't worry. It's the legal document that spells out to your app's users what they're agreeing to do in order to use your app. Fortunately the iTunes Store has a standard agreement, which has been time-tested — but you should read it anyway before you use it.

- *Availability Date:* When your app will be available for download (for free apps) or purchase-and-download.

- *Application Price:* Free is easier, but later on, in "You're not done yet," I show you what you have to do if you want to get *paid* (what a concept) for all the work you did getting your app to the public.

- *Localization:* Additional languages (besides English) for your metadata. You can have your text and images in Italian in all Italian-speaking stores, for example.

- *App Store Availability:* The territories in which you would like to make your app available. (The default is all countries iTunes supports.)

✔ **Artwork:** A picture is worth a thousand words, so the App store gives you the opportunity to dazzle your app's potential users with some nice imagery:

- *iPad Home Screen Icon:* Your built app must include an icon sized at 72 x 72 pixels. You can add the icon directly to the app following the procedure I describe in Chapter 9. This icon is what will be displayed on the iPad home screen. You also need to supply a smaller version of this icon, at 48 x 48 pixels, for display in Spotlight search results and in the Settings application (if you provide settings).

- *Large Application Icon:* This icon will be used to display your app on your App Store page and other App Store pages. It needs to meet the following requirements, although the version you see in the App Store is resized by Apple:

  512 x 512 pixels (a square image)

  72 dots-per-inch (dpi)

  JPEG or TIFF format (saved without separate layers)

- *Primary Screenshot:* This shot will be used on your application product page in the App Store.

  Apple doesn't want you to include the iPad status bar in your screenshot.

  Up to four additional optional screenshots can appear on the application product page. These may be resized by Apple to fit the space provided. Follow the same requirements from the preceding list.

  To take a screenshot on an iPad, quickly press and release the Sleep/Wake and Home buttons at the same time. The screen flashes (and if your volume is up, you can hear a shutter click). This flash indicates that the screen was saved in the Saved Images album — choose the album in the Photos app to see the image. You can take as many screen shots as you like. The next time you sync your iPad, your photo application (such as iPhoto) launches to receive these new images.

  You can also capture a screenshot using the Xcode Organizer window. Open Xcode and choose Window⇨Organizer. Plug in your iPad and in a few seconds, it should appear in the list of devices on the left. Click the Screenshot tab at the top of the Organizer window, get the device to the point that you want a screenshot, and then click the Capture button. To make that screenshot your application's default image, click Save As Default Image. To get a PNG file of the screenshot, drag it to the desktop.

- *Additional Artwork:* (Optional) If you're really lucky — I mean *really* lucky (or that good) — you may be included on featured pages in the App Store. Apple will want "high-quality layered artwork with a title treatment for your application," which will then be used in small banners to feature your app in the App Store.

You're not done yet

If you're going to charge for your app, you have to provide even more information. Most of it is pretty straightforward, except for some of the banking information, which you *do* need to have available. To change this information after you've entered it, you have to e-mail iTunes technical support. It behooves you to get it right the first time.

Here's what I'm talking about:

- ✔ **Bank name**
- ✔ **Bank address**
- ✔ **Account number**
- ✔ **Branch/Branch ID**
- ✔ **ABA/Routing Transit Number:** Generally, this number is the first nine digits of that long number at the bottom of your checks that also contains the account number. If you aren't sure what the routing number is, contact your bank.
- ✔ **Your Bank SWIFT Code:** SWIFT is an acronym for Society for Worldwide Interbank Financial Telecommunication . You have to get this code from your bank.

Take it from me: It's far easier if you have all bits and pieces together *before* you start the actual upload process, rather than having to scramble at 3 a.m. to find some obscure piece of information it wants. (The Bank Swift Code was the one that got co-author Neal.)

Uploading your information

At this point, you could start the app-upload process. But hold it. Better to look before leaping: Check out the requisite Contracts, Tax & Banking Information.

Here's why: If you plan on selling your app, you need to have your paid commercial agreement in place and signed before your apps can be posted to the App Store.

If your app is free, you've already entered into the freeware distribution agreement by being accepted into the iPhone Developer Program. You may not want to charge for your app now, but just like with anything else at Apple, contract approval can take a while, so you should probably fill out the contract information just to get it out of the way.

Start by clicking the Contracts, Tax & Banking Information link on the iTunes Connect main page. The Manage Your Contracts page appears. You use this page to create a contract for your paid app. You can also see that you already have, by default, a contract in effect for free apps. To create a new contract, select the box under Request Contract in the Request New Contracts section, and you're taken though a series of pages that ask you to provide the information Apple needs, including all the bank information I call your attention to up there in the section right before this one. (You were wondering where you had to put all that stuff? Well, wonder no more.)

Uploading your app and its data

After you've set the wheels of commerce in motion, you can then go back to the iTunes Connect main page and upload your data. Click the Manage Your Applications link (refer to Figure 6-7) to call up the Manage Your Applications page, as shown in Figure 6-8. In that page, click the Add New Application button and go to town. Fill in all the blanks, using all that info I ask you to collect in the "Supplying the Information Required for the App Store" section earlier in the chapter. Along the way, you'll upload your metadata and the app itself to Apple.

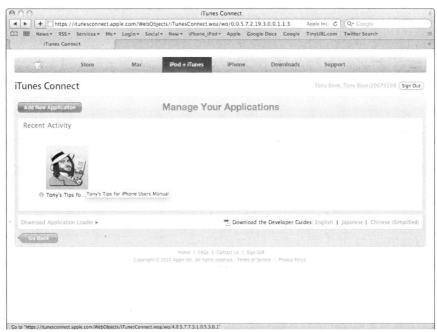

Figure 6-8:
Add your
application.

Click the Download the Developer Guide link at the bottom of the Manage Your Applications page in iTunes Connect (refer to Figure 6-9) to obtain comprehensive information about submitting apps to the App Store.

Apple offers Application Loader, a Mac application that analyzes your app's zip file and verifies all the certificates and icons before uploading your app. Using the Application Loader minimizes your chances of app rejection. To download it, scroll down the Manage Your Applications page to the bottom and then click the Get Application Loader link. To use it, go ahead with the process of adding a new app to the App Store, but when iTunes Connect asks you to upload your app, select the Check Here to Upload Your Binary Later check box. Complete the rest of the information required for uploading an app. Then, to begin uploading, start Application Loader and choose File➪New. You're asked to log in, and if all is well, you see a dialog with a drop-down menu of all the apps iTunes Connect recognizes that are waiting for a binary. Follow the instructions to upload.

To edit your app's information, manage in-app purchasing, remove the app from the store, or update the app, click the app's icon (as shown in Figure 6-8) to see your choices, as shown in Figure 6-9.

Figure 6-9:
Manage
your appli-
cation.

Click Edit Information to edit the information about your app in the store. You can also click Remove from Sale to remove the app from the store, or Update Application to submit an update to your app. Click the Crash Reports, App Details, or View in App Store links to see more information about your app.

Avoiding the App Store Rejection Slip

While no one knows the true figure, the vast majority of submitted apps are accepted into the App Store. Besides the typical rejections (mostly for bugs or for improper use of artwork or trademarks in the app), some apps were rejected for pornographic images, some were rejected for being too similar to Apple's own apps, while others fell into some gray area that Apple hadn't anticipated — for instance, apps that are intended to help people cheat at gambling in casinos. For guidelines on how to avoid rejection due to coding or user interface issues, see Chapter 2.

Before you upload your app and its data, make sure you haven't run afoul of any of Apple's rules about trademarks, copyrights, and artwork. Be sure to peruse Apple's posted Guidelines for Using Apple's Trademarks and Copyrights, which you can find here:

```
www.apple.com/legal/trademark/guidelinesfor3rdparties.html
```

Here are some tips:

- ✔ **Use the same icon for the app (the bundle icon) and the App Store page icon.** Make sure the 72 x 72 pixel icon for your app, and the 48 x 48 pixel version for Spotlight search and Settings, is the same image as the 512 x 512 pixel version for your App Store page.

- ✔ **Icons must be different for *lite* and *pro* versions (such as free and paid versions).** Use a different icon image for app and page for a lite version than the one you use for the pro version. Using the same icon image for both sends your app straight to the rejection bin.

- ✔ **Don't use any part of an Apple image and certainly none of the company's trademark images or names.** Your app can't include any photos or illustrations of the iPad, including icons that resemble the iPad, or any other Apple products (including the Apple logo itself). I've heard of projects being rejected for using the Bonjour logo, as well as Apple's network icon (the little picture of the globe with all the glowing lines). Your app can't include the word *iPad* in its title (although the iPhone app title *Tony's Tips for iPhone Users* is okay because the app's content is about the iPhone), and its use in the title or description of any components or features is very strict and probably not worth the trouble.

✔ **If you use any of Apple's user interface graphics, you must use them in the way they were intended.** For example, the blue + button should be used only to add an item to a list.

✔ **Don't infringe on other trademarks, either.** Your app's title, description, and content must not potentially infringe upon other non-Apple trademarks or product likenesses. I've heard of an app rejected for using an icon resembling Polaroid photos.

✔ **Keywords can get you in trouble.** Keyword terms must be related to your app's content. It should be obvious, but some developers do it: You can't use offensive terms. And it's a big no-no to refer to other apps, competitive or not.

✔ **Don't include pricing information in your app's description and release notes.** Your app's marketing text — the application description and release notes — should not include pricing information, mostly because it would cause confusion in other countries due to pricing differences.

✔ **Don't mention Steve.** Apple will reject any app that mentions Steve Jobs in any context, even as a clue in a puzzle — it does not matter how trivial the reference; just the name is enough.

✔ **Don't try to fool the ratings.** Apps are rated accordingly for the highest (meaning most adult) level of content that the user is able to access. If you hide it, they will find it, and if Apple's review indicates that the app's content is in any way inconsistent with the information you provided, out you go!

Now What?

You wait for your app's approval or rejection. The timeframe is, on average, about two weeks, though some developers have claimed much longer, and I can attest to it taking much shorter for my app.

So it varies, but if you follow my advice about submitting your app in the section "Avoiding the App Store Rejection Slip" in this chapter, and you take my advice in Chapter 2 about development and user interface practices to avoid, it shouldn't take longer than a few weeks. Use the time wisely to set up your marketing campaigns, as I describe in Chapter 3.

Finally, at what may seem at long last (although it's really been only a few chapters), you're ready to look behind the screen and see exactly how an iPad app works. So take a break if you need to, but come back ready to explore Part III.

Part III
Understanding Apps

The 5th Wave   By Rich Tennant

"You ever notice how much more streaming media there is than there used to be?"

In this part . . .

This part, although short, offers a peek behind the curtain of the great and powerful OS (the iPhone OS for the iPad, that is — and Toto, we're not in Kansas anymore). Your app, in a sense, becomes the Wizard of the iPhone OS, conjuring up blazing content and performing amazing tricks on the iPad.

Beware! The secrets described herein are not for the uninitiated; one must embark on a soul-searching journey through Part I of this book to discover the True Meaning of the Killer iPad App, and then one must register with an oath of confidentiality, join the cadre of iPad developers, and train with the SDK tools that perform the alchemy of app development, as described in Part II. At some point in this quest, you may experience the rapture of what your killer app might be, in which case you are ready to read the following:

✔ Chapter 7 explains the SDK frameworks for the iPhone OS that form the raw material of your iPad app (which you then refine with your code and user interface objects), and the design patterns that you should adopt to make use of these frameworks. It also shows how windows, views, and view controllers work on the iPad.

✔ Chapter 8 describes in detail the (possibly) short and happy life of an iPad app, from launch to termination. You see how an application object is created and connected to the window object. You find out all about the event loop and how it all starts with the main nib file, which you can select in Xcode and look at in Interface Builder. When you finish, you should have enough information to get started coding your app.

Chapter 7

Looking Behind the Screen

. . . .

. . . .

*O*ne thing that makes iPad software development so appealing is the richness of the tools and frameworks provided in the Apple's iPhone Software Development Kit (SDK). The *frameworks* are especially important; each one is a distinct body of code that actually implements your application's generic functionality — gives the application its basic way of working, in other words. This is especially true of one framework in particular: the UIKit framework, which is the heart of the user interface.

In this chapter, you find out about most of the iPad's user interface architecture, which is a mostly static view that explains what the various pieces are, what each does, and how they interact with each other. This chapter lays the groundwork for developing the DeepThoughts app's user interface, which you get a chance to tackle in Chapter 9.

Using Frameworks

A *framework* offers common code providing generic functionality. The iPhone OS for the iPad provides a set of frameworks for incorporating technologies, services, and features into your apps. For example, the UIKit framework gives you event-handling support, drawing support, windows, views, and controls you can use in your app.

A framework is designed to easily integrate your code that runs your game or delivers the information that your user wants. Frameworks are similar to software libraries, but with an added twist: They also *implement* a program's flow of control (unlike a software library whose components are arranged by the programmer into a flow of control). This means that, instead of the programmer deciding the order that things should happen — such as which messages are sent to which objects and in what order when an application launches, or when a user touches a button on the screen — the order is a part of the framework and doesn't need to be specified by the programmer.

When you use a framework, you provide your app with a ready-made set of basic functions; you've told it, "Here's how to act." With the framework in place, all you need to do is *add* the specific functionality that you want in the app — the content as well as the controls and views that enable the user to access and use that content — *to* the frameworks.

The frameworks and the iPhone OS for the iPad provide some pretty complex functionality, such as

- ✔ Launching the app and displaying a view
- ✔ Displaying controls and responding to a user action — such as tapping a toggle switch, or flicking to scroll a list.
- ✔ Accessing sites on the Internet, not just through a browser, but from within your own app
- ✔ Managing user preferences
- ✔ Playing sounds and movies
- ✔ The list goes on — you get the picture

Some developers talk in terms of "using a framework" — but your app doesn't use frameworks so much as the frameworks *use your app.* Your app provides the functions that the framework accesses; the framework needs your code in order to become an app that does something other than start up, display a blank view, and then end. This perspective makes figuring out how to work with a framework much easier. (For one thing, it lets the programmer know where he or she is essential.)

If this seems too good to be true, well, okay, it is — all that complexity (and convenience) comes at a cost. It can be really difficult to get your head around the whole thing and know exactly where (and how) to add your app's functionality to that supplied by the framework. That's where *design patterns* come in. Understanding the design patterns behind the frameworks gives you a way of thinking about a framework — especially UIKit — that doesn't make your head explode.

Using Design Patterns

A major theme of this chapter is the fact that, when it comes to iPad app development, the UIKit framework does a lot of the heavy lifting for you. That's all well and good, but it's a little more complicated than that: The framework is designed around certain programming paradigms, also known as *design patterns*. The design pattern is a model that your own code must be consistent with. In programming terms, a design pattern is a commonly used template that gives you a consistent way to get a particular task done.

To understand how to take best advantage of the power of the framework — or (better put) how the framework objects want to use *your app* best — you need to understand design patterns. If you don't understand them or if you try to work around them because you're sure you have a "better" way of doing things, your job will actually be much more difficult. (Developing software can be hard enough, so making your job more difficult is definitely something you want to avoid.) Getting a handle on the basic design patterns used (and expected by) the framework helps you develop an app that makes the best use of the framework. This means the least amount of work in the shortest amount of time.

The design patterns can help you to understand not only how to structure your code, but also how the framework itself is structured. They describe relationships and interactions between classes or objects, as well as how responsibilities should be distributed amongst classes so the iPad does what you want it to do.

You need to be comfortable with these three basic design patterns:

- ✔ Model-View-Controller (MVC)
- ✔ Delegation
- ✔ Target-Action

Of these, the Model-View-Controller design pattern is the key to understanding how an iPad app works. I defer the discussion of the last two until after you get the MVC under your belt.

The Model-View-Controller (MVC) pattern

The iPhone OS frameworks for iPad development are *object-oriented*. The easiest way to understand what that really means is to think about a team. The work that needs to get done is divided up and assigned to individual team members (objects). Every member of a team has a job and works with other team members to get things done. What's more, a good team doesn't butt in on what other members are doing — just like how an object in object-oriented programming spends its time taking care of business and not caring what the object in the virtual cubicle next door is doing.

Object-oriented programming was originally developed to make code more maintainable, reusable, extensible, and understandable (what a concept!) by tucking all the functionality behind well-defined interfaces. The actual details of how something works (as well as its data) are hidden, which makes modifying and extending an application much easier.

Great — so far — but a pesky question still plagues programmers:

Exactly how do you decide on the objects and what each one does?

Sometimes the answer to that question is pretty easy — just use the real world as a model. (Eureka!) In the iPadTravel411 app that serves as an example in Part V, some of the classes of model objects are `Airport` and `Currency`. But when it comes to a generic program structure, how *do* you decide what the objects should be? That may not be so obvious.

The MVC pattern is a well-established way to group application functions into objects. Variations of it have been around at least since the early days of Smalltalk, one of the very first object-oriented languages. The MVC is a high-level pattern — it addresses the architecture of an application and classifies objects according to the general roles they play in an application.

The MVC pattern creates, in effect, a miniature universe for the application, populated with three kinds of objects. It also specifies roles and responsibilities for all three objects and specifies the way they're supposed to interact with each other. To make things more concrete (that is, to keep your head from exploding), imagine a big, beautiful, 60-inch flat screen TV. Here's the gist:

- ✔ **Model objects:** These objects together comprise the content "engine" of your app. They contain the app's data and logic — making your app more than just a pretty face. In the iPadTravel411 application, for example, the model "knows" the various ways to get from Heathrow Airport to London as well as some logic to decide the best alternative based on time of day, price, and some other considerations. (You find out about adding data models in Chapter 17.)

  You can think of the *model* (which may be one object or several that interact) as a particular television program, one that, quite frankly, does not give a hoot about what TV set it is being shown on.

  In fact, the model shouldn't give a hoot. Even though it owns its data, it should have no connection at all to the user interface and should be blissfully ignorant about what is being done with its data.

✔ **View objects:** These objects display things on the screen and respond to user actions. Pretty much anything you can see is a kind of view object — the window and all the controls, for example. Your views know how to display information that they get from the model object and how to get any input from the user the model may need. But the view objects themselves should know nothing about the model. A view object may handle a request to tell the user the fastest way to London, but it doesn't bother itself with what that request means. It may display the different ways to get to London, although it doesn't care about the content options it displays for you.

You can think of the *view* as a television screen that doesn't care about what program it is showing or what channel you just selected.

The UIKit framework provides many different kinds of views, as you'll find out later on in this chapter.

If the view knows nothing about the model, and the model knows nothing about the view, how do you get data and other notifications to pass from one to the other? To get that conversation started (Model: "I've just updated my data." View: "Hey, give me something to display," for example), you need the third element in the MVC triumvirate, the controller.

✔ **Controller objects:** These objects connect the application's view objects to its model objects. They supply the view objects with what they need to display (getting it from the model) and also provide the model with user input from the view.

You can think of the *controller* as the circuitry that pulls the show off of the cable and then sends it to the screen or requests a particular pay-per-view show.

The MVC in action

Imagine that an iPad user is at Heathrow Airport, and he or she starts the handy iPadTravel411 app mentioned so often in these pages. The view will display his or her location as "Heathrow Airport." The user may tap a button (a view) that requests the weather. The controller interprets that request and tells the model what it needs to do by sending a message to the appropriate method in the model object with the necessary parameters. The model accesses the appropriate Web site (or fails to access it, due to the lack of an Internet connection), and the controller then delivers that information to the view, which promptly displays the information — either the appropriate page from the Web site, or the Weather is not available offline message.

All this is illustrated in Figure 7-1.

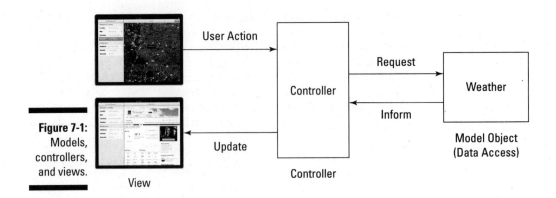

Figure 7-1:
Models,
controllers,
and views.

When you think about your application in terms of Model, View, and Controller objects, the UIKit framework starts to make sense. It also begins to lift the fog from where at least part of your application-specific behavior needs to go. Before I get more into that, however, you need to know a little more about the classes provided to you by the UIKit that implement the MVC design pattern — windows, views, and view controllers.

Working with Windows and Views

After an app is launched, it's going to be the only app running on the system — aside from the operating system software, of course. iPad apps have only a single window, and your application interface takes over the entire screen. When your application is running, it's all the user is doing with the iPad.

Looking out the window

The single window you see displayed on the iPad is an instance of the UIWindow class. This window is created at launch time, either programmatically by you or automatically by UIKit loading it from a *nib* file — a special file that contains instant objects that are reconstituted at runtime. (You can find out more about nib files in Chapter 5.) You then add views and controls to the window. In general, after you create the Window object (that is, if you create it instead of having it done for you), you never really have to think about it again.

A user can't directly close or manipulate an iPad window. It's your app that manages the window.

Although your app never creates more than one window at a time, the iPhone OS can use additional windows on top of your window. The system status bar is one example. You can also display alerts on top of your window by using the supplied Alert views.

Figure 7-2 shows the window layout on the iPad for the iPadTravel411 app.

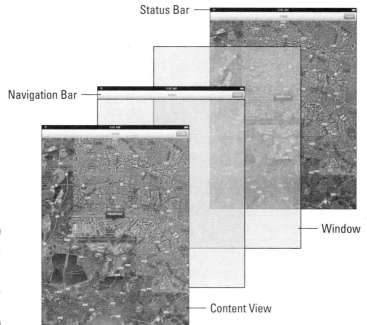

Status Bar

Navigation Bar

Window

Content View

Admiring the view

In an iPad app world, view objects are responsible for the view functionality in the Model-View-Controller architecture.

A view is a rectangular area on the screen (on top of a window). The *Content view* is that portion of data and controls that appear between the upper and lower bars shown in Figure 7-2.

In the UIKit framework, windows are really a special kind of view, but for purposes of this discussion, I'm talking about views that sit on top of the window.

What views do

Views are the main way for your app to interact with a user. This interaction happens in two ways:

- ✔ **Views display content.** For example, by making drawing and animation happen onscreen.

  In essence, the view object displays the data from the model object.

- ✔ **Views handle touch events.** They respond when the user touches a button, for example.

  Handling touch events is part of a *responder chain* (a special logical sequence detailed in Chapter 8).

The view hierarchy

Views and subviews create a view hierarchy. There are two ways of looking at it (no pun intended this time): visually (how the user perceives it) and hierarchically (how you structure it). You must be clear about the differences, or you will find yourself in a state of confusion that resembles Times Square on New Year's Eve.

Looking at it visually, the window is at the base of this hierarchy with a *Content view* on top of it (a transparent view that fills the window's Content rectangle). The Content view displays information and also allows the user to interact with the application, using (preferably standard) user-interface items such as text fields, buttons, toolbars, and tables, all of which are specialized kinds of views.

In your program, that relationship is different. The Content view is added to the window view as a *subview.*

- ✔ Views added to the Content view become *subviews* of it.

- ✔ Views added to the Content view become the *superviews* of any views added to them.

- ✔ A view can have one (and only one) superview and zero or more subviews.

It seems counterintuitive, but a subview is displayed *on top of* its parent view (that is, on top of its superview). Think about this relationship as containment: A superview *contains* its subviews. Figure 7-3 shows an example of a view hierarchy — "A Content View", with A, B, and C subviews.

Controls — such as buttons, text fields, and the like — are really view subclasses that become subviews. So are any other display areas you may specify. The view must manage its subviews, as well as resize itself with respect to its superviews. Fortunately, much of what the view must do is already coded for you. The UIKit framework supplies the code that defines view behavior.

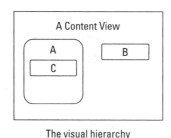

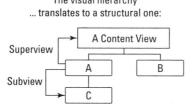

Figure 7-3:
The view
hierarchy is
both visual
and struc-
tural.

The visual hierarchy
... translates to a structural one:

The view hierarchy plays a key role in both drawing and event handling. When a window is sent a message to display itself, the window asks its sub-view to render itself first. If that view has a subview, it asks *its* subview to render itself first, going down the structural hierarchy (or up the visual structure) until the last subview is reached. It then renders itself and returns to its caller, which renders itself, and so on.

You create or modify a view hierarchy whenever you add a view to another view with Interface Builder (or if you add a view programmatically). The UIKit framework automatically handles all the relationships associated with the view hierarchy.

Developers typically gloss over this visual versus hierarchical view when starting out — and without understanding this, it's really difficult to get a handle on what's going on.

The kinds of views you use

The UIView class defines the basic properties of a view, and you may be able to use it as is — like you do in the DeepThoughts app — by simply adding some controls.

The framework also provides you with a number of other views that are sub-classed from UIView. These views implement the kinds of things that you as a developer need to do on a regular basis.

It's important to use the view objects that are part of the UIKit framework. When you use an object such as a UISlider or UIButton, your slider or button behaves just like a slider or button in any other iPad app. This enables the consistency in appearance and behavior across apps that users expect. (For more on how this kind of consistency in a user interface is one of the characteristics of a great app, see Chapter 2.)

Container views

Container views are a technical (Apple) term for Content views that do more than just lie there on the screen and display your controls and other content.

The UIScrollView class, for example, adds scrolling without you having to do any work.

UITableView inherits this scrolling capability from UIScrollView and adds the ability to display lists and respond to the selections of an item in that list. Think of the Contacts application (and a host of others).

Another container view, the UIToolbar class, contains button-like controls — and you find those everywhere on the iPad. In Mail, for example, you touch an icon button in the toolbar to respond to an e-mail. Toolbars can be positioned at the top and bottom of a view. If you are familiar with iPhone apps, keep in mind that the iPad's increased screen size makes it possible to include more items on a toolbar.

Controls

Controls are the fingertip-friendly graphics you see extensively used in a typical application's user interface. Controls are actually subclasses of the UIControl superclass, a subclass of the UIView class. They include touch-able items like buttons, sliders, and switches, as well as text fields in which you enter data.

Controls make heavy use of the Target-Action design pattern, which you get to see with the Done button in the DeepThoughts app in Chapter 11.

Display views

Think of display views as controls that look good, but don't really do anything except, well, look good. These include UIImageView, UILabel, UIProgressView, and UIActivityIndicatorView. (You use UILabel in the DeepThoughts app in Chapter 10 to display the area in which the falling words appear.)

Text and Web views

Text and *Web views* provide a way to display formatted text in your application. The UITextView class supports the display and editing of multiple lines of text in a scrollable area. The UIWebView class provides a way to display HTML content. These views can be used as the Content view, or they can also be used in the same way as a display view above, as a subview of a Content view. You encounter `UIWebView` in the iPadTravel411 app in Chapter 17, which you use to display the Weather view. `UIWebView` also is the primary way to include graphics and formatted text in Text display views.

Alert views and action sheets

Alert views and *action sheets* present a message to the user, along with buttons that allow the user to respond to the message. Alert views and action sheets are similar in function but look and behave differently. For example, the `UIAlertView` class displays a blue alert box that pops up on the screen, and the `UIActionSheet` class displays a box that slides in from the bottom of the screen.

Navigation views

Tab bars and *Navigation bars* work in conjunction with view controllers to provide tools for navigating in your app. Normally, you don't need to create a `UITabBar` or `UINavigationBar` directly — it's easier to use Interface Builder or configure these views through a tab bar or Navigation bar controller.

The window

A *window* provides a surface for drawing content and is the root container for all other views.

Controlling View Controllers

View controllers implement the controller component of the Model-View-Controller design pattern. These Controller objects contain the code that connects the app's view objects to its model objects. They provide the data to the view. Whenever the view needs to display something, the view controller goes out and gets what the view needs from the model. Similarly, view controllers respond to controls in your Content view and may do things like tell the model to update its data (when the user adds or changes text in a text field, for example); or compute something (the current value of, say, your U.S. dollars in British pounds); or change the view being displayed (as with choosing Weather in the iPadTravel411 app).

As shown in "The Target-Action pattern" section later in this chapter, a view controller is often the (target) object that responds to the on-screen controls. The Target-Action mechanism is what enables the view controller to be aware of any changes in the view, which can then be transmitted to the model. For example, Figure 7-4 shows what happens when the user taps the Weather entry in the iPadTravel411 app to request the current weather conditions.

1. A message is sent to that view's view controller to handle the request.

2. The view controller's method interacts with the Weather model object.

3. The model object processes the request from the user for the current weather.

4. The model object sends the data back to the view controller.

5. The view controller creates a new view to present the information.

View controllers have other vital iPad responsibilities as well, such as:

✔ Managing a set of views — including creating them, or flushing them from memory during low-memory situations.

✔ Responding to a change in the device's orientation — say, landscape to portrait — by resizing the managed views to match the new orientation.

✔ Creating a *Modal* view, which is a child window that displays a dialog requiring the user to do something (touch the Yes button, for example) before returning to the application.

You would use a Modal view to ensure the user has paid attention to the implications of an action (for example, "Are you *sure* you want to delete all your contacts?").

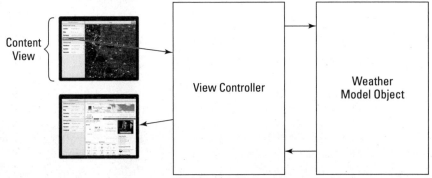

Figure 7-4:
The world of the view controller (as used in the iPad Travel411 app).

Content View

View Controller

Weather Model Object

In addition to the base `UIViewController` class, `UIKit` includes subclasses such as `UITabBarController`, `UINavigationController`, `UITableViewController`, and `UIImagePickerController` to manage the tab bar, Navigation bar, Table views, and to access the Photo library on the user's iPad.

Using naming conventions

When creating your own classes, it's a good idea to follow a couple of standard framework-naming conventions:

✔ Class names (such as `View`) should start with a capital letter.

✔ The names of methods (such as `view-DidLoad`) should start with a lowercase letter.

✔ The names of instance variables (such as `frame`) should start with a lowercase letter.

When you do it this way, it makes it easier to understand what something actually is just from the name.

Apple recommends that apps should support all iPad landscape and portrait orientations (this differs slightly from the iPhone, which doesn't require apps to support both portrait and landscape). You'll want to use a view controller just to manage a single view and auto-rotate it when the device's orientation changes. The app's window and view controllers provide the basic infrastructure needed to support rotations — you can use the existing infrastructure as-is, or customize the behavior to suit the particulars of your app, as you do with the iPadTravel411 app in Chapter 15.

What about the Model?

As this chapter shows (and as you will continue to discover), a lot of the functionality you need is already in the frameworks.

But when it comes to the model objects, for the most part, you're pretty much on your own. You need to design and create model objects to hold the data and carry out the logic. In the iPadTravel411 app in Chapter 14, for example, you create an `Airport` object that knows the different ways to get into the city that it supports.

You may find classes in the framework that help you get the nuts and bolts of the model working. But the actual content and specific functionality is up to you. As for actually implementing model objects, you find out how to do that in Chapter 17.

Adding Your Own Application's Behavior

Earlier in this chapter (by now it probably seems like a million years ago), I mention two other design patterns used in addition to the Model-View-Controller (MVC) pattern. If you have a photographic memory, you don't need me telling you that those two patterns are the Delegation pattern and the Target-Action pattern. These patterns, along with the MVC pattern and subclassing, provide the mechanisms for you to add your app-specific behavior to the UIKit (and any other) framework.

The first way to add behavior is through model objects in the MVC pattern. Model objects contain the data and logic that make, well, your application.

The second way, the way people traditionally think about adding behavior to an object-oriented program, is through *subclassing,* where you first create a new (sub) class that inherits behavior and instance variables from another (super) class and then add additional behavior, instance variables, and *properties* to the mix until you come up with just what you want. (I explain properties in Chapter 11.) The idea here is to start with something basic and then add to it — kind of like taking a deuce coupe (1932 Ford) and turning it into a hot rod. You'd subclass a view controller class, for example, to respond to controls.

The third way to add behavior involves using the Delegation pattern, which allows you to customize an object's behavior without subclassing by basically forcing another object to do the first object's work for it. For example, the Delegation design pattern is used at application startup to invoke a method applicationDidFinishLaunching: that gives you a place to do your own application-specific initialization. All you do is add your code to the method.

The final way to add behavior involves the Target-Action design pattern, which allows your application to respond to an event. When a user touches a button, for example, you specify what method should be invoked to respond to the button touch. What is interesting about this pattern is that it also requires subclassing — usually a view controller (refer to Figure 7-4) — in order to add the code to handle the event.

The next few sections go into a little more detail about Delegation patterns and Target-Action patterns.

The Delegation pattern

Delegation is a pattern used extensively in the iPhone OS frameworks for iPad and iPhone apps, so much so that it's very important to clearly understand it. In fact, once you understand it, your life will be much easier.

Delegation, as I mention in the previous section, is a way of customizing the behavior of an object without subclassing it. Instead, one object (a Framework object) delegates the task of implementing one of its responsibilities to another object. You're using a behavior-rich object supplied by the framework *as is,* and putting the code for program-specific behavior in a separate (delegate) object. When a request is made of the Framework object, the method of the delegate that implements the program-specific behavior is automatically called.

For example, the UIApplication object handles most of the actual work needed to run the application. But, as you will see in Chapter 8, it sends your application delegate the applicationDidFinishLaunching: message to give you an opportunity to restore the application's window and view to where it was when the user previously left off. You can also use this method to create objects that are unique to your app.

When a Framework object has been designed to use delegates to implement certain behaviors, the behaviors it requires (or gives you the option to implement) are defined in a *protocol.*

Protocols define an interface that the delegate object implements. Protocols can be formal or informal, although I concentrate solely on the former because it includes support for things like type checking and runtime checking to see whether an object conforms to the protocol.

In a formal protocol, you usually don't have to implement all the methods; many are declared optional, meaning you only have to implement the ones relevant to your app. Before it attempts to send a message to its delegate, the host object determines whether the delegate implements the method (via a respondsToSelector: message) to avoid the embarrassment of branching into nowhere if the method is not implemented.

You can find out much more about delegation and the Delegation pattern when you develop the DeepThoughts app in Part IV and especially the iPadTravel411 app in Part V.

The Target-Action pattern

You use the *Target-Action* pattern to let your app know that a user has done something. He or she may have tapped a button or entered some text, for example. The control — a button, say — sends a message (the Action message) that you specify to the target you have selected to handle that particular action. The receiving object, or the Target, is usually a view controller object.

If you wanted to develop an app that could start a car from an iPad (not a bad idea for those who live in a place like Minneapolis in winter), you could display two buttons, Start and Heater. You could use Interface Builder to specify, when the user taps Start, that the target is the `Car Controller` object and that the method to invoke is `ignition`. Figure 7-5 shows the Target-Action mechanism in action. (If you're curious about `IBAction` and `(id) sender`, I explain what they are when I show you how to use the Target-Action pattern in your application.)

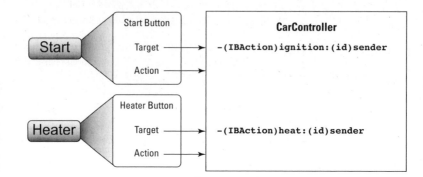

Figure 7-5:
The Target-
Action
mechanism.

The Target-Action mechanism enables you to create a control object and tell it not only what object you want handling the event, but also the message to send. For example, if the user touches a Ring Bell button onscreen, you want to send a Ring Bell message to the view controller. But if the Wave Flag button on the same screen is touched, you want to be able to send the Wave Flag message to the same view controller. If you couldn't specify the message, all buttons would have to send the same message. It would then make the coding more difficult and more complex because you would have to identify which button had sent the message and what to do in response. It would also make changing the user interface more work and more error prone.

When creating your app, you can set a control's action and target through the Interface Builder. This setting allows you to specify what method in which object should respond to a control without having to write any code.

You can also change the target and action dynamically by sending the control or its cell `setTarget:` and `setAction:` messages.

For more on the Interface Builder, check out Chapter 9.

Doing What When?

The `UIKit` framework provides a great deal of ready-made functionality, but the beauty of `UIKit` lies in the fact that — as this chapter explains — you can customize its behavior using three distinct mechanisms.

✔ Subclassing

✔ Target-Action

✔ Delegation

One of the challenges facing a new developer is to determine which of these mechanisms to use when. (That was certainly the case for me.) To ensure that you have an overall conceptual picture of the iPad application architecture, check out the Cheat Sheet for *iPhone Application Development All-in-One For Dummies,* which offers a summary of which mechanisms are used when. You can find the Cheat Sheet at www.dummies.com/cheatsheet/iphone applicationdevelopment.

You still have quite a bit more background information to explore before you get started building the DeepThoughts app in Chapter 9. It helps a great deal to know more about how an app runs in the iPad's iPhone OS — the *runtime scenario.* Although that sounds like the title of a prison escape movie, it's really about what goes on inside the iPad when the user launches your app, and you find out all about that in the next chapter, along with how Interface Builder nib files work. What fun!

Chapter 8

Understanding How an App Runs

- -

In This Chapter

▶ Watching how the template-based app works at runtime

▶ Following what goes on when the user launches your app

▶ Getting a handle on how nib files work

▶ Remembering memory management

▶ Knowing what else you should be aware of at runtime

- -

*W*hen you create an Xcode project and select a template, as I show in Chapter 5, you get a considerable head start on the process of coding your very own iPad app. In that chapter, I choose the View-based Application template for the DeepThoughts app, and as a result, I have a working app that offers a view.

As the wise sage (and wisecracking baseball player) Yogi Berra once said, "You can observe a lot just by watching." Before you add anything more to this skeleton of an app, it helps to look at *how* it does what it already does. By uncovering the mysteries of what this template does at runtime, you can learn a bit more about where to put *your* code.

As you find out in Chapter 7, a *framework* offers common code providing generic functionality. The iPhone OS for the iPad provides a set of frameworks for incorporating technologies, services, and features into your apps. The framework is designed to easily integrate your code; with the framework in place, all you need to do is *add* the specific functionality that you want in the app — the content as well as the controls and views that enable the user to access and use that content — *to* the frameworks.

App Anatomy 101 — The Lifecycle

The short-but-happy life of an iPad app begins when a user launches it by tapping its icon on the iPad Home screen. The system launches your app by calling its `main` function, which you can see in the Xcode Editor window in Figure 8-1.

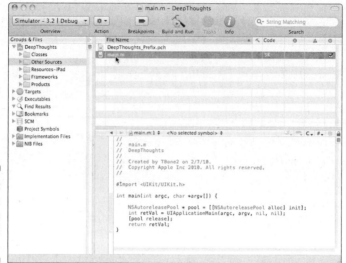

Figure 8-1:
The main
function is
where it all
begins.

The `main` function does only three things:

- ✔ Sets up an autorelease pool:

  ```
  NSAutoreleasePool * pool = [[NSAutoreleasePool alloc]
           init];
  ```

- ✔ Calls the `UIApplicationMain` function to create the application object
  and delegate and set up the event cycle. The template uses the first `nil`
  as the principle class name so that `UIApplication` is the assumed
  name, and it specifies the second `nil` to load the delegate object from
  the application's main nib file:

  ```
  int retVal = UIApplicationMain(argc, argv, nil, nil);
  ```

- ✔ At termination, releases the autorelease pool:

  ```
  [pool release];
  return retVal;
  ```

(As Objective-C programmers already know, the lines beginning with `//` in
the code are comments that don't do anything.)

To be honest, this whole `main` function thing isn't something you
even need to think about. What's important is what happens *when* the
`UIApplicationMain` function is called. Here's the play-by-play:

1. **The main nib file is loaded.**

   A *nib file* is a resource file that contains the specifications for one or
   more objects. The main nib file usually contains a window object of
   some kind, the application delegate object, and any other key objects.

When the file is loaded, the objects are reconstituted (think "instant application") in memory.

In the DeepThoughts app you just started (with a little help from the aforementioned View-based Application template), this is the moment of truth when the DeepThoughtsAppDelegate and DeepThoughtsViewController objects are created along with the main window.

For more on the application delegate and view controller objects and the roles they play in apps, see Chapter 7.

2. **The *application delegate* (DeepThoughtsAppDelegate) receives the application:didFinishLaunchingWithOptions: message.**

You can see the DeepThoughtsAppDelegate.m implementation file in Figure 8-2, as provided by the template — see how much code is already written for you!

The application:didFinishLaunchingWithOptions: message tells the delegate when the application has launched. In this step, you initialize and set up your application. The application delegate object is a custom object that you code. It's responsible for some of the application-level behavior of your application. (Delegation is an extensively used design pattern that I introduce in Chapter 7.)

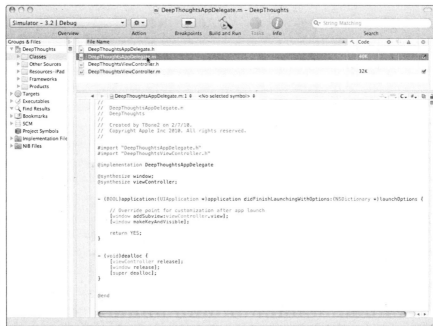

Figure 8-2:
The application delegate implementation as provided by the template.

3. The UIKit framework sets up the event loop.

The *event loop* is the code responsible for polling input sources — the screen, for example. Events, such as touches on the screen, are sent to the object — say, a controller — that you have specified to handle that kind of event, as shown in Figure 8-3. These handling objects contain the code that implements what you want your app to do in response to that particular event. A touch on a control may result in a change in what the user sees in a view, a switch to a new view, or even the playing of the song "Don't Touch Me."

4. When the user performs an action that would cause your app to quit, UIKit notifies your app and begins the termination process.

Your app delegate is sent the applicationWillTerminate: message, and you have the opportunity to add code to do whatever you want to do before termination, including saving the state the user was in. Saving is important, because then, when the app is launched again (refer to Step 2) and the UIApplicationMain sends the app delegate the applicationDidFinishLaunching message, you can restore the app to the state the user left it (such as a certain view).

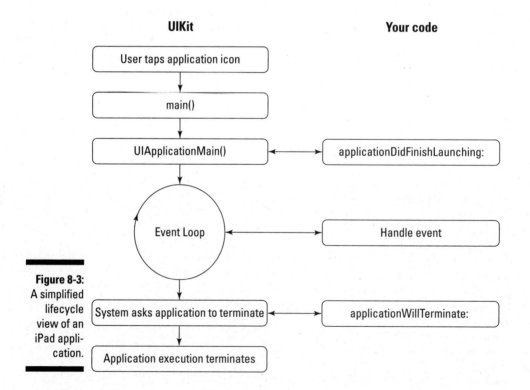

Figure 8-3:
A simplified lifecycle view of an iPad application.

It all starts with the main nib file

When you create a new project using a template — quite the normal state of affairs, as I show in Chapter 5 — the basic application environment is included. That means when you launch your app, an application object is created and connected to the window object, the run loop is established, and so on — despite the fact that you haven't done a lick of coding.

Most of this work is done by the `UIApplicationMain` function, as illustrated back in Figure 8-3. To take advantage of this once-in-a-lifetime opportunity to see how all this works, go back to your project window in Xcode and select the Resources-iPad folder in the Groups & Files list on the left. (You do have a project already started, right? If not, check out Chapter 5.) Here's a blow-by-blow description of what the `UIApplicationMain` function actually does:

1. **An instance of `UIApplication` is created.**

2. **`UIApplication` looks in the `info.plist` file, trying to find the main nib file.**

   To see the `info.plist` file, select `DeepThoughts-Info.plist` in the Detail view of the Xcode window, as shown in Figure 8-4. The content of the file appears in the Editor view below the Detail view.

   `UIApplication` makes its way down the Key column of the `info.plist` file until it finds the Main Nib File Base Name entry. Eureka! It peeks over at the Value column and sees that the value for the Main Nib File Base Name entry is `MainWindow`. (See Figure 8-4.)

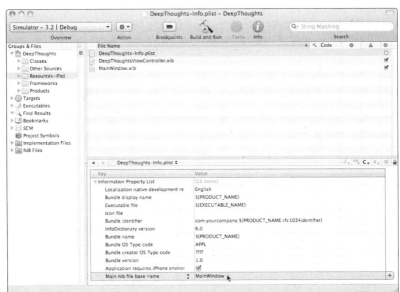

Figure 8-4: The info. plist file holds the key to the Main Nib File entry.

3. UIApplication loads MainWindow.xib.

Figure 8-5 illustrates this process of loading the main window's nib file.

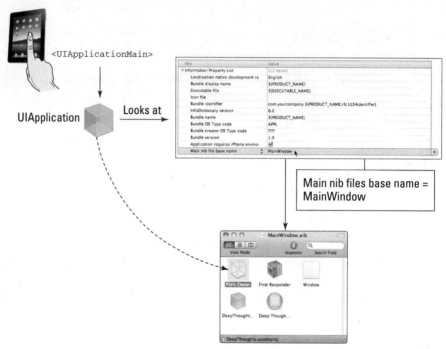

Figure 8-5:
The application is launched.

The nib file MainWindow.xib is what causes your application's delegate, window, and view controller instances to get created at runtime. Remember, this file is provided as part of the project template. You don't need to change or do anything here. This is just a chance to see what's going on behind the scenes.

To see the nib file (MainWindow.xib) in Interface Builder, double-click MainWindow.xib in the Xcode project window's Detail view, as shown in Figure 8-6.

When Interface Builder opens, take a look at the nib file's main window — the one labeled MainWindow.xib (as shown in Figure 8-7). Select File's Owner in the window, click the Inspector button at the top of the window, and then click the Identity tab of the Inspector window if it's not already selected (or choose Tools⇨Identity Inspector to show the Identity tab of the Inspector window).

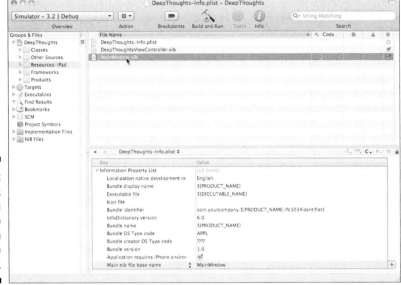

Figure 8-6:
Double-click
the Main
Window.xib
file to open
Interface
Builder.

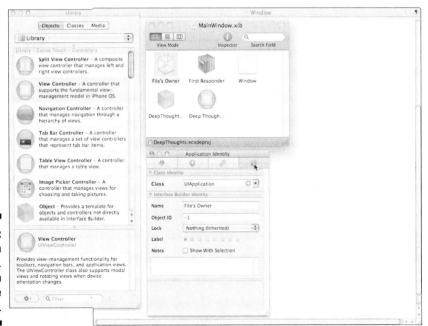

Figure 8-7:
The Main
Window.
xib file in
Interface
Builder.

The `MainWindow.xib` window shows four icons, but you can view them in
a list by clicking the center View Mode button in the upper-left corner of the
window, as shown in Figure 8-8. The interface objects are as follows:

✔ **File's Owner (proxy object):** The File's Owner — the object that's going to use (or *own*) this file — is of the class `UIApplication`. This object isn't created when the file is loaded, as are the window and views — it's already created by the `UIApplicationMain` object before the nib file is loaded.

`UIApplication` objects have a delegate object that implements the `UIApplicationDelegate` protocol. Specifying the delegate object can be done from Interface Builder by setting the `delegate` outlet of a `UIApplication` object. To see that this has already been done for you in the template, click File's Owner, and then click the Connections tab of the Inspector window (or choose Tools⇨Connections Inspector). The `delegate` outlet is set to "Deep Thoughts App Delegate," as shown in Figure 8-8 — click the outlet connection in the Inspector window and DeepThoughts App Delegate is highlighted in the `MainWindow.xib` window.

✔ **First Responder (proxy object):** This object is the first entry in an application's responder chain, which is constantly updated while the application is running — usually to point to the object that the user is currently interacting with. If, for example, the user were to tap a text field to enter some data, the first responder would become the text field object.

✔ **Window:** The window has its background set to white and status bar set to black, as shown in Figure 8-9, and is set to *not* be visible at launch. To see the window's attributes, click Window in the MainWindow.xib window, and click the Attributes tab in the Inspector window.

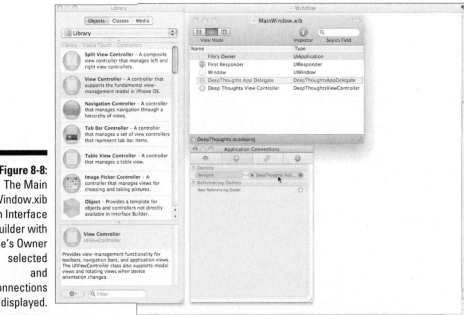

Figure 8-8: The Main Window.xib in Interface Builder with File's Owner selected and Connections displayed.

✔ **An instance of `DeepThoughtsAppDelegate` set to be the application's delegate.**

You can see the header and implementation of `DeepThoughtsApp Delegate` in Listing 8-1 and 8-2. This is where you can put code that restores the app after launch to its previous *state* (see "Termination" in this chapter for the meaning of this), or performs any other custom application initialization.

✔ **An instance of `DeepThoughtsViewController` set to be the application's view controller.**

The view controller is where you put your code to control the views of your app, as you find out in Chapter 10.

The following section spells out what happens to these objects when `UIApplication` loads `MainWindow.xib`.

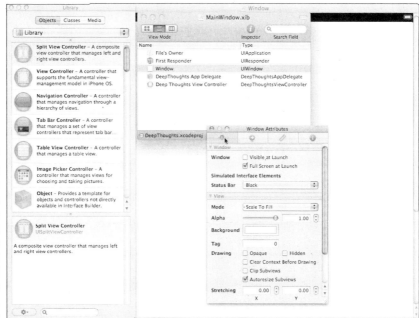

Figure 8-9:
The Main Window.xib in Interface Builder with Window selected and Attributes displayed.

Initialization

`UIApplication` loads the parts of the `MainWindow.xib` file as follows:

1. **Creates `DeepThoughtsAppDelegate`.**

2. **Creates `Window`.**

3. Sends the `DeepThoughtsAppDelegate` the `application:didFinish LaunchingWithOptions:` message.

4. `DeepThoughtsAppDelegate` initializes the window.

I show the header and implementation of `DeepThoughtsAppDelegate` in Listings 8-1 and 8-2. All this is done for you as part of the Xcode template.

Listing 8-1: DeepThoughtsAppDelegate.h

```
#import <UIKit/UIKit.h>

@class DeepThoughtsViewController;

@interface DeepThoughtsAppDelegate : NSObject
        <UIApplicationDelegate> {
    UIWindow *window;
    DeepThoughtsViewController *viewController;
}

@property (nonatomic, retain) IBOutlet UIWindow *window;
@property (nonatomic, retain) IBOutlet
        DeepThoughtsViewController *viewController;


@end
```

Listing 8-2: DeepThoughtsAppDelegate.m

```
#import "DeepThoughtsAppDelegate.h"
#import "DeepThoughtsViewController.h"

@implementation DeepThoughtsAppDelegate

@synthesize window;
@synthesize viewController;

- (BOOL)application:(UIApplication *)application didF
        inishLaunchingWithOptions:(NSDictionary *)
        launchOptions {

    // Override point for customization after app launch
    [window addSubview:viewController.view];
    [window makeKeyAndVisible];

        return YES;
}

- (void)dealloc {
    [viewController release];
    [window release];
    [super dealloc];
```

```
}

@end
```

In Listing 8-2, the view controller is initialized with the `initWithNibName:bundle:` method. You could use the `applicationDidFinishLaunching` method to do any other application initialization as well — such as returning everything to what it was like when the user last used the application.

Your goal during startup should be to present your application's user interface as quickly as possible — quick initialization = happy users. Don't load large data structures that your application won't use right away. If your application requires time to load data from the network (or perform other tasks that take noticeable time), get your interface up and running first and then launch the slow task on a background thread. Then you can display a progress indicator or other feedback to the user to indicate that your application is loading the necessary data or doing something important.

The application delegate object (refer to Listing 8-1) is usually derived from `NSObject`, the root class (the very base class from which all iPad application objects are derived), although it can be an instance of any class you like, as long as it adopts the `UIApplicationDelegate` protocol. The methods of this protocol correspond to behaviors that are needed during the application lifecycle and are your way of implementing this custom behavior. Although you aren't required to implement all the methods of the `UIApplicationDelegate` protocol, every application should implement the following critical application tasks:

- ✔ Initialization, which I've just covered
- ✔ Handling events, which I cover in the next chapter
- ✔ Handling termination, which I cover next
- ✔ Responding to interruptions and low memory warnings, which I cover later in this chapter

Termination

When your app quits, you should save any unsaved data or *state* (where the user is in the app — the current view, options selected, and stuff like that) to a temporary cache file or to the preferences database. The next time the user launches your app, your code can use that information to restore your app to its previous state.

Getting stuff to (safely) shut down is another application delegate responsibility. Although I don't do this in DeepThoughts, your app's delegate can implement the delegate method `applicationWillTerminate:` to save the current state and unsaved data to disk. (Yes, the disk in the iPad is not *really* a disk — it's a solid state drive that Apple *calls* a disk.) You can also use this method to perform additional cleanup operations, such as deleting temporary files. I show you how to use the `applicationWillTerminate:` method to save and restore the iPadTravel411 app in Chapter 16.

The state information you save should be as minimal as possible but still let you accurately restore your app to an appropriate point. You don't have to display the exact same screen used previously — for example, if a user edits a contact and then leaves the Contacts app, upon returning, the Contacts app displays the top-level list of contacts, rather than the editing screen for the contact.

Other Runtime Considerations

Launch, initialize, process, terminate, launch, initialize, process, terminate . . . it has a nice rhythm to it, doesn't it? And those *are* the four major stages of the application's lifecycle. But life isn't simple — and neither is runtime. To mix things up a bit, your application will also have to come to terms with interruptions and memory management.

Responding to interruptions

On an iPad, various events besides termination can interrupt your app to allow the user to respond — for example, calendar alerts or the user pressing the Sleep/Wake button. Such interruptions may only be temporary. If the user chooses to ignore an interruption, your app continues running as before. If the user decides to tap the alert to deal with it, your app will be terminated.

Figure 8-10 shows the sequence of events that occurs during the arrival of an alert. Here's what that looks like step by step:

1. **An event occurs, such as a calendar alert.**

2. **The system sends your application delegate the `applicationWill ResignActive:` message.**

    Because these interruptions cause a temporary loss of control by your app — meaning that touch events, as I describe in Chapter 11, are no longer sent to your app — it's up to you to prevent what's known in the trade as a "negative user experience." For example, if your app is a game, you should pause the game.

3. **The system displays an alert panel with information about the event.**

The user can choose to ignore the event or respond to it.

4. **If the user ignores the event, the system sends your application delegate the `applicationDidBecomeActive:` message and resumes the delivery of touch events to your app.**

    You can use this delegate method to restore the app to the state it was in before the interruption. What you do depends on your app. In some apps, it makes sense to resume normal processing. In others — if you've paused a game, for example — you could leave the game paused until the user decides to resume play.

5. **If the user responds to the event, instead of ignoring it, the system sends your application delegate the `applicationWillTerminate:` message.**

    Your app should do what it needs to do in order to terminate gracefully.

The way the Sleep/Wake button is handled is a little different. When the app enters or resumes from a sleep state, two messages are sent to the application delegate: `applicationWillResignActive:` and `applicationDidBecomeActive:`, respectively. In this case, your app always resumes, though the user might immediately launch a different app.

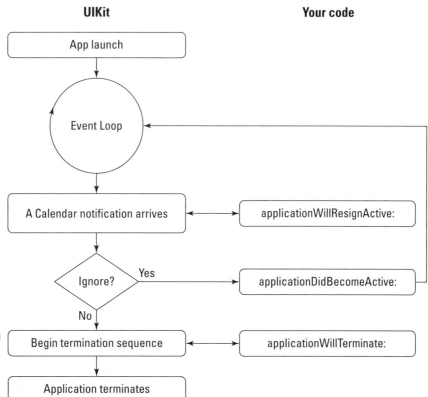

Figure 8-10:
Handling an
interruption.

Seeing how memory management works on the iPad

One of the main responsibilities of all good little applications is to deal with low memory. So the first line of defense is (obviously) to understand how you as a programmer can help them *avoid* getting into that state.

In the iPhone OS for the iPad, each program uses the virtual-memory mechanism found in all modern operating systems. But virtual memory is limited to the amount of physical memory available. This is because the iPhone OS doesn't store changeable memory (such as object data) on the disk to free up space, and then read it in later when it's needed. Instead, the iPhone OS tries to give the running application the memory it needs — freeing memory pages that contain read-only contents (such as code), where all it has to do is load the "originals" back into memory when they're needed. Of course, this may be only a temporary fix if those resources are needed again a short time later.

If memory continues to be limited, the system may also send notifications to the running application, asking it to free up additional memory. This is one of the critical events that all applications must respond to.

Observing low-memory warnings

When the system dispatches a low-memory notification to your application, it's something you must pay attention to. If you don't, it's a reliable recipe for disaster. (Think of your low-fuel light going on as you approach a sign that says, "Next services 100 miles.") UIKit provides several ways of setting up your application so that you receive timely low-memory notifications:

✔ Implement the applicationDidReceiveMemoryWarning: method of your application delegate. Your application delegate could then release any data structure or objects it owns — or notify the objects to release memory they own. Apple recommends this approach.

✔ Override the didReceiveMemoryWarning: method in your custom UIViewController subclass. The view controller could then release views — or even other view controllers — that are off-screen. For example, in your new project (DeepThoughts) created with the View-based Application template, the template already supplies the following in DeepThoughtsViewController.m, ready for you to customize:

```
- (void)didReceiveMemoryWarning {
    // Releases the view if it doesn't have a
        superview.
    [super didReceiveMemoryWarning];

    // Release any cached data, images, etc that aren't
        in use.
}
```

```
- (void)viewDidUnload {
    // Release any retained subviews of the main view.
    // e.g. self.myOutlet = nil;
}
```

✔ Register to receive the UIApplicationDidReceiveMemoryWarning Notification: notification. Such notifications are sent to the notification center, where all notifications are centralized. An object that wants to get informed about this notification registers itself to the notification center by telling which notification it wants to get informed and which method should be invoked when the notification is raised. A model object could then release data structures or objects it owns that it doesn't need immediately and can re-create later. However, this approach is beyond the scope of this book.

Each of these strategies gives a different part of your application a chance to free up the memory it no longer needs (or doesn't need right now). As for how you actually get these strategies working for you, that's dependent on your application's architecture. That means you'll need to explore it on your own.

Not freeing up enough memory will result in the iPhone OS sending your iPad application the applicationWillTerminate: message and shutting you down. For many apps, though, the best defense is a good offense, and you need to manage your memory effectively and eliminate any memory leaks in your code. (A memory leak is how programmers describe a situation in which an object is unable to release the memory it has acquired — it can diminish performance by reducing the amount of available memory.)

Avoiding the warnings

When you create an object — a window or button for example — memory is allocated to hold that object's data. The more objects you create, the more memory you use — and the less there is available for additional objects you might need. Obviously, it's important to make available (that is, *de-allocate*) the memory that an object was using when the object is no longer needed. This task is called *memory management.*

Objective-C uses reference counting to figure out when to release the memory allocated to an object. It's your responsibility (as a programmer) to keep the memory-management system informed when an object is no longer needed.

Reference counting is a pretty simple concept. When you create the object, it's given a reference count of 1. As other objects use this object, they use methods to increase the reference count, and decrease it when they're done. When the reference count reaches 0, the object is no longer needed, and the memory is de-allocated.

Some basic memory-management rules you shouldn't forget

Here are the fundamental rules when it comes to memory management:

- Any object you create using `alloc` or `new`, any method that contains `copy`, and any object you send a `retain` message to is *yours* — you own it. That means you're responsible for telling the memory-management system when you no longer need the object and that its memory can now be used elsewhere.

- Within a given block of code, the number of times you use `new`, `copy`, `alloc`, and `retain` should equal the number of times you use `release` and `autorelease`. You should think of memory management as consisting of pairs of messages. If you balance every `alloc` and every `retain` with a `release`, your object will eventually be freed up when you're done with it.

- When you assign an instance variable using an accessor with a property attribute of `retain`, `retain` is automatically invoked — that is, you now own the object. Implement a `dealloc` method to release the instance variables you own.

- Objects created any other way (through convenience constructors or other accessor methods) are not your problem.

If you have a solid background in Objective-C memory management (all three of you out there), following those rules should be straightforward or even obvious. If you don't have that background, no sweat: See *Objective-C For Dummies* for some background.

Reread this section!

Okay, there are some aspects of programming that you can skate right past without understanding what's really going on, and you can still create a decent iPad app. But memory management is *not* one of them!

A direct correlation exists between the amount of free memory available and your application's performance. If the memory available to your application dwindles far enough, the system will be forced to terminate your application. To avoid such a fate, keep a few words of wisdom in mind:

- Minimize the amount of memory you use — make that a high priority of your implementation design.

- Be sure to use the memory-management functions.

- In other words, be sure to clean up after yourself, or the system will do it for you, and it won't be a pretty picture.

Whew!

Congratulations — in the last chapter and this chapter, you've just gone through the "Classic Comics" version of another several hundred pages of Apple documentation, reference manuals, and how-to guides.

Although there's a lot left unsaid (though less than you might suspect), the details in the previous chapter and this chapter are enough to not only to get you started but also to keep you going as you develop your own iPad apps. It provides a frame of reference on which you can hang the concepts I throw around with abandon in upcoming chapters — as well as the groundwork for a deep enough understanding of the application lifecycle to give you a handle on the detailed documentation.

Time to move on to the really fun stuff: building DeepThoughts into an app that actually does something.

Part IV
Building DeepThoughts

ORICHTENNANT

iPad
APPLICATION
DEVELOPMENT

"Stop working on the Priority Parking Spot Allocation app. They want to fast track the Coffee Pot/Cubicle Proximity app."

In this part . . .

To wrap your head around the entire process of build-ing an app, I present to you DeepThoughts, a sample app, which you find out how to build in this part. These chapters demonstrate enough of the building blocks for creating a sophisticated iPad app that you should pay attention and follow along with these chapters:

- ✔ Chapter 9 takes you on a tour of the View-based Application template, on which DeepThoughts is based. You also find out how to add an image to your first iPad view-based app, and add an inter-face element (an Info button). You also do one of the more important graphical tasks: supply an icon for the app for the iPad display.

- ✔ Chapter 10 dives right into custom-coding your app. You find out how to use Xcode's documenta-tion and help windows while adding code, and you discover the answer to that monumental question, where does my code go? The code you add controls and animates the view and sets up the methods and variables for applying user pref-erence settings.

- ✔ Chapter 11 gets you right into the thick of iPad development, creating a modal view for users to change their preference settings, connecting interface objects, and adding recognition for ges-tures. At the end of this chapter, DeepThoughts is done (except for bugs).

- ✔ Chapter 12 shows you how to swat the bugs in your apps using the Debugger, the Mini Debugger, the Console, and even the Static Analyzer. You find out all about setting breakpoints that stop your app cold in the Simulator so that you can examine the contents of variables and messages to objects. At the end of this chapter, DeepThoughts is actu-ally finished, and you know how to debug apps with Xcode.

Chapter 9

Building the User Interface

In This Chapter

▶ Inspecting an app with a view

▶ Using Interface Builder to add graphics and buttons

▶ Adding an application icon

Steve Jobs said it best: "Design is not just what it looks like and feels like. Design is how it works." That's why you should know how an iPad app works before trying to design a user interface for one.

For one thing, you need to consider the memory limitations and display orientation of the iPad. That's why the Xcode templates are so useful — they take care of the display and memory management so that you can focus on what your app can do. After seeing how easy it is to add graphics and interface elements to the template-based project, you may think the user interface for your app will be a piece of cake — and to some extent, it probably will be, thanks to Interface Builder.

The template you select for your Xcode project (as I show in Chapter 5) provides the skeleton of a user interface. For example, the View-based Application template for the DeepThoughts app offers a view and a view controller that you can customize. Other templates offer rudimentary interface objects — for example, the Navigation-based Application template offers a Navigation controller, and the Utility-based Application template offers a Flipside view that a user opens by tapping an Info button and closes by tapping a Done button. The Split View-based Application template offers a Split view controller as well as the two view controllers you'd use to manage a master-detail-style display.

Make sure you choose the appropriate template so that you don't have to reinvent the wheel. And before you start coding, examine how the template's interface works and how to add your custom interface objects and graphics. That's what this chapter is all about.

Running the View-Based Application Template

When you start a project with the View-based Application template, you get the Main window, a view (using a white background) scaled to fill the entire Main window, and a black status bar at the top. The view and status bar automatically change orientation for you when the user rotates the iPad.

You can see this in action in the Simulator, even before writing any code — after choosing the template to create your project (as I describe in Chapter 5), build and run the template project by choosing Build⟳Build and Run from the Xcode main menu. (I also show you how to build, run, and use the Simulator in Chapter 5.)

After a user launches your app, the functionality provided in the `UIKit` framework manages most of the application's infrastructure. Part of the initialization process mentioned in Chapter 8 involves setting up the main run loop and event-handling code, which is the responsibility of the `UIApplication` object. When the application is onscreen, it's driven by external events — such as stubby fingers touching sleek buttons.

As you discover in Chapter 8, the nib file `MainWindow.xib` causes the application's delegate, window, and view controller instances to get created at runtime, and both `MainWindow.xib` and the view controller's nib file, `DeepThoughtsViewController.xib`, are provided as part of the View-based Application template. An instance of `DeepThoughtsViewController` is set to be the application's view controller, and that's where you put your code to control the view.

Before doing that, however, you can build this view to have a background image and some interface elements. To see what you have in the view now, you can inspect the view in Interface Builder.

Inspecting the View

To see how the view is created and connected to the template code, start up Interface Builder from Xcode by clicking Resources-iPad in the Groups & Files list; then double-clicking the `DeepThoughtsViewController.xib` file to launch Interface Builder.

To inspect the view, click the Identity tab of the Inspector window (or choose Tools⟳Identity Inspector), and then click the View icon in the `DeepThoughtsViewController.xib` window to see the identity of the view, as shown in Figure 9-1.

The four icons across the top of the Inspector window from left to right correspond to the Attributes, Connections, Size, and Identity Inspectors, respectively, in the Tools menu.

Figure 9-1:
The view's identity in Interface Builder.

You can see that the view belongs to the UIView class, and that user interaction has been enabled. UIView is an abstract superclass that provides concrete subclasses with a structure for drawing and handling events. The UIView class provides common methods you can use to create all types of views as well as access their properties.

You can also click the Attributes tab of the Inspector window (or choose Tools⇨Attributes Inspector) to see the view's attributes — and you find that it includes a black status bar and a white background.

To get info about the class that uses, or *owns*, this view, click File's Owner in the DeepThoughtsViewController.xib window and then click the Identity tab of the Inspector window (or choose Tools⇨Identity Inspector). In the Class pop-up menu, you can see that the File's Owner — the object that's going to use (or *own*) this file — is set to the class DeepThoughtsView Controller (as shown in Figure 9-2). Click the circled arrow next to DeepThoughtsViewController in the Class pop-up menu to display the class in the Library window along with its description. (Refer to Figure 9-2.)

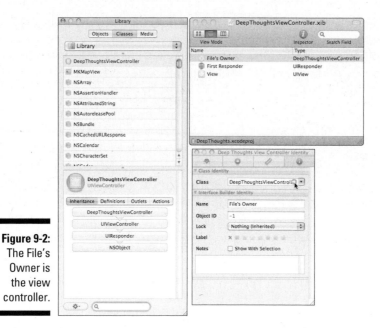

Figure 9-2:
The File's
Owner is
the view
controller.

How does this work? The template set this all up for you, without you having to lift a finger.

Understanding How the View Is Initialized

If you look back to Chapter 8, you can see that the template supplies the following code in `DeepThoughtsAppDelegate.h`:

```
@class DeepThoughtsViewController;
@interface DeepThoughtsAppDelegate : NSObject
          <UIApplicationDelegate> {
    UIWindow *window;
 DeepThoughtsViewController *viewController;
}
```

This sets up the `UIApplicationDelegate` protocol with `window`. The template also declares an accessor method for `window` and tags it with an `IBOutlet` so that Interface Builder can discover it, while also declaring an accessor method for `viewController`:

```
@property (nonatomic, retain) IBOutlet UIWindow *window;
@property (nonatomic, retain) DeepThoughtsViewController
          *viewController;
```

In the file DeepThoughtsAppDelegate.m, the @synthesize statements tell the compiler to create accessor methods for you — one for each @property declaration (window and viewController). After the delegate receives notification that the application has launched in the application:didFinish LaunchingWithOptions: method, the code uses the addSubview and makeKeyAndVisible methods to display the view:

```
@implementation DeepThoughtsAppDelegate
@synthesize window;
@synthesize viewController;

- (BOOL)application:(UIApplication *)application didF
        inishLaunchingWithOptions:(NSDictionary *)
        launchOptions {

    // Override point for customization after app launch
    [window addSubview:viewController.view];
    [window makeKeyAndVisible];

        return YES;
}
```

The view controller is initialized, and addSubView adds viewController. view to window in order to display the view. Calling makeKeyAndVisible on window makes the window visible as well as making it the main window and the first responder for events (touches).

In DeepThoughtsViewController.h, you find this:

```
@interface DeepThoughtsViewController : UIViewController {
}
```

This tells you that DeepThoughtsViewController is a subclass of UIViewController. The UIViewController class provides the fundamental view-management model for iPad apps. You use each instance of UIViewController to manage a full-screen view.

In DeepThoughtsViewController.m near the top, you find the code that sets up the view initialization:

```
@implementation DeepThoughtsViewController
- (id)initWithNibName:(NSString *)nibNameOrNil
        bundle:(NSBundle *)nibBundleOrNil {
    if (self = [super initWithNibName:nibNameOrNil
        bundle:nibBundleOrNil]) {
        // Custom initialization
    }
    return self;
}
```

The `DeepThoughtsViewController` object is created by a nib file directly passed on to `UIViewController` to handle the initialization. (You can add custom initialization at the point where the `//` comment appears.)

Adding an Image to the View

So far, the DeepThoughts app displays a white view with a black status bar — for the entire 1,024 x 768 pixels (at up to 24 bits per pixel). You need to put those pixels to work! A compelling iPad app needs to immerse the user in an experience, even if that experience is the appearance of a leather-bound address book rather than a simple contact entry form. The basis of any kind of immersive experience is the image you display in the view.

To place an image in your app, first you need the image. While you have plenty of pixels to work with, you should create artwork for the final image in a larger multiple of the pixel dimensions you need so that you can add depth and details before scaling it down accurately to the iPad display size.

The preferred format for the image is `.png`. Although most common image formats, such as `.jpg` (JPEG) will display correctly, Xcode automatically optimizes `.png` images at build time to make them the fastest and most efficient image type for use in iPad applications.

After you have your image (in my case, I'm using a JPEG image), do the following:

1. **In Xcode, drag the image file into the Resources-iPad folder in the Groups & Files list, as shown in Figure 9-3.**

   Although you can drag it to any location in the Groups & Files list, I like to keep my projects uncluttered, and I use the Resources-iPad folder to hold all interface-related files.

   An alternative is to click the Resources-iPad folder in Xcode, choose Project➪Add to Project, and then navigate to the file you want to add.

   After dragging or adding the file, Xcode displays a dialog for making a copy of the file and specifying its reference type, text encoding, and other options, as shown in Figure 9-4.

2. **Check the Copy Items into Destination Group's Folder check box to copy the file and then click Add to finish copying the image file into your project.**

   If you don't make a copy of the file, Xcode simply creates a pointer to the file. The advantage of using a pointer is that if you modify the image later, Xcode will use that modified version. The disadvantage is that Xcode won't be able to find the image file if you move it.

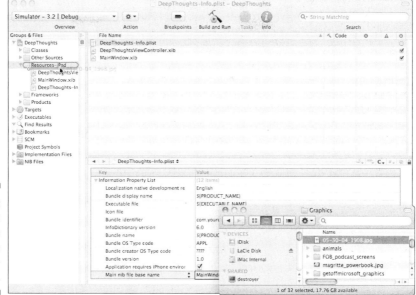

Figure 9-3: Drag an image file into the Resources-iPad folder.

Figure 9-4: Tell Xcode to make a copy of the file and add it to the project.

I'm all for copying. If you change the image, use the same name for the changed file and drag it back into Resources-iPad to replace the older file. Then build the project again.

You don't need to change the default settings for Reference Type, Text Encoding, or Recursively Create Groups for Any Added Folders.

3. **Double-click DeepThoughtsViewController.xib in the Resources-iPad folder to open Interface Builder.**

The Interface Builder windows should appear (refer to Figure 9-1). If the Library window doesn't appear with the other windows, choose Tools➪Library to show it.

4. **Click the Objects tab at the top of the Library window and select Data Views from the drop-down menu below the Objects tab.**

   Selecting Objects and then Data Views narrows your search through the Library window so that you can find the object you need quickly.

   It turns out that, to place the image in the view, you need the Image View object, as shown in Figure 9-5.

5. **Drag the Image View object from the Library onto the View window.**

   If the View window is obscured by other windows, just drag the Image View object directly on top of the View icon in the `DeepThoughtsView Controller.xib` window as I do in Figure 9-5, so that it appears underneath and part of the view.

Figure 9-5:
Adding the Image View object to the view.

6. **Select Image View in the `DeepThoughtsViewController.xib` window and click the Attributes tab of the Inspector window (or choose Tools➪Attributes Inspector).**

   The Attribute Inspector shows the Image View attributes.

7. **In the Attribute Inspector, choose the image file in the Image drop-down menu, as shown in Figure 9-6.**

That Inspector window's a handy little critter, isn't it? Just select the image file you dragged into your project in Step 1. Your Image View object does what it's told, and loads your view so that it ends up looking something like Figure 9-7.

TIP

If you don't see the image file in the Image drop-down menu, choose File⇨Reload All Class Files. It should appear the next time you use the Image drop-down menu.

8. **Choose File⇨Save to save your changes to the `DeepThoughtsView Controller.xib` file.**

Figure 9-6: Select the image file for the Image View object.

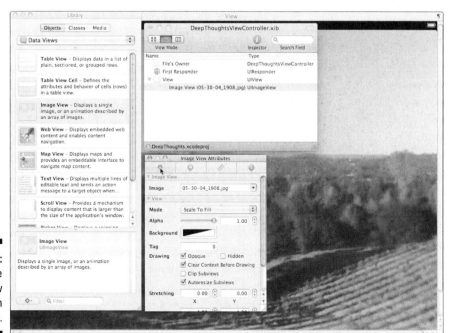

Figure 9-7: The image file now appears in the view.

This example uses a full-screen image. If you place images that are smaller, as I show in the next section when I place an Info button, Interface Builder gives you help placing the image in the view.

Adding an Info Button

The DeepThoughts app is supposed to display an animation of text flowing down the view, and the user (after the app is finished) will be able to change the text and the speed of the animation either by tapping an Info button (which is similar to the iPhone version of this app), or by tapping the view itself. I show you how to connect the Info button to your code in Chapter 11 so it can show a modal dialog for changing the text and setting the speed, but you need to first add the Info button to the user interface, as I show here.

To add a user interface button and set it to be an Info button, follow these steps:

1. **Make your way over to the Groups & Files list and double-click `DeepThoughtsViewController.xib` in the Resources-iPad folder to open the file in Interface Builder (if it isn't already open).**

   Interface Builder should appear with the `DeepThoughtsView Controller.xib` window, the Library window, the Inspector window, and the View window. (Refer to Figure 9-7.) If you followed the steps of the previous section, the Library window should already be open; if it isn't already open, choose Tools⇨Library to show it.

2. **Click the Classes tab at the top of the Library window and then select `UIResponder` from the drop-down menu below the Classes tab.**

   Selecting Classes and then `UIResponder` narrows your search through the Library window so that you can find the class you need quickly. To place the Info button in the view, you need the `UIButton` class, as shown in Figure 9-8.

3. **Drag the `UIButton` class object from the Library onto the View window.**

   Again, if the View window is obscured by other windows, just drag the `UIButton` class object directly on top of the View icon in the `DeepThoughtsViewController.xib` window as I do in Figure 9-8, so that it appears underneath the image you added in the previous section (which is also part of view).

   After all this dragging, the `UIButton` class object appears under View in the `DeepThoughtsViewController.xib` window as a Rounded Rect Button, as shown in Figure 9-9, which is its default setting.

Figure 9-8:
Add the UIButton class object to the view.

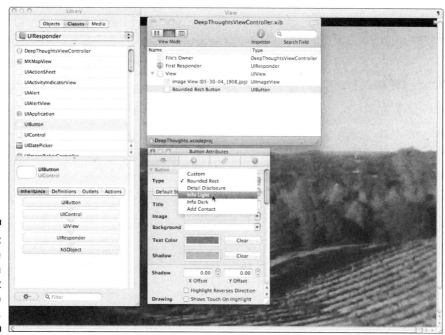

Figure 9-9:
Change the UIButton class object to an Info Light button.

4. **Select the Rounded Rect Button item in the `DeepThoughtsView Controller.xib` window and then click the Attributes tab of the Inspector window (or choose Tools⇨Attributes Inspector) if it isn't already selected.**

   The Attribute Inspector shows Button Attributes (refer to Figure 9-9).

5. **In the Attribute Inspector, choose Info Light from the Type drop-down menu. (Refer to Figure 9-9.)**

   The Rounded Rect Button item transforms itself into the Light Info Button item in the `DeepThoughtsViewController.xib` window.

6. **Drag the Light Info Button to its position in the View window.**

   Notice the lines displayed by Interface Builder. They're there to make it easy to place the interface element. Interface Builder also displays lines at the borders to help you stay within Apple's User Interface Guidelines. (The lines are actually blue, but that's kind of hard to see in a black and white illustration.)

7. **Choose File⇨Save to save your changes to the `DeepThoughtsView Controller.xib` file.**

   You can also close Interface Builder and save changes to the file by choosing Interface Builder⇨Quit Interface Builder and then clicking Save while closing it.

I placed the Info button in the upper-left corner of the app's view so that when the iPad is rotated (either left or right), and the display orientation switches from portrait to landscape (or vice-versa), the Info button would still be in the upper-left corner.

It's extremely important with iPad apps to design your app's view to take into consideration both portrait and landscape orientations — that's one of the features of the iPad that truly improves the user experience with the content.

When placing the button, you get to see what the Light Info button looks like in its Default State Configuration. Click the pop-up menu under the Type pop-up menu in the Attributes Inspector window to choose other configurations, such as Highlighted State Configuration or Selected State Configuration, to see what the button looks like when highlighted or selected. You can also change the text color, shadow, background, and other attributes in the Attributes Inspector.

While you're in a graphical mindset — especially if you're in the middle of processing graphic images for your app or designing interface elements — take the time to create your app icon and add it to your app, as spelled out in the next section.

Adding an Application Icon

You shouldn't procrastinate about adding an application icon. A well-designed icon adds a professional touch, and it takes time to get it right. You may start out with a "placeholder" icon until you've had a chance to explore the App Store and look at other icons, but whether or not you have a finished icon, it helps you identify the app in the Simulator (in case you've installed other projects), and psychologically, it boosts your confidence that the app is real.

An application icon is simply a 57 x 57-pixel .png graphics file. Add the file in the same way you added the image in the "Adding an Image to the View" section, earlier in this chapter. Follow these steps:

1. **In Xcode, drag the graphics file into the Resources-iPad folder in the Project window's Groups & Files list. (Refer to Figure 9-3.)**

   An alternative is to click the Resources-iPad folder in Xcode, choose Project⇨Add to Project, and then navigate to the file you want to add.

   After dragging or adding the file, Xcode displays a dialog for making a copy of the file. (Refer to Figure 9-4.)

2. **Check the Copy Items into Destination Group's Folder checkbox to copy the file and then click Add to finish copying the graphics file into your project.**

   You don't need to change the default settings for Reference Type, Text Encoding, or Recursively Create Groups for Any Added Folders.

After you add the icon's graphics file, you also need to specify that this file is what you want used as the application's icon. You do that by using one of those other mysterious files you see in the Resources-iPad folder: DeepThoughts-Info.plist. The "plist" part is your clue: the file is a *property list,* which are used extensively by applications as a uniform and convenient means of organizing, storing, and accessing data such as the filename for the app's icon. Xcode lets you edit property lists directly so that you can create and change them as you need to. Here's how:

1. **In the Resources-iPad folder, click the `DeepThoughts-Info.plist` file, as shown in Figure 9-10.**

   The contents of the info.plist file are displayed in the Editor pane. You're treated to some information about the application, including an item in the Key column labeled Icon file.

2. **Double-click in the empty space in the Value column next to Icon file.**

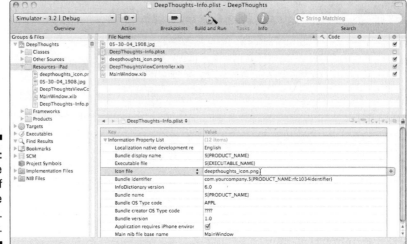

Figure 9-10:
Enter the
name of
the icon file
in the info.
plist.

3. **Type in the name of your `.png` graphics file and then build the project as you normally would.**

   You know, clicking the Build and Run button in the Project Window toolbar, choosing Build⇨Build and Go (Run) from the main menu, or pressing ⌘+Return. Building the project gives you the opportunity to save it. (You could also quit Xcode, which also gives you the opportunity to save the project.)

After building and running the project, you see your new app icon for the app rather than a blank icon in the Simulator. Now your project looks serious! Which means it's now time to add some serious code that does something interesting with the view, as I show in the next chapter.

Chapter 10

Animating the View

. . . .

In This Chapter

▶ Using your friendly Xcode Text editor

▶ Accessing documentation for quick help with coding

▶ Searching through your code and establishing markers

▶ Adding a Constants.h file

▶ Adding code to the view controller

▶ Creating animation in the view

. . . .

I wanted to keep the DeepThoughts sample app as simple as possible so that you can focus on how to build any iPad app with Xcode. As Albert Einstein said, "Everything should be as simple as it is, but not simpler." As you can see by the detail of the previous chapters, building *any* type of iPad app is not *simple* by any means.

But most iPad apps start off with a view, and the View-based Application template creates a skeleton for a fully functioning iPad app, as you find out in this chapter. You also get to flesh out the template with some code that transforms it from an app that just sits there and looks pretty to an app that actually *does* something.

DeepThoughts is supposed to display falling words — text flowing down the view in different sizes, starting with the words "Peace Love Groovy Music" — at a speed the user can change. DeepThoughts should also allow the user to enter text to substitute different words for "Peace Love Groovy Music" as well as set the speed in advance.

As you add the code to DeepThoughts, I also explain some of the features of the Xcode Text editor.

Using the Xcode Text Editor

The main tool you use to write code for an iPad application is the Xcode Text editor. Apple has gone out of its way to make the Text editor as user-friendly as possible, as evidenced by the following list of (quite convenient) features:

- ✔ **Code Sense:** Code Sense is a feature of the editor that shows arguments, placeholders, and suggested code as you type statements. Code Sense can be really useful, especially if you're like me and forget exactly what the arguments are for a function. When Code Sense is active (it is by default), Xcode uses the text you typed, as well as the context within which you typed it, to provide suggestions for completing what it thinks you're *going to* type. You can accept suggestions by pressing Tab or Return. You may also display a list of completions by pressing the Escape key. You can set options for code sensing by choosing Xcode⇨Preferences and clicking the Code Sense tab.

- ✔ **Code folding in the Focus ribbon:** With code folding, you can collapse code that you're not working on and display only the code that requires your attention. You do this by clicking in the Focus Ribbon column to the left of the code you want to hide to show a disclosure triangle. Clicking the disclosure triangle hides or shows blocks of code. (Not sure where the Focus Ribbon column is? Look right there between the gutter, which displays line numbers and breakpoints, and the editor.)

- ✔ **Switching between header and implementation windows:** On the toolbar above the Text editor, click the last icon before the lock to switch from the `.h` (header) file to the `.m` (implementation) file, and vice versa. While the header declares the class's instance variables and methods, the implementation holds the logic of your code. If you look inside the `Classes` section of the Groups & Files list of the Project window, you can see the separate `.h` and `.m` files for the `DeepThoughtsAppDelegate` and `DeepThoughtsViewController` view classes.

- ✔ **Opening a file in a separate window:** Double-click the filename to open the file in a new window. If you have a big monitor, or multiple monitors, this new window enables you to look at more than one file at a time. You can, for example, look at the method of one class *and* the method it invokes in the same class or even a different class.

Accessing Documentation

Like many developers, you may find yourself wanting to dig deeper when it comes to a particular bit of code. That's when you'll really appreciate Xcode's Quick Help, header file access, Documentation window, Help menu, and Find tools. With these tools, you can quickly access the documentation for a particular class, method, or property.

To see how this works, say you have the Project window open with the code displayed in Figure 10-1. What if you want to find out more about `UIApplicationDelegate`? What, practically speaking, could you do?

Quick Help

Quick Help is an unobtrusive window that provides the documentation for a single symbol. It pops up inline, although you can use Quick Help as a symbol inspector (which stays open) by moving the window after it opens. You can also customize the display in Documentation preferences in Xcode preferences.

To get Quick Help for a symbol, double-click to select the symbol in the Text editor (in this case, `UIApplicationDelegate`; see Figure 10-1) and then choose Help➪Quick Help. Alternatively, ⌘-click (right-click) and choose Quick Help from the contextual menu that appears.

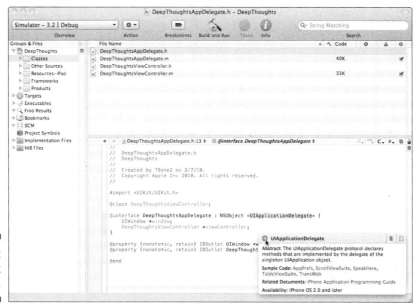

Figure 10-1:
Get Quick
Help.

The header file for a symbol

Headers are a big deal in code because they're the place where you find the class declaration, which includes all of its instance variables and method declarations. To display the header file for a symbol, press ⌘ while double-clicking the symbol in the Text editor. For example, in Figure 10-2, I pressed ⌘ and then double-clicked `UIApplicationDelegate`. This trick works for the classes you create as well.

To return to the previous view in the Text editor, click the Go Back button (refer to Figure 10-2).

Go Back button

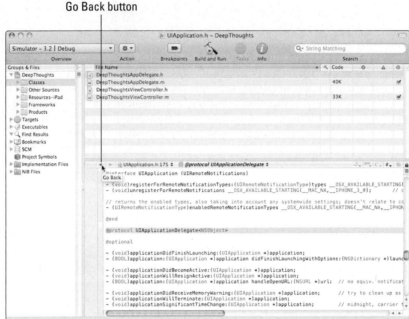

Figure 10-2:
The header
file for UI
Application
Delegate.

Documentation window

The Documentation window lets you browse and search items that are part of the Apple Developer Connection Reference Library (a collection of developer documentation and technical notes) as well as any third-party documentation you have installed.

You access the documentation by pressing ⌘+Option while double-clicking a symbol. Among other pieces of valuable information, you get access to the Application Programming Interface (API) reference that provides information about the symbol. This access enables you to get the documentation about a method to find out more about it or the methods and properties in a framework class. In Figure 10-3, I pressed ⌘+Option while double-clicking `UIApplicationDelegate`.

Using the Documentation window, you can browse and search the developer documentation — the API references, guides, and article collections about particular tools or technologies — installed on your computer. It's the go-to place for getting documentation about a method or more info about the methods and properties in a framework class.

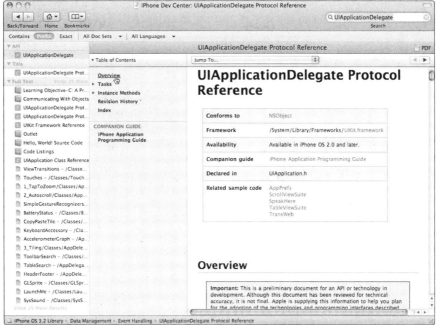

Figure 10-3:
The
Document-
ation
window.

Help menu

The Help menu's search field also lets you search Xcode documentation as well as open the Documentation window and Quick Help.

You can also ⌘-click (right-click) a symbol to display a contextual pop-up menu that gives you similar options to what you see in the Help menu, including Quick Help (and other related functions).

Find

Xcode can also help you find things in your own project. You'll find that, as your classes get bigger, sometimes you'll want to find a single symbol or all occurrences of a symbol in a file or class. You can easily do that by choosing Edit⇨Find⇨Find or pressing ⌘+F, which opens a Find toolbar to help you search the file in the editor window.

For example, in Figure 10-4, I first press ⌘+F and then type **viewController** in the Find toolbar. Xcode finds all the instances of `viewController` in that file and highlights them in the Text editor.

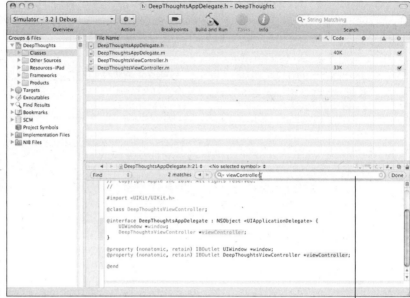

Figure 10-4:
Find "view-
Controller"
in the file
open in the
Text editor.

Find toolbar

You can also use Find to go through your whole project by choosing
Edit⇨Find⇨Find in Project, or by pressing ⌘+Shift+F, which opens the
Project Find window shown in Figure 10-5. You can type something like **view
Controller** in the Find field, and then choose In Project — or, as I chose in
Figure 10-5, In All Open Files — in the drop-down menu on the right side of
the field. (Project Find is a great feature for tracking down something in your
code — you're sure to use it often.)

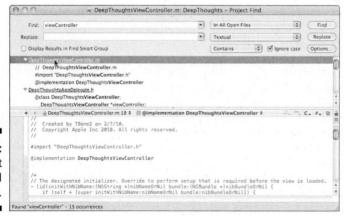

Figure 10-5:
The Project
Find
window.

If you select a line in the top pane of the Project Find window, as you can see in Figure 10-5, the file in which that instance occurs is opened in the bottom pane and the reference highlighted.

Your searches are saved in your project. Click the triangle next to Find Results in the Groups & Files list to reveal your searches, as shown in Figure 10-6 (my search for "viewController"). Select a search to see the search results.

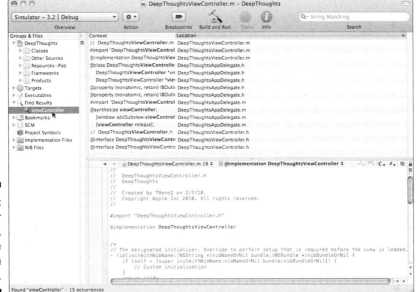

Figure 10-6: Revisit your searches, which are saved in your project.

Now that you have some idea of how to use the Xcode Text editor, it's time to write some code.

Figuring Out Where Your Code Goes

One of the biggest challenges facing a developer working with an unfamiliar framework and template is figuring out where in the *control flow* — the sequence in which messages are sent during execution — to put the code to get something done.

The delegate object

Okay, here's how the template set up the DeepThoughts app: UIApplication loads the parts of the MainWindow.xib to create DeepThoughtsAppDelegate and the window, and sends DeepThoughtsAppDelegate the application: didFinishLaunchingWithOptions: message. The application:did FinishLaunchingWithOptions: method in DeepThoughtsAppDelegate initializes the view (viewController).

The application:didFinishLaunchingWithOptions: message is sent at the very beginning, before the user can even see anything on the screen. Here's where you'd insert your code to initialize your application — where you'd load data, for example, or restore the state of the application to where it was the last time the user exited. (For DeepThoughts, you don't need to change anything here; it's all supplied by the template.)

The view controller object

DeepThoughtsViewController is the controller responsible for *managing* the view. Select DeepThoughtsViewController.m to see its code in the Text editor. Then click the Methods list pop-up menu in the Xcode Text Editor's Navigation bar (to the left of the Bookmarks menu), as shown in Figure 10-7, to see the controller object's methods.

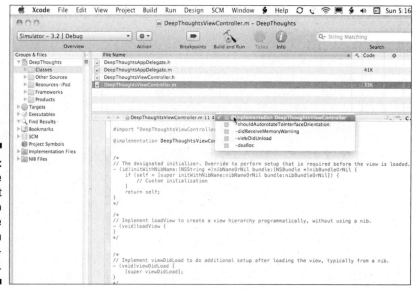

Figure 10-7: Click the Methods list pop-up to see all the methods in the controller object.

What you see in the pop-up menu is a list of active methods in the controller object.

You can also see that the code in the Text editor starts off with sections of comments that include code you can implement if you want to, simply by removing the comments. (As Objective-C programmers already know, the lines beginning with // are single-line comments that don't do anything. A line beginning with /* followed by a line ending with */ marks an entire comment section that doesn't do anything.)

The first of these (commented out) sections starts off with "The designated initializer", the second with "Implement loadView", and the third with "Implement viewDidLoad."

After those comment sections, you encounter the first active method:

```
- (BOOL)shouldAutorotateToInterfaceOrientation:
          (UIInterfaceOrientation)interfaceOrientation {
    return YES;
}
```

This method (which appears as shouldAutorotateToInterfaceOrien tation: in the Methods list pop-up, as shown in Figure 10-7) starts your app with the default portrait orientation, unless you override it. The comment above this code says "Override to allow orientations other than the default portrait orientation."

For DeepThoughts, you don't have to do anything with this code because you *want* the app to start off in portrait orientation, but for other apps you may create, you can override the code by simply adding comment markers to *comment it out*"(make the code inactive). To add comment markers, insert /* before the beginning of the statement (right before – (BOOL)), and insert */ on a line after the last bracket (}).

Marking code sections in the view controller

Before adding your code to DeepThoughtsViewController.m, it helps to know what each section of the template-provided code does and to mark off each section so that you can navigate quickly to the sections you're interested in. You can do so by marking each of the code territories.

The # pragma mark statement marks each territory, and the marks themselves appear in the Methods list pop-up menu. You use the # pragma mark statement with a label (such as View life cycle or Orientation) to add the label in bold to the Methods list so that you can identify and keep separate the methods logically in the list.

For example, in Figure 10-8, I add two # pragma mark statements above the commented sections containing the initialization and load-view code:

```
#pragma mark -
#pragma mark View life cycle
```

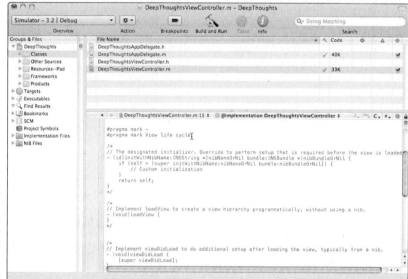

Figure 10-8:
Add markers for the first major section of code.

The first mark (with a space and a dash) places a one-pixel horizontal line with space around it in the Methods list, to separate list items — you don't have to include these, but they make the list easier to navigate. The second mark places View life cycle in the Methods lists.

In Figure 10-9, I add two # pragma mark statements above the should AutorotateToInterfaceOrientation: method to mark the section as Orientation, and then I put two more # pragma mark statements above the didReceiveMemoryWarning method to mark that section as Memory Management.

You can now click the Methods list pop-up menu, as shown in Figure 10-10, to see these markers and to navigate to each section quickly. This trick is useful for finding code sections, organizing your code, and adding new code in the proper sections.

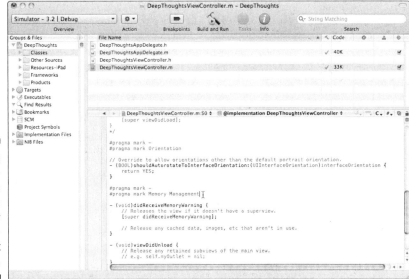

Figure 10-9:
Add markers for the Orientation and Memory Management sections.

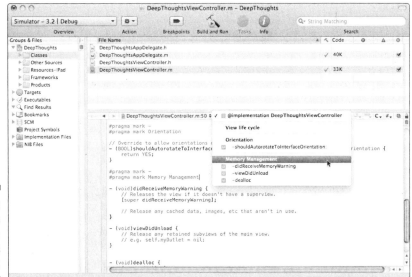

Figure 10-10:
The markers appear in the Methods list.

Preparing for User Settings

Before diving into the code that animates the view in DeepThoughts, keep in mind one of the important tenets of object-oriented programming. Yes, I'm talking about *encapsulation,* the idea that you should keep the details of how an object works hidden from the other objects that use it.

In the case of DeepThoughts, the actual text that is shown in animation as well as the actual speed of the animation are details that should not be hard-coded into your view controller. In Chapter 11, I show you how to enable the user to change the text and the speed setting, so you want to keep these details generic in the code you add to the view controller.

You also need to add a method to the view controller that connects to the Light Info button added to the user interface in Chapter 9. This button will enable the user to change the text and speed settings. For now, this method will be a placeholder until you fill it out with code in Chapter 11.

Editing the view controller header

With DeepThoughts, the idea is to enable the user to enter his or her own words for the falling words animation, as well as change the speed of the animation. The Light Info button, added in Chapter 9, is supposed to react to a Touch Up Inside event — which occurs when the button is touched and then released, symbolizing a click. When that happens, it invokes a method in the view controller to display a *Modal view*, which is a view presented like a dialog where the user has to interact with the view— enter new words or change the speed setting, for example — before the workflow can continue. (For more on Modal views, see Chapter 11.)

For now, you need to declare an action method by using the `IBAction` quali-fier in `DeepThoughtsViewController.h` and add a placeholder method corresponding to it in `DeepThoughtsViewController.m`. You need to use the `IBAction` type qualifier, which is used by Interface Builder to synchro-nize actions added programmatically with its internal list of action methods defined for a project. You also need to add the code needed to display the falling words at a certain speed.

First open `DeepThoughtsViewController.h` (the header file) and insert the code in bold in Listing 10-1.

Listing 10-1:   DeepThoughtsViewController.h

```
@interface DeepThoughtsViewController : UIViewController
            {

    UIImage      *fallingImage;
    NSString     *fallingWords;
    UIImageView  *imageView;
    double        speed;
}
- (IBAction)settings;
```

```
@property (readwrite)   double speed;
@property (nonatomic, retain) UIImageView *imageView;

@end
```

This code establishes the falling image itself (fallingImage), which will contain the text string in fallingWords and will flow down the display according to the speed.

Following that code is the action method declaration using the IBAction qualifier. In Chapter 11, you use Interface Builder to specify the fact that, when the user taps the Light Info button, the target is the DeepThoughtsView Controller object and the method to invoke is settings. This is an example of the Target-Action pattern described in Chapter 7.

The @property declarations declare that there are accessor methods for the compiler to create, and the corresponding @synthesize statements you add in the next section tell the compiler to actually create them for you. I explain accessor methods in Chapter 11.

You're done with the DeepThoughtsViewController.h file for this chapter, but before you edit the code in DeepThoughtsViewController.m, you need to add the keys for your settings in a Constants.h file.

Adding a Constants.h file

To save and read settings in your app, you can use a built-in, easy-to-use class that lets you read and set user preference settings from your app — NSUserDefaults. The class is also used by the Settings app that comes with your iPad (which Apple has graciously consented to let us peons use).

You use NSUserDefaults to read and store preference data to a default database, using a key value — just as you would access keyed data from an NSDictionary. I explain how this works in Chapter 11, but for now, the particular keys you will use are kWordsOfWisdom for the falling words replacement text, kSpeed for the animation speed, and kMaxSpeed for the maximum speed possible.

To use keys like kWordsOfWisdom, kSpeed, or kMaxSpeed, you need to first define them in a Constants.h file. To implement the Constants.h file in your project, do the following:

1. **Select the project name (DeepThoughts) in the Groups & Files list and then choose File⇨New File from the Xcode main menu.**

2. **In the New File dialog that appears, choose Other from the listing on the left (under the Mac OS X heading) and then choose Empty File in the main pane, as shown in Figure 10-11.**

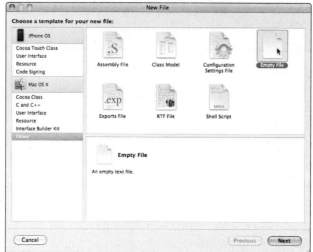

Figure 10-11:
Create an
empty file.

3. **In the new dialog that appears, name the file `Constants.h` (as shown in Figure 10-12) and then click Finish.**

Don't make any other changes — just the name.

The new empty `Constants.h` file is saved in your project, as shown in Figure 10-13.

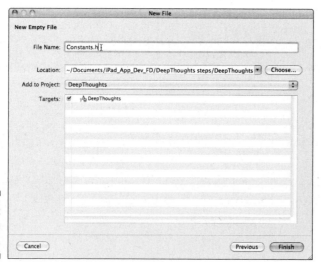

Figure 10-12:
Name the
new file.

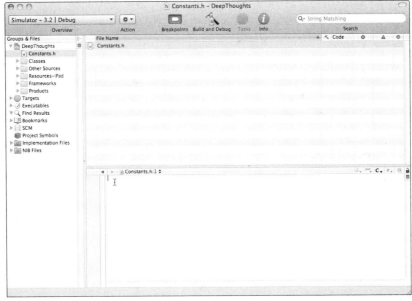

Figure 10-13:
The empty
Constants.h
file.

With a new home for your constants all set up and waiting, all you have to do is add the constants you need, as shown in Figure 10-14:

```
#define kWordsOfWisdom    @"wordsOfWisdomPreference"
#define kSpeed                      @"speedPreference"
#define kMaxSpeed                              20.0
```

Having a `Constants.h` file in hand is great, but you have to let `DeepThoughtsViewController.m` know that you plan to use it, as I show in the next section.

It may seem like starting at the end and working backwards, but it makes sense to show the code in DeepThoughts that uses these settings first, and then show in Chapter 11 how you can enable the user to change and save these settings.

To put the settings to use in the app's view, you have to link it up with the view's controller — in this case, `DeepThoughtsViewController`. The best place to do that is `viewDidLoad`, which is invoked right after the view has been loaded from the nib file. `viewDidLoad` is found in the `DeepThoughtsViewController.m` file, so that's where you'd go to insert your code to use the settings to control the animated view. The next section shows you how that's done.

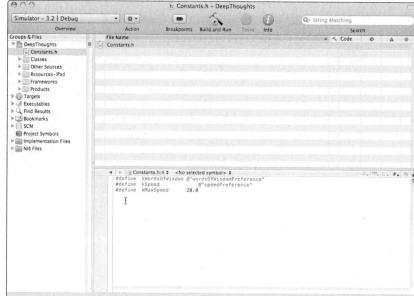

Figure 10-14:
Define the
keys in the
Constants.h
file.

Controlling the View

Select the `DeepThoughtsViewController.m` file so that it appears in
the Text editor, and insert the code in bold in Listing 10-2. (The code that's
not in bold is supplied by the View-based Application template, except
the `#pragma mark` markers, which you added earlier in this chapter, in
"Marking code sections in the view controller.")

Listing 10-2: DeepThoughtsViewController.m

```
#import "DeepThoughtsViewController.h"
#import "Constants.h"

@implementation DeepThoughtsViewController
@synthesize speed, imageView;

#pragma mark -
#pragma mark View life cycle
/*
// The designated initializer. Override to perform setup
        that is required before the view is loaded.
- (id)initWithNibName:(NSString *)nibNameOrNil
        bundle:(NSBundle *)nibBundleOrNil {
```

```
        if (self = [super initWithNibName:nibNameOrNil
               bundle:nibBundleOrNil]) {
           // Custom initialization
        }
        return self;
}
*/
/*
// Implement loadView to create a view hierarchy
            programmatically, without using a nib.
- (void)loadView {
}
*/
/*
// Implement viewDidLoad to do additional setup after
            loading the view, typically from a nib.
- (void)viewDidLoad {
    [super viewDidLoad];
}
*/
- (void)viewDidLoad {

  [super viewDidLoad];
  [NSTimer scheduledTimerWithTimeInterval:.5 target:self
           selector:@selector(onTimer) userInfo:nil
           repeats:YES];
  if (![[NSUserDefaults standardUserDefaults]
           objectForKey:kWordsOfWisdom]) {
    [[NSUserDefaults standardUserDefaults]
           setObject:@"Peace Love Groovy Music"
           forKey:kWordsOfWisdom];
    fallingWords = @"Peace Love Groovy Music";
  }
  else {
    fallingWords = [[NSUserDefaults standardUserDefaults]
           stringForKey:kWordsOfWisdom];
  }
  if (![[NSUserDefaults standardUserDefaults]
           objectForKey:kSpeed] ){
    [[NSUserDefaults standardUserDefaults]setDouble:10.0
           forKey:kSpeed];
    speed = kMaxSpeed-10.0;}
  else {
    speed = kMaxSpeed-[[NSUserDefaults
           standardUserDefaults] doubleForKey:kSpeed] ;
  }
}

#pragma mark -
#pragma mark Animation
```

(continued)

Listing 10-2 *(continued)*

```
- (void)onTimer{

  UILabel *fallingImageView = [[UILabel alloc]
          initWithFrame:CGRectMake(0, 0, 100, 30)];
  fallingImageView.text = fallingWords;
  fallingImageView.textColor = [UIColor  purpleColor];
  fallingImageView.font = [UIFont systemFontOfSize:30];
  fallingImageView.backgroundColor = [UIColor
          clearColor];

  fallingImageView.adjustsFontSizeToFitWidth = YES;

  int startX = round(random() % 400);
  int endX =  round(random() % 400);
  //speed of falling
  double randomSpeed = (1/round(random() % 100) +1)
          *speed;
  // image size;
  double scaleH = (1/round(random() % 100) +1) *60;
  double scaleW = (1/round(random() % 100) +1) *200;

  [self.view addSubview:fallingImageView];

  fallingImageView.frame = CGRectMake(startX, -100,
          scaleW, scaleH);

  fallingImageView.alpha = .75;

  [UIView beginAnimations:nil context:fallingImageView];
  [UIView setAnimationDuration:randomSpeed];
  [UIView setAnimationDelegate:self];
[UIView setAnimationDidStopSelector:@selector(animationDon
      e:finished:context:)];

  fallingImageView.frame = CGRectMake(endX, self.view.
          frame.size.height, scaleW, scaleH);


  [UIView commitAnimations];
}

-(void)animationDone:(NSString *)animationID
          finished:(NSNumber *)finished context:(id)
          context {
  UIImageView *fallingImageView = context;
  [fallingImageView removeFromSuperview];
  [fallingImageView release];
}
```

```
#pragma mark -
#pragma mark Controls

- (IBAction)settings {

}

#pragma mark -
#pragma mark Orientation

// Override to allow orientations other than the default
        portrait orientation.
- (BOOL)shouldAutorotateToInterfaceOrientation:(UIInterfac
        eOrientation)interfaceOrientation {
    return YES;
}

#pragma mark -
#pragma mark Memory Management

- (void)didReceiveMemoryWarning {
        // Releases the view if it doesn't have a
        superview.
    [super didReceiveMemoryWarning];

        // Release any cached data, images, etc that
        aren't in use.
}

- (void)viewDidUnload {
        // Release any retained subviews of the main view.
        // e.g. self.myOutlet = nil;
}


- (void)dealloc {
    [super dealloc];
}

@end
```

That's a lot to swallow at once, but I explain how all this works in the rest of this chapter and in Chapter 11.

The first statement you add imports the Constants.h file:

```
#import "Constants.h"
```

You can now use the keys you set up in "Adding a Constants.h file" in this chapter with NSUserDefaults in the subsequent code to retrieve the user settings.

Although the `@property` declarations way back in Listing 10-1 tell the compiler that there are accessor methods (which I describe in more detail in Chapter 11), these methods still have to be created. Fortunately, Objective-C will create these accessor methods for you whenever you include an `@syn thesize` statement — the next bolded item in Listing 10-2:

```
@synthesize speed, imageView;
```

The `@synthesize` statement tells the compiler to create accessor methods for you — one for each `@property` declaration (`speed` and `imageView`).

At the end of the bolded code you add in Listing 10-2 is a new `#pragma mark` section titled `Controls` that includes the placeholder `settings` method for connecting the Light Info button to the view controller:

```
#pragma mark -
#pragma mark Controls

- (IBAction)settings {

}
```

This is the action method using the `IBAction` qualifier. In Chapter 11, you use Interface Builder to specify that when the user taps the Light Info button, the target is the `DeepThoughtsViewController` object, and the method to invoke is `settings`. This is an example of the Target-Action pattern described in Chapter 7.

The viewDidLoad method

Now let's look at the bolded code section you add in Listing 10-2 marked as `View life cycle` which includes the following commented-out code near the end of the section:

```
/*
// Implement viewDidLoad to do additional setup after
         loading the view, typically from a nib.
- (void)viewDidLoad {
[super viewDidLoad];
}
*/
```

The `viewDidLoad` message is sent right after the view has been loaded from the nib file (the `.xib` file you can modify in Interface Builder) — check out Chapter 8 for a complete explanation of that loading process. This is the place where you insert your code for *view initialization,* which in this case means displaying the DeepThoughts' falling words.

This would also be the place to insert your code to do anything needed before the view becomes visible. Although I don't use it in this example, you could take advantage of the commented-out `loadView` statement to create a view hierarchy programmatically, *without* using a nib file. However, that info is beyond the scope of this book. You could also include a `viewWillAppear` message, which is sent right before the view will appear. Both `viewDidLoad` and `viewWillAppear` are methods declared in the `UIViewController` class and are invoked at the appropriate times by the framework.

Although I left the commented-out code in place to show where you would insert your version of the `viewDidLoad` method (right below it), you can delete the commented-out code.

The `viewDidLoad` method you inserted (in bold in Listing 10-2) starts out by setting up a timer for the interval between each display of falling words:

```
- (void)viewDidLoad {

[super viewDidLoad];
[NSTimer scheduledTimerWithTimeInterval:.5 target:self
        selector:@selector(onTimer) userInfo:nil
        repeats:YES];
```

You use the `NSTimer` class to create timers. A timer waits until a certain time interval has elapsed and then fires, sending a specified message to a target object. I use the `scheduledTimerWithTimeInterval:target:selector:userInfo:repeats:` class method to create the timer and schedule it on the current run loop in the default mode. The interval is 0.5 seconds, the *target* is `self`, and the *selector* is the message to send to the target when the timer fires — in this case, `onTimer`. The *userInfo* is the user info for the timer (set to `nil`), and the timer is set to `repeat` — that is, it will repeatedly reschedule itself until invalidated.

Next, the code checks to see whether the `kWordsOfWisdom` setting has been moved into `NSUserDefaults`:

```
if (![[NSUserDefaults standardUserDefaults]
        objectForKey:kWordsOfWisdom]) {
   [[NSUserDefaults standardUserDefaults]
        setObject:@"Peace Love Groovy Music"
        forKey:kWordsOfWisdom];
   fallingWords = @"Peace Love Groovy Music";
}
else {
   fallingWords = [[NSUserDefaults standardUserDefaults]
        stringForKey:kWordsOfWisdom];
}
```

```
if (![[NSUserDefaults standardUserDefaults]
        objectForKey:kSpeed] ){
  [[NSUserDefaults standardUserDefaults]setDouble:10.0
        forKey:kSpeed];
  speed = kMaxSpeed-10.0;}
else {
  speed = kMaxSpeed-[[NSUserDefaults
        standardUserDefaults] doubleForKey:kSpeed] ;
}
```

The code moves the user's preferences into `NSUserDefaults` only *after* the application runs for the first time. However, if you decide to make user preference settings available in the Settings app (as shown in Chapter 16), Settings will update preferences in `NSUserDefaults` if the user makes any changes.

If the settings have not been moved into `NSUserDefaults` yet, the code uses the initial preference value (`"Peace Love Groovy Music"`) for `fallingWords`.

```
[[NSUserDefaults standardUserDefaults]setObject:@"Peace
        Love Groovy Music" forKey:kWordsOfWisdom];
  fallingWords = @"Peace Love Groovy Music";
```

If the settings *have* been moved into `NSUserDefaults`, the code reads them in and then sets `fallingWords` to whatever the user's preference is.

```
else {
    fallingWords = [[NSUserDefaults standardUserDefaults]
        stringForKey:kWordsOfWisdom];
```

The code then repeats this check with the `speed` setting.

You use `standardUserDefaults` (a `NSUserDefaults` class method) to gain access to the standard user default settings. You can store data there, as you discover in Chapter 11.

Drawing the view

Connecting the timer to the actual drawing of the display is the `onTimer` method. Take a good look at the code for this method (from the bold code in Listing 10-2), which starts with a new `#pragma` marker titled `Animation`:

```
- (void)onTimer{

  UILabel *fallingImageView = [[UILabel alloc]
        initWithFrame:CGRectMake(0, 0, 100, 30)];
  fallingImageView.text = fallingWords;
```

```
fallingImageView.textColor = [UIColor  purpleColor];
fallingImageView.font = [UIFont systemFontOfSize:30];
fallingImageView.backgroundColor = [UIColor clearColor];
fallingImageView.adjustsFontSizeToFitWidth = YES;

int startX = round(random() % 400);
int endX =  round(random() % 400);
//speed of falling
double randomSpeed = (1/round(random() % 100) +1)
        *speed;
// image size;
double scaleH = (1/round(random() % 100) +1) *60;
double scaleW = (1/round(random() % 100) +1) *200;

[self.view addSubview:fallingImageView];

fallingImageView.frame = CGRectMake(startX, -100,
        scaleW, scaleH);

fallingImageView.alpha = .75;

[UIView beginAnimations:nil context:fallingImageView];
[UIView setAnimationDuration:randomSpeed];
[UIView setAnimationDelegate:self];
    [UIView
 setAnimationDidStopSelector:@selector(
 animationDone:finished:context:)];

fallingImageView.frame = CGRectMake(endX, self.view.
        frame.size.height, scaleW, scaleH);

[UIView commitAnimations];
}

-(void)animationDone:(NSString *)animationID
        finished:(NSNumber *)finished context:(id)
        context {
 UIImageView *fallingImageView = context;
 [fallingImageView removeFromSuperview];
 [fallingImageView release];
}
```

The UILabel class implements a read-only text view. You can use this class to draw one or multiple lines of static text. In this case, the block of code uses the initWithFrame method with CGRectMake to create a rectangle, with the x-coordinate and y-coordinate of the rectangle's origin point at (0, 0) and a specified width and height (100, 30).

The code converts the fallingWords string to fallingImageView for display; sets up the text color, font, and background color; and adjusts the font size for the width. The font and textColor properties apply to the entire text string.

The next block of code uses the random function for the starting and ending points (startX and endX), for speed, and for width (scaleW) and height (scaleH) for fallingImageView. The random function uses a non-linear additive-feedback random number generator, with a default table of size 31 long integers, and returns successive pseudo-random numbers in the range from 0 to 2,147,483,647. Then, addSubview adds a view so that it's displayed above its siblings, and frame specifies the rectangle in the super-layer's coordinate space, using startX, -100, scaleW, and scaleH.

The animation block

The UIView class provides common methods you use to create all types of views. In this particular code, it's used for a block of animation. The beginAnimations:context: method starts the animation block, and the commitAnimations method ends the block. Inside the block, the code sets property values to make visual changes that comprise the animation. In this case, the code changes the rectangle's starting coordinates from startX to endX, and from -100 to self.view.frame.size.height:

```
fallingImageView.frame = CGRectMake(endX, self.view.frame.
            size.height, scaleW, scaleH);
```

The setAnimationDuration method sets the animation duration, and setAnimationDidStopSelector sets the message to send to the animation delegate when animation stops. The animation delegate is animationDone, which uses removeFromSuperview (an instance method of the UIView class) to remove fallingImageView from its superview, its window, and from the responder chain; and then uses release (an instance method of the NSAutoreleasePool class) to release fallingImageView. Remember, you own any object you create with alloc, which means you're responsible for releasing it when you're done.

Testing the View

Save your Xcode project by choosing File⇨Save. Then, to see the magic you've just wrought, click the Build and Run button. You should see the Simulator launch, run the app, and display the falling words, as shown in Figure 10-15.

The animation is quite impressive, but now is not the time to sit on your laurels. There's more work to be done — setting up the modal controller so that users can change the text and speed for the animation and then saving these new preferences, for example. All that and more are covered in Chapter 11.

Figure 10-15:
The view
in the
Simulator.

Chapter 11

Adding User Settings and Gestures

*O*ne reason why it's easy to extend and enhance your iPad app is the fact that the template sets you up to take advantage of *delegation* — you're using a behavior-rich object supplied by the framework *as is,* and you're putting the code for program-specific behavior in a separate (delegate) object. You're basically using delegation to get the framework objects to do the work for you, as I describe in Chapter 7.

Government and military leaders know all about delegation. Ronald Reagan could have been talking about extending the functionality of apps object-oriented programming when he said "Surround yourself with the best people you can find, delegate authority, and don't interfere." And General George S. Patton seemed to know all about combining delegation with encapsulation to enhance applications when he said, "Never tell people *how* to do things. Tell them *what* to do and they will surprise you with their ingenuity."

Encapsulation, you'll recall, is about keeping the details of how an object works hidden from the other objects that use it — and you practice encapsulation in the code you add to animate the view in Chapter 10. That code doesn't know (or care) where the user's preference settings for text or animation speed come from; it simply does its job well.

In object-oriented programming, you can essentially copy all the characteristics of an existing class to make a new class — the new class *inherits* the methods and data structure of the existing class. When you combine delegation, encapsulation, and inheritance, changing or enhancing objects or their functionality becomes much easier because it reduces the impact of those changes on the rest of your application.

Inheritance allows you to do a number of things that make your programs more extensible — in a subclass, you can add new methods and instance variables to what is inherited from a superclass, refine or extend the behavior of an inherited method, and change the behavior of an inherited method. With encapsulation, you're hiding *how* things are being done from *what* is being done. Combining inheritance and encapsulation gives you *polymorphism* — using objects that do the same thing in different ways. (See *Objective-C For Dummies* for background info on these programming patterns.)

With DeepThoughts, the idea is to enable the user to enter his or her own words for the falling words animation, as well as change the speed of the animation. In this chapter, you enhance the DeepThoughts app to enable the user to change these preference settings using a *Modal view* — a child window, such as a dialog in Mac OS X, that appears on top of the parent window (the Main view) and requires the user to interact with it before returning to the parent window.

For these functions to work, you need to enable the app to save data entered by a user for the next time he or she fires up the app. In Chapter 10, you added code that uses these preference settings in your app to animate the view, but now you find out how to save data entered by the user using a modal controller that displays a view — a modal dialog — on top of the animated view. You create another view controller and use the inherited methods of the `UIViewController` superclass to implement the modal dialog that the user can use to enter text and change the animation speed. Because you've encapsulated the details of how to set the falling words and speed, it's a piece of cake to add code for setting and saving user preference settings.

Setting Up User Preference Settings

Most people these days have spent enough time around computers that they know what I mean when I throw the term *preferences* around. On your desktop, for example, you can set preferences at the system level for things like security, screen savers, printing, and file sharing — just to name a few. You can also set preferences for applications. For example, you can set all sorts of preferences in Xcode — not to mention all those preferences in your browser and word-processing programs.

The latter are application-specific settings used to configure the behavior or appearance of an application. You can create and save preference settings in your app, but you can also use the supplied Settings app to display and set your app-specific preferences (the Settings app icon looks like a bunch of gears). Whatever separate settings feature you come up with has to function within the framework of the Settings app; in effect, the Settings app makes you color within the lines.

What guidelines does the iPad impose for preference settings? Here's a short summary:

- ✔ **If you have preference settings that are typically configured once and then rarely changed:** Leave the task of setting preferences to the Settings app. On an iPad, this would apply to things like enabling/disabling Wi-Fi access, setting wallpaper displays, setting up Mail accounts, and any other preference settings you would set and then leave in place for a while.

- ✔ **If you have preference settings that the user might want to change regularly:** In this situation, you should consider having users set the options themselves in your app.

The Weather app is a good example: Suppose you have this thing for Dubrovnik — where it happens to be 48° F as I'm writing this — and you'd like to add it to your list of preferred cities that you want the Weather app to keep tabs on. To load Dubrovnik into the Weather app, all you would have to do is tap the Info button, and you can add it to your list of cities. That's a lot easier than going back to the Home screen, launching Settings, adding the new city, and then launching the Weather app again.

With DeepThoughts, the idea is to change settings on the fly, whenever you feel like it, so it makes more sense to set up preferences from inside the app (because they are changed frequently). To find out how to set up your app to save preferences in a Settings bundle for the Settings app, see Chapter 16.

To save and read preference settings, you use a built-in, easy-to-use class that lets you read and set user preferences from your app — NSUserDefaults. In Chapter 10, you use NSUserDefaults to read and store preference data to a default database, using a key value — just as you would access keyed data from an NSDictionary. The difference here is that NSUserDefaults data is stored in the file system rather than in an object in memory — objects, after all, go away when the application terminates.

By the way, don't ask why the language experts put Defaults in the name rather than something to do with preference settings — fewer letters, maybe — but that's the way it is. Just don't let their naming idiosyncrasies confuse you.

Storing the data in the file system rather than in memory gives you an easy way to store application-specific information. With the help of NSUserDefaults, you can easily store the state the user was in when he or she quit the application — or store something simple like a text string — which just so happens to be precisely what you did in the code you added in Chapter 10 for DeepThoughts.

Identifying preference settings for NSUserDefaults

It's really easy to both access and update a preference — as long as you have NSUserDefaults by your side. The trick in this case is that you use the NSUserDefaults class to read and update the replacement text and speed. NSUserDefaults is implemented as a *singleton,* meaning there's only one instance of NSUserDefaults running in your application. To get access to that one instance, you invoke the class method standardUserDefaults:

```
[NSUserDefaults  standardUserDefaults]
```

standardUserDefaults returns the NSUserDefaults object. As soon as you have access to the standard user defaults, you can store data there and then get it back when you need it. To store data, you simply give it a key and tell it to save the data using that key.

The way you tell it to save something is by using the setObject:forKey: method. In case your knowledge of Objective-C is a little rusty (or not there at all), that's the way any message that has two arguments is referred to.

The first argument, setObject:, is the object you want NSUserDefaults to save. This object must be NSData, NSString, NSNumber, NSDate, NSArray, or NSDictionary. In this case, savedData is an NSString, so you're in good shape.

The second argument is forKey:. In order to get the data back, and in order for NSUserDefaults to know where to save it, you have to be able to identify it to NSUserDefaults. You can, after all, have a number of preferences stored in the NSUserDefaults database, and the key tells NSUserDefaults which one you're interested in.

The keys you use are kWordsOfWisdom for the falling words replacement text, kSpeed for the animation speed, and kMaxSpeed for the maximum speed possible. You added them to the Constants.h file in Chapter 10.

Reading preferences into the app

To use the preference settings for the app's view, you link it up with the view controller — in this case, DeepThoughtsViewController. As Chapter 10 explains, the best place to do that is viewDidLoad, which is invoked right after the view has been loaded from the nib file.

After using the NSTimer class to create timers, the code checks to see whether the kWordsOfWisdom and speed settings have been moved into NSUserDefaults. The code moves the user's preferences into NSUserDefaults only *after* the application runs for the first time. If the settings haven't been moved into NSUserDefaults yet, the code uses the initial preference value ("Peace Love Groovy Music") for fallingWords. If the settings *have* been moved into NSUserDefaults, the code reads them in and then sets fallingWords and speed to whatever the user's preference is. The rest of the code that animates the view can now use the preference settings.

Now that you've added the code to use the preference settings (in Chapter 10), you need to now decide how to enable the user to change these settings. One easy way for your app to offer the preference settings is in a modal dialog, which the user can use to enter the replacement text for falling Words and change the speed.

Setting Up a Modal View Controller

You've encountered Modal views before — whenever you had to click OK in a dialog box to allow a system or application workflow to continue. A *Modal view* provides self-contained functionality in the context of the current task or workflow. Think of it as a child window that requires the user to interact with it before returning to the parent.

A Modal view interrupts the workflow, but if the context shift is clear and temporary (so that the user doesn't lose sight of the main task), a modal view can be the most agreeable way to offer the ability to change settings. As a design goal, keep tasks in a M view fairly short and narrowly focused. You don't want your users to experience a Modal view as a mini application within your application. Avoid creating a modal task that involves a hierarchy of Modal views, because people can get lost and forget how to retrace their steps. And always provide an obvious and safe way to exit a Modal view — such as a Done button.

The goal with DeepThoughts is to display a Modal view over the animated view when the user taps the Light Info button (which you added to the user interface in Chapter 9). In that Modal view, the user can enter text to replace the existing text for fallingWords and drag a speed slider for speed. The user can then tap a Done button to gracefully exit the Modal view. You add these interface elements to the Modal view using — you guessed it — Interface Builder.

First, you need to add a new view controller for the Modal view, to be called SettingsViewController. That's the topic of the next section.

Adding a new view controller

The Modal view, just like the animated Main view, is accessed by a subclass of `UIViewController`.

To add the subclass, do the following:

1. **Select the Classes group (if it's not already selected) in the Xcode project window's Groups & Files list and then choose File⇨New File.**

2. **In the New File dialog that appears (as shown in Figure 11-1), select Cocoa Touch Class in the left column under iPhone OS and select UIViewController Subclass in the row of icons on the right.**

3. **Select the Targeted for iPad check box (so that you get the appropriate subclass), select the With XIB for User Interface check box as well (so that the `.xib` file is created along with the new view controller files), and then click Next.**

4. **In the next New File screen, enter the filename for the implementation file (`SettingsViewController.m`), as shown in Figure 11-2. Be sure to also select the Also Create "SettingsViewController.h" check box. Finally, click Finish.**

Figure 11-1:
Create
a new
subclass of
UIView
Controller.

Xcode creates `SettingsViewController.h` and `SettingsView Controller.m` in the Classes group. Xcode also creates `SettingsView. xib` in the Classes group. You may want to drag `SettingsView.xib` from that group into the Resources-iPad group, as I do in Figure 11-3, just to be consistent. (That's where the other nib files are located.)

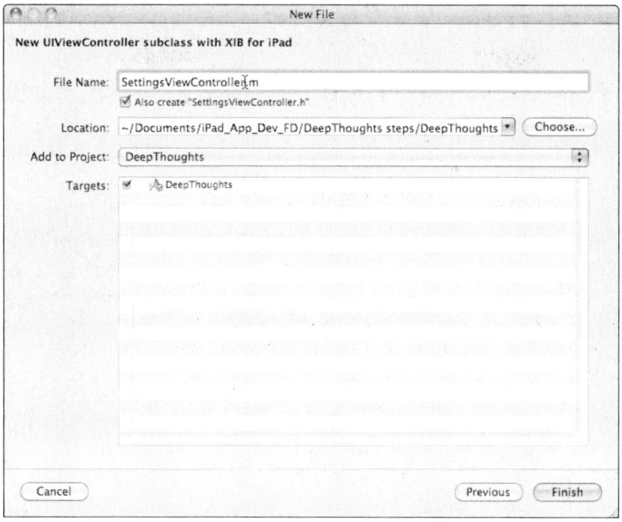

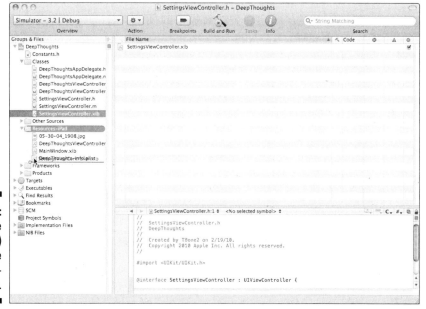

Figure 11-2:
Here you name the subclass.

Figure 11-3:
Move the nib (.xib) file to the Resources-iPad group.

You now have a bare-bones view controller for the Modal view, called `SettingsViewController`.

Next, you need to add the code to the `SettingsViewController.h` (header) and `SettingsViewController.m` (implementation) files that connect to the interface elements (speed slider and text entry field) to offer the ability to change the speed and enter replacement text.

Adding outlets to the view controller

Before using Interface Builder to create the elements for the Modal view, you should first put *outlets* in the code that will connect your methods to the Interface Builder interface objects.

The fact that a connection between an object and its outlets exists is actually stored in a nib file. When the nib file is loaded, each connection is reconstituted and reestablished, thus enabling you to send messages to the object. IBOutlet is the keyword that tags an instance-variable declaration so the Interface Builder application knows that a particular instance variable *is* an outlet — and can then enable the connection to it with Xcode.

In your code, it turns out that you need to create *two* outlets: one to point to the text entry field and one to point to the speed slider. To get this outlet business started, you need to *declare* each outlet, which you do with the help of the aforementioned IBOutlet keyword.

Add the bold lines of code in Listing 11-1 to the SettingsViewController.h file.

Listing 11-1:   SettingsViewController.h

```
#import <UIKit/UIKit.h>
@protocol SettingsViewControllerDelegate;

@interface SettingsViewController : UIViewController {
<SettingsViewControllerDelegate>  delegate;
  NSString                       *wordsOfWisdom;
  float                           sliderValue;
  IBOutlet UITextField           *theTextField;
  IBOutlet UISlider              *slider;
}

- (IBAction) done;
- (IBAction) speedChanged:  (id) sender;
@property (nonatomic, assign) id
          <SettingsViewControllerDelegate> delegate;
@property (nonatomic, assign) NSString* wordsOfWisdom;
@property (nonatomic, assign) UISlider* slider;

@end

@protocol SettingsViewControllerDelegate
- (void) settingsViewControllerDidFinish:(SettingsViewCont
          roller *)controller;
- (void) changeSpeed: (double) newSpeed;

@end
```

Two action methods (done and speedChanged) for Interface Builder elements are declared (with IBAction), along with the IBOutlet statements, which declare the outlets that will be automatically initialized with a pointer to the UITextField (theTextField) and the UISlider (slider) when the application is launched. But while this will happen automatically, it won't *automatically* happen automatically. You have to help it out a bit.

In procedural programming — you know, all that Linux Kernel stuff — variables are generally fair game for all. But in object-oriented programming, a class's instance variables are tucked away inside an object and shouldn't be accessed directly. The only way for them to be initialized is for you to create what are called *accessor methods,* which allow the specific instance variable of an object to be read and (if you want) updated. Creating accessor methods is a two-step process that begins with a @property declaration, which tells the compiler that there are accessor methods. And that's what you did in Listing 11-1; you coded corresponding @property declarations for each IBOutlet declaration.

The methods that provide access to the instance variables of an object are called *accessor methods,* and they effectively get (using a *getter method*) and set (using a *setter method*) the values for an instance variable. Although you can code those methods yourself, it can be rather tedious. This is where properties come in. The Objective-C Declared Properties feature provides a simple way to declare and implement an object's accessor methods. The compiler can synthesize accessor methods according to the way you told it to in the property declaration. Objective-C creates the getter and setter methods for you by using an @property declaration in the interface file, combined with the @synthesize declaration in the implementation file.

All that being said, at the end of the day, you need to do three things in your code to have the compiler create accessors for you:

1. **Declare an instance variable in the interface file.**

2. **Add an @property declaration of that instance variable in the same interface file (usually with the nonatomic attribute).**

   The declaration specifies the name and type of the property as well as some attributes that provide the compiler with information about how exactly you want the accessor methods to be implemented.

   For example, the declaration

   ```
   @property (nonatomic, assign) NSString* wordsOfWisdom;
   ```

   declares a property named wordsOfWisdom, which is a pointer to an NSString object. As for the two attributes — nonatomic and assign — nonatomic tells the compiler to create an accessor to return the value directly, which is another way of saying that the accessors can be interrupted while in use. (This works fine for applications like this one.)

The second value, `assign`, tells the compiler to create an accessor method that sends an `assign` message to any object that's assigned to this property.

3. **Use @synthesize in the implementation file so that Objective-C generates the accessors for you.**

   The `@property` declaration only declares that there *should be* accessors. It's the `@synthesize` statement that tells the compiler to *create* them for you. You add this statement in the next section, along with more code, to the `SettingsViewController.m` implementation file.

Using delegation

Delegation is a design pattern used extensively in the `UIKit` and `AppKit` frameworks to customize the behavior of an object without subclassing. Instead of having to bother with subclassing, one object delegates the task of implementing one of its methods to another object. You can use delegation to create a class that implements the `changeSpeed` method of the `DeepThoughtsViewController` (the *delegator*) class, for example, one that will behave in the same way as a subclass. You can use Interface Builder to connect objects to their delegates; or you can set the connection programmatically through the delegating object's `setDelegate:` method or `delegate` property.

To implement a delegated method, you put the code for your application-specific behavior in a separate (*delegate*) object. When a request is made of the delegator, the delegate's method that implements the application-specific behavior is invoked by the delegator.

The methods that a class delegates are defined in a *protocol*. You declared protocols in Listing 11-1 with the `@protocol` directive:

```
@protocol SettingsViewControllerDelegate
- (void) settingsViewControllerDidFinish:(SettingsViewCont
         roller *)controller;
- (void) changeSpeed: (double) newSpeed;

@end
```

Protocols declare methods that can be implemented by any class. They are useful for declaring methods that other delegate objects are expected to implement.

Adding methods for the interface objects

Next, you need to add the methods to the `SettingsViewController.m` (implementation) file for managing the Modal view and performing actions connected to the slider, the text field, and the Done button (all of which get added in the "Connecting the Interface Objects in Interface Builder" section, later in this chapter).

Before adding your code to this View Controller object, it helps to know what each section of the template-provided code does, and it's especially helpful if you use `# pragma mark` statements to mark off each section so you can quickly jump to the relevant section when needed. (For more on how to use `# pragma mark` statements, check out Chapter 10.) I added these statements along with the new code (in bold) in Listing 11-2.

The `# pragma mark` statement is simply a way to organize your methods in the Method list pop-up in the Xcode Text Editor's navigation bar (to the left of the Bookmarks menu). You use it with a label (such as `View life cycle`) to add the label in bold to the Method list so that you can identify and keep separate the methods logically in the list.

Add the bold statements in Listing 11-2 to the skeletal view controller code in the new `SettingsViewController.m` file.

Listing 11-2:   SettingsViewController.m

```
#import "SettingsViewController.h"
#import "DeepThoughtsViewController.h"
#import "Constants.h"

@implementation SettingsViewController

@synthesize delegate, wordsOfWisdom, slider ;

#pragma mark -
#pragma mark View life cycle

/*
 // The designated initializer.  Override if you create
            the controller programmatically and want to
            perform customization that is not appropriate
            for viewDidLoad.
- (id)initWithNibName:(NSString *)nibNameOrNil
            bundle:(NSBundle *)nibBundleOrNil {
    if ((self = [super initWithNibName:nibNameOrNil
            bundle:nibBundleOrNil])) {
        // Custom initialization
    }
    return self;
}
```

(continued)

Listing 11-2 *(continued)*

```
*/

/*
// Implement viewDidLoad to do additional setup after
        loading the view, typically from a nib.
- (void)viewDidLoad {
  [super viewDidLoad];
}
*/
- (void)viewDidLoad {
  [super viewDidLoad];
  self.view.backgroundColor = [UIColor clearColor];
  slider.value = + kMaxSpeed -
          ((DeepThoughtsViewController*) (self.
          parentViewController)).speed;
}

#pragma mark -
#pragma mark textField

-(BOOL)textFieldShouldBeginEditing:(UITextField *)
        textField {
  [textField setReturnKeyType:UIReturnKeyNext];
  return YES;
}

-(BOOL)textFieldShouldReturn:(UITextField *)textField {
  [textField resignFirstResponder];
        return YES;
}
- (void)textFieldDidEndEditing:(UITextField *)textField {
  wordsOfWisdom = textField.text;
}

#pragma mark -
#pragma mark Controls

- (IBAction) speedChanged: (id) sender {
  [delegate changeSpeed: [(UISlider *)sender value] ];
}

- (IBAction)done {
  if(! [theTextField.text isEqualToString: @"" ])
          wordsOfWisdom = theTextField.text;
          [self.delegate settingsViewControllerDidFinish:s
          elf];
}
```

```
#pragma mark -
#pragma mark Orientation

- (BOOL)shouldAutorotateToInterfaceOrientation:
            (UIInterfaceOrientation)interfaceOrientation {
    // Overriden to allow any orientation.
    return YES;
}


#pragma mark -
#pragma mark Memory management

- (void)didReceiveMemoryWarning {
    // Releases the view if it doesn't have a superview.
    [super didReceiveMemoryWarning];

    // Release any cached data, images, etc that aren't in
        use.
}

- (void)viewDidUnload {
    [super viewDidUnload];
    // Release any retained subviews of the main view.
    // e.g. self.myOutlet = nil;
}

- (void)dealloc {
    [super dealloc];
}

@end
```

Okay, let me walk you through this one. Although the @property declaration in the header file in Listing 11-1 tells the compiler that there are accessor methods, they still have to be created. Fortunately, Objective-C will create these accessor methods for you whenever you include an @synthesize statement for a property, which is what you did near the top of Listing 11-2:

```
@synthesize delegate , wordsOfWisdom, slider;
```

The @synthesize statement tells the compiler to create accessor methods for you — one for each @property declaration.

Next, you add the viewDidLoad method to set the background and speed for the slider:

```
- (void)viewDidLoad {
    [super viewDidLoad];
    self.view.backgroundColor = [UIColor clearColor];
    slider.value = + kMaxSpeed -
            ((DeepThoughtsViewController*) (self.
            parentViewController)).speed;
}
```

Following that code (in Listing 11-2), you add the text field methods to obtain the wordsOfWisdom:

```
#pragma mark -
#pragma mark textField

- (BOOL)textFieldShouldBeginEditing:(UITextField *)
            textField {
  [textField setReturnKeyType:UIReturnKeyNext];
  return YES;
}
- (BOOL)textFieldShouldReturn:(UITextField *)textField {
  [textField resignFirstResponder];
   return YES;
}
- (void)textFieldDidEndEditing:(UITextField *)textField {
  wordsOfWisdom = textField.text;
}
```

The UITextFieldDelegate protocol defines the messages sent to a text field delegate as part of the sequence of editing its text. When the user performs an action that would normally start an editing session, the text field calls the textFieldShouldBeginEditing: method first to see whether editing should actually proceed. In most circumstances, you would simply return YES from this method to allow editing to proceed.

The text field calls the textFieldShouldReturn: method whenever the user taps the Return button on the keyboard to find out whether it should process the Return. You can use this method to implement any custom behavior when the Return button is tapped, but for your purposes, you simply return YES (which is the default), although you could return NO to ignore the Return button.

After saying "yes" to this and that, the real action happens with the text FieldDidEndEditing: method, which is called after the text field resigns its first responder status to tell the delegate that editing has stopped for the specified text field, so that you now have the edited wordsOfWisdom.

Next, you provide a speedChanged method (of type IBAction) to handle a change in speed, which uses the delegate's changeSpeed method to immediately change the speed of the animation in the view as the user changes it in the Modal view:

```
#pragma mark -
#pragma mark Controls

- (IBAction) speedChanged: (id) sender {
  [delegate changeSpeed: [(UISlider *)sender value] ];
}
```

```
- (IBAction)done {
 if(! [theTextField.text isEqualToString: @"" ])
     wordsOfWisdom = theTextField.text;
     [self.delegate settingsViewControllerDidFinish:self];
 }
```

You also supply a done method that handles the possibility of a blank text field. The code assigns the text field's text to wordsOfWisdom *only* if the field is *not* theTextField.text isEqualToString: @"".

Initializing and setting the Modal view style

Fine so far, but there are still a few problems: Where is this Modal view initialized and set up? And how would DeepThoughtsViewController even know about the new speed setting and change it accordingly?

Here's the deal: You need to modify the code in DeepThoughtsView Controller.h (header) and DeepThoughtsViewController.m (implementation) files to add the method for initializing and setting up the Modal view when the user taps the Light Info button. You also need to add the code to change the speed. Add the bold lines of code in Listing 11-3 to the DeepThoughtsViewController.h file.

Listing 11-3: DeepThoughtsViewController.h

```
#import <UIKit/UIKit.h>
#import "SettingsViewController.h"

@interface DeepThoughtsViewController : UIViewController
         <SettingsViewControllerDelegate> {

   UIImage     *fallingImage;
   NSString    *fallingWords;
   UIImageView *imageView;
   double       speed;
}
- (IBAction)settings;
- (void) changeSpeed: (double) newSpeed;
- (void) settingsViewControllerDidFinish:
          (SettingsViewController *)controller;

@property (readwrite)  double speed;
@property (nonatomic, retain) UIImageView *imageView;

@end
```

You modify the declarations to include the `SettingsViewController.h` declarations, and you add the `SettingsViewControllerDelegate` protocol so that you can use the delegate's methods. You then declare the `change Speed` and `settingsViewControllerDidFinish:` methods.

Next, you add the bold lines of code in Listing 11-4 to the `DeepThoughtsView Controller.m` file in the `Controls` section (marked by `#pragma mark Controls` in Chapter 10).

Listing 11-4:   DeepThoughtsViewController.m (Controls Section)

```
#pragma mark -
#pragma mark Controls

- (IBAction)settings {
  SettingsViewController *controller =
  [[SettingsViewController alloc] initWithNibName:@"Setti
  ngsViewController" bundle:nil];

 controller.modalTransitionStyle =
    UIModalTransitionStyleFlipHorizontal;
 controller.modalPresentationStyle =
    UIModalPresentationFormSheet;
 controller.delegate = self;

 [self presentModalViewController:controller animated:YES];

 [controller release];
}

- (void) changeSpeed: (double) newSpeed {
 speed = kMaxSpeed-newSpeed;
 [[NSUserDefaults standardUserDefaults]setDouble: newSpeed
    forKey:kSpeed];
}

- (void) settingsViewControllerDidFinish:(SettingsViewCont
          roller *)controller {

 if (controller.wordsOfWisdom ) {
   fallingWords = controller.wordsOfWisdom;
   [[NSUserDefaults standardUserDefaults]
   setObject:fallingWords  forKey:kWordsOfWisdom];
   [fallingWords retain];
 }
   [self dismissModalViewControllerAnimated:YES];
}
```

The settings method (of type IBAction) initializes the Modal view. The UIViewController class offers the modalTransitionStyle property to set the transition to use when the Modal view appears (I chose UIModalTransitionStyleFlipHorizontal to do a horizontal 3D flip from right-to-left, a fairly standard transition).

You could choose other transitions, such as a *partial-curl* (UIModal TransitionStylePartialCurl), in which one corner of the current view curls up to reveal the modal view underneath. When the user leaves the Modal view, the current view uncurls to its original position. (Of course, a Modal view revealed by a partial-curl can't itself reveal *another* Modal view with a partial-curl — that would be a wipe-out, in surfer terms.)

The UIViewController class also offers the modalPresentationStyle property that specifies the appearance of the Modal view on the iPad. Options for this property let you present the Modal view so that it fills the entire iPad display, or only part of the display:

✔ UIModalPresentationFullScreen: This option uses the entire display, which is good for something that is complex — such as choosing a Genius mix from your music playlists in the iPod app.

✔ UIModalPresentationPageSheet: This option offers a fixed width of 768 points; the sheet height is the current height of the display. In portrait, the page sheet view covers the entire display; in landscape orientation, the area of the display that is visible on both sides of the page sheet view is dimmed to prevent user interaction. Some apps use this style for composing a text message or note.

✔ UIModalPresentationFormSheet: I use this option (in Listing 11-4) for DeepThoughts. The form sheet is a fixed-dimension view of 540 x 620 points centered in the display. The area of the display that is visible outside the form sheet view is dimmed to prevent user interaction. When the keyboard is visible in landscape orientation, the form sheet view moves up to just below the status bar so that you can still see it.

✔ UIModalPresentationCurrentContext: This option uses the same size as its parent view. This style is good for displaying a Modal view within a Split view pane, popover, or other view that doesn't fill the display.

After setting the transition and presentation style for the Modal view, the code uses the presentModalViewController:animated: instance method to present the animated Modal view (and attach it to the view hierarchy). At the end of the code (in Listing 11-4), you use the dismiss ModalViewControllerAnimated: method to animate the view as it's dismissed.

Saving the preference settings

The code in Listing 11-4 then implements the `changeSpeed` method to change the animation speed if the slider in the Modal view changes. After this, you add the `settingsViewControllerDidFinish:` method to save the user preference settings. Although the user can change the speed and see the results on the fly, the speed setting is saved (for later use when the app runs again) only after the user taps Done in the Modal view. (You connect the Done button in the "Adding the Done button" section, later in this chapter.)

As you'll recall from earlier in this chapter in "Identifying preference settings for NSUserDefaults," you use `standardUserDefaults` (a `NSUserDefaults` class method) to gain access to the standard user defaults; you can store data there and then get it back when you need it. To store data, you use the `setObject;forKey:` method. The first argument, `setObject:`, is the object you want `NSUserDefaults` to save (`fallingWords`); the second argument is `forKey:` (`kWordsOfWisdom`), which is how `NSUserDefaults` identifies it. For the slider value, `setDouble: controller.slider.value forKey:` sets the value of the specified default key to the double value.

The next step is to create the interface elements for the Done button, speed slider, and text field elements of the Modal view and then *connect* these interface elements — along with the Light Info button in the animated view — to the methods in your view controllers.

Don't forget to save your changes in Xcode; otherwise, Interface Builder won't be able to find the new code. Choose File⇨Save.

Connecting the Interface Objects in Interface Builder

You've created the outlets and their accessor methods in your code. The next sections are about wiring the two nib (.xib) files to your code using Interface Builder — so that when the nib files are loaded, the nib loading code will create these connections automatically.

To start, open the Modal view controller in Interface Builder: click Resources-iPad in the Groups & Files list and then double-click the `SettingsViewController.xib` file to launch Interface Builder.

You can then click the View icon in the `SettingsViewController.xib` window of Interface Builder so that you can add the user interface objects to it. If the Library window isn't already open, choose Tools➪Library.

Adding the Done button

To add the Done button, click the Classes tab at the top of the Library window, and select `UIResponder` from the drop-down menu below the Classes tab. (This narrows your search through the Library window so that you can find the class you need quickly.) You need the `UIButton` class, the same class you used for the Info button in Chapter 9.

Drag the `UIButton` class object from the Library onto the View window in the top-left corner, as shown in Figure 11-4. Horizontal and vertical guides appear to help you place the object where you want it.

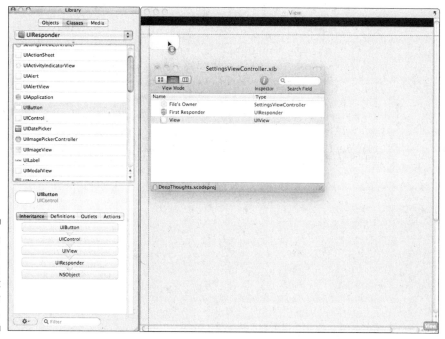

Figure 11-4:
Drag the
UIButton
class object
to the View
window.

After dragging it, the `UIButton` class object appears under View in the `SettingsViewController.xib` window as a Rounded Rect Button, which is its default setting.

Select Rounded Rect Button in the `SettingsViewController.xib` window, and click the Attributes tab of the Inspector window (or choose Tools⇨Attributes Inspector) if it is not already selected. The Attribute Inspector shows Button Attributes, as shown in Figure 11-5. Choose Custom in the Type drop-down menu in Button Attributes and then click the Text Color tile to change it to white, and click the Clear button next to Shadow to remove the shadow. Don't forget to type **Done** for the button's title. (See Figure 11-5.)

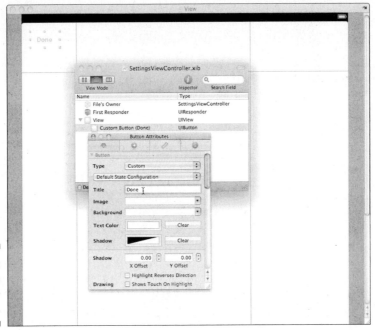

Figure 11-5: Change the button attributes.

To connect the Done button to your code, select Custom Button (Done) in the `SettingsViewController.xib` window, and click the Connections tab in the Inspector window (or choose Tools⇨Connections Inspector) and scroll down to the bottom of the Events section (above Referencing Outlets). Drag from the connection point for a Touch Up Inside event to File's Owner, as shown in Figure 11-6. Then choose `done` from the pop-up menu that appears to connect the object to your code's outlet (`done`), as shown in Figure 11-7.

That's it; the Done button is done.

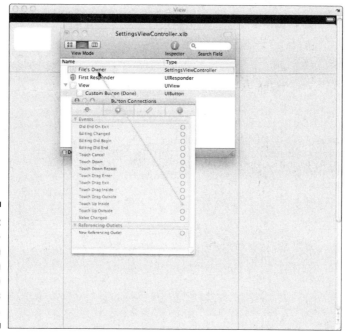

Figure 11-6:
Make a connection from the custom button to the File's Owner.

Figure 11-7:
Connect the custom button to the done method.

Adding the slider and text field

Next, select Inputs & Values from the Interface Builder Library pop-up menu to see the input objects you can use. Information about each object appears in the lower portion of the Library window. The slider, for example, is of the `UISlider` class; it displays a horizontal bar representing a range of values.

Drag the slider from the Library window over to the View window, just like you did with the `UIButton` class object. (Refer to Figure 11-4.) Once again, horizontal and vertical guides appear to help you place the slider where you want it in the View window.

You can select the horizontal slider in the View window and then drag its edges to make it longer. To set the slider's values, click the Attributes tab in the Inspector window (or choose Tools⇨Attributes Inspector) and then change the Minimum, Maximum, and Initial values, as shown in Figure 11-8.

Figure 11-8:
Set the slider's Minimum, Maximum, and Initial values.

To connect the horizontal slider to your code, first click the triangle next to the View icon in the `SettingsViewController.xib` window to reveal its contents (which now includes Horizontal Slider) and then select Horizontal Slider. Then click the Connections tab in the Inspector window (or choose Tools⇨Connections Inspector) and scroll down to the Referencing Outlets section. Drag from the connection point for a new referencing outlet to File's Owner, as shown in Figure 11-9. Then choose `slider` from the pop-up menu that appears to connect the object to your code's outlet (`slider`), as shown in Figure 11-10.

Because you want to capture the speed setting when the user slides the slider and then immediately use that new setting with the view controller, scroll down to the bottom of the Events section (above Referencing Outlets) in the Connections Inspector, and drag from the connection point for a Value Changed event to File's Owner, as shown in Figure 11-11. Then choose speedChanged from the pop-up menu that appears to connect the object to your code's outlet (speedChanged), as shown in Figure 11-12.

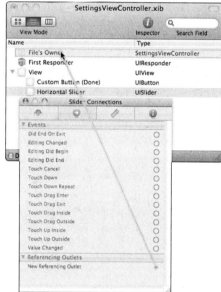

Figure 11-9:
Make a connection from the Horizontal Slider to the File's Owner.

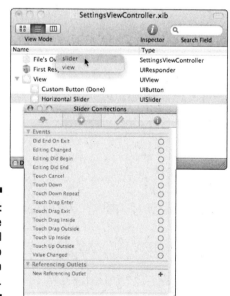

Figure 11-10:
Connect the Horizontal Slider to slider in your code.

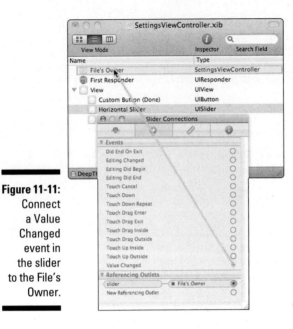

Figure 11-11:
Connect
a Value
Changed
event in
the slider
to the File's
Owner.

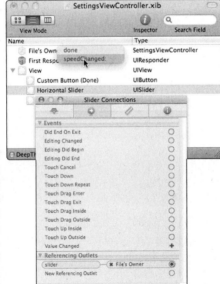

Figure 11-12:
Connect
the Value
Changed
event to
the speed-
Changed
method.

Now, perform a similar procedure with the Text Field object in the Interface Builder Library window (if the Library window isn't already open, choose Tools➪Library). Drag the Text Field for text entry from the Library window to the View window. Horizontal and vertical guides appear to help you place it where you want it.

You can then select your new text field in the View window and then
drag its edges to make it longer. To change its attributes, first select
Bezel Style Text Field (which is now underneath Horizontal Slider) in the
`SettingsViewController.xib` window. Then click the Attributes tab in
the Inspector window (or choose Tools⇨Attributes Inspector), as shown in
Figure 11-13.

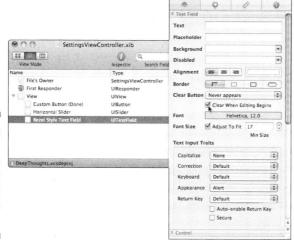

Figure 11-13:
After drag-
ging the
Text Field
you can
change its
attributes.

To connect the text field's Delegate connector to `SettingsViewController`,
click the Connections tab in the Inspector window (or choose Tools⇨
Connections Inspector) and drag from the connection point for `delegate`
(at the top of the Text Field Connections window) to File's Owner, as shown
in Figure 11-14.

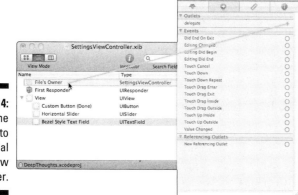

Figure 11-14:
Connect the
Text Field to
the Modal
view
controller.

Finally, with Bezel Style Text Field still selected, scroll down the Text Field Connections window to the Referencing Outlets section. Drag from the connection point for a new referencing outlet to File's Owner, as shown in Figure 11-15. Then choose `theTextField` from the pop-up menu that appears to connect the object to your code's outlet (`theTextField`), as shown in Figure 11-16.

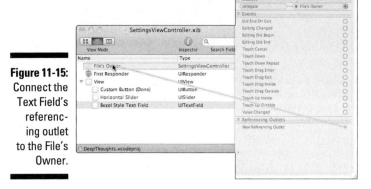

Figure 11-15:
Connect the Text Field's referencing outlet to the File's Owner.

Figure 11-16:
Connect the Text Field outlet to theTextField in your code.

Don't forget to save your changes in Interface Builder — you can choose File➪Save if you are continuing to edit the same file, or you can click Save in the warning dialog if you close the file or quit Interface Builder.

For the next step, you need to close the `SettingsViewController.xib` file and double-click the `DeepThoughtsViewController.xib` file to launch Interface Builder again.

Connecting the Info button

You have one more chore: to connect the Light Info button, which you added to the user interface in Chapter 9, to the method in `DeepThoughtsViewController` that initializes the Modal view.

To connect the Light Info button to this method, double-click the `DeepThoughtsViewController.xib` file to launch Interface Builder (if you haven't done this already). Next, click the triangle next to View in the `DeepThoughtsViewController.xib` window to open it, select Light Info Button underneath View, click the Connections tab in the Inspector window (or choose Tools⇨Connections Inspector), and drag the outlet for a Touch Inside Up event to the File's Owner to make a connection, as shown in Figure 11-17. The `settings` method pops up so that you can select it for the Info button, as shown in Figure 11-18.

Figure 11-17: Connect the Touch Up Inside event for the Light Info button.

Figure 11-18:
Connect
the Touch
Up Inside
event to
the settings
method.

Understanding event processing

What actually happens when the Info button reacts to a Touch Up Inside event? The event is processed. Here's a rundown of how such events drive a process inside the app:

1. **You have an event — the user taps a button, for example.**

   The touch of a finger (or lifting it from the screen) adds a touch event to the application's event queue, where it's *encapsulated* in — placed into, in other words — a UIEvent object. There's a UITouch object for each finger touching the screen, so you can track individual touches. As the user manipulates the screen with his or her fingers, the system reports the changes for each finger in the corresponding UITouch object.

2. **The run loop monitor dispatches the event.**

   When there's something to process, the event-handling code of the UIApplication processes touch events by dispatching them to the appropriate *responder* object — the object that has signed up to take responsibility for doing something when an event happens (when the user touches the screen, for example). Responder objects can include instances of UIApplication, UIWindow, UIView, and its subclasses (all which inherit from UIResponder).

3. **A responder object decides how to handle the event.**

For example, a touch event occurring with a button in a view is delivered to the button object. The button object handles the event by sending an action message to another object — in this case, the `UIViewController` object. Setting it up this way enables you to use standard button objects without having to muck about in their innards — just tell the button what method you want invoked in your view controller, and you're basically set.

Processing the message may result in changes to a view, or a new view altogether, or some other kind of change in the user interface. When this happens, the view and graphics infrastructure takes over and processes the required drawing events.

4. **You're sent back to the event loop.**

After an event is handled or discarded, control passes back to the run loop. The run loop then processes the next event or puts the thread to sleep if there's nothing more for it to do.

Testing the new Modal view

So it looks like you now have all the pieces in place for the DeepThoughts application. Save your Xcode project by choosing File⇨Save. Then, to test the Modal view, click the Build and Run button. You should see the Simulator launch, run the app, and display the falling words over the image.

Now click the Info button in the upper-left corner. The Modal view should appear, as shown in Figure 11-19. Click inside the text box to make the keyboard appear, and type new words for the falling words. Drag the slider to change the animation speed, and the falling words should move slower or faster in the view behind the Modal view. Cool!

In the Simulator, choose Hardware⇨Rotate Right to see what DeepThoughts looks like in landscape orientation. After clicking inside the text box to edit the falling words, you should notice that in landscape orientation, the keyboard is much larger, and the Modal view automatically slides up to accommodate it — thanks to the Form Sheet Modal view style you chose in the "Initializing and setting the Modal view style" section, earlier in this chapter.

As you experiment with code and build and run your project, you need to delete the application and its data from the Simulator if you change anything of significance — before building and running again. The consequences of not doing so will become obvious when things don't work like you would expect them to. See Chapter 5 for details on deleting specific apps from the Simulator. For a fast reset of all apps and all data in the simulator, choose iPhone Simulator⇨Reset Contents and Settings, and then click Reset. Note that this removes *all* apps and data that you have installed in the simulator.

Figure 11-19:
Run Deep
Thoughts
and click
the Info
button to
see the
Modal view.

You can now enter a new phrase and speed up or slow down the animation. Your preferences are saved when you leave the app, so that they're used when you launch the app again later.

Ah, but there's a bit more you can do with this little app, as you see in the next section.

Adding Tap and Swipe Recognizers

To put a finer point on touch events, let's examine gestures. No sample iPad application would be complete without some gesture control, because with an iPad you have a large display that begs to be tapped, pinched, and even swiped.

To offer a finer grain of control over what happens when fingers touch the display, you can use a delegate of the UIGestureRecognizer class that recognize gestures and customizes their actions. This class defines a set of common behaviors that can be configured for all gesture recognizers, and it can also communicate with its delegate (an object that adopts the UIGestureRecognizerDelegate protocol) for even finer control. With a

Gesture-Recognizer object, you can separate the logic for recognizing a gesture from the action that should occur. When one of these objects recognizes a common gesture or, in some cases, a change in the gesture, it sends an action message to each designated target object.

To improve DeepThoughts, you can add a Tap recognizer to the view that brings up the Modal view for changing settings (and thereby dispense with the Info button if you want). You can also create Swipe Gesture recognizers to recognize right and left swipes. You add this code to the view controller for the animated view — which means the files to be modified are `DeepThoughtsViewController.h` and `DeepThoughtsViewController.m`.

Add the bold lines of code in Listing 11-5 to the `DeepThoughtsView Controller.h` file. First, add `UIGestureRecognizer` within the angle brackets of the `@interface` statement (be sure to include the comma before it) to declare the `UIGestureRecognizer` delegate, and then add a declaration for a new `addGestures` method, which you'll set up later in DeepThoughtsController.m to recognize gestures.

Listing 11-5:   DeepThoughtsViewController.h

```
#import <UIKit/UIKit.h>
#import "SettingsViewController.h"

@interface DeepThoughtsViewController : UIViewController
          <SettingsViewControllerDelegate ,
          UIGestureRecognizerDelegate>  {

  UIImage      *fallingImage;
  NSString     *fallingWords;
  UIImageView *imageView;
  double        speed;
}
- (IBAction)settings;
- (void) changeSpeed: (double) newSpeed;
- (void) settingsViewControllerDidFinish:
          (SettingsViewController *)controller;
- (void) addGestures;

@property (readwrite)  double speed;
@property (nonatomic, retain) UIImageView *imageView;

@end
```

Next, add the bold line of code in Listing 11-6 to the `DeepThoughtsView Controller.m` file at the end of the `viewDidLoad` method, which is at the end of the `View life cycle` section (the section we marked using `#pragma mark View life cycle` in Chapter 10).

Listing 11-6:   DeepThoughtsViewController.m (View life cycle Section)

(The `View life cycle` *section marked by* `#pragma mark View life cycle` *appears here. See Chapter 10 for the complete code.)*

```
- (void)viewDidLoad {

    [super viewDidLoad];
    [NSTimer scheduledTimerWithTimeInterval:.5 target:self
            selector:@selector(onTimer) userInfo:nil
            repeats:YES];
    if (![[NSUserDefaults standardUserDefaults]
            objectForKey:kWordsOfWisdom]) {
        [[NSUserDefaults standardUserDefaults]
            setObject:@"Peace Love Groovy Music"
            forKey:kWordsOfWisdom];
        fallingWords = @"Peace Love Groovy Music";
    }
    else {
        fallingWords = [[NSUserDefaults standardUserDefaults]
            stringForKey:kWordsOfWisdom];
    }
    if (![[NSUserDefaults standardUserDefaults]
            objectForKey:kSpeed] ){
        [[NSUserDefaults standardUserDefaults]setDouble:10.0
            forKey:kSpeed];
        speed = kMaxSpeed-10.0;}
    else {
        speed = kMaxSpeed-[[NSUserDefaults
            standardUserDefaults] doubleForKey:kSpeed] ;
    }

    [self addGestures];
}
```

(The rest of the code would appear here. See Chapter 10 for the complete code.)

You have now added the `addGestures` method to the view, so it's time to specify what that method actually does.

Add the bold lines of code in Listing 11-7 to the `DeepThoughtsView Controller.m` file — between the end of the `Controls` section (marked by `#pragma mark Controls` in Chapter 10) and the beginning of the Orientation section (marked by `#pragma mark Orientation` in Chapter 10).

Listing 11-7:   DeepThoughtsViewController.m (View life cycle Section)

(The `Controls` *section marked by* `#pragma mark Controls` *appears here. See Listing 11-4 for the Controls section, and Chapter 10 for the complete code.)*

```objc
     [self dismissModalViewControllerAnimated:YES];
}

#pragma mark -
#pragma mark Responding to gestures

- (void) addGestures {

  /*
   Create and configure the gesture recognizers. Add each
         to the view as a gesture recognizer.
   */
  UIGestureRecognizer *recognizer;
  /*
   Create a tap recognizer and add it to the view.
   Keep a reference to the recognizer to test in gestureRe
         cognizer:shouldReceiveTouch:.
   */
  recognizer = [[UITapGestureRecognizer
         alloc] initWithTarget:self action:@
         selector(handleTapFrom:)];
  [self.view addGestureRecognizer:recognizer];
  // self.tapRecognizer = (UITapGestureRecognizer *)
         recognizer;
  recognizer.delegate = self;
  [recognizer release];

  /*
   Create a swipe gesture recognizer to recognize right
         swipes (the default).
   */
  recognizer = [[UISwipeGestureRecognizer
         alloc] initWithTarget:self action:@
         selector(handleSwipeFrom:)];
  [self.view addGestureRecognizer:recognizer];
  [recognizer release];
  /*
   Create a swipe gesture recognizer to recognize left
         swipes.
   */
  recognizer = [[UISwipeGestureRecognizer
         alloc] initWithTarget:self action:@
         selector(handleSwipeFrom:)];
  ((UISwipeGestureRecognizer *)recognizer).direction =
         UISwipeGestureRecognizerDirectionLeft;
  [self.view addGestureRecognizer:recognizer];
  [recognizer release];
}
```

(continued)

Listing 11-7 *(continued)*

```
- (BOOL)gestureRecognizer:(UIGestureRecognizer *)
          gestureRecognizer shouldReceiveTouch:(UITouch
          *)touch {
  return YES;
}

/*
 In response to a tap gesture, show settings modal view.
 */
- (void)handleTapFrom:(UITapGestureRecognizer *)recognizer
          {
  [self settings];
}

/*
 In response to a swipe gesture, change the speed.
 */
- (void)handleSwipeFrom:(UISwipeGestureRecognizer *)
          recognizer {

  if (recognizer.direction ==
          UISwipeGestureRecognizerDirectionLeft) {
    if (speed <= kMaxSpeed) speed = speed+2;
  }
  else {
    if (speed > 0) speed = speed-2;
  }
}

#pragma mark -
#pragma mark Orientation
```

(The Orientation section appears here. See Chapter 10 for the complete code.)

The code initializes a Tap recognizer and adds it to the view using the addGestureRecognizer: instance method that's part of UIGestureRecognizer. (UITapGestureRecognizer is a subclass of UIGestureRecognizer that looks for single or multiple taps.)

The code then initializes two Swipe recognizers to handle left and right swipes and adds them to the view. (UISwipeGestureRecognizer is a concrete subclass of UIGestureRecognizer that looks for swiping gestures in one or more directions.) The default direction is a right swipe, so you don't have to specify the direction. For a left swipe, you specify a direction property with UISwipeGestureRecognizerDirectionLeft.

Through this code, you also keep a reference to the `recognizer` so that you can test it using `gestureRecognizer:shouldReceiveTouch:`, which asks the delegate if a Gesture recognizer should receive an object representing a touch. `YES` (the default) lets the Gesture recognizer examine the Touch object.

Finally, you specify what the `handleTapFrom` method does: in response to a Tap gesture (from `UITapGestureRecognizer`), the method uses `settings` to display the Modal view. You also specify what the `handleSwipeFrom` method does: if the direction is to the left (`recognizer.direction == UISwipeGestureRecognizerDirectionLeft`), the method reduces the animation speed; if not (which means the direction must be to the right, which is the default), the method increases the speed.

Save your Xcode project by choosing File⇨Save. Then, to test the gestures, click the Build and Run button. You should see the Simulator launch, run the app, and display the falling words over the image.

Now click anywhere in the animated view. The Modal view should appear, and you can click inside the text box and type new words for the falling words, and drag the slider to change the animation speed. Click the Done button to return to the animated view. Now drag across the view to the right, and the animation should speed up — dragging is the equivalent of a swipe. Drag across to the left, and the animation should slow down. Very cool!

A Lot Accomplished Very Quickly

So it looks like you have all the pieces in place for the DeepThoughts application. The user can now tap anywhere to bring up a Modal view and enter a new phrase for the flowing words (so you can either keep or get rid of the Light Info button, which does the same thing) and control the animation speed. The user can also control the speed by swiping the animated view left or right.

Appearances can be deceiving, though.

Reality check: Some how-to books on software development should really be housed in the Fiction section of your local bookstore because all their examples work flawlessly. In the real world, everything doesn't always go as planned; occasionally your software program blows up on you. That's why an essential part of software development is the debugging phase — teasing as many flaws out of your app as possible so you can squash 'em. The next chapter shows you how to work through the debugging phase of your project and introduces you to the SDK's very own debugging tool, something that's sure to make your software-development life a lot easier.

Chapter 12

Getting the Bugs Out

. . . .

In This Chapter

▶ Understanding the kinds of errors that may come up

▶ Using Xcode's Debugger and Build windows

▶ Setting breakpoints and examining objects and variables

▶ Using the Static Analyzer to analyze your code for memory leaks

. . . .

*W*hen you're developing an application, sometimes things don't work out quite the way you planned — especially when you knock over a can of Jolt Cola on the keyboard and fry it out of existence.

Murphy was an optimist about computer programming with his law that there's always one more bug. It took Weinberg's Second Law to put debugging into perspective: If builders built buildings the way that programmers program programs, the first woodpecker to come along would destroy civilization.

As I learned the hard way (indeed, I wrote *Murphy's Computer Laws* in 1980 for Celestial Arts, only to violate most of them in subsequent projects), debugging is not something to put off until later, after the warnings and error messages pile up. Keep in mind Bove's Theorem: The remaining work required to finish a project increases as the deadline approaches. It's best to tackle any errors and warnings you get immediately.

So, what does it take to tackle the inevitable errors that will find their way into your code? In a word, *debugging:* the process of analyzing your code line by line to view your program's state at a particular stage of execution. To debug a program, you run it under the control of a debugger, which lets you pause the program and examine its state. In this chapter, I show you how to use the Xcode Debugger to understand, locate, and fix bugs.

Understanding Bugs

"Stuff happens," in the immortal words of a famous ex-U.S. Secretary of Defense. When it comes to developing your own programs, that "stuff" comes in three categories:

✔ **Syntax errors:** Compilers — the Objective-C compiler in Xcode is a case in point — expect you to use a certain set of instructions in your code; those instructions make up the language it understands. When you type If instead of if, or the subtler [view release} (with a curly closing bracket) instead of [view release] (with a straight closing bracket), the compiler suddenly has no idea what you're talking about and generates a syntax error. Objective-C is case sensitive, which means that Speedchanged and speedChanged are treated differently. Class, category, and protocol names generally begin with an uppercase letter (such as NSUserDefaults); the names of methods and instance variables typically begin with a lowercase letter (such as speedChanged).

Syntax errors are the most obvious, simply because your program won't compile (and therefore won't run) until all of them are fixed. Generally, syntax errors spring from typographical errors. (And yes, the errors can be pretty penny-ante stuff — an *I* for an *i*, for goodness sake — but it doesn't take much to stump a compiler.)

In Figure 12-1, you can see an example of a syntax error — simply forgetting to put a semicolon at the end of the fallingWords statement. This one is kindly pointed out by Xcode's friendly Debugger feature. After choosing Build⟿Build and Run to build and run the application (and saving all changes in the process), the build fails — a tiny hammer icon and Failed appears in the notification section (in the bottom-right corner of the Xcode window), and the compiler highlights the statement after the syntax error with three (count 'em) red exclamation marks: one in the gutter to the left of the statement after the syntax error, one in the strip of debugging information that appears around the statement after the syntax error, and one in the notifications section of the Xcode window.

A syntax error in a different place in the code might not be explained so easily by Xcode and might therefore wreak havoc with subsequent code, thus causing the build to fail. For example, in Figure 12-2, I forget to include an asterisk in front of recognizer in the UIGestureRecognizer recognizer statement (which should be UIGestureRecognizer *recognizer). As a result, the compiler found a problem with subsequent code. Click the exclamation mark, and Xcode brings up the Build Results window, as shown in the upper part of Figure 12-3, with a long list of errors starting with Statically allocated instance of Objective-C class 'UIGestureRecognizer'. The Build Results window can show a more detailed view of the consequences of an error.

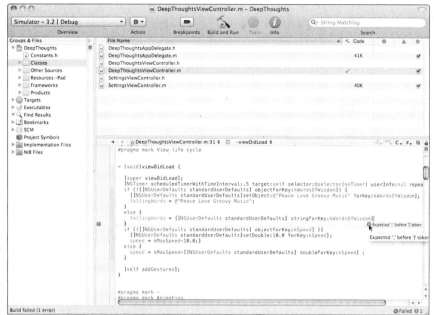

Figure 12-1:
A syntax
error. Oops.

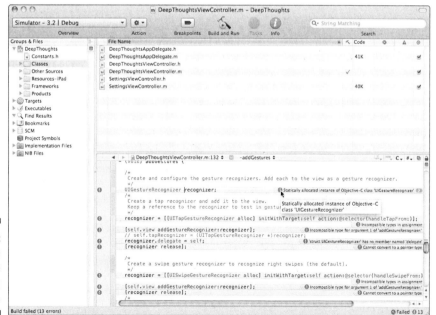

Figure 12-2:
A subtle
but more
damaging
syntax error.

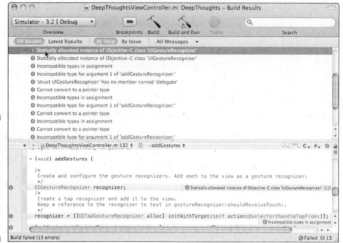

Figure 12-3:
The Build Results window lists the damage from this one error.

It's generally better to ignore the subsequent errors after a syntax error because they may be the result of that first error.

✔ **Runtime errors:** *Runtime errors* cause your program to stop executing — it *crashes,* in other words, as in "crash and burn to much wailing and gnashing of teeth." Something might have come up in the data that you hadn't expected (a division-by-zero error, for example), or the result of a method dealt a nasty surprise to your logic, or you sent a message to an object that doesn't have that message implemented. Sometimes you even get some build warnings for these errors; often the application simply stops working or *hangs* (stops and does nothing), or shuts down.

✔ **Logic errors:** Your literal-minded application does exactly what you tell it to, but sometimes you unintentionally tell it the wrong thing, and it coughs up a *logic error.* For example, in Figure 12-4, I deliberately created a logic error by dividing by zero. Xcode warns you about the divide-by-zero error but goes ahead anyway and builds and runs the app.

I typed the divide-by-zero error (`speed = kMaxSpeed/0-10.0`) to make the point that you may be able to build and run your app, but it may not work as intended.

You can see in Figure 12-4 the yellow exclamation point, which is a warning (rather than a red one, which is an error), and the message `Division by zero`. Clicking the exclamation point brings up the Build Results window, as shown in Figure 12-5, with the `Division by zero` warning and the steps of compiling and building the app.

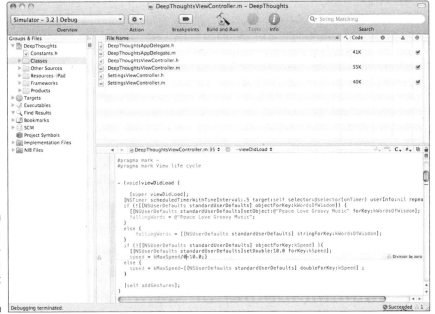

Figure 12-4:
Oh, great —
it builds
but doesn't
work.

Figure 12-5:
The Build
Results
window
shows what
happened.

TIP

With a complex app, you might be pelted with compiler warnings that you don't have time to take care of because they have no impact on the execution of the program. One reason to set your preferences so that Xcode always opens the Build Results window is that you'll get continually reminded about these warnings if you haven't fixed them. To set this preference, choose

Xcode⇨Preferences⇨Building and choose Always from the Open During Builds pop-up menu.

Syntax errors, runtime errors, and logic errors can all be pains in the behind, but there's no need to think of them as insurmountable roadblocks. You're still on your way to a cool iPad app.

Using the Debugger

The Debugger can be really useful when your program isn't doing what you expect. For the blatant errors, the Debugger can show you exactly what was going on when the error occurred. It provides you with a trail of how you got to where you are, highlights the problem instruction, and it shows you your application's variables and their values at that point.

If you've been following the examples in Chapters 9 through 11 for developing the DeepThoughts app, you're ready to debug the app, and your configuration should still be set to `Simulator-3.2 | Debug` in the pop-up menu in the upper left corner of the Xcode Project window. (Refer to Figure 12-4.) If you've been developing a project with a different configuration, you must change it to the Debug build configuration. (Before you can take advantage of the Debugger, the compiler must collect information *for* the Debugger, and the Debug build configuration generates the debugging symbols for that purpose.)

You can tap the Debugger from the Xcode Text Editor, as I show in the next section, and set breakpoints that stop execution at any point and trace the messages sent up to that point (as I describe in "Setting breakpoints" in the next section), so that you can step through the program's execution and view the contents of variables. The Debugger window offers even more control over the process and provides detailed information. You can also use the Mini Debugger — a floating window — that offers many of the functions of the Debugger window, as I show later in this chapter.

You can even use the Mac OS X Console utility application to view messages and interact with the GNU Source-Level Debugger with typed commands, as I explain in "Using the Console" in this chapter.

Debugging in the Text Editor

As shown earlier, a syntax error can stop a build in its tracks, and you can see both the compiler and the debugger at work behind the scenes in the Text Editor. A red exclamation point in the Text Editor, as shown in Figure 12-6, points to the instruction that caused the program to stop building — that's the Debugger pointing out the problem.

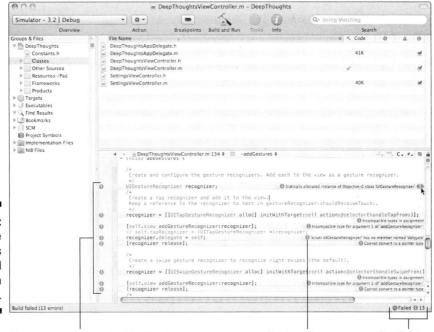

Figure 12-6:
Xcode highlights an error and displays a datatip.

Syntax errors recognized by Xcode   Debugger datatip   Notifications

There's even some information about the error. The Debugger offers a strip of information called a *datatip,* which you can see in Figure 12-6 right next to the offending line. The datatip says `Statically allocated instance of Objective-C class 'UIGestureRecognizer'` and ends with a 2, which means another error or warning is there. In Figure 12-7 I click the 2, and it reveals a second warning, which happens to be the same error again. Other datatips show errors about incompatible types and that `'struct UIGestureRecognizer' has no member named 'delegate'`.

What this all means is that the compiler "thinks" I'm trying to allocate the object (`recognizer`) statically, rather than as a pointer — and that's because I forgot to include an asterisk in front of `recognizer`.

If your app manages to build and run (which can happen even with a warning, as you can see back in Figure 12-4), that means it has passed through the compiler without syntax errors. But you aren't out of the woods yet — even if you don't see evidence of runtime errors that crash the app, you certainly haven't tried all the app's functions yet. You also don't know whether there are logic errors. But don't despair; you have options.

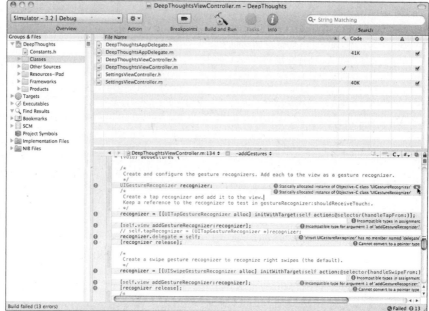

Figure 12-7:
The datatip
shows a
second
warning.

Setting breakpoints

Breaking down may be a bad situation in real life, but in the life of your app, getting a break is a good thing. A *breakpoint* is an instruction to the Debugger to stop execution at that instruction and wait for further instructions (no pun intended). By setting breakpoints at various methods in your program, you can step through its execution — at the instruction level — to see exactly what it's doing. You can also examine the variables the program is setting and using. If you're stymied by a logic error, setting breakpoints is a great way to break that logjam.

To set a breakpoint in the Xcode Text Editor, click inside the far-left column of the Editor pane, as shown in Figure 12-8. I set a breakpoint to stop execution right before the `int startX = round(random() % 400)` statement.

To get rid of a breakpoint, simply drag it off to the side. You can also right-click the breakpoint and choose Remove Breakpoint from the pop-up menu that appears.

You can set the Xcode Text Editor to recognize breakpoints by clicking the Breakpoints button in the Project window toolbar — the Build and Run button changes to Build and Debug. Click Build and Debug to build and run the program.

Figure 12-8:
Setting a
breakpoint
in the Text
Editor.

Using the Debugger strip

When you build and run the program with breakpoints, the Debugger strip
appears in the Text Editor as the program runs in the Simulator. The program stops executing at the first breakpoint. The process counter (PC) red
arrow points to the line of code in the Text Editor immediately following the
breakpoint. The Debugger strip appears just above the Text Editor, as shown
in Figure 12-9, while the app is running in the Simulator but stopped at the
breakpoint.

When you move your pointer over a variable in a datatip (refer to Figure 12-9),
its contents are revealed. You can modify the contents of mutable variables,
as I do in Figure 12-9 with `startX`. This is a powerful way to find out the value
of variables at any given point during execution. (And yes, a slip of the datatip
can sink a shipping app.)

The Debugger strip offers several buttons for your pushing pleasure:

✔ **Thread list:** Displays a list of the threads in your program. I explain this
in "Using the Debugger Window," later in this chapter.

✔ **Breakpoints:** Activates or deactivates breakpoints, which I describe in
"Setting breakpoints" earlier in this section.

✔ **Continue:** Continues execution of a paused process in your program.

✔ **Step Over:** Steps over the current line of code. The *process counter* (PC), which is identified by the red arrow in the gutter (refer to Figure 12-9), moves to the next line of code to be executed in the current file.

✔ **Step Into:** Steps into a function or method in the current line of code. If possible, the Text Editor shows the source file with the called routine. The PC (red arrow) points to the line of code to be executed next.

✔ **Step Out:** Steps out of the current function or method. The Text Editor shows the source file with the function's caller.

✔ **Show Debugger:** Opens the Debugger proper.

✔ **Show Console:** Opens the Mac OS X Console, which I describe in "Using the Console," later in this chapter

✔ **Call list:** Displays a list of the called functions or methods in the *stack,* which I explain next.

Thread list   Debugger strip

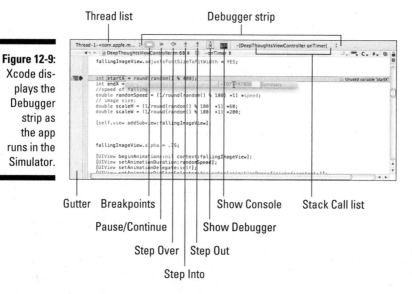

Figure 12-9:
Xcode displays the Debugger strip as the app runs in the Simulator.

Gutter   Breakpoints   Show Console   Stack Call list

Pause/Continue   Show Debugger

Step Over | Step Out

Step Into

Click the up and down arrows next to `DeepThoughtsViewController onTimer` in the Debugger strip (refer to Figure 12-9), or whatever else is displayed in that section of the Debugger strip, so that you can see the *stack* — a trace of the objects and methods that got you to where you are now, as shown in Figure 12-10.

Although the stack is about as useful as a stack of pancakes in this particular context, the stack *can* be very useful in a more complex application — it can help you understand the path that you took to get where you are. Seeing how one object sent a message to another object — which sent a message to a third object — can be really helpful, especially if you didn't expect the program flow to work that way.

Getting a look at the stack can also be useful if you're trying to understand how the framework does its job, and in what order messages are sent. You can stop the execution of your program at a breakpoint and trace the messages sent up to that point.

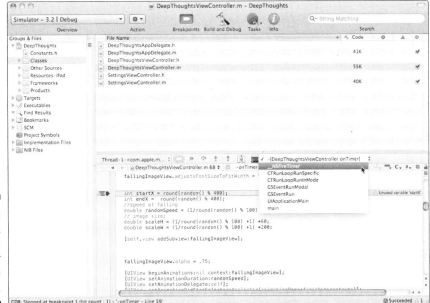

Figure 12-10:
The stack in the Debugger strip in the Text Editor.

You can play with your app in the Simulator and then switch back to the Text Editor to launch the Debugger window — click the Show Debugger button in the Debugger strip (refer to Figure 12-9), or choose Run⇨Debugger, to bring up the Debugger window.

Using the Debugger Window

After clicking the Show Debugger button in the Debugger strip, or choosing Run⇨Debugger (or pressing ⌘+Shift+Y), the Debugger window appears as shown in Figure 12-11. (Even though the Debugger is officially running, you have to open the Debugger window explicitly.) You can then click the Pause button along the top of the Debugger window to stop execution, unless execution is already stopped at a breakpoint. (The Restart button replaces the Pause button after clicking Pause or stopping at a breakpoint, as shown in Figure 12-11.)

The Debugger window has everything the Text Editor has, but you can also see your stack and the variables in scope at a glance.

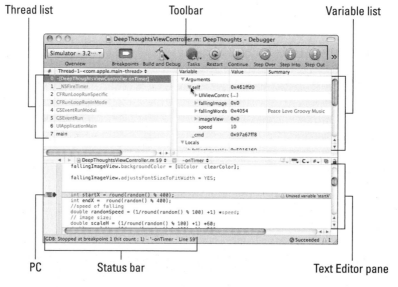

Thread list   Toolbar   Variable list

Figure 12-11:
The
Debugger
window.

PC   Status bar   Text Editor pane

Here's what you see in the Debugger window:

- ✔ **Toolbar:** Offers buttons for controlling the program's execution, including Pause/Restart, Continue, Step Over, Step Into, and Step Out. (Restart starts execution from the beginning, whereas Continue continues execution from a breakpoint.)

- ✔ **Thread list:** Shows the call stack of the current thread. For each function or method call that your program makes, the Debugger stores information about it in a stack frame. These stack frames are stored in the call stack. When you pause execution at a breakpoint or when you click the Pause button on the toolbar, Xcode displays the call stack for the currently running process in the Thread list and puts the most recent call at the top. The pop-up menu above this view lets you select different threads to view when debugging a multi-threaded application.

✔ **Variable list:** Shows information — such as name, type, and value — about the variables for the selected stack frame. To see the contents of a structured variable (including arrays and vectors) or an object, click the triangle next to the variable.

✔ **Text Editor pane:** Displays the source code you are debugging. When you pause execution by clicking the Pause button in the Toolbar, the Debugger highlights the line of source code where execution paused and displays the PC red arrow indicator.

✔ **Status bar:** Displays the current status of the debugging session. For example, in Figure 12-11, Xcode indicates that GDB (the GNU Source-Level Debugger) is stopped at breakpoint 1.

Your window may not look exactly like Figure 12-11 — that's because Xcode gives you lots of different ways to customize the look of the Debugger window. You can, for example, choose Run⇨Debugger Display from the main menu and then choose Horizontal Layout or Vertical Layout to change the window's layout.

You might want to choose Run⇨Debugger Display⇨Source and Disassembly if you have a hankering for checking both the source code *and* the assembly language (if you really care about assembly language); in that case, the Text Editor pane divides down the center into two panes, with the source code on the left and the assembly code in the right. The option I choose for Figure 12-11 is Source Only — so that only the source code appears in the Text Editor pane.

You can click the Step Into button in the Debugger window to go through your code line by line. The Debugger window also gives you other options for making your way through your program:

✔ **Step Over** gives you the opportunity to skip over a line of code.

✔ **Step Into** takes you step by step into a function or method in the current line of code.

✔ **Step Out** takes you out of the current method.

✔ **Continue** tells the program to keep on with its execution.

✔ **Restart** restarts the program. (You were hoping maybe if you tried it again it would work?)

Showing datatips for variables and objects

In the Debugger window, as shown in Figure 12-12, you can move your pointer over an object or variable in the Text Editor pane to show its contents in a datatip, and you can move your pointer over other disclosure triangles to see even more information in the datatip. In Figure 12-12, I move the pointer over `wordsOfWisdom` to show that it's an `NSString` set to `0x0`, and then I move the pointer over the triangle to reveal its class (`NSObject`) information.

Expanding the view of objects not only helps you check variables, but also checks messages sent to object reference instance variables. Objective-C, unlike some other languages, allows you to send a message to a `nil` object *without* generating a runtime error. If you do that, you should expect to subsequently see some sort of logic error because a message to a `nil` object simply does nothing. But it's possible that an object reference hasn't been set, and you're sending the message into the ether. If you look at an object reference instance variable and its value is `0x0`, (as in `NSString * wordsOfWisdom 0x0 out of scope` in the very top line of the datatip in Figure 12-12), any messages to that object are simply ignored. So when you get a logic error, the first thing you may want to check is whether any of the object references you're using have `0x0` as their values, informing you that the reference was never initialized.

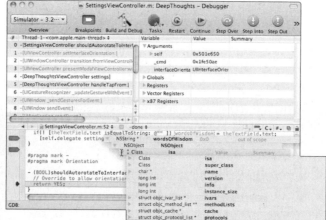

Figure 12-12: Show the contents of an object or variable.

As you can see, the Debugger can be really useful when your program isn't doing what you expect. For the blatant errors, the Debugger can show you exactly what was going on when the error occurred. It provides you with a trail of how you got to where you are, highlights the problem instruction, and shows you your application's variables and their values at that point.

What's just as valuable is how the Debugger can help you with logic errors. You may have mistakenly attached the slider interface object in Interface Builder to `theTextField` rather than `slider`. Sending a message to `nil` is not uncommon, especially when you're making changes to the user interface and forget to set up an outlet, for example. In such situations, the ability to look at the object references can really help.

Using the Mini Debugger

The Mini Debugger is a floating window that provides debugging controls similar to those of the Xcode Text Editor. It can make debugging a bit easier, because you don't have to switch back and forth between your running application and your Xcode Project window and Debugging window.

To show the Mini Debugger while running your program, choose Run⇨Mini Debugger. The Mini Debugger appears as shown in Figure 12-13, with buttons to stop or pause the program, open the Xcode project, or activate or deactivate breakpoints.

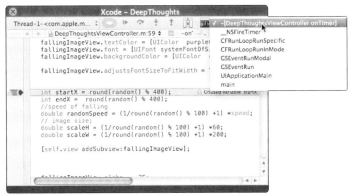

Figure 12-13: Use the Mini Debugger to pause program execution and check out the code.

After pausing or stopping the program (or reaching a breakpoint), the Mini Debugger displays the same information you would see when debugging in the Text Editor. As you can see in Figure 12-13, you can click the rightmost pop-up menu along the top of the window to see the call stack.

Using the Console Application

The Console utility application, supplied with Mac OS X, lets you to watch error and status messages as they appear. If your computer appears to be stalled or is acting in an unusual manner, Console might be producing information that can help debug the problem. While the Xcode Debugger provides a graphical interface for GDB (the GNU Source-Level Debugger), Console lets you interact directly with GDB using a command line. You can type commands using Console to perform simple debugging tasks, and you can include code in your app to use NSLog statements to log messages to Console before and after variables are set.

To open the Console window, choose Run⇨Console. After building and running the Xcode project, the messages appear in the Console window in bold, as you can see in Figure 12-14.

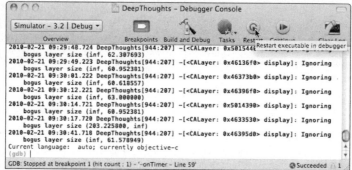

Figure 12-14: Use the Console window to monitor error and status messages.

You can use the Console window to see the commands that Xcode sends to GDB or the Java command-line debugger, to actually send commands directly to GDB or the Java command-line debugger, and to look at the debugger output for those commands. To enter commands, click in the Console window and type at the gdb or JavaBug prompt. To get help with GDB and Java debugging commands, type **help**. (To get the gdb or JavaBug prompt, the program you're debugging must be paused.)

Using the Static Analyzer

Xcode offers the Build and Analyze feature (the Static Analyzer) that analyzes your code for memory leaks. The results show up like warnings and errors, with explanations of where and what the issue is. You can also see the flow of control of the (potential) problem.

To show how this works, I deliberately created a memory leak in DeepThoughtsAppDelegate. I copied the following line of code in DeepThoughtsAppDelegate.h:

```
DeepThoughtsViewController *viewController;
```

I then added the following statement below the statement you see above, changing `viewController` to `viewController2`:

```
DeepThoughtsViewController *viewController2;
```

And a few lines down, I did the same thing — I copied the `@property` statement for `viewController` to make one for `viewController 2`:

```
@property (nonatomic, retain) IBOutlet
         DeepThoughtsViewController *viewController2;
```

Then, in `DeepThoughtsAppDelegate.m`, I added the following line of code after setting up the view with the view controller:

```
DeepThoughtsViewController *viewController2 =
         [DeepThoughtsViewController alloc];
```

Allocating a new object without doing anything with it is sure to cause a memory leak warning.

To run the Static Analyzer, choose Build➪Build and Analyze. Sure enough, the changes I made to the code cause the warning shown in Figure 12-15. I get a warning (ignore the unused variable warning) with a little blue icon that says

```
Potential leak of an object allocated on line 23 and
              stored into 'viewController2'
```

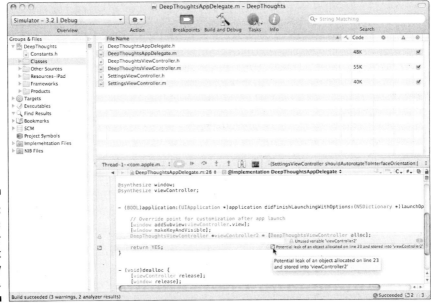

Figure 12-15:
The Static
Analyzer
warns about
a memory
leak.

If you click on the little blue icon for the warning (refer to Figure 12-15), you get a "trace" of what happened, as I show in Figure 12-16.

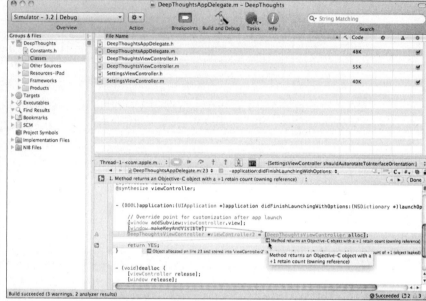

First you get the following warning, which you can see by moving your pointer over the blue arrow icon in the trace (as shown in Figure 12-16):

```
Method returns an Objective-C object with a +1 retain
count (owning reference)
```

Then, in the next line, if you move your pointer over the blue arrow icon as shown in Figure 12-17, you can see this:

```
Object allocated on line 23 and stored into
'viewController2' is no longer referenced after
this point and has a retain count of +1 (object leaked)
```

Notice that the results refer to line numbers. That's why I made a point of explaining how to turn on line numbers in Xcode back in Chapter 5.

As you know by now, memory management is a big deal on the iPad.

Before you attempt to get your app into the App Store or even run it on anyone's iPad, you need to make sure it's behaving properly. By that I mean not only delivering the promised functionality, but also avoiding the unintentional misuse of iPad resources. Keep in mind that the iPad, as cool as it may very well be, is nevertheless somewhat resource-constrained when it comes to memory usage and battery life. Such restraints can have a direct effect on what you can (and can't) do in your application.

Now that you've meditated on DeepThoughts long enough to know the secrets of iPad app development, you're ready to tackle a truly industrial-strength application, which is displayed in all its glittering detail in Part V.

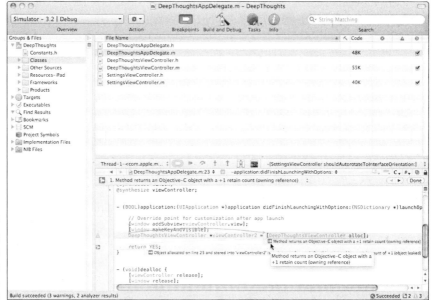

Figure 12-17: More secrets revealed.

Part V
Building an Industrial-Strength Application

The 5th Wave   By Rich Tennant

"You can lay on it if you want, but my channeling energy through your body's chakras isn't going to increase your iPad's battery life."

In this part . . .

In this part, I explain the design of an application that has big muscles: a context-driven user interface, lots of functionality, Web access, an annotated custom map, and an application architecture that you can use to build your own version of The Next Great Thing.

- ✔ Chapter 13 takes you on a tour of how to start the whole process of designing and then building your app. You put yourself in the user's shoes and then take that understanding and transform it into a program architecture — one you can actually implement.

- ✔ Chapter 14 helps you find your way with maps. You find out about creating maps with MKMapView, centering them, displaying a region, and even pinpointing where you are. And yes, you discover how to work with all those cute annotations that makes maps more useful. You also learn to geocode — how to get GPS coordinates for an address, as well as an address from GPS coordinates.

- ✔ Chapter 15 introduces you to spilt screen controllers, popovers, and table views — the primary ways that the user will discover all those neat thing your app can do for them. You discover how to create and display them and then respond to a tap and navigate to where the user wants to go.

- ✔ Chapter 16 pays more attention to the user experience. You find out how to save the state of the application when the user quits and then restore it when he returns. You also get more into Settings and give the user option of real-time data or data you have saved from the last time he was online.

- ✔ Chapter 17 shows you how to get to all that content that makes the iPad a superb user experience. You use data you've stored locally in your application bundle as well as data you have on a server someplace in the cloud (and want to save for later use when the user is no longer online), and you even display a Web page and allow a user to navigate out into the Internet and then back without ever leaving your app.

Chapter 13

Designing Your Application

Although the iPad can do almost anything that the iPhone can do (except the making calls stuff, and yeah, some models can only use Wi-Fi), there are some things you'll want to do only on the iPad. (There are also some things you'll really prefer to do on the iPhone, and I'll leave that for you to explore on your own).

In this chapter, I take you through an overview of the design cycle of a more complex application (iPadTravel411), and I show you how to take an idea that was developed for the iPhone and expand it to take advantage of the iPad's capabilities. Although I can't develop the entire application within the confines of this book, I show you how to take a subset of it and how to use the iPad's capabilities to implement it.

I start by explaining the app itself.

Defining the Problems

Innovation is usually born of frustration, and the iPadTravel411 project was no exception. It just turns out that my frustration was linked to a trip to beautiful Venice rather than, say, the vacuum cleaner doing a terrible job of picking up cat hair.

My wife and I were going to arrive late at night, and rather than trying to get into Venice at that hour, we decided we'd stay at a hotel near the airport and then go into Venice the next day. We were going to meet some friends who were leaving the day after that, and we wanted to get a relatively early start so we could spend the day with them.

I was a little concerned about the logistics. I thought we would have to go back to the airport terminal from the hotel and then get on a water bus or water taxi. Both the water taxi stand and the water bus stop are a distance from the terminal, and that meant more time and more trudging about. The water taxi was the fastest way, but very pricey (around $140 USD at the time). The water bus was much cheaper but more confusing — and only ran once an hour. It seemed like a major excursion.

My friends said, "Why not take a taxi or a bus?"

I said, "A bus to Venice it's an island the last time I checked."

Okay, it *is* an island, but there's a causeway running from the mainland to Piazzale Roma, where you can then get a water bus or water taxi — or meet your friends.

Although it's more romantic to arrive by sea, it's a lot easier by land. Having been to Venice a couple times before, and considering our time constraints, we opted for the land route.

Now, I'm sure that information was in a guidebook someplace, but it would have taken a lot of work to dig it out; most guidebooks focus on attractions. Also, guidebooks go out of date quickly; the one I had for Venice was already two years old. Of course, I could have used the Internet before I left home to find the information, but that can also be a real chore. And, as I like to remember, "The great thing about the Internet is that some of the information and advice is true."

What I wanted was something that made it easier to travel by reducing all the hassles — getting to and from a strange airport, getting around the city, getting the best exchange rate, knowing how much I should tip in a restaurant — that sort of thing. (Not too much to ask, right?)

Don't get me wrong — I actually do a lot of research before I go someplace, and often I have that information handy already. But I end up with lots of paper because I usually don't take a laptop with me on vacation; even when I do, it's terribly inconvenient to have to take it out on a bus or in an airline terminal to find some information. And then there's the challenge of finding a Wi-Fi connection when you really need it.

I kept that idea in the back of my mind because at the time there was no real solution.

But then . . . enter the iPhone. After taking a look at the SDK, I realized I could write an app (without too much real difficulty) to do everything I thought would make traveling no more painful that a root canal. (Hey, my dentist does wonderful things with Novocain and nitrous oxide these days.)

Although I initially developed this application for the iPhone, when the iPad made its debut I realized that — for at least some parts of the application —

the iPad was an even better solution. So I started by simply trying to "port" the application to the iPad. What I learned is valuable for anyone from the I-never-developed-anything-before developer to someone who already has an iPhone application in the App Store — so valuable, in fact, that I'm going to highlight here:

> The iPad is *not* simply a bigger iPhone, which means a simple Port Strategy is going to end up being an unmitigated disaster.

So, even though the goal of the iPadTravel411 app will remain the same, I take you through the process of designing the same solution to a user's problem for the iPad. (If you're curious about how I set up the original iPadTravel411 app, get yourself a copy of *iPhone Application Development For Dummies* and take a look at the MobileTravel411 and iPhoneTravel411 apps.) Much of the stuff is similar, but the user experience is far different, given both the size of the display as well as the available functionality in the SDK.

Categorizing the problems and defining the solutions

On desktop or laptop machines, features are often categorized by function, but given the way the iPad is designed to be used (as I describe in Chapter 1 and explain further in this chapter), categorizing by *context* makes more sense. So after I settled on the information and functionality I needed when I was traveling, I grouped things into the following contexts.

- ✔ **Getting and using money:** What is the country's currency (including denominations and coins), and what's the best way to exchange my currency for it? I want to understand the costs of using credit cards versus an ATM card, or exchanging at a *bureau de change.* I also want to be able to understand how the dreaded VAT (value-added tax) really works.

- ✔ **Getting to and from the airport:** What choices do I really have when it comes to things terminal? What are the costs, advantages, and disadvantages — and logistics — of each? Do I have to buy a ticket in advance? How do I find said ticket? What's the schedule?

- ✔ **Getting around the city:** Same kind of pickle as getting to and from the airport — what's available *and* best for a traveler's purposes? I once spent several days in Barcelona before I realized there was a subway system.

- ✔ **Seeing what's happening right now in the city:** Guidebooks are fine for visiting the sights, and I might want to (some day) re-create one on the iPad. But what I *would* like to know now is if there's anything special happening when I'm in some particular place at some particular time. Bastille Day in Paris can be fun if you know about the Bastille Day parade, and less of a hassle if you know you can't cross the Champs-Élysées for a few hours.

✔ **Knowing the practical day-to-day stuff:** How do you make calls into, out of, and within a given city? How much and when should I tip? What is acceptable and unacceptable behavior? For example, that it's considered impolite to eat or drink something while walking down the street in Japan might not occur to someone from New York City.

✔ **Staying safe:** Being immediately informed of breaking news that could make things unsafe — large demonstrations or terrorist attacks, for example — would be high on my wish list. But even the more mundane things like the "dangerous" neighborhoods are important. What should you do in an emergency? A friend of mine had her passport stolen in Prague — at times like that, it would be nice to have the locations and phone numbers of embassies or consulates. This is stuff you hardly ever need, but when you need it, you need it right away.

✔ **What to do before I go:** In the past, I've forgotten to call my cell phone company before I leave home to get a roaming package and notify my credit card company that I'll be out of the country or far from home, so please, _please_ don't decline my hotel charge in Vladivostok. I also want to be able to download all the information before I leave so I can look at it on the plane, or as part of my strategy for avoiding roaming charges or handling an unexpected lack of connections.

✔ **Knowing where I am:** In all of these situations, I also want to be able to get my bearings by seeing where I am — and where I might need to get to — on a map.

I also wanted to make the app easy to use for someone who isn't intimately involved with the design — and perhaps doesn't immediately share my take on the best way to organize the information. So, for each choice in the main window, I wanted to be able to add a few words of explanation about what each category contained.

All great ideas, but as I said, the important thing is to know how to make an app actually fulfill the promise of all these great ideas. For that, you need someone to walk you through the design cycle of the application — and I'm nominating myself. Although you could use at least half a dozen models for the process (I'm a recovering software development methodologist myself), the one I go through here is pretty simple and is well suited for the iPad to boot. Here goes:

1. Defining the problems

2. Categorizing the problems and defining the solutions

3. Designing the user experience

   a. Leveraging the iPad's strengths

   b. Seeing what you have to work with when it comes to the device

   c. Recognizing the constraints of the device

4. Creating the program architecture

    a. Content views

    b. View controllers

    c. Models

5. Writing the code (and testing it along the way)

6. Doing it until you get it right

Of course, the actual analysis, design, and programming (not to mention testing) process has a bit more to it than this — and coming up with the specifications and design definitely involve more than what you see in these few pages. But from a process perspective, it's pretty close to the real thing. It does give you an idea of the questions you need to ask — and have answered — in order to develop an iPad application.

A word of caution, though. Even though iPad apps are smaller and much easier to get your head around than, say, a full-blown enterprise service-oriented architecture, they come equipped with a unique set of challenges. Between the iPad capabilities, which ironically become a kind of requirement for creating a good app, and the high expectation of iPad users, you have your hands full.

Designing the User Experience

Because you've already been through Steps 1 and 2 of my handy-dandy iPad application development design cycle — see the previous section — what I do next is talk about the user experience. After I've gone through all of that, I show you how to develop a subset of the application (I call the resulting app the iPadTravel411) in Chapters 14 through 17.

To be honest, I actually started the process of defining the user experience process earlier in the chapter when I defined the kinds of contexts I was interested in and the information and capabilities I wanted in each of them. (That's yet more proof that it's hard to compartmentalize experience into discrete steps.) But to get the actual *design* ball of my application rolling, I started out by thinking a bit more about what else (besides the features, of course) I wanted from the application — in other words, I started thinking about what the *experience* of using the application should be like.

To further the process, you would actually want to model the user *workflow,* so to speak — how the user would want to use the information and capabilities you could provide in each of those contexts I identified in the "Categorizing the problems and defining the solutions" section, earlier in this chapter.

Although sketching out such a workflow completely is beyond the scope of this book, I do want to explain how knowing what you have to work with (the iPad's strengths and features) as well knowing what the device won't let you do (or, at least, not do without a fight) can help you define what your (and the user's) options are. To start that process of knowledge acquisition off, I want to review some of the things that the iPad is really good at.

Leveraging the iPad's strengths

Although I've had a lot of experience designing, developing, and writing about iPhone applications, soon after the iPad was announced I began to realize that — contrary to what many of the pundits have said — the device isn't simply a larger iPhone or iPod touch. In fact, even though iPhone/iPod touch applications could be ported to the iPad without too much trouble, in order to offer real value on that device, many would have to be redesigned. (In fact, some iPhone/iPod touch applications weren't even relevant for the iPad.)

Although the iPad shares some features with the iPhone — portability, ease of use and convenience, its awareness of your location, and its ability to connect seamlessly to the Internet from most places — it is also significantly different. Two differences jumped out at me:

- ✔ The iPad is not as compact as an iPhone, for example, so the user is less likely to have the device with them all of the time, as they would with a cell phone or smart phone.

- ✔ The screen size is great for displaying lots and lots of content — not one of the iPhone's strengths, if I'm being totally honest.

What I realized is that these two differences when put together provide for the ability to allow the user to explore whatever interests them in a more intimate or personal way. So rather than a device that was ideal for short, ad hoc tasks, what you have is a device well-suited for longer-term, more intensive exploration of a subject.

Not that you can't do that on an iPhone; it's just that the iPhone is better for really short-term tasks that require no more than a limited amount of specific information that can be delivered on the small screen. In that sense, iPhones and other small screen devices are all about execution as opposed to planning and/or immersion in a subject. Which is, on the other hand, the long suit for the large screen iPad.

So what do you get when you combine the iPad's form factor, touch interface, ease of use, and portability, with its ability to beautifully display rich content, its awareness of your location, and its ability to connect seamlessly to the Internet from most places? A more intimate device with a better way to access information — one that allows the user to explore topics in the way they want to and one on which you can create a more natural interface that is consistent with the way the user wants to work.

Just think about it: The iPad is meant to be able to be used in any orientation, and the ability to flip the device over to share it with someone is a natural extension of that.

It starts with the last thing I mentioned in a previous paragraph — creating a user experience that's based on the way people naturally want to work. Among other things, you become the champion of relevance, searching out and destroying anything that isn't relevant to what the user is doing while he or she is using a particular part of your application.

Knowing the location of the user enables you to further refine the context by including the actual physical location and adding that to that crucial "relevance" filter. If you're in London, the iPad is well aware of that fact, meaning your application can "ask" the user whether he or she wants to use London as a filter for relevant information.

The idea is to focus on delivering rich content, understanding that the quality of information has to be better than the alternative — what you get by using the application has to have more value than alternative ways of doing the same thing. I can find airport transportation in a guidebook, but it's not up-to-date. I can get foreign exchange information from a *bureau de change,* but unless I know the bank rate, I don't know whether I'm being ripped off. I can get restaurant information from a newspaper, but I don't know whether the restaurant has subsequently changed hours or is closed for vacation. If the application can consistently provide me with better, more up-to-date information, it's the kind of application that's tailor-made for a context-driven design. This sort of design is possible on a mobile device because the device can access the Internet, which allows you to provide real-time, up-to-date information. In addition, it enables you to transcend the CPU and memory limitations of the iPad by offloading processing and data storage out to a server in the cloud.

What you have to work with

Okay, it's time to check the windows situation. On the Mac (or any other PC) you have lots of windows, and lots of different kinds. On the iPhone, on the other hand, you have a single window with an occasional action sheet or alert.

The iPad falls somewhere in between the superabundant and the almost non-existent— with the following in your bag of tricks:

1. Full-screen views

2. Split-screen views

3. Popover views

4. Controls, less than full-screen modal dialogs, action sheets and alerts

Full-screen views

On the iPad, you have the luxury of a large 9.7-inch (diagonal), LED-backlit, glossy, widescreen, Multi-Touch display with 1,024 x 768-pixel resolution at 132 pixels per inch.

Figure 13-1 shows one of the things you could fill it with.

Although one of the constraints on your application design for the iPhone and other mobile devices is the small screen, ironically the large screen on the iPad can also be thought of as a constraint. If you don't fill it (correctly) it can look really bad.

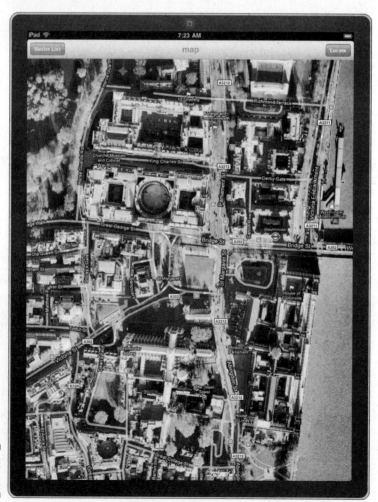

Figure 13-1:
Nice view.

Split-screen views

The iPhone SDK 3.2 introduces a split-screen view, as you can see in Figure 13-2. You'll definitely be taking advantage of split-screen views as you build the subset of iPadTravel411.

The split screen enables you to display two views side by side. In this example, the user has an opportunity to navigate to a particular part of the application while looking at a map of London. In Figure 13-2, the view on one side of the split is a Navigation view whereas the view on the other side is a Content view (I get to that next), but you can display anything you'd like.

Popovers

Although split-screen views work well for landscape mode, in portrait mode the left side disappears. Instead of a split screen, you can create a Popover view that displays the same information that you had in the split-screen view (in Figure 13-2 for example), or actually anything else would like. You can see an example of that in Figure 13-3, where you have a nice little Map view of Paddington Station in London in the background and instructions on how to get there from Heathrow airport on the Heathrow Express making up the Popover view.

Figure 13-2:
Split screen.

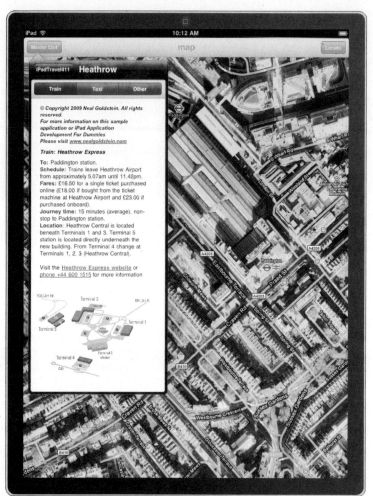

Figure 13-3:
A Popover
view.

Controls, less than full-screen modal dialogs, action sheets, and alerts

Controls, small modal dialogs, action sheets, alerts — all of these items let the user navigate the application. Controls allow the user to control the application — determining what they want to see, for example, or even letting them enter data. You work with controls such as text edit, buttons, and sliders, as well as delivering some of them in a modal dialog in Part IV. In this part (Chapter 17, to be precise), I introduce you to the control you see in Figure 13-3. This fellow is known as a *segmented control,* and as you can see, it enables the user to choose the transportation information he or she wants to see in the Popover view — Train, Taxi, or Other.

Device constraints

Although there are a host of possibilities on the iPad, you also need to live within some constraints. This means that you not only have to take into account the user context when designing an application, but you also need to take into account the device context.

After all, the device is also a context for the user. He or she, based on individual experience, expects applications to behave in a certain way. As I explain in Chapter 1, this expectation provides another perspective on why staying consistent with the user interface guidelines is so important.

If you want to maximize the user experience, you have to take the following into account (I know I went through these in Chapter 1, but remembering them is critical):

- **Filling screen real estate:** On the iPhone, you may have had the problem of *too much* content. Although scrolling is built in to an iPhone and is relatively easy to do, folks don't particularly like to scroll on an iPhone, meaning you should require as little scrolling as possible, especially on navigation pages, and especially on the main page. On the iPad, the opposite situation *not enough* content — may end being a real challenge. You need to fill that big beautiful screen with rich, useful content. This means that many of the things you used on the iPhone to minimize screen displays works against you on the iPad. If you flip ahead to Figure 13-7 for example, you can see what happened when I tried to do a simple port of my app. There is no reason to devote all of this screen space to this view. I should fill it up with useful information for the user — other than what he or she can do next

- **Limitations of a touch-based interface:** Although the Multi-Touch interface is an iPhone feature, it brings with it limitations as well. Fingers aren't as precise as a mouse pointer, and user interface elements need to be large enough and spaced far enough apart so that the user's fingers can find their way around the interface comfortably. You also can do only so much with fingers. There are definitely fewer possibilities using fingers than when using the combination of multi-button mouse and keyboard. Even though the iPad does offer a "real" keyboard option, for most applications you'll want to take advantage of the touch-based interface.

✔ **Limited computer power, memory, and battery life:** As an application designer for the iPad, you have to keep practical issues like power and memory limitations in mind. Although the iPad definitely has more going for it in these matters than the iPhone, you still need to be realistic about what it has under the hood.

✔ **Connection limitations:** There's always a possibility that the user may be out of range, or on a plane, or has decided not to pay exorbitant roaming fees, or is using an iPad model that doesn't have Internet access except via Wi-Fi. You need to account for that possibility in your application and preserve as much functionality as possible. This usually means allowing the user to download and use the current real-time information, where applicable.

Coming up with a final design

After carefully thinking about all of the things I wanted the app to be able to do as well as meditating on the possibilities available to me on the iPad, the limitations of the device (and a few glasses of wine with my partners in crime), the final user interface I came up with looks like Figure 13-4.

In Figure 13-5, you can see the subset of features that I show you how to implement in Chapters 14 through 17. I choose this subset because it gives me the opportunity to show you the most how-to-do-that without it being overwhelming.

Part of making the app easy to use involves giving users a way to set their preferences for how the app should work. In Figure 13-6, you can see the iPadTravel411 Settings view. This setting allows the user to specify that he or she wants to work in a *stored data mode* — using previously stored data, rather than the current real-time version that would require Internet access. The idea is to download the information the user needs before he or she leaves the safe world of Wi-Fi. This is a requirement for iPad models without 3G, and a necessity for 3G models when the user is abroad and he or she wants to avoid data roaming charges and thus be able to afford food other than ramen noodles on the trip.

Figure 13-4:
The full
application.

Figure 13-5:
You user-
friendly
subset.

Figure 13-6:
Stored data
mode.

Creating the Program Architecture

After you've come up with a user interface capable of delivering the kind of the user experience you've defined, you need to map that onto a program architecture.

Keeping things at a basic level, you can think of the iPadTravel411 application architecture as being made up of the following:

✔ **Models:** Model objects encapsulate the logic and (data) content of the application. (You may remember that there was no model object in the app DeepThoughts from Part IV, per se.) For iPadTravel411, I show you how to design, implement, and use model objects.

✔ **Views:** Views present the user experience; you have to decide what information to display and how to display it. In the DeepThoughts application, there was a Content view and a Modal view with controls as subviews. Now, with the iPadTravel411 app, you're going to be working with a Navigation view and several Content views. You'll also want to add a toolbar (control) in one set of views to allow the user to specify which type of airport transportation he or she would like information about — train, taxi, or other.

✔ **Controllers:** (They're known as view controllers in the IPhone SDK.) Controllers manage the user experience. They connect the views that present the user experience with the models that provide the necessary content. In addition (as you'll see), controllers also manage the way the user navigates the application.

No big surprises here — especially because the MVC model (Model-View-Controller) is pretty much the basis for *all* iPad application development projects. The trick here is coming up with just the right views, controllers, and model objects to get your project off the ground. Within the requirements I spell out in the "Designing the User Experience" section earlier in the chapter, I came up with the elements highlighted in the next few sections.

I'm going to start with the views because they determine the functionality and information available in a given context — being at an airport and needing to get into the city, for example.

Views

Views offer the application's face to the world. They enable a user to

✔ See content.

✔ Navigate the application.

✔ Provide input into the application (both instructions and data) through controls.

Views can be categorized even further, as the next sections make clear.

Content views

Content views display the information the user wants — show me where I am on a map, or tell me the best way to get from Heathrow Airport to London.

Earlier in the chapter, the view in Figure 13-1, the view on the right side of Figure 13-2, and both views in Figure 13-3 are Content views, for example.

As I explain in Chapter 7, there are several kinds of views you can use on the iPad to display the various kinds of information you want to provide your users. In Chapters 14 through 17, I show you how to use the following view classes that come with the SDK:

- ✔ UIWebView
- ✔ MKMapView
- ✔ UIImageView

For now, I just want to highlight some of the main features of each view class.

UIWebView

UIWebView is especially good for displaying two specific kinds of content: text-based formatted data and Web content.

Highlighting text-based formatted data in this context may have come as a bit of a surprise, but Web views make it easy to access data from a central repository on the Internet. (Client-server is alive and well!) Because some of what I want to do needs to be updated regularly — if I want the current price and schedule of the Heathrow Express, for example, data from last year (or even last week) may not help me — being able to grab the most up-to-date information from the Web is a definite plus. I also want the most current information about what's happening in the city I plan to visit.

As for other benefits of Web views, keep in mind that real-time access isn't always necessary — sometimes it's perfectly fine to store some data on the iPad (and you will). It turns out that Web views can easily display formatted data that's locally stored — very handy. For example, the basics of foreign exchange are what they are — they're not going to change from today to tomorrow. That means the user doesn't need up-to-the-minute information on that particular topic.

The fact that UIWebView is great at displaying Web content should come as no surprise. If users want more information on the Heathrow Express, they can get to the Heathrow Express Web site by simply touching a link. Web views allow you manage the navigation out from your app, on to the Internet, back and forward in the history of Web pages, and then back to the originating view, without ever leaving the app.

MKMapView

MKMapView enables you to easily display maps similar to the one provided by the iPad's own Maps application. You use this class to display map information and to manipulate whatever gets displayed on the map from your application. You can center the map on a given coordinate, specify the size of the area you want to display, and annotate the map with custom information.

UIImageView

UIImageView allows you to display either a single image or animate a series of images. For animating the images, the UIImageView class provides controls to set the duration and frequency of the animation. You can also start and stop the animation freely.

In Chapter 9 you've already used an UIImage view in the DeepThoughts application. In iPadTravel411, you can use Image views in a number of ways — displaying pictures of what you're talking about comes to mind. In the case of the subset of the application that you develop in Chapter 14 through 17, you'll display a graphic image that allows the user to navigate the maze known as Heathrow Airport, as you can see in Figure 13-3.

It turns out that there's one more view that you can use to display content — UITableView. But because you will be primarily using it for navigation, I cover it in the following section.

Navigation views

Because of the screen real-estate on the iPhone, most applications were designed around a Main view (which was primarily navigation based) and additional views (which could be content or navigational or even both).

In the iPad, the need for a main Navigation view disappears and in fact having one would probably result in a pretty bad application interface. After all, who wants to see something like Figure 13-7 with all that dull and empty space when it would be so much nicer to fill some of that valuable space with some actual content?

On the other hand, offering some kind of navigation help, as shown earlier in Figure 13-2, can be useful to a user trying to make her way through your app. The help you see in Figure 13-2 is provided by UITableView.

An instance of UITableView (or simply, a Table view) is a means for displaying and editing hierarchical lists of information. As such, they're used a lot in iPad applications to do two specific things:

- **Display hierarchal data:** Think of the iPod application, which gives you a list of albums, and if you select one, a list of songs.

- **Act as a table of contents (or for my purposes, contexts):** Now think of the Settings application, which gives you a list of applications that you can set preferences for. When you select one of those applications from the list, it takes you to a view that lists what preferences you're able to set as well as a way to set them.

You find out all about Table views — and using them as well — in Chapter 16.

Controls, less than full-screen modal dialogs, action sheets, and alerts

Controls are things the user can manipulate in order to "tell" the application what he or she wants it to do. Controls are derived from UIControl. They can operate on the data or even provide navigations. You're already quite familiar with controls from the DeepThoughts app. The controls you see on the iPad — and the ones you used in the DeepThoughts application — are views as well, and as I explain in Chapter 7, are a subclass of `UIControl`.

In the design of the iPadTravel411 app, for example, you would use a control to allow a user to enter a dollar value and then display the amount in British pounds.

Although I won't be showing you that particular trick, I will be showing you how to use a `UISegmentedControl` to allow the user to choose the transportation information he or she wants to see in the Popover view — Train, Taxi, or Other. (You can see that segmented control in the Popover view back in Figure 13-3.) This particular control resides in a toolbar, which can also hold buttons, but the segmented control can actually be placed anywhere in a view.

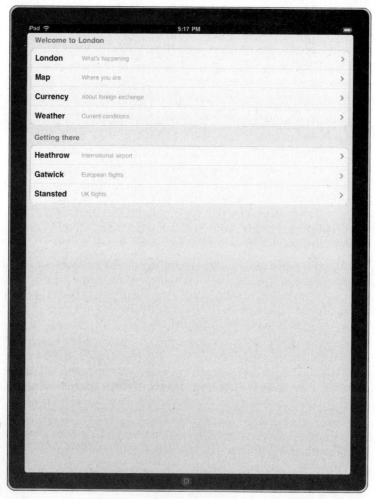

Figure 13-7:
Don't do
this!

Modal dialogs (those windows that display a dialog requiring the user to do something before they can get on with whatever they're doing in the app) are also views but what makes them special are their view controllers. Action sheets and alerts are also views and the same is true of them. I show you how to use an alert in Chapter 16, and action sheets are very similar.

View controllers

View controllers are responsible for not only providing the data for a view to display, but also for responding to user input and navigation requests.

They connect together the model, which owns the data, with the view that displays the data and receives user input. The view controllers you will use are all going to be derived from (a subclass of) `UIViewController`. You'll create custom view controllers to manage the data displayed in your Map view and Web views by sub classing `UIViewController`. These view controller subclasses will also implement delegate protocols as needed.

In addition, you'll be subclassing `UITableViewController` to manage the data displayed — take a look at the left side view in Figure 13-4 — as well as any user selection in a Table view, and create instances of `UISplitViewController` and `UIPopoverController` to manage the Split view you see in Figure 13-2 and the popover in Figure 13-3, respectively.

Models

Although you could write a book on model design (in fact, I've written a couple, not to mention an Apple video — but that's another story), I want to concentrate on a couple things now to keep you focused.

The *models* own the data and the application logic. In the iPadTravel411 application, for example, a model object would convert U.S. dollars to pounds (or any other currency) and vice versa. This kind of model is closely tied to the functionality of the view it supports. The How Many Zimbabwean Dollars Can I Get For $2.75 (US) view requires a model that can compute exchange rates, and here's where the real-world objects associated with object-oriented programming come into play. In the full-blown iPadTravel411 app, I have a Currency (model) object that knows how to compute exchange rates, and a VAT (value-added tax) object that does something similar. So for each view like those two, I create a model object.

You have a couple of options when it comes to creating the model objects needed by the view controllers. One way is to have the view controllers themselves create the ones they'll use. For example, the `AirportController` would create the `Airport` object, and so on.

Although this does work, and I've actually done that in past versions, I'd like you to consider a different approach that results in a more extensible program. This approach is based upon creating a single modal class that provides an interface to the view controllers, hiding from them any knowledge of how the model is constructed as well as which specific objects make up the model. (I explain this whole process in detail in *Objective-C For Dummies,* so if you're curious, you might want to pick up a copy of that book.)

One of the advantages of the MVC design pattern I explain in Chapter 2 is that it allows you to separate these three groups — the model, the view, the controller — in your application and work on them separately. If each group has a well-defined interface, it encapsulates many of the kinds of changes that are often made so that they don't affect the other groups. This is especially true of the model and view controller relationship.

If the view controllers have minimal knowledge about the model, you can change the model objects with minor impact on the view controllers.

As I said, what makes this possible is a well-defined interface. In Chapters 14 through 17 you create such a well-defined interface between the model and the controllers by using a technique called *composition,* which is a useful way to create interfaces.

Composition uses individual objects to carry out the roles and responsibilities declared in the model interface, so you don't need to have all of the functionality in one bloated object. But it makes things easy to change by hiding those objects from the other objects that really end up using them. I'm a big fan of composition because it's another way to hide what's really going on behind the curtain. It keeps the objects that use the composite object ignorant of the objects the composite object uses and actually makes the components ignorant of each other, allowing you to switch components in and out at will.

The Destination class is going to be the basis for such an architecture, and even though I don't fully implement it here, Chapters 14 through 17 should give you enough background so you can understand the structure and have no trouble extending it on your own.

When it comes to the various Content views you need for the iPadTravel411, some of them clearly have more complex data requirements than others. For example, when transportation data is needed, if the user is in a real-time mode (that is, not using stored data), the data is downloaded from a server and then stored in file on the device. When the Internet is unavailable or the user has specified stored data mode in preferences, the data that was previously saved in the file is used. In a complex case like this, Destination creates and uses a model object (in this case, Airport), encapsulating the knowledge of what objects make up the model from the object that use it. In less complex situations, the Destination object manages the data itself.

All the model objects are of a subclass NSObject, because NSObject provides the basic interface to the runtime system. It already has methods for allocation, initialization, memory management, introspection (what class am I?), encoding and decoding (which makes it quite easy to save objects as "objects"), message dispatch, and a host of other equally obscure methods that I don't get into but are required for objects to be able to behave like they're expected to behave in an iPhone OS/Objective-C world.

What I'm going to do in the iPadTravel411 application is actually have you create a model interface object and several model objects and view controllers to illustrate what you need to know about the model, view, and (view) controller relationship, how to access and display data stored locally or on a server, as well as how to simply display a Web site. That will be enough to keep you busy for a while.

Stored data mode, saving state, and localization

Using the application design I've described, adding all the features I mention in this section's little heading is easy; I explain them as I work through the implementation in Chapters 16 and 17. Although I don't dig too deeply into localization in this book, I show you how to build your application so that you can easily include that handy feature in your app.

Writing the Code

For me, writing the code is the fun part. I've been known to start working at 5 a.m. and quit at 2 a.m. the next morning because I was having so much fun. I help you have that kind of fun in Chapters 14 through17.

The iterative nature of the process

If there's one thing I can guarantee about development, it's that *nobody gets it right the first time.* Although object-oriented design and development are in themselves fun intellectual exercises (at least for some folks), they're also very valuable. An object-oriented program is relatively easier to modify and extend, not just during initial development, but also over time from version to version. (Actually, "initial development" and "version updating" are the same things; they differ only by a period of rest and vacation between them.)

The design of my iPadTravel411 application evolved over time, as I learned the capabilities and intricacies of the platform and the impact of my design decisions. What I've tried to do in this chapter, and the ones following, is to help you avoid (at least most of) the blind alleys I stumbled down while developing my first application. So get ready for a stumble-free experience. On to Chapters 14 through 17.

Chapter 14

Delighting the User at Application Launch

*Y*ou've heard me say it before, and I'll say it again: The iPad is about content. For an app bearing the name iPadTravel411, there's no better place to start dealing with content than with a map. In this chapter, I introduce you to MKMapView and have you create a UIViewController subclass (MapController) to manage the map display. In addition, you get to add the Destination model object to manage some of the data associated with the map as well as specify how you want the map displayed.

Content First

The iPad is about delivering content, and that's what you'll want your user to experience when he launches your app — *real* content, rather than some sort of screen that enables you to navigate the app that you'd normally get in a mobile device with a smaller screen.

Although this book doesn't go on and on about what *kind* of content you should be providing in your app, you should know that the SDK does make it really easy to deliver certain types of content — in this case, maps. In this chapter, I take you on a tour of MKMapKit and show you how to create really useful annotated maps that contain the information the user needs. (*Annotated* in this context means those cute pins in the map that display a callout to describe that location when you touch them.)

Because the goal of iPadTravel411 is to reduce the hassles involved with traveling, it should come as no surprise that one thing you can do right off the bat is present the users with a handy map that should be able to help them in whatever situation they're in. In Figure 14-1, you can see the iPad displaying a map that includes the airport (in this case, Heathrow) and the user's destination (London).

Including the ability to display a map in iPadTravel411 became important as people begin to realize the kinds of solutions that can be delivered on the iPad. To many travelers, nothing brands you more as a tourist than unfolding a large map (except of course looking through a thick guidebook). In this chapter, I show you how to take advantage of the iPad's built-in capability to display a map of virtually anywhere in the world, as well as determine your location and then indicate it in the map. As I mention earlier, its awareness of your location is one of the things that enables you to develop a totally new kind of application and really differentiate an iPad application from a desktop one.

Oh, and by the way, it turns out that working with maps is one of the most fun things you can do on the iPad because Apple makes it so easy. In fact, you can display a map that supports those great panning and zooming gestures you find on all the Big Boy apps by simply creating a view controller and a nib file. (You do that soon.)

In this chapter, you do much more than that, though. I show you how to center your map on an area you want to display (Heathrow airport or London, for example, or both), add annotations (and even show the user's current location.

My running example here will be the iPadTravel411 application described in Chapter 13. Space prohibits dotting every *i* and crossing every *t* in implementing the application, but I can show you how to use the technology you're going to need to do the detailed work on your own. And even though I don't have the complete listings in this book, the listings are available on my Web site — www.nealgoldstein.com.

Your users (and Apple) will insist that they be able to use the iPad in any orientation. Later I show you how to make sure both Heathrow Airport and London are both visible on the map no mater what orientation the user chooses.

Figure 14-1:
Where's
Waldo?

Ladies and Gentlemen, Start Your Engines

To begin, just as you did in the DeepThoughts application in Part IV, you
need to create an Xcode project. With that in mind, fire up Xcode and
officially launch the iPadTravel411 project. (If you need a refresher on how
to set up a project in Xcode, take another look at Chapter 4.) As Figure 14-2
shows, you need to go with a View-based Application template and then save
the project as iPadTravel411 in a folder. (I have it on my desktop.) Be sure to
choose iPad in the Product drop-down menu.

It's also better at this point not to do anything with the `iPhoneTravel 411ViewController` file (like open it) — you'll see why in a moment.

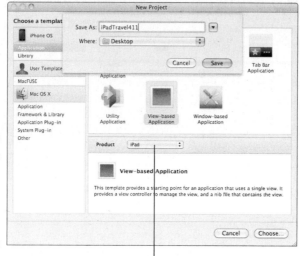

Figure 14-2:
The
Navigation-
based
Application
template.

Be sure to select iPad here.

One thing left to do; you have to add a new framework.

Up until now, all you've needed is the framework that more or less came supplied when you created a project — the `UIKit` framework you've been working with since Chapter 4. But now you need a new framework to enable the Map view.

1. **With your project open in Xcode, click the disclosure triangle next to Targets in the Groups & Files list and then right-click iPadTravel411.**

   Be sure to do this using the Targets folder, or Step 3 won't work!

2. **From the submenu that appears, choose Add and then choose Existing Frameworks as I have in Figure 14-3.**

3. **Select `MapKit.framework` from the window that appears, click Add, as shown in Figure 14-4, and then drag the newly added `MapKit. framework` (you'll find it just above the Targets group) into the Frameworks folder.**

Yea! You're done with all the tedium! Now you can get on to the more interesting stuff.

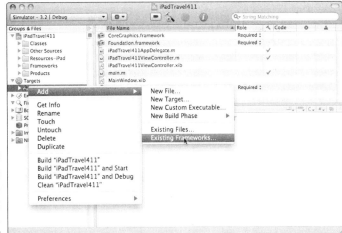

Figure 14-3:
Select an existing Framework.

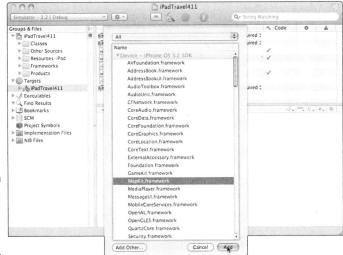

Figure 14-4:
Adding the MapKit. Framework.

Changing the name to protect the innocent

While Xcode creates a Main view controller for you in the template you've just chosen, your application is going to be a bit more sophisticated that that. More specifically, the controller you'll use to work with the map will be only one of a number of view controllers, so I'm going to have you rename it to something more representative of its role.

To do that, you'll take advantage of an Xcode feature called *Refactor*. This guy does your work for you by changing the name of your class in all the places it occurs — well, almost all.

1. **Click the disclosure triangle next to Classes in the Groups & Files list, then click the `iPadTravel411ViewController.m` file so it's displayed in the editor, and then (finally) double-click `iPadTravel 411ViewController.`to select it.**

   You end up with what you can see in Figure 14-5.

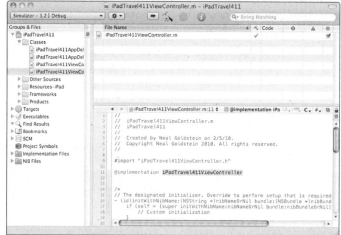

Figure 14-5:
Select iPad
Travel411
View
Controller
in iPad
Travel411
View
Controller.m.

2. **With `iPadTravel411ViewController.m` selected, choose Edit⇨ Refactor from the Xcode main menu.**

   The Refactoring window appears onscreen.

3. **Enter MapController into the text field in the top-right of the window, as I've done in Figure 14-6, and then select Preview (leave the check boxes the way they are).**

   You should see what I see in Figure 14-7.

4. **Click the Apply button.**

   All references to `iPadTravel411ViewController` (except one) are replaced with `MapController`.

5. **Click the disclosure triangle next to Resources – iPad in the Groups & Files list.**

Doing so reveals the `iPadTravel411ViewController.xib`. This one is the holdout, stubbornly refusing to change its name to `MapController`. You have to change by renaming it — as spelled out in the next step.

6. **Right-click `iPadTravel411ViewController.xib` and choose Rename. Then type in** MapController.xib **and then hit return.**

7. **Save all the files and you'll be ready to get to work.**

Figure: 14-6:
Refactor
your class.

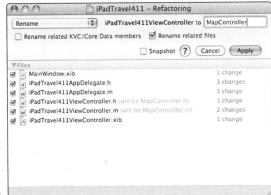

Figure 14-7:
Click Apply.

Please, please, please do this refactoring business exactly this way. If you don't, you may find that not all the references you wanted to change were in fact changed. If that happens, you'll need to do a global search (⌘+Shift+F) for `iPadTravel411ViewController` and change each instance to `MapController`.

Setting up the nib file

For the iPadTravel411 application, you'll use a `MKMapView` to display the information you think your users will need. You'll set the `MKMapView` up using Interface Builder, but you'll also need a reference to it from the `MapController` so you'll be able to tell the map what you want displayed and how you want to display it.

To do that, you need to create an *outlet* (a special kind of instance variable that can refer to objects in the nib) in the view controller, just as you did back in Chapter 9 when you were working on the DeepThoughts application. The outlet reference will be filled in automatically — based on all those connections you made in Interface Builder — when your application is initialized.

1. **Within Xcode, add a `mapView` (`MKMapView`) outlet to the `MapController.h` interface file.**

   You declare an outlet by using the keyword `IBOutlet` in the `MapController` interface file.

   ```
   IBOutlet MKMapView    *mapView;
   ```

2. **Even though you just added the `MapKit` framework, you still have to tell `MapController` to actually *use* it. To do that, add the following to `MapController.h`:**

   ```
   #import <MapKit/MapKit.h>
   ```

3. **While your cursor is still in the `MapController.h` window, be sure to save your `MapController.h` file by choosing File⇨Save or pressing ⌘+S.**

4. **Use the Groups & Files list on the left in the Project window to drill down to the `MapController.xib` file; then double-click the file to launch it in Interface Builder.**

   If the Attributes Inspector window is not open, choose Tools⇨Inspector or press ⌘+Shift +I. If the View window isn't visible, double-click the View icon in the `MapController` window.

   If you can't find the `MapController.xib` window (you may have minimized it — accidentally, on purpose, whatever) you can get it back by choosing Window⇨MapController.xib or whichever nib file you're working on.

5. **Click in the View window and then choose `MKMapView` from the Class drop-down menu in the Identity Inspector.**

Doing so changes the title of the View window to Map View in the `MapController` window as well as in the View window proper the next time you open it.

6. **Back in the `MapController.xib` window, right-click File's Owner to call up a contextual menu with a list of connections.**

   You can get the same list using the Connections tab in the Attributes Inspector.

7. **Drag from the little circle next to the `mapView` outlet in the list onto the Map View window.**

   Doing so connects the `MapController`'s `mapView` outlet to the Map view.

   When you're done, the File's Owner contextual menu should look like what you see in Figure 14-8.

Figure 14-8:
The Map
Controller
connections
are all in
place.

You're not done with Interface Builder yet, though. Because you changed the name of `iPadTravel411ViewController`, you're going to have to change the way Interface Builder sets up its initial load. Although this may seem like a lot of unnecessary work (maybe you're saying "forget this name business and let's get on with it"), I want to show you this because it's usually one of the more difficult things for beginning programmers to figure out - essentially, how do all these nib files work together and how do you change the template if you want to do something a little different. Although this isn't something you may do often, when you need to do it, you need to do it.

With that explanation out of the way, it's time to tweak the `MapController` initial load.

1. **Use the Groups & Files list on the left in the Project window to drill back down to the `MainWindow.xib file`; then double-click the file to launch it in Interface Builder.**

2. **Click `MapController` in the `MainWindow.xib` window.**

   If the Map Controller Attributes Inspector window is not open, choose Tools⇨Inspector or press ⌘+Shift +I.

3. **In the Map Controller Attributes window, select MapController from the Nib Name drop-down menu, as shown in Figure 14-9.**

4. **Be sure to save your file by choosing File⇨Save or pressing ⌘+S.**

Figure 14-9:
Changing
the Main
Window
nib file.

Now compile your project. Be sure to select the Simulator in the editor. What you'll see is what you get in Figure 14-10 — a real, honest-to-goodness map that supports the standard panning and zooming gestures. You really didn't have to do much to get it (after you got past the renaming, that is).

Figure 14-10:
The easy
part of
displaying
a map.

Using MapKit

One of the great features of iPhone 3.2 SDK and beyond is the MapKit framework. It enables you to bring up a simple map as well as actually *do* things with your map without having to do much work at all.

The map looks just like the maps in the fancy built-in applications and creates a seamless mapping experience across multiple applications.

The essence of mapping on the iPad is the `MKMapView`. It's a subclass of `UIView`, and you can use it out of the box to create a map, just like you did in the previous section. You use this class as-is to display map information and to manipulate the map contents from your application. It enables you to center the map on a given coordinate, specify the size of the area you want to display, and annotate the map with custom information.

When you initialize a Map view, you can specify the initial region for that map to display. You do this by setting the *region* property of the map. A region is defined by a center point and a horizontal and vertical distance, referred to as the *span*. The span defines how much of the map will be visible and results in a zoom level. The smaller the span, the greater the zoom.

The Map view supports the standard map gestures.

- ✔ Scroll
- ✔ Pinch zoom
- ✔ Double-tap zoom in
- ✔ Two-finger–tap zoom out (You might not even know about that one.)

You can also specify the map type — regular, satellite, or hybrid — by changing a single property. In Chapter 13, all of the Map views are in regular mode (the default). In Figure 14-11, you can see the hybrid mode. For many applications, one mode may work better than the other; in iPadTarvel411, my sense is that the regular view works better for the user in most situations, so I use that. Feel free to use the type that suits you (and your users) the best.

What you could — and should — do is provide a control for the users to specify which type they'd actually want. Although in the full-blown iPadTravel411 app I do that, I leave that for you to do on your own here. The line of code (you can put it anywhere in `viewDidLoad` in `MapController.m`) that would specify a hybrid map is

```
mapView.mapType = MKMapTypeHybrid;
```

Because `MapKit` was written from scratch, it was developed with the limitations of the iPhone in mind. As a result, it optimizes performance on the iPhone by caching data as well as managing memory and seamlessly handling connectivity changes (like moving from 3G to Wi-Fi, for example).

The map data itself is Google-hosted map data, and network connectivity is required. And because the `MapKit` framework uses Google services to provide map data, using it binds you to the Google Maps/Google Earth API terms of service.

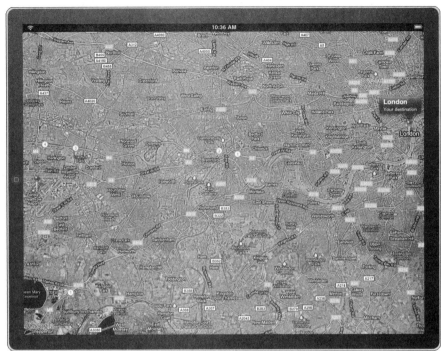

Figure 14-11:
Hybrid
mode.

Although you should not subclass the MKMapView class itself, you can tailor a Map view's behavior by providing a delegate object — which can be any object in your application as long as it conforms to the MKMapViewDelegate protocol. While you will not be using any of the delegate methods in this application (you'll need them when you start creating your own Annotation views and managing the user interactions with those views) they allow you to receive map-related update messages.

Adding the Destination Model

Before you go any further, you need to add the Destination model I mention back in Chapter 13 — it is the main interface for the view controllers into the model.

It would be a good idea to add a new folder in the Groups & Files list to hold all your new model classes. (Don't worry; you really have only a couple more to deal with.) To do so, select the iPadTravel411 project icon and then choose Project⇨New Group. You get a brand-spanking-new folder named New Group added to the Groups & Files list, already selected and waiting for you to type in the name you want. To change what folder a file is in, select it and then drag the file to the folder you want it to occupy. The same goes for folders as well. (After all, they can go into other folders.)

To add a `Destination` model, do the following:

1. **Select File⇨New File from the main menu (or press ⌘+N) to get the New File dialog.**

2. **In the leftmost column of the dialog, first select Cocoa Touch Classes under the iPhone OS heading and then select the *Objective-C class* template in the topmost pane — making sure that `NSObject` is selected in the Subclass drop-down menu. Then click Next.**

   You see a new dialog asking for some more information.

3. **Enter Destination.m in the File Name field and then click Finish.**

As I said, I'm a big fan of *composition* and the `Destination` class will own the relationship between the view controllers and the model. To do that, though, you need to create a `Destination` *object* someplace, and the logical candidate, since its there at launch time, is the `iPadTravel411App Delegate`.

To do that, add the code in bold in Listing 14-1 to `iPadTravel411AppDelegate.m`.

Listing 14-1:   Modifying didFinishLaunchingWithOptions:

```
#import "iPadTravel411AppDelegate.h"
#import "MapController.h"
#import "Destination.h";

@implementation iPadTravel411AppDelegate

@synthesize window;
@synthesize viewController;


- (BOOL)application:(UIApplication *)
          application didFinishLaunchingWithOptions:
                         (NSDictionary *)launchOptions {

  destination = [[Destination alloc]
                             initWithName:@"England"];
  viewController =
    [[MapController alloc] initWithDestination:destination];

  [window addSubview:viewController.view];
  [window makeKeyAndVisible];
   return YES;
}
```

What you've done in Listing 14-1 is create the `Destination` object. The `MapController` will use that object to get the information it needs — the initial coordinates for the map, for example, as well as the annotations that should be displayed.

```
destination =
            [[Destination alloc] initWithName:@"England"];
```

The next thing you do is create the `MapController` explicitly, rather than having the nib loader so it. You're doing this so you can initialize the `MapController` with the `Destination` object you just created.

```
viewController =
    [[MapController alloc] initWithDestination:destination];
```

To make sure the accessors are created for you by the compiler for the property that property you're going to create in just a sec — you also have to add a `synthesize` statement to `iPadTravel411AppDelegate.m`.

```
@synthesize destination;
```

To make `destination` a property, add the code in bold in Listing 14-2 to `iPadTravel411AppDelegate.h`.

Listing 14-2:   Add destination as a Property to iPadTravel411AppDelegate.h

```
#import <UIKit/UIKit.h>

@class MapController;
@class Destination;

@interface iPadTravel411AppDelegate : NSObject
        <UIApplicationDelegate> {

  UIWindow *window;
  MapController *viewController;
  Destination    * destination;
}
@property (nonatomic, retain) IBOutlet UIWindow
          window;
@property (nonatomic, retain) IBOutlet MapController
          *viewController;
@property (nonatomic, retain) Destination    *destination;
@end
```

The next step is to add the new initialization method and pass the `Destination` object to the `MapController`. Add the code in bold in Listing 14-3 to `MapController.h` and the code in bold in Listing 14-4 to `MapController.m`.

Before you do that, though, there is one other thing I want to point out.

If you have a couple app development projects under your belt by this time, you may have become used to using a method called `applicationDidFinish Launching:`. You'll notice here that you're using `application:didFinish LaunchingWithOptions:`. The difference between the two is that the later includes an additional argument, which is an `NSDictionary`. This method is used when the application has launched due to a remote notification or the opening of a URL resource — situations that are beyond the scope of this book. I still recommended, though, that you go ahead and use `application: didFinishLaunchingWithOptions:`. When the application is launched "normally" (by the user touching the app icon on the main screen), the two methods are virtually the same.

By now, you probably understand that

1. If you add a new method, you need to add the declaration to the header (or `.h`) file

2. If you add a reference to a new class in a header (or `.h`) file, you have to add a corresponding `@class` statement.

3. If you add a reference to a new class in the implementation (or `.m`) file, you have to add a corresponding `#import` statement.

So I don't always tell you to do all that (but I remind you once in a while).

Listing 14-3:   Adding Destination and the initWithDestination: Method to MapController.h

```
#import <UIKit/UIKit.h>
#import <MapKit/MapKit.h>

@class Destination;

@interface MapController : UIViewController {

  IBOutlet MKMapView    *mapView;
  Destination           *destination;
}
- (id) initWithDestination: (Destination*) aDestination;

@end
```

Listing 14-4: Adding the InitWithDestination: Method

```
#import "MapController.h"

#import "Destination.h"

@implementation MapController

- (id) initWithDestination: (Destination*) aDestination {
  if (self =
    [super initWithNibName:@"MapController" bundle:nil]) {
    destination = aDestination;
  }
  return self;
}
```

The first thing this method does is invoke its superclass's initialization
method.

```
if (self =
    [super initWithNibName:@"MapController" bundle:nil]) {
```

You pass it the nib filename (the one you just created in a previous section)
and `nil` as the bundle, telling it to look in the main bundle for the information it needs.

Note that the message to `super` precedes the initialization code added in the
method. This sequencing ensures that initialization proceeds in the order of
inheritance. Calling the superclass's `initWithNibName:bundle:` method
initializes the controller, loads and initializes the objects in the nib file (views
and controls, for example), and then sets all its outlet instance variables and
Target-Action connections for good measure.

The `init…:` methods all return a pointer to the object created. Although not
the case here, the reason you assign whatever comes back from an `init…:`
method to `self` is that some classes actually return a different class than
what you created. The assignment to `self` becomes important if your class
is derived from one of those kinds of classes. Keep in mind as well that an
`init…:` method can also return `nil` if there's a problem initializing an object.
If you're creating an object where that's a possibility, you have to take that
into account. (Both of those situations are beyond the scope of this book.)

After the superclass initialization is completed, the `MapController` is ready
to do its own initialization, including saving the `aDestination` argument to
the `destination` instance variable.

I get to the `Destination` class in the "It's about the region" section, later in
the chapter.

Enhancing the Map

Having this nice global map centered on the United States is kind of interesting, but not very useful if you're planning to go to London. The following sections look at what you would have to do to make the map more useful as well as how to center the map on Heathrow and London.

Adding landscape mode and the current location

I've said it before and I'll say it again: An iPad app has to be able to work effectively in any orientation. It turns out, though, that when it comes to the MKMapView, it's already done for you. If you go back to Xcode, you'll see the following method is part of MapController.m:

```
- (BOOL)shouldAutorotateToInterfaceOrientation:
            (UIInterfaceOrientation)toInterfaceOrientation {

  return YES;
}
```

That's all it takes.

What about showing your location on the map? That's just as easy! You'll add some code to a method called viewDidLoad.

This method was included for you in MapController.m by the UIViewController subclass template (albeit, commented out) you chose in the "Ladies and Gentlemen, Start Your Engines" section, earlier in the chapter. Here's the code that was automatically added:

```
/*
// Implement viewDidLoad to do additional setup after
          loading the view, typically from a nib.
- void)viewDidLoad {
  [super viewDidLoad];
}
*/
```

Simply uncomment out this method and then add the code after [super viewDidLoad] in Listing 14-5:

Listing 14-5:   viewDidLoad

```
- (void)viewDidLoad {
  [super viewDidLoad];

  mapView.showsUserLocation = YES;
}
```

showsUserLocation is a MKMapView property that tells the Map view whether to show the user location. If YES, you get the same blue pulsing dot showing user location you see displayed in the built-in Map application.

If you were to compile and run the application as it stands (which you actually can't yet because you haven't added the Destination class method init WithName:), you'd get a map of the USA with a blue dot that represents the iPad's current location. (There may be a lag until the iPad is able to determine that location, but you should see it eventually.) You can see that in Figure 14-12.

 That's the current location *if you're running the app on the iPad.* If you're running the app in on the Simulator, that location is Apple's home base of Cupertino, CA. Touching the blue dot also displays a nice little annotation. You'll find out how to customize the text to display whatever you cleverly come up with — including as you'll see, the address of the current location — in the later section "Annotations."

It's about the region

Pulsing blue dots and little red annotation pins are cute but still not useful enough for the purposes of the app.

As I mention at the beginning of this chapter, ideally when you land at Heathrow (or wherever), you should see a map that centers on Heathrow as opposed to the United States. To get there from here, however, is also pretty easy.

First look at how you center the map.

```
- (void)updateRegionLatitude:(float) latitude
          longitude:(float) longitude
          latitudeDelta:(float) latitudeDelta
                    longitudeDelta:(float) longitudeDelta {

  MKCoordinateRegion region;
  region.center.latitude = latitude;
  region.center.longitude = longitude;
  region.span.latitudeDelta = latitudeDelta;
  region.span.longitudeDelta = longitudeDelta;
  [mapView setRegion:region animated:NO];
}
```

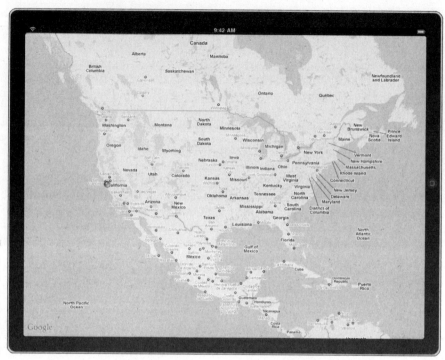

Figure 14-12:
Displaying a map in land-scape mode with a user location.

Start by adding the above code to `MapController.m` and its declaration to `MapController.h`.

Setting the *region* is how you center the map and set the zoom level. All of this accomplished by the statement

```
[mapView setRegion:region animated:NO];
```

A region is a Map view property that specifies four things (as illustrated in Figure 14-13).

1. `region.center.latitude` specifies the latitude of the center of the map.

2. `region.center.longitude` specifies the longitude of the center of the map.

    For example, if I were to set those values as

    ```
    region.center.latitude = 51.471184;
    region.center.longitude = -0.452542;
    ```

    the center of the map would be at Heathrow airport.

3. `region.span.latitudeDelta` specifies the north-to-south distance (in degrees) to display on the map. One degree of latitude is always approximately 111 kilometers (69 miles). A `region.span.latitudeDelta` of

0.0036 would specify a north-to-south distance on the map of about a quarter of a mile. Latitudes north of the equator have positive values, and latitudes south of the equator have negative values.

4. `region.span.longitudeDelta` specifies the east-to-west distance (in degrees) to display on the map. Unfortunately, the number of miles in one degree of longitude varies based on the latitude. For example, one degree of longitude is approximately 69 miles at the equator but shrinks to 0 miles at the poles. Longitudes east of the zero meridian (by international convention, the zero or Prime Meridian passes through the Royal Observatory, Greenwich, in east London) have positive values, and longitudes west of the zero meridian have negative values.

Although the span values provide an implicit zoom value for the map, the actual region you see displayed may not equal the span you specify because the map will go to the zoom level that best fits the region that is set. This also means that even if you just change the center coordinate in the map, the zoom level may change because distances represented by a span change at different latitudes and longitudes. To account for that, those smart developers at Apple included a property you can set that will change the center coordinate without changing the zoom level.

```
@property (nonatomic) CLLocationCoordinate2D
            centerCoordinate
```

When you change this property, the map is centered on the new coordinate and updates span values to maintain the current zoom level.

That `CLLocationCoordinate2D` type is something you'll be using a lot, so I'd like to explain that before I take you any further.

`CLLocationCoordinate2D` type is a structure that contains a geographical coordinate using the WGS 84 reference frame (the reference coordinate system used by the Global Positioning System).

```
typedef struct {
CLLocationDegrees latitude;
CLLocationDegrees longitude;
} CLLocationCoordinate2D;
```

✔ `latitude` is the latitude in degrees. This is the value you set in the code you just entered (`region.center.latitude = latitude;`).

✔ `longitude` is the longitude in degrees. This is the value you set in the code you just entered (`region.center.longitude = longitude;`).

To center the map display on Heathrow, you send the `updateRegion Latitude:longitude: latitudeDelta:longitudeDelta` message (the code you just entered) when the view is loaded, that is, in the `viewDidLoad:` method. You already added some code there to display the current location, so add the following code in bold:

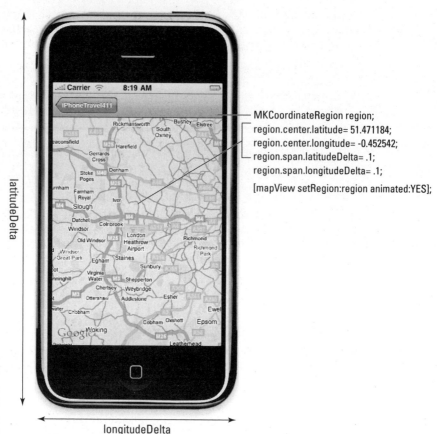

MKCoordinateRegion region;
region.center.latitude= 51.471184;
region.center.longitude= -0.452542;
region.span.latitudeDelta= .1;
region.span.longitudeDelta= .1;

[mapView setRegion:region animated:YES];

latitudeDelta

Figure 14-13:
How regions
work.

longitudeDelta

```
-  (void)viewDidLoad {

   [super viewDidLoad];
   mapView.showsUserLocation = YES;
   CLLocationCoordinate2D initialCoordinate =
                           [destination initialCoordinate];
   [self updateRegionLatitude: initialCoordinate.latitude
         longitude: initialCoordinate.longitude
                           latitudeDelta:.1 longitudeDelta:.1];
   self.title = [destination mapTitle];
}
```

Take a look at what this code does:

1. The `initialCoordinate` message is sent to the `Destination` object to get the initial coordinates you want displayed. You're adding some additional functionality to the model, whose responsibility now includes

specifying that location. The user may have requested that location when he or she set up the trip (I don't cover that topic in this book, leaving it as an exercise for you to do), or it may have been a default location that you decided on when you wrote the code (an airport specified in the destination, for example).

2. The map title is set by sending the `mapTitle` message to the `Destination` object — adding another model responsibility.

For all of this to work of course, you have to add some code to the `Destination` class.

Start by adding the initialization method to `Destination.m`.

```
- (id) initWithName: (NSString*) theDestination {

  if ((self = [super init])) {
    destinationName = theDestination;
  }
  return self;
}
```

This is a standard way to initialize objects and includes saving a reference to the destination name.

Next add the `initialCoordinate` method to `Destination.m`.

```
- (CLLocationCoordinate2D) initialCoordinate {

  CLLocationCoordinate2D startCoordinate;
  startCoordinate.latitude=51.471184;
  startCoordinate.longitude=-0.452542;
  return startCoordinate;
}
- (NSString*) mapTitle{

  return @" map";
}
```

You have to include the `MapKit` in `Destination`, so add the following to `Destination.h`:

```
#import <MapKit/MapKit.h>
```

When you're done, the `Destination.h` file should look like Listing 14-6.

Tracking location changes

You can also track changes in user location by using *key-value observing*. This will enable you to move the map as the user changes location. I don't go into detail on key-value observing other than to show you the code.

First, you add the code in bold to `viewDidLoad:` in `MapController.m` to add an observer that's to be called when a certain value is changed — in this case `userLocation`.

```
- (void)viewDidLoad {
  [super viewDidLoad];
  mapView.showsUserLocation = YES;
  CLLocationCoordinate2D initialCoordinate =
                                          [map
   initialCoordinate];
  [self updateRegionLatitude: initialCoordinate.latitude
   longitude:
            initialCoordinate.longitude
            latitudeDelta:.2 longitudeDelta:.2];

  self.title = [destination mapTitle];
  [mapView.userLocation addObserver:self
   forKeyPath:@"location"
                                        options:0
   context:NULL];
}
```

Adding that code causes the `observeValueForKeyPath::` message to be sent to the observer (self or the `MapController`). To implement the method in `MapController.m`, enter the following:

```
- (void)observeValueForKeyPath:(NSString *) keyPath
            ofObject:(id)object change:(NSDictionary *) change
            context:(void *) context {

  NSLog (@"Location changed");
}
```

In this method, the `keyPath` field returns `mapView.userLocation.location`, which you can use to get the current location. In this example, I am simply displaying a message on the Debugger Console, but as I said, once the user moves a certain amount, you may want to re-center the map.

Technical Stuff: This isn't exactly the same location you'd get from `CLLocationManager` — it's optimized for the map, while `CLLocationManager` provides the raw user location.

Of course, you have to run this on the iPad for the location to change.

Listing 14-6:   Destination.h

```
#import <Foundation/Foundation.h>
#import <MapKit/MapKit.h>
```

```
@interface Destination : NSObject {

  NSString   *destinationName;
}
- (id) initWithName: (NSString*) theDestination;
- (CLLocationCoordinate2D)initialCoordinate;
- (NSString*)mapTitle;

@end
```

If you compile and build your project (you should also add the method declaration to MapController.h), you should see what's shown in Figure 14-14.

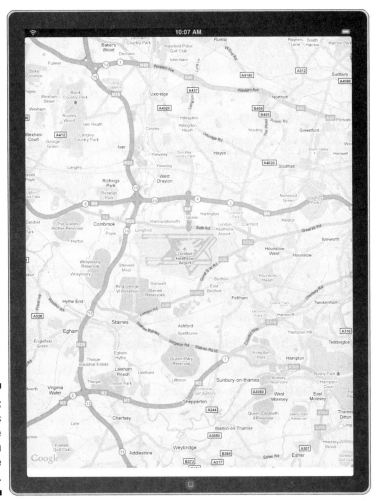

Figure 14-14:
Regions
determine
what you
see on the
map.

Although this is better, I'd rather be able to see both the airport (Heathrow) and my destination (London) at the same time. Although I could pinch to reduce the map, I show you in the section "Displaying both annotations" how to ensure that two (or more) locations are visible at the initial launch.

At this point, when the user touches Map in the Main view, iPadTravel411 displays a map centered on Heathrow, and if you pan over (a tedious task you'll fix soon) to Cupertino (or wherever you are), you can see the blue dot.

If you tap the dot, as shown back in Figure 14-12, you see a callout known as an *annotation* displaying the message Current Location. You can also add annotations on your own, which is what you'll do in the next section.

Annotations

The MKMapView class supports the ability to annotate the map with custom information. There are two parts to the annotation, the annotation itself, which contains the data for the annotation, and the Annotation view that displays the data.

Understanding annotations

An annotation acts as a model for the Map view, with a view controller connecting the two.

Annotation objects are any objects that conform to the MKAnnotation protocol and are typically existing classes in your application's model. The job of an annotation object is to know its location (coordinate) on the map along with the text to be displayed in the callout. The MKAnnotation protocol requires a class that adopts that protocol to implement the coordinate property. In this case, it will make sense for the Airport and City model objects that you will use in Chapter 17 to add the responsibilities of an annotation object to their bag of tricks. After all, the Airport and City model objects already know what airport or city they represent, respectively. It makes sense for these objects to have the coordinate and callout data as well.

In this case however, those classes are just a glimmer in your eye, so I show you how to create a class that does nothing but act as an annotation. Then when you create the Airport and City classes, you can just incorporate the code you have written here in those classes.

Here's what you need to do to make that happen:

Adding an MapAnnotation class

To start, you need to create a MapAnnotation class.

1. **Choose File⇨New File from the main menu (or press ⌘+N) to get the New File dialog.**

2. **In the leftmost column of the dialog, first select Cocoa Touch Classes under the iPhone OS heading and then select the *Objective-C class* template in the topmost pane, making sure that NSObject is selected in the Subclass drop-down menu. Then click Next.**

   You see a new dialog asking for some more information.

3. **Enter** MapAnnotation **in the File Name field and then click Finish.**

This class will be adopting the MKAnnotation protocol. There are three elements to this protocol:

1. A required property coordinate

2. An optional title method

3. An optional subtitle method

As you can see in Listing 14-7, the MapAnnotation header file shows that MapAnnotation includes both the required property and optional methods. Add the code in bold to MapAnnotation.h.

Listing 14-7: MapAnnotation.h

```
#import <Foundation/Foundation.h>
#import <MapKit/MapKit.h>

@interface MapAnnotation : NSObject <MKAnnotation> {

  CLLocationCoordinate2D coordinate;
  NSString *annotationTitle;
  NSString *annotationSubTitle;
}
@property (nonatomic) CLLocationCoordinate2D coordinate;
- (id) initWithTitle:(NSString*) title
          subTitle:(NSString*) subTitle
          coordinate:(CLLocationCoordinate2D) aCoordinate;

@end
```

Implementing these methods is similarly straightforward. Add the code in bold in Listing 14-8 to MapAnnotation.m.

Listing 14-8: Implementing Annotations

```
#import "MapAnnotation.h"

@implementation MapAnnotation
@synthesize coordinate;

- (id) initWithTitle: (NSString*) title
        subTitle:(NSString*) subtitle
        coordinate:(CLLocationCoordinate2D) aCoordinate {

  if ((self = [super init])) {
    coordinate = aCoordinate;
    annotationTitle = title;
    [annotationTitle retain];
    annotationSubTitle = subtitle;
    [annotationSubTitle retain];
  }
  return self;
}

-(NSString*) title {

  return annotationTitle;
}

-(NSString*) subtitle {

  return annotationSubTitle;
}

@end
```

When you create a `MapAnnotation` object, you initialize it with a title, sub-title, and coordinate. As you'll see, you'll pass the annotation objects to the Map view and, when it needs to, it uses each annotation's `location` property to place a pin on the map. If a user selects an annotation, the Map view sends the `title` and `subtitle` messages to the `MapAnnotation` objects, and displays the results in the annotation callout.

As you can see, `MapAnnotation` assigns the latitude and longitude it was passed to the `coordinate` property, which will be used by the Map view to position the annotation.

So how do the `MapAnnotation` objects get to the Map view, and even more importantly, where do the `coordinate`, `title`, and `subtitle` values come from?

You start by giving the `Destination` object the responsibility of creating these annotations by adding the code in Listing 14-9 to `Destination.m`.

Listing 14-9:   Creating the MapAnnotation Objects

```
- (NSMutableArray*) createAnnotations {

  CLLocationCoordinate2D theCoordinate;
  theCoordinate.latitude = 51.471184;
  theCoordinate.longitude = -0.452542;
  MapAnnotation* sampleAnnotation =
      [[MapAnnotation alloc] initWithTitle: @"Heathrow"
        subTitle: @"International Airport"
                               coordinate: theCoordinate];
  NSMutableArray* mapAnnotations =
  [[NSMutableArray alloc] initWithCapacity:1];
  [mapAnnotations addObject:sampleAnnotation];
  [sampleAnnotation release];
  theCoordinate.latitude = 51.500153;
  theCoordinate.longitude= -0.126236;
  sampleAnnotation = [[MapAnnotation  alloc]
          initWithTitle: @"London"
          subTitle: @"Your destination" coordinate:
          theCoordinate];
  [mapAnnotations addObject:sampleAnnotation];
  [sampleAnnotation release];
  return mapAnnotations;
}
```

So far, so good. You have two MapAnnotation objects that have been
arbitrarily created with the title, subtitle, and coordinates of Heathrow and
London. Normally you would get these values from something like a file or
database, or even via user input, but that's outside of the scope of this book.

The only thing left to do is to put them in an array and send the array to the
Map view to get the annotations displayed.

Don't forget to add the #import "MapAnnotation.h" to Destination.m
as well as - (NSMutableArray*) createAnnotations; to
Destination.h.

Displaying the annotations

Displaying the annotations is easy. All you have to do is add the line of code
in bold to viewDidLoad in MapController.m.

```
- (void)viewDidLoad {

  [super viewDidLoad];
  mapView.showsUserLocation = YES;
  CLLocationCoordinate2D initialCoordinate =
```

```
    [destination initialCoordinate];
    [self updateRegionLatitude: initialCoordinate.latitude
            longitude: initialCoordinate.longitude
                latitudeDelta:.1 longitudeDelta:.1];
    self.title = [destination mapTitle];
    [mapView.userLocation addObserver:self
            forKeyPath:@"location" options:0 context:NULL];
    [mapView addAnnotations:
                        [destination createAnnotations]];
}
```

The MapController sends the addAnnotations: message to the Map view, passing it an array of objects that conform to the MKAnnotation protocol; that is, each one has a coordinate property and an optional title (and subtitle) method if you want to display something in the annotation callout.

The Map view places annotations on the screen by sending its delegate (in this case, the MapController) the mapView:viewForAnnotation: message. This message is sent for each annotation object in the array. Here you can create a custom view, or return nil to use the default view. (If you don't implement this delegate method — which you won't for the iPadTravel411 app — the default view is also used.)

Creating your own Annotation views is beyond the scope of this book (although I will tell you that the most efficient way to provide the content for an Annotation view is to set its image property). Fortunately, the default Annotation view is fine for your purposes. It displays a pin in the location specified in the coordinate property of the annotation delegate (City and Airport, in this case), and when the user touches the pin, the optional title and subtitle text will display if the title and subtitle methods are implemented in the selfsame annotation delegate.

You can also add callouts to the annotation callout, such as a Detail Disclosure button (the one that looks like a white chevron in a blue button in a Table View cell), or the info button (like the one you see in many of the utility apps) without creating your own Annotation view. Again, another exercise for you to take on if you'd like to explore that avenue.

If you compile and build your project, you can check out one of the annotations you just added in Figure 14-15. (See it smack dab in the middle of Heathrow Airport?)

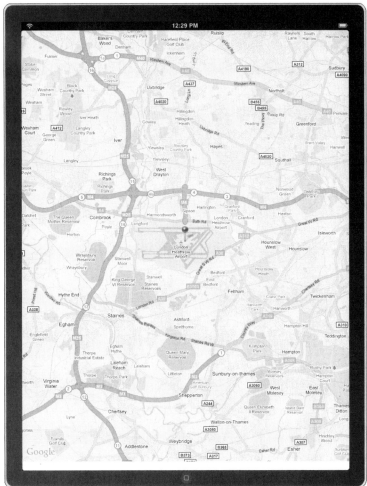

Figure 14-15:
An
annotation —
close but no
banana.

Displaying Both Annotations

Although what you see in the Map view is good, under some circumstances (like when you just arrived at the airport, for example) it would really be better if the user could automatically see both Heathrow and London (and their respective annotations) on the map without hard-coding the region as you have been doing so far. This isn't that difficult to do. Add the code in Listing 14-10 to `MapController.m`.

Listing 14-10:   regionForAnnotationGroup

```
- (MKCoordinateRegion)
             regionForAnnotationGroup: (NSArray*) group {

   double maxLonWest= 0;
   double minLonEast = 180;
   double maxLatNorth = 0;
   double minLatSouth = 180;

   for (MapAnnotation* location in group) {
     if (fabs(location.coordinate.longitude ) >
           fabs(maxLonWest))
        maxLonWest = location.coordinate.longitude;
     if (fabs(location.coordinate.longitude ) <
           fabs(minLonEast))
        minLonEast = location.coordinate.longitude;
     if (fabs(location.coordinate.latitude ) >
           fabs(maxLatNorth))
        maxLatNorth = location.coordinate.latitude;
     if (fabs(location.coordinate.latitude ) <
           fabs(minLatSouth))
        minLatSouth = location.coordinate.latitude;
   }

   double centerLatitide =
        maxLatNorth - (((maxLatNorth) - (minLatSouth))/2);
   double centerLongitude =
        maxLonWest - (((maxLonWest) - (minLonEast))/2);

   MKCoordinateRegion region;
   region.center.latitude =  centerLatitide;
   region.center.longitude = centerLongitude;
   region.span.latitudeDelta =
                         fabs(maxLatNorth - minLatSouth);
   if (fabs(maxLatNorth - minLatSouth) <= .005) region.
        span.latitudeDelta = .01;
   region.span.longitudeDelta =
                         fabs(maxLonWest - minLonEast);
   if (fabs(maxLonWest - minLonEast) <= .005) region.span.
        longitudeDelta = .01;

   return region;
}
```

This code computes the region that includes both annotations. Frankly, this is really beyond the scope of this book, but it's handy to be able to know how to do this so I have included here. I'll just summarize how it works and leave it for you to go through it step by step.

In general terms, here's how the code works: You want both annotations to fit on one screen, so the code goes through each annotation and determines the maximum north and south latitudes and the maximum east and west longitudes. The only trick here is that, because latitude and longitude can be negative, it uses a function fabs to get the absolute value of a floating point number. After that, it's simply a matter of finding the center latitude and longitude and setting the region center and then taking the maximum west and maximum east longitude and the maximum north and maximum south latitude and using that as the span. I decided that I didn't want the span to ever be less than .005, so if it is, I arbitrarily make it .01.

All that is left is to change the MapController viewDidLoad method to use this method instead of the Destination initialCoordinate and updateRegionLatitude:::::.

To do that, add the stuff in bold and delete the stuff in strikethrough in viewDidLoad as shown in Listing 14-11.

Listing 14-11:   viewDidLoad Now Results in the Annotations Being Visible

```
- (void)viewDidLoad {

    [super viewDidLoad];
    mapView.showsUserLocation = YES;
//   CLLocationCoordinate2D initialCoordinate =
//   [destination initialCoordinate];
//  [self updateRegionLatitude: initialCoordinate.latitude
            longitude: initialCoordinate.longitude
//                     latitudeDelta:.1 longitudeDelta:.1];
    self.title = [destination mapTitle];
    [mapView.userLocation addObserver:self
            forKeyPath:@"location" options:0 context:NULL];
    [mapView addAnnotations:
                         [destination createAnnotations]];
    NSArray* annotations = [destination createAnnotations];
    [mapView addAnnotations:annotations];
    [mapView setRegion:[self regionForAnnotationGroup:
            annotations] animated:NO];
}
```

You also have to import MapAnnotation.h. You can see the results in Figure 14-16.

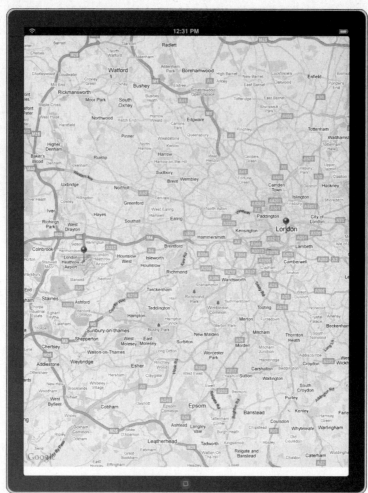

Figure 14-16:
A better
way to
compute a
region.

After you make regions something you compute rather than something you hard-code, all of a sudden you're confronted with another issue, and that's the requirement that the iPad has to work equally well in both landscape and portrait mode. The problem is that if the application opens in landscape mode and computes the correct region, then when you switch to portrait mode the annotations will no longer be visible.

So this is a good time to introduce you to `didRotateFromInterfaceOrientation`. This message is sent to the `MapController` when the user inference orientation changes. Fortunately, all you have to do to get this to work for you is add the code in Listing 14-12 to `MapController.m`.

Listing 14-12:   Accounting for User Rotation Changes

```
- (void)didRotateFromInterfaceOrientation:
        (UIInterfaceOrientation)fromInterfaceOrientation {

    [mapView setRegion:[self regionForAnnotationGroup:
            [destination createAnnotations]] animated:YES];
}
```

All you need to do is compute the new region size (you do that in `regionFor AnnotationGroup:animated:`) and the map will do the rest for you.

Working equally well in any orientation is a major iPad requirement. There are several other `UIViewController` methods you be able to use that will give you the opportunity to rearrange things as the orientation changes, but you'll have to explore them on your own.

Going to the Current Location

Although you can pan to the user location on the map, in this case, it's kind of annoying, unless you're actually coding this at or around London or Heathrow. To remove at least that annoyance from the user's life, I want to show you how easy it is to add a button to the Navigation bar to zoom you in to the current location and then back to the map region and span you're currently displaying.

1. **To add the handy Zoom button to the Navigation bar, add the following code at the end of the `MapController` method `viewDidLoad`.**

   You have quite a bit of code there, so this is just what to add:

   ```
   UIBarButtonItem *locateButton =
        [[UIBarButtonItem alloc] initWithTitle: @"Locate"
        style:UIBarButtonItemStylePlain target: self
        action:@selector(goToLocation:)];
   self.navigationItem.rightBarButtonItem = locate
            Button;
   [locateButton release];
   ```

   When the user taps the button, you've specified that the `goToLoca tion:` message is to be sent (`action:@selector(goToLocation:)`) to the `MapController` (`target:self`).

2. **Next add the `goToLocation:` method in Listing 14-13 to `MapController.m`.**

Listing 14-13:   goToLocation:

```
- (IBAction)goToLocation:(id)sender{
  MKUserLocation *annotation = mapView.userLocation;
  CLLocation *location = annotation.location;
  if (nil == location)
     return;
  CLLocationDistance distance =
               MAX(4*location.horizontalAccuracy,500);
  MKCoordinateRegion region =
          MKCoordinateRegionMakeWithDistance
          (location.coordinate, distance, distance);
 [mapView setRegion:region animated:NO];

  self.navigationItem.rightBarButtonItem.action =
                               @selector(goToTrip:);
  self.navigationItem.rightBarButtonItem.title =
                               @"Map";
}
```

When the user presses the Locate button, you first check to see whether the location is available. (It may take a few seconds after you start the application for the location to become available.) If not, you simply `return`. (You could, of course, show an alert informing the user what's going on and to try again in 10 seconds or so — I'll leave that up to you.)

If the location is available, you compute the span for the region you'll be moving to. In this case, the code

```
CLLocationDistance distance =
            MAX(4*location.horizontalAccuracy,1000);
```

computes the span to be four times the `horizontalAccuracy` of the device (but no less than 1000 meters). `horizontalAccuracy` is a radius of uncertainty given the accuracy of the device; that is, the user is somewhere within that circle.

You then call the `MKCoordinateRegionMakeWithDistance` function that creates a new `MKCoordinateRegion` from the specified coordinate and distance values. `distance` and `distance` correspond to `latitudinalMeters` and `longitudinalMeters`, respectively.

If you hadn't wanted to change the span, you could have simply set the Map view's `centerCoordinate` property to `userLocation`, and, as I said earlier in the "It's about the region" section, that would have centered the region at the `userLocation` coordinate without changing the span.

3. **Finally, you change the title on the button to Map and the `@selector` to (`goToTrip:`), which means that the next time the user touches the**

button, the `goToTrip:` message will be sent — so you had better add the code in Listing 14-14 to `MapController.m`.

Listing 14-14:   goToTrip

```
- (void) goToTrip:(id)sender{

    NSArray* annotations =
                    [destination createAnnotations];
    [mapView addAnnotations:annotations];
    [mapView setRegion:
        [self regionForAnnotationGroup:annotations]
                                        animated:NO];
    self.navigationItem.rightBarButtonItem.title =
                                        @"Locate";
    self.navigationItem.rightBarButtonItem.action =
                            @selector(goToLocation:);
}
```

The only problem here, of course, is that we have not yet managed to place an actual Navigation bar on the map. To give the button a safe and secure home, you'll have to add a Navigation bar (and its controller) to the `MapController`. I talk more about Navigation controllers in Chapter 17, so for now just make the modifications you see in Listing 14-15 (adding the bold and deleting the strikethrough) to `didFinishLaunchingWithOptions:` in `iPadTravel411AppDelegate.m`.

Listing 14-15:   Adding a Navigation Bar and Controller to MapController

```
- (BOOL)application:(UIApplication *)
    application didFinishLaunchingWithOptions:
                        (NSDictionary *)launchOptions {

    Destination * destination =
            [[Destination alloc] initWithName:@"England"];
    viewController =
    [[MapController alloc] initWithDestination:destination];
    UINavigationController *navigationController =
            [[UINavigationController alloc]
                initWithRootViewController:viewController];
//  [window addSubview:viewController.view];
    [window addSubview:navigationController.view];
    [window makeKeyAndVisible];

    return YES;
}
```

Figure 14-17 shows you what happens when you touch the Locate button. (Hello, Cupertino!)

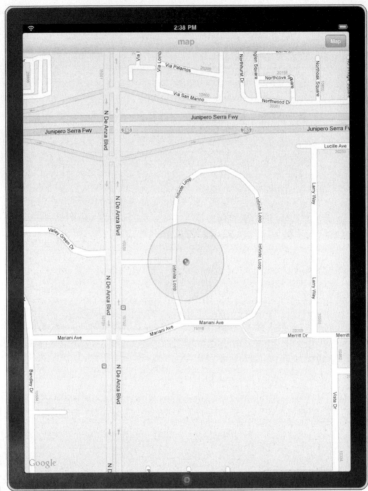

Figure 14-17:
Go to
current
location.

Geocoding

Demanding man that I am, I'm not satisfied with just seeing where I am on the map; I'd also like to know the address. (If I have the address, I could also write some code to turn the iPad's current address into an Address Book contact, but I'll allow you the pleasure of figuring that out.)

Being able to go from a coordinate on a map to an address is called *reverse geocoding,* and thankfully the ability to do that is supplied by the `MapKit`. *Forward geocoding* (also called just geocoding), which converts an address to a coordinate, does not come with the `MapKit`, although many free and commercial services are available.

Keep in mind that the location may not be completely accurate — remember `horizontalAccuracy` in the earlier "Going to the Current Location" section. For example, since my office is very close to my property line, my location sometimes shows up with my next-door neighbor's address.

Adding reverse geocoding to iPadTravel411 enables you to display the address of the current location. Just follow these steps:

1. **Import `MKReverseGeocoder` into `MapController.h` and have `MapController` adopt the `MKReverseGeocoderDelegate` protocol.**

   ```
   #import <MapKit/MKReverseGeocoder.h>

   @interface MapController : UIViewController

        <MKReverseGeocoderDelegate> {
   ```

2. **Add an instance variable to hold a reference to the geocoder object.**

   ```
   MKReverseGeocoder *reverseGeocoder;
   ```

   You'll use this later to release the `MKReverseGeocoder` once you get the current address.

3. **Add the methods in Listing 14-16, `reverseGeocoder:didFind Placemark:` and `reverseGeocoder:didFailWithError:`, to `MapController.m`.**

Listing 14-16: The Reverse Geocoder Methods

```
- (void)reverseGeocoder:(MKReverseGeocoder *) geocoder
        didFindPlacemark:(MKPlacemark *) placemark {

  NSMutableString* addressString =
          [[NSMutableString alloc]
          initWithString: placemark.subThoroughfare];
  [addressString appendString: @" "];
  [addressString appendString:placemark.thoroughfare];
  mapView.userLocation.subtitle = placemark.locality;
  mapView.userLocation.title = addressString;
  [addressString release];
}

- (void)reverseGeocoder:(MKReverseGeocoder *) geocoder
               didFailWithError:(NSError *) error{

      NSLog(@"Reverse Geocoder Errored");
}
```

The reverseGeocoder:didFindPlacemark: message to the delegate is sent when the MKReverseGeocoder object successfully obtains *placemark* information for its coordinate. An MKPlacemark object stores placemark data for a given latitude and longitude. Placemark data includes the properties that hold the country, state, city, and street address (and other information) associated with the specified coordinate, for example. Here's a (far from complete) listing:

- country: Name of country

- administrativeArea: State

- locality: City

- thoroughfare: Street address (name)

- subThoroughfare: Additional street-level information, such as the street number

- postalCode: Postal code

In this implementation, you're setting the user location annotation (userLocation) title (supplied by MapKit) to a string you create made up of the subThoroughfare and thoroughfare (the street address). You assign the subtitle the locality (city) property.

MKReverseGeocoder also includes a placemark property so that you can also access the placemark after the results are reported to the delegate object.

A placemark is also an annotation and conforms to the MKAnnotation protocol, whose properties and methods include the placemark coordinate and other information. Because they're annotations, you can add them directly to the Map view.

The reverseGeocoder:didFailWithError: message is sent to the delegate if the MKReverseGeocoder couldn't get the placemark information for the coordinate you supplied to it. (This is a required MKReverseGeocoderDelegate method.)

Of course, to get the reverse geocoder information, you need to create an MKReverseGeocoder object. Make the MapController a delegate, send it a start message, and then release it when you're done with it. Here are the details:

1. **Allocate and start the reverse geocoder and add the MapController as its delegate in the MapController goToLocation: method by adding the code in bold.**

```
- (void)goToLocation:(id)sender{

    MKUserLocation *annotation = mapView.userLocation;
```

```
CLLocation *location = annotation.location;
if (nil == location)
  return;
CLLocationDistance distance =
MAX(4*location.horizontalAccuracy,500);
MKCoordinateRegion region =
MKCoordinateRegionMakeWithDistance
(location.coordinate, distance, distance);
[mapView setRegion:region animated:NO];

self.navigationItem.rightBarButtonItem.action =
@selector(goToTrip:);
self.navigationItem.rightBarButtonItem.title =
@"Map";
reverseGeocoder = [[MKReverseGeocoder alloc]
      initWithCoordinate:location.coordinate];
reverseGeocoder.delegate = self;
[reverseGeocoder start];
}
```

Notice you initialize the `MKReverseGeocoder` with the coordinate of the current location.

2. **Release the MKReverseGeocoder by adding the code in bold in `goTo Trip:`.**

```
- (void) goToTrip:(id)sender{

[reverseGeocoder release];
NSArray* annotations =
                  [destination createAnnotations];
[mapView addAnnotations:annotations];
[mapView setRegion:
    [self regionForAnnotationGroup:annotations]
                                animated:NO];
self.navigationItem.rightBarButtonItem.title =
                                @"Locate";
self.navigationItem.rightBarButtonItem.action =
                    @selector(goToLocation:);
}
```

You release the `MKReverseGeocoder` in this method because while you start the `MKReverseGeocoder` in the `goToLocation:` method, it actually does not return the information in that method. It operates asynchronously; and when it either constructs the placemark or gives up, it sends the message `reverseGeocoder:didFindPlacemark:` or `rev erseGeocoder:didFailWithError:`, respectively. If you're returning to the original Map view, however, you no longer care if it succeeds or fails, since you no longer need the placemark, and you release the `MKReverseGeocoder`.

Figure 14-18 shows the result of your adventures in reverse geocoding. You see the call out when you tap the pin (annotation).

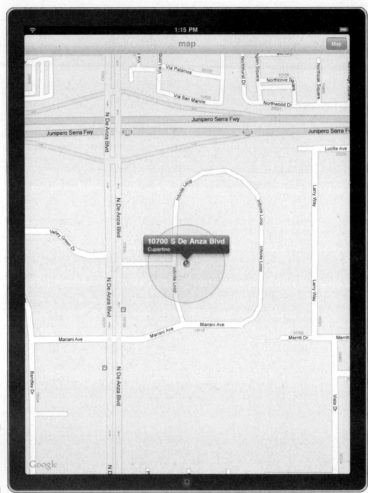

Figure 14-18:
Reverse
geocoding.

Chapter 15

Navigating Your Application

· ·

· ·

*B*ack in Chapter 13, I show you a screen shot of the iPadTravel411 application with a Map view on one side of the screen and a Table view — acting as a Navigation view — on the other. In that particular case, I set up the Navigation view to provide a kind of table of contents or directory to the application content and functionality. In this chapter, I show you how to take a Table view like the one back in Chapter 13 and implement it as one of the views in a Split view controller.

My advice to you: Keep an eye on the Split view controller. It's sure to come in handy one day because it's a very powerful class that allows you to first display the Table view in landscape mode and then, when the user has turned the iPad to portrait mode, take the same Table view and display it in a Popover window. (Neat.)

Adding a Split Screen Controller

The `UISplitViewController` class is a view controller that simply manages the presentation of two side-by-side view controllers — it is, in this respect, a container controller. Using this class, you create a view controller on the left (the *Master view,* as it's called) which presents a list of items and one on the right which presents the details, or content, of the selected item (the *Detail view,* as it's called).

After you create and initialize a UISplitViewController object, you assign two view controllers to it by using the viewController property. The Split view controller has no interface — its job is to coordinate the presentation of its two view controllers and to manage the transitions between different orientations.

What's more, your new friend the Split view controller doesn't manage the communication between the two view controllers you assign to it. It's your responsibility to determine the best way to do that. I show you one way in this chapter.

To manage transitions between orientations, the Split view controller not only takes care of the mechanism of the transition, but also changes the display to accommodate the orientation most effectively. In a landscape orientation, you can see both view controllers' views side by side. When the Split view controller rotates between portrait and landscape orientations, however, it can either hide or show the first view controller (the Master view controller by definition) in its array of view controllers. When the view controller is hidden, you can add a button to the toolbar of the remaining view controller that will display the hidden view controller in a popover.

The adding of a button is implemented in a delegate protocol, and the popover sends its delegates messages to coordinate the display of a popover with the hidden view controller — the methods of this protocol are designed to be invoked at the right time so that you can add and remove the button.

Getting your views

To start with, you need to create the Master view controller. You're going to go with a Table view, which should be familiar to anyone who's used an iPhone.

Master view controllers are not just for navigation, and in Chapter 17, I show you how to display content in the Master view controller as well.

Kick things off by creating the MasterViewController class. Select the Classes group if you want to have it end up in there (or really go for it and create your own group)

1. **Choose File⇨New File from the main menu (or press ⌘+N) to get the New File dialog.**

2. **In the leftmost column of the dialog, first select Cocoa Touch Classes under the iPhone OS heading and then select the UIViewController Subclass template in the topmost pane.**

3. **Make sure that the following check boxes are all selected:**

   - UITableViewController Subclass

   - XIB for User Interface

   - Targeted for iPad

4. **Click Next.**

   You see a new dialog asking for some more information.

5. **Enter MasterViewController in the File Name field and then click Finish.**

   Three files will be added @md `MasterViewController.h`, `MasterViewController.m`, and `MasterViewController.xib`. (You might want to move that last one to the Resources group.)

Now that you have two view controllers to work with: the `MasterView Controller` and the first Detail view controller you created and named `MapController` back in Chapter 14. (See, there *was* a good reason to change the name.) I show you how to create a Split view controller and add both views to it. It will require a bit of change in `iPadTravel411AppDeleagte`, so give your fingers a good stretch and then get started.

Creating a Split View Controller

Start by making the following changes (adding the bolded stuff and deleting the strikethrough stuff) to `iPadTravel411AppDelegate.m` shown in Listing 15-1.

Listing 15-1:   Creating a Split View Controller

```
#import "iPadTravel411AppDelegate.h"
#import "MapController.h"
#import "Destination.h";
#import "MasterViewController.h"

@implementation iPadTravel411AppDelegate

@synthesize window;
@synthesize viewController;
@synthesize destination;
@synthesize splitViewController, masterViewController,
            detailViewController, initialController;

-(BOOL)application:(UIApplication *)
```

(continued)

Listing 15-1 *(continued)*

```
application didFinishLaunchingWithOptions:
                         (NSDictionary *)launchOptions {
Destination *destination =
      [[Destination alloc] initWithName:@"England"];
masterViewController = [[MasterViewController alloc]
         initWithDestination: destination];
UINavigationController *navigationController =
      [[UINavigationController alloc]
      initWithRootViewController:masterViewController];
//viewController = [[MapController alloc] initWithDestinat
         ion:destination];
//UINavigationController *navigationController =
         [[UINavigationController alloc] initWithRootVie
         wController:viewController];
detailViewController = [[MapController alloc]
                       initWithDestination:destination];
initialController = [[UINavigationController alloc]
      initWithRootViewController:detailViewController];
splitViewController =
                   [[UISplitViewController alloc] init];
splitViewController.viewControllers =
      [NSArray arrayWithObjects:navigationController,
                           initialController, nil];
splitViewController.delegate =
   (<UISplitViewControllerDelegate>)detailViewController;
//[window addSubview:navigationController.view];
[window addSubview:splitViewController.view];
[window makeKeyAndVisible];
return YES;
}
```

Although some of this code is pretty straightforward and similar to what you've already done, some of it is also new.

Because a Split view controller requires two view controllers, the first thing you do is add code for creating the MasterViewController.

```
masterViewController = [[MasterViewController alloc]
                       initWithDestination: destination];
UINavigationController *navigationController =
      [[UINavigationController alloc]
      initWithRootViewController:masterViewController];
```

The next thing you do is create the initial controller for the Detail view. All you have done here is change the instance variable that refers to the Map controller and added an instance variable and property to hold the reference to the Navigation controller.

```
//viewController = [[MapController alloc] initWithDestina
          tion:destination];
//UINavigationController *navigationController =
          [[UINavigationController alloc] initWithRootVi
          ewController:viewController];
detailViewController = [[MapController alloc]
                     initWithDestination:destination];
initialController = [[UINavigationController alloc]
     initWithRootViewController:detailViewController];
```

Next you create the Split view controller and add its two child controllers — the `navigationController` (which holds the `MasterViewController`) and the `initialController` which holds the `MapController`.

```
splitViewController =
                  [[UISplitViewController alloc] init];
splitViewController.viewControllers =
       [NSArray arrayWithObjects:navigationController,
                            initialController, nil];
```

Finally, you assign the `splitViewController` delegate and then the `splitViewController` to the window, like so:

```
splitViewController.delegate =
   (<UISplitViewControllerDelegate>)detailViewController;
[window addSubview:splitViewController.view];
[window makeKeyAndVisible];
```

This strange construct:

```
(<UISplitViewControllerDelegate>)detailViewController;
```

casts the `detailViewController` as a `UISplitViewController Delegate`. Because the `detailViewController` is defined to be a `UIViewController`, you need to cast it as a `UISplitViewController Delegate` so the compiler won't complain.

Also notice that the Master view controller has an initialization method — `initWithDestination`. You have to add that baby to the `MasterViewController.m`. No big deal, though. Just add the code in Listing 15-2 to `MasterViewController.m` and that bit of business is taken care of.

Listing 15-2: initWithDestination:

```
- (id) initWithDestination: (Destination*) aDestination {
    if (self = [super initWithNibName:@"MasterViewControl
            ler" bundle:nil]) {
        destination = aDestination;
    }
    return self;
}
```

Listing 15-3 shows you what you must also add to `MasterViewController.h`.

Listing 15-3: Add to MasterViewController.h

```
#import <UIKit/UIKit.h>
@class Destination;

@interface MasterViewController : UITableViewController {

    Destination *destination;
}

- (id) initWithDestination: (Destination*) aDestination;

@end
```

The `Destination` is the model used by the view controllers to get the content needed by the view that is created when the user selects a row in the Table view.

You also have to add an `#import "Destination.h"` statement to the `MasterViewController.m` file.

Next you need to add the plumbing to the interface to support these changes. To do that, make the changes you see in Listing 15-4.

Listing 15-4: iPadTravel411Appdelegate.h

```
#import <UIKit/UIKit.h>
@class Destination;
@class MasterViewController;


@class MapController;
```

```
@interface iPadTravel411AppDelegate : NSObject
         <UIApplicationDelegate> {

  UIWindow                 *window;
  MapController             *viewController;
  Destination               *destination;
  UISplitViewController    *splitViewController;
  MasterViewController     *masterViewController;
  UIViewController          *detailViewController;
  UINavigationController   *initialController;
}

@property (nonatomic, retain) IBOutlet UIWindow *window;
@property (nonatomic, retain) IBOutlet MapController
         *viewController;
@property (nonatomic, retain) IBOutlet Destination    *
         destination;
@property (nonatomic,retain)
         UISplitViewController *splitViewController;
@property (nonatomic,retain)
         MasterViewController *masterViewController;
@property (nonatomic,retain)
             UIViewController *detailViewController;
@property (nonatomic,retain)
         UINavigationController  *initialController;


@end
```

If you want to compile your project at this point, you'll have to delete bits of two lines of code in `MasterViewController.m`, as follows. (I talk about what those two lines are about next.)

```
- (NSInteger)numberOfSectionsInTableView:(UITableView *)
         tableView {
    // Return the number of sections.
    return 1; //<#number of sections#>;
}


- (NSInteger)tableView:(UITableView *)tableView numberOfRo
         wsInSection:(NSInteger)section {
    // Return the number of rows in the section.
    return 2; //<#number of rows in section#>;
}
```

What you would see when you rotate it to landscape mode is shown in Figure 15-1 — an empty Table view on the left (the Master view controller), and your trusty Map view on the right (the Detail view controller).

Figure 15-1:
A Split view
controller.

Unfortunately, you have no way to get to that view when the device is in portrait mode — yet. To do that you'll need to use a Popover view.

Popovers

One of the user interface elements you'll want to add to your application is the popover. Although there are a number of uses for popovers, I am going to show you how to display the Master view that you see in landscape mode in a Popover view in portrait mode.

The Split view controller you just implemented displays both the Master and Detail view in landscape orientations but only the Detail view controller is displayed in portrait orientations. When the Master view controller is hidden, it is standard practice to add a button to the toolbar of the Detail view controller that the user can then use to display the Master view controller in a popover. All this is accomplished by making the Detail view controller a delegate of the Split view controller, which sends its delegate messages at the appropriate times to add and remove the button (and a few other times as well, which I'm not going to get into).

The UIPopoverController class manages the presentation of content in a popover. The content is provided in the same way you provide content in any other view — using a view controller that you provide to the popover. Popovers present information temporarily, but they don't take over the entire screen like a Modal view does. This information is layered on top of your existing content in a special type of window. It remains visible until the user taps outside the Popover window or you explicitly dismiss it.

You also can/should specify the size of the Popover window by assigning a value to the popoverContentSize property or by calling the setPopoverContentSize:animated: method. You should be aware that the size you specify is just the preferred size for your view. The actual size may be reduced to make the popover fit on the screen and not collide with the keyboard.

When displayed, taps outside of the Popover window cause the popover to be dismissed automatically. You can, however, allow the user to interact with the specified views and not dismiss the popover, using the passthrough Views property (although you won't be doing that here). Taps inside the Popover window do not dismiss the popover and, as you'll see, your Master view controller will include code to dismiss the popover explicitly.

So, before you add any more views, you'll add a popover to the Map controller you've been working with. Fortunately, much of what you have to do is already taken care of by the Split view controller. Your job is simple. Just add the button to launch the Popup controller in the portrait mode, and then remove the button in the landscape mode.

As I mentioned, the Split view controller handles most of this and calls its delegate as necessary.

To start with, you need to make the MapController a UISplitView Delegate. Whoops, you actually did that already when I had you add the line of code in the didFinishLaunchingWithOptions: method for iPadAppTravel411AppDelegate:

```
splitViewController.delegate = (
    <UISplitViewControllerDelegate> )detailViewController;
```

Moving on, you to need specify the fact that MapController is a UISplitViewControllerDelegate by adding the bolded, and protocol name MapController.h.

```
@interface MapController : UIViewController
<MKReverseGeocoderDelegate,
                          UISplitViewControllerDelegate> {
```

Now, all you have to do is implement two delegate methods in the MapController.

```
splitViewController:willHideViewController:
             withBarButtonItem:forPopoverController:
splitViewController:willShowViewController:
                          invalidatingBarButtonItem:
```

The first of these methods is invoked when the Split view controller rotates from a landscape to portrait orientation and hides the Master view controller. When that happens, the Split view controller sends this message to add a button to the toolbar (or Navigation bar) of the Detail controller. To have the message called in Listing 15-5 to `MapController.m`. (You also need to import `iPadTravel411AppDelegate`.)

Listing 15-5:   Adding the Button

```
- (void)splitViewController: (UISplitViewController*)svc
willHideViewController:(UIViewController *)aViewController
withBarButtonItem:(UIBarButtonItem*)barButtonItem
          forPopoverController: (UIPopoverController*)pc {

   barButtonItem.title = @"Master List";
   self.navigationItem.leftBarButtonItem = barButtonItem;
   self.popoverController = pc;
   iPadTravel411AppDelegate *appDelegate =
          (iPadTravel411AppDelegate *)[[UIApplication
          sharedApplication] delegate];
   appDelegate.popoverController = pc;
}
```

All you really do here is add the button to the Navigation bar and save a reference to the `popoverController`.

I'm having you save a reference to the `popoverController` in the app delegate so you can access it later when you want to dismiss it when the user makes a selection in the popover containing the `MasterViewController`. To do that, you also need to import the `iPadTraver411AppDelegate` in `MapController.m` and add an instance variable and property — `popover-Controller`, to be precise — to both the `MasterViewController` and the `iPadTraver411AppDelegate`. You have already added properties earlier in this chapter so this is like lots of programming — more of the same.

As you may have noticed, I came up with the catchy title, @`"Master List"`, for the button label in the code in Listing 15-5. Although this is probably not the most user-friendly title, I went with it because that's the name you'll find if you use the template to create a Split view controller project

The second of the `MapController` delegate methods is invoked when the view controller rotates from a portrait to landscape orientation; it shows its hidden view controller once more. If you added the specified button to your toolbar to facilitate the display of the hidden view controller in a popover, you must implement this method and use it to remove that button.

To do this, add the code in Listing 15-6 to `MapController.m`.

Listing 15-6: Removing the Button

```
- (void)splitViewController: (UISplitViewController*)svc
        willShowViewController:(UIViewController *)
        aViewController invalidatingBarButtonItem:(UIBa
        rButtonItem *)barButtonItem {

  self.navigationItem.leftBarButtonItem = nil;
  self.popoverController = nil;
  iPadTravel411AppDelegate *appDelegate =
        (iPadTravel411AppDelegate *)[[UIApplication
        sharedApplication] delegate];
  appDelegate.popoverController = nil;
}
```

Finally, specify the size of the popover in `MasterController.m` by adding the following method.

Listing 15-7: Specifying Popover Size

```
- (CGSize)contentSizeForViewInPopoverView {

  return CGSizeMake(kPopoverWidth, 600.0);
}
```

You want to make it 320 pixels wide to match the size of the `master Controller` view.

Of course, I could have just hard-coded in the 320 pixels here, but instead, in the interest of showing you how to implement a robust application, I'm going to use a constant for the popover width. (I'll leave it up to you to deal with the height.) I'll put those constants in `Constants.h`, which you will create next, which will eventually contain other constants. I do this for purely defensive reasons: This value will be used again in this application (I know that because hindsight is 20-20), and declaring it as a constant makes keeping both in synch easier.

I show you some techniques here that make life much, much easier later. It means paying attention to some of the less-glamorous application nuts and bolts functionality — can you say "memory management"? — that may be annoying to implement along the way but that are *really* difficult to retrofit later. I want to head you away from the boulder-strewn paths that so many developers have gone down (me included), much to their later sorrow.

To implement the `Constants.h` file, you do the following:

1. **Choose File⇨New File from the Xcode main menu.**

   I recommend having the `Classes` folder selected in the Groups & Files list so the file will be placed in there.

2. **In the New File dialog that appears, choose Other from the listing on the left (under the Mac OS X heading) and then choose Empty File in the main pane.**

3. **In the new dialog that appears, name the file `Constants.h` and then click Finish.**

   The new empty file is saved in the Classes folder.

With a new home for your constants all set up and waiting, all you have to do is add the first constant.

```
#define kPopoverWidth 320.0
```

Having a `Constants.h` file in hand is great, but you have to let `MasterViewController.m` know that you plan to use it. To include `Constants.h` in `MasterViewController.m`, open `MasterViewController.m` in Xcode and add the following statement:

```
#import "Constants.h"
```

That's really all there is to it.

The Table view will act as a table of contents for your application's functionality. So go ahead and get started with filling it out.

Working with Table Views

Table views are front and center in several applications that come with the iPad as well as the iPhone. Table views also play a major role in many of the more complex applications you can download from the App Store. (Obvious examples: Almost all the [Master] views in the Mail, iPod, and Contacts applications are Table views.) Table views not only display data, but also serve as a way to navigate a hierarchy.

If you take a look at an application such as Mail or iPod, you'll find that Table views present a scrollable list of *items* (or *rows* or *entries* — I use all three terms interchangeably) that may be divided into *sections*. A row can display text or images. So, when you select a row, you may be presented with another Table view, or you may end up with some other view that may display a Web page or even some controls such as buttons and text fields. You can see an illustration of this diversity in Figure 15-2. Selecting Weather on the left leads to a Content view displaying the weather — very handy in London.

Figure 15-2:
A table and
Web view.

But even though a Table view is an instance of the class UITableView, each visible row of the table uses an UITableViewCell to draw its contents. Think of a Table *view* as the object that creates and manages the table structure, and the Table view *cell* as being responsible for displaying the content of a single row of the table.

Although powerful, Table views are surprisingly easy to work with. To create a Table view, you need only to do four — count 'em, four — things, in the following order:

1. **Create and format the view itself.**

   This includes specifying the table style and a few other parameters — most of which can be done in Interface Builder.

2. **Specify the Table View configuration.**

   Not too complicated, actually. You let UITableView know how many sections you want, how many rows you want in each section, and what you want to call your section headers. You do that with the help of the numberOfSectionsInTableView: method, the tableView:number OfRowsInSection: method, and the tableView:titleForHeader InSection: method, respectively.

3. **Supply the text (or graphic) for each row.**

   You return that from the implementation of the `tableView:cellForRowAtIndexPath:` method. This message is sent for each visible row in the Table view, and you return a Table view cell to display the text or graphic.

4. **Respond to a user selection of the row.**

   You use the `tableView:didSelectRowAtIndexPath:` method to take care of this task. In this method, you create a view controller and a new view. For example, when the user selects Weather in Figure 15-2, this method is called, and then a Weather controller and a Weather view are created and displayed.

A `UITableView` object must have a *data source* and a *delegate*. The data source supplies the content for the Table view, and the delegate manages the appearance and behavior of the Table view. The data source adopts the `UITableViewDataSource` protocol and the delegate adopts the `UITableViewDelegate` protocol — no surprises there. Of the preceding methods, only the `tableView:didSelectRowAtIndexPath:` is included in the `UITableViewDelegate` protocol. All the others I list earlier are included in the `UITableViewDataSource` protocol.

The data source and the delegate are often (but not necessarily) implemented in the same object — which is often a subclass of `UITableViewController`. I plan to use the `MasterViewController` for my iPad411Travel app.

Implementing these five (count 'em, five) methods — and taking Interface Builder for a spin or two, along with the same kind of initialization methods and the standard memory-management methods you used in the DeepThoughts application — creates a table view that can respond to a selection made in the table.

Not bad.

Creating and formatting a grouped table view

Table views come in two basic styles. The default style is called *plain* and looks really unadorned — plain vanilla. It's a list: just one darn thing after another. You can index it, though, just as the Table view in the Contacts application is indexed, so it can be a pretty powerful tool. Plain is the style you see earlier in Figure 15-1; it's the default when you created the `MasterViewController` from the template in Step 2 of the step list found in the "Getting your views" section, earlier in the chapter.

The other style is the *grouped* Table view; unsurprisingly, it allows you to clump entries into various categories. That's the view you see back in Figure 15-2.

Grouped tables cannot have an index.

When you configure a grouped Table view, you can also have header, footer, and section titles. (A plain view, on the other hand, can obviously have only section headers and footers, since it doesn't have sections.) I show you how to do section titles shortly.

Inquisitive type that you are, if you look up UITableViewController in the Documentation reference by right-clicking its entry and choosing Find Selected Text in Documentation from the pop-up menu that appears, the Class reference tells you that UITableViewController conforms to the UITableViewDelegate and UITableViewDataSource protocols (and a few others). These two protocols just happen to be the ones I said were necessary to implement table views. What luck. (Kidding. It's all intentional.)

Always on the lookout for more information, you continue down the Groups & Files list to open your project's Resources folder (if that's where you put it, as I suggested earlier), where you double-click the MasterViewController.xib file to launch Interface Builder. You're reassured to see a Table view set up in front of you — admittedly, a plain Table view rather than the grouped Table view we want, but a Table view nonetheless. To get the final duck in a row, choose Grouped from the Style drop-down menu in the Attributes Inspector, as shown in Figure 15-3, to make the switch from plain to grouped. Be sure to save the file after you do this.

At this point, if you build and run this project; it will look like you've taken a step backwards. You'll no longer see all those empty cells; in fact, you won't see anything at all except the background. Although you do have a basic framework, now you have to fill in all the blanks.

Making UITableViewController work for you

The data source and the delegate for Table views are often (but not necessarily) the same object — and that object is frequently a custom subclass of UITableViewController. For the iPadTravel411 project, the MasterViewController is a subclass of UITableViewController — and the UITableViewController has adopted the UITableViewDelegate and UITableViewDataSource protocols. So you're free to implement those handy methods I mention in the "Working with Table Views" section, earlier in the chapter. (Just remember that you need to implement them in MasterViewController to make your table usable.) You should start with the methods that format the table the way you'd like, as spelled out in the very next section.

Adding sections

In a grouped Table view, each group is referred to as a *section*.

In an indexed table, each indexed grouping of data is also called a section. For example, in the iPod application, all the albums beginning with *A* would be one section, those beginning with *B* another section, and so on. Although it uses the same name, this isn't the same thing as sections in a grouped table (which doesn't have an index).

The two methods you need to start things off are as follows:

```
numberOfSectionsInTableView:(UITableView *)tableView
tableView:(UITableView *)tableView
        numberOfRowsInSection:(NSInteger)section
```

Each of these methods returns an integer and that tells the Table view something — the number of sections and the number of rows in a given section, respectively.

In Listing 15-8, you can see the code that results in two sections with four rows in the first section and three in the second.

These methods are already implemented for you by the Navigation-Based Application template in the `MasterViewController.m` file (and you modified each a bit just to see the Table view). You just need to remove all of the existing code and replace it with what you see in Listing 15-8.

Listing 15-8:   Modifying numberOfSectionsInTableView:
and tableView:numberOfRowsInSection:

```
-  (NSInteger)numberOfSectionsInTableView:(UITableView *)
                                              tableView {

    return kSections;
}

-  (NSInteger)tableView:(UITableView *)tableView
                  numberOfRowsInSection:(NSInteger)section {

    NSInteger rows;
    switch (section) {
      case 0:
        rows = kSection1Rows;
        break;
      case 1:
        rows = kSection2Rows;
        break;
      default:
        break;
    }
    return rows;
}
```

You implement `tableView:numberOfRowsInSection:` by using a simple
`switch` statement:

```
switch (section) {
```

Keep in mind that the first section is zero, as is the first row.

As I did with popover width back in the "Popovers" section, earlier in this
chapter, I'm going to use constants to represent the number of sections *and*
the number of rows in each section. I'll put those constants in `Constants.h`,
which you've already created (and you'll have to import `Constants.h` to
in `MasterViewController.m`). Just as with popover width, I do this for
purely defensive reasons: Both of these values will be used often in this application, and declaring them as constants makes changing the number of rows
and sections easy, and it also helps avoid hard-to-detect typing mistakes.

You need to add the following to the `Constants.h` file:

```
#define kSections      2
#define kSection1Rows  4
#define kSection2Rows  3
```

When you build and run this (provisional) app, you get what you see on the left in Figure 15-4 — two sections, the first with four rows and the second with three.

Although using constants and a `switch` statement does make your program more extensible, it does require you to change the `switch` statement if you want to add or change the layout. An even better solution (although not implemented in this version) is to create an array in `awakeFromNib` that looks like this:

```
sectionsArray = [[NSMutableArray alloc]
                                initWithCapacity:2];
[sectionsArray addObject:[[ NSNumber alloc]
                                initWithInt:4]];
[sectionsArray addObject:[[ NSNumber alloc]
                                initWithInt:3]];
```

Then you could use the array count `[sectionsArray count]` to return the number of sections and index into the array for the number of rows in a section `[sectionsArray objectAtIndex:section]`.

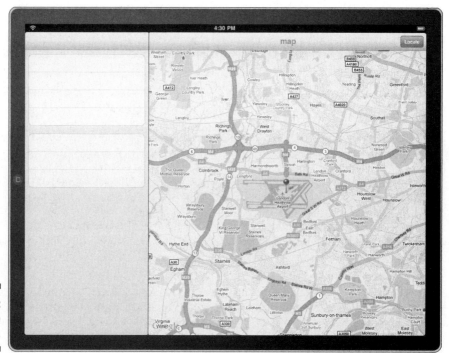

Figure 15-4:
Now I have
sections.

Adding titles for the sections

With sections in place, you now need to title them so users know what the sections are for. Luckily for you, the UITableViewdataSource protocol has a handy method — titled, appropriately enough, the tableView:titleFor HeaderInSection: method — that enables you to add a title for each section. Listing 15-9 shows one way to implement the method.

Listing 15-9:   Adding Section Titles

```
- (NSString *)tableView:(UITableView *)tableView
            titleForHeaderInSection:(NSInteger)section {

  NSString *title = nil;
  switch (section) {
    case 0:
      title = @"Welcome to London";
      break;
    case 1:
      title =  @"Getting there";
      break;
    default:
      break;
  }
  return title;
}
```

This (again) is a simple switch statement. For case 0, or the first section, you want the title to be "Welcome to London", and for case 1, or the second section, you want the title to be "Getting there".

Okay, this, too, was really easy — so you probably won't be surprised to find out that it's *not* the best way to tackle the whole titling business. Another path not to take — in fact, a really *important* one not to take. Really Serious Application Developers insist on catering to the needs of an increasingly global audience, which means — paradoxically — that they have to *localize* their applications. In other words, an app must be created in such a way that it presents a different view to different, local audiences. The next section explains how localization is done.

Localization

Localizing an application isn't difficult, just tedious. To localize your application, you create a folder in your application bundle (I get to that in a bit) for each language you want to support. Each folder has the application's translated resources.

In the Settings application for the iPadTravel411 app, you're going to set things up so the user can set the language — Spanish or Italian, for example — and the region format.

For example, if the user's language is Spanish, available regions range from Spain to Argentina to the United States and lots of places in between. When a localized application needs to load a resource (such as an image, a property list, or a nib), the application checks the user's language and region and looks for a localization folder that corresponds to the selected language and region. If it finds one, it loads the localized version of the resource instead of the *base* version — the one you're working in.

Showing you all the ins and outs of localizing your application is a bit too Byzantine for this book. But I *do* show you what you must do to make your app localizable when you're ready to tackle the chore on your own.

What you have to get right — right from the start — are the strings you use in your application that get presented to the user. (If the user has chosen Spanish as his or her language of choice, what's expected in the main view is now *Moneda*, not *Currency*.) You ensure that the users see what they're expecting to see by storing the strings you use in your application in a `strings` text file; this file contains a list of string pairs, each identified by a comment. You would create one of these files for each language you support.

Here's an example of what an entry in a `strings` file might look like for this application:

```
/*Airport choices */
"Getting there"  = "Getting there";
```

The values between the `/*` and the `*/` characters are just comments for the (human) translator you task with creating the right translation for the phrase — assuming, of course, that you're not fluent in the ten-or-so languages that you'll probably want to include in your app and therefore will need some translating help. You write such comments to provide some context — how that string is being used in the application.

Okay, this example has two strings: The one to the left of the equals sign is used as a key; the one to the right of the equals sign is the one displayed. In the example, both strings are the same — but in the `strings` file used for a Spanish speaker, here's what you'd see:

```
/*Airport choices */
"Getting there"  = "Cómo llegar";
```

Looking up such values in the table is handled by the `NSLocalizedString` macro in your code.

To show you how to use the macro, I take one of the section headings as an example. Instead of

```
title = Getting there;
```

I code it as follows:

```
title = NSLocalizedString(@"Getting there",
                                @"Airport choices");
```

As you can see, the macro has two inputs: The first is the string in your language; the second is the general comment for the translator. At runtime, `NSLocalizedString` looks for a `strings` file named `localizable.strings` in the language that has been set: Spanish, for example. (A user would have done that by going to Settings and choosing General⇨Internati onal⇨Language⇨Español.) If `NSLocalizedString` finds the `strings` file, it searches the file for a line that matches the first parameter. In this case, it would return "Cómo llegar," and that is what would be displayed as the section header. If the macro doesn't find the file or a specified string, it returns its first parameter — and the string will appear in the base language.

To create the `localizable.strings` file, you run a command-line program named `genstrings`, which searches your code files for the macro and places them all in a `localizable.strings` file (which it creates), ready for the (human) translator. `genstrings` is beyond the scope of this book, but it's well documented. When you're ready, I leave you to explore it on your own.

Okay, sure, it's really annoying to have to do this sort of thing as you write your code. (Yes, I know, *really, really* annoying.) But that's not nearly as annoying as having to go back and *find and replace all the strings you want to localize* after the application is almost done. Take my word for it!

Listing 15-10 shows how to use the `NSLocalizedString` macro to create localizable section titles. Add this code to MasterViewController.m.

Listing 15-10:   Adding Localizable Section Titles

```
- (NSString *)tableView:(UITableView *)tableView
             titleForHeaderInSection:(NSInteger)section {

   NSString *title = nil;
   switch (section) {
```

(continued)

Listing 15-10 *(continued)*

```
  case 0:
    title = NSLocalizedString(@"Welcome to London",
                                     @"City name");
    break;
  case 1:
    title = NSLocalizedString(@"Getting there",
                                    @"Airport choices");
    break;
  default:
    break;
  }
  return title;
}
```

Creating the row model

As all good iPad app developers should know, the Model-View-Controller (MVC) design pattern is the basis for the design of the framework you use to develop your applications. In this design pattern, each element (model, view, or controller) concentrates on the task at hand; it doesn't much care what the other elements are doing. For Table views, that means the method that draws the content doesn't know what the content is — and the method that decides what to do when a selection is made in a particular row is equally ignorant of what the selection is. The important thing is to have a model object — one for each row — to hold and provide that information.

In this kind of situation, you usually want to deal with the model-object business by creating an array of models, one for each row. In this case, the model object will be a dictionary that holds the following two items:

✔ **The selection text:** Heathrow, for example

✔ **The description text:** International airport, for example

You can see both items illustrated in Figure 15-5.

In more complex applications, you could provide a dictionary *within* the dictionary and use it to provide the same kind of information for the next level in the hierarchy. The iPod application is an example: It presents you with a list of albums, and then when you select an album, it shows you a list of songs on that album.

Following is the code that shows you how to create a single dictionary for a row. Later, I show you how to create all the dictionaries and where all this code needs to go.

```
menuList = [[NSMutableArray alloc] init];

[menuList addObject:[NSMutableDictionary
                             dictionaryWithObjectsAndKeys:
    NSLocalizedString(@"Heathrow",
                        @"Heathrow Section"), kSelectKey,
    NSLocalizedString(@"International airport",
                        @"Heathrow Explain"), kDescriptKey,
    nil]];
```

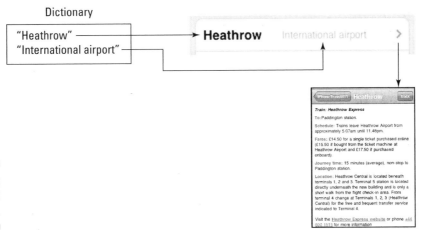

Figure 15-5:
The model
for a row.

Here's the blow-by-blow account:

1. **Create an array to hold the model for each row.**

   An NSMutableArray is a good choice here because it allows you to easily insert and delete objects.

   In such an array, the position of the dictionary corresponds to the row it implements — that's to say relative to row zero in the table and not taking into account the section.

2. **Create an NSMutableDictionary with two entries and the following keys:**

   - kSelectKey: The entry that corresponds to the main entry in the Table view ("Heathrow," for example).

   - kDescriptKey: The entry that corresponds to the description in the Table view ("International Airport," for example).

3. Add the keys to the `Constants.h` file.

```
#define kSelectKey      @"selection"
#define kDescriptKey    @"description"
```

The @ before each of the preceding strings tells the compiler that this is an NSString.

You'll want to create this array and all of the dictionaries in the MasterViewController viewDidLoadMethod method that you can see in Listing 15-11. As I mention in Chapter 14, this method was included for you in MasterViewController.m by the UIViewController subclass template (albeit, commented out). Simply uncomment out this method and then add the code in Listing 15-11.

You might think you could do this in awakeFromNib. When the MasterViewController nib file is loaded, the awakeFromNib message is sent to the MasterViewController after all the objects in the nib file have been loaded and the MasterViewController outlet instance variables have been set. Typically, the object that owns the nib file (File's Owner, in this case the MasterViewController) implements awakeFromNib to do initialization that requires that outlet and target-action connections be set. However, this will need to be set up earlier — as you'll see in Chapter 16, when you find out how to save and restore state.

You could argue that you really should create a model class that creates this data-model array and get its data from a file or property list. For simplicity's sake, I do it in the viewDidLoad: method for the iPadTravel411 app.

Listing 15-11:   viewDidLoad

```objc
- (void)viewDidLoad {
  [super viewDidLoad];
  self.title = [[[NSBundle mainBundle] infoDictionary]
                          objectForKey:@"CFBundleName"];
  menuList = [[NSMutableArray alloc] init];
  [menuList addObject:[NSMutableDictionary
                          dictionaryWithObjectsAndKeys:
    NSLocalizedString(@"London", @"City Section"),
                                          kSelectKey,
    NSLocalizedString(@"What's happening",
                @"City Explain"), kDescriptKey, nil]];
  [menuList addObject:[NSMutableDictionary
                          dictionaryWithObjectsAndKeys:
    NSLocalizedString(@"Map", @"Map Section"),
                                          kSelectKey,
    NSLocalizedString(@"Where you are",
                @"Map Explain"), kDescriptKey, nil]];
```

```
[menuList addObject:[NSMutableDictionary
                          dictionaryWithObjectsAndKeys:
  NSLocalizedString(@"Currency", @"Currency Section"),
                                           kSelectKey,
  NSLocalizedString(@"About foreign exchange",
          @"Currency Explain"), kDescriptKey, nil]];
[menuList addObject:[NSMutableDictionary
                          dictionaryWithObjectsAndKeys:
  NSLocalizedString(@"Weather", @"Weather Section"),
                                          kSelectKey,
  NSLocalizedString(@"Current conditions",
          @"Weather  Explain"), kDescriptKey, nil]];
[menuList addObject:[NSMutableDictionary
                          dictionaryWithObjectsAndKeys:
  NSLocalizedString(@"Heathrow", @"Heathrow Section"),
                                          kSelectKey,
  NSLocalizedString(@"International airport",
          @"Heathrow Explain"), kDescriptKey, nil]];
[menuList addObject:[NSMutableDictionary
                          dictionaryWithObjectsAndKeys:
  NSLocalizedString(@"Gatwick", @"Gatwick Section"),
                                          kSelectKey,
  NSLocalizedString(@"European flights",
          @"Gatwick Explain"), kDescriptKey, nil]];
[menuList addObject:[NSMutableDictionary
                          dictionaryWithObjectsAndKeys:
  NSLocalizedString(@"Stansted",
                     @"Stansted Section"), kSelectKey,
  NSLocalizedString(@"UK flights",
          @"Stansted Explain"), kDescriptKey, nil]];
}
```

Going through the code, you can see that the first thing you do is get the application name from the bundle so you can use it as the Main view title.

```
self.title = [[[NSBundle mainBundle] infoDictionary]
                          objectForKey:@"CFBundleName"];
```

"What bundle," you ask. Well, when you build your iPad application, Xcode packages it as a bundle containing the following:

✔ The application's executable code

✔ Any resources that the app has to use (for instance, the application icon, other images, and localized content)

✔ The info.plist, also known as the information property list, which defines key values for the application, such as bundle ID, version number, and display name `infoDictionary` returns a dictionary that's constructed from the bundle's `info.plist`. `CFBundleName` is the key to the entry that contains the (localizable) application name on the home page. The title is what will be displayed in the Navigation bar at the top of the screen.

Going through the rest of the code, you can see that for each entry in the Main view, you have to create a dictionary and put it in the `menuList` array. (You're putting it there so you can use it later when you need to provide the row's content.)

You also need to add the new `menuList` instance variable to `MasterViewController.h`.

Seeing how cells work

I've been going steadily from macro to micro, so it makes sense that after setting up a model for each row, I get to talk about cells, the individual constituents of each row.

Cell objects are what draw the contents of a row in a Table view. The method `tableView:cellForRowAtIndexPath:` is called for each visible row in the table. It's expected that the method will configure and return a `UITableViewCell` object for each row. The `UITableView` object uses this cell to draw the row.

When providing cells for the Table view, you have three general approaches you can take:

- Use vanilla (not subclassed) `UITableViewCell` cell objects.
- Add subviews to a `UITableViewCell` cell object's Content view.
- Use cell objects created from a custom subclass of `UITableViewCell`.

The next few sections take a look at these options, one by one.

Using vanilla cell objects

Using the `UITableViewCell` class directly, you can create cell objects with text and an optional image. (If a cell has no image, the text starts near the left edge of the cell.) You also have an area on the right of the cell for accessory views, such as disclosure indicators (the one shaped like a regular chevron), detail disclosure controls (the one that looks like a white chevron in a blue button), and even control objects such as sliders, switches, or custom views. If you like, you can format the font, alignment, and color of the text, as well as have a different format when the row is selected. The layout of a cell is shown in Figure 15-6.

Display Mode

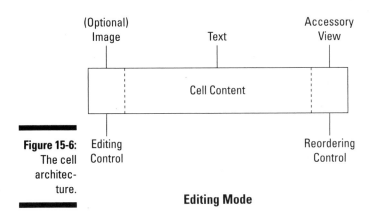

Figure 15-6:
The cell architecture.

Editing Mode

Adding subviews to a cell's Content view

Although you can specify the font, color, size, alignment, and other characteristics of the text in a cell by using the UITableViewCell class directly, the formatting is applied to all the text in the cell. To get the variation that I suspect you want between the selection and description text (and, it turns out, the alignment as well), you have to create subviews within the cell.

A cell that a Table view uses for displaying a row is, in reality, a view in its own right. UITableViewCell inherits from UIView, and it has a Content view. With Content views, you can add one subview (containing, say, the selection text "Weather") formatted the way you want — and a second subview (holding, say, the description text, "Current conditions") formatted an entirely different way. You may remember that you already experienced adding subviews (the button, text field, and labels) in creating the DeepThoughts application's Main view, although you may not have known you were doing that at the time. Well, now it can be told.

Creating a custom subclass UITableViewCell

Finally, you can create a custom cell subclass when your content requires it — usually when you need to change the default behavior of the cell.

Creating the cell

As I mention in the previous section, you're going to use the UITableView Cell class to create the cells for your Table views and then add the subviews you need in order to do the formatting you want. The place to create the cell is tableView:cellForRowAtIndexPath:. This method is called for each visible row in the Table view, as shown in Listing 15-12 (add the code to `MasterViewController.m`). You'll find that a code stub is already included in the `MasterViewController.m` file, courtesy of the template.

Listing 15-12:   Drawing the Text

```
- (UITableViewCell *)tableView:(UITableView * )tableView
        cellForRowAtIndexPath:(NSIndexPath *)indexPath {

  UITableViewCell *cell = [tableView
      dequeueReusableCellWithIdentifier:kCellIdentifier];

  if (cell == nil) {
    cell = [[[UITableViewCell alloc]
            initWithStyle:UITableViewCellStyleDefault
            reuseIdentifier:kCellIdentifier] autorelease];

    cell.accessoryType =
            UITableViewCellAccessoryDisclosureIndicator;

    CGRect subViewFrame = cell.contentView.frame;
    subViewFrame.origin.x += kInset;
    subViewFrame.size.width = kInset+kSelectLabelWidth;

    UILabel *selectLabel = [[UILabel alloc]
                            initWithFrame:subViewFrame];
    selectLabel.textColor = [UIColor blackColor];
    selectLabel.highlightedTextColor = [UIColor
                                        whiteColor];
    selectLabel.font = [UIFont boldSystemFontOfSize:18];
    selectLabel.backgroundColor = [UIColor clearColor];
    [cell.contentView addSubview:selectLabel];

    subViewFrame.origin.x += kInset+kSelectLabelWidth;
    subViewFrame.size.width = kDescriptLabelWidth;

    UILabel *descriptLabel = [[UILabel alloc]
                            initWithFrame:subViewFrame];
    descriptLabel.textColor = [UIColor grayColor];
    descriptLabel.highlightedTextColor = [UIColor
                                        whiteColor];
    descriptLabel.font = [UIFont systemFontOfSize:14];
    descriptLabel.backgroundColor = [UIColor clearColor];
    [cell.contentView addSubview:descriptLabel];

    int menuOffset = (indexPath.section*kSection1Rows)+
                                        indexPath.row;
```

```
    NSDictionary *cellText = [menuList
                                objectAtIndex:menuOffset];

    selectLabel.text = [cellText objectForKey:kSelectKey];
    descriptLabel.text = [cellText
                                objectForKey:kDescriptKey];
    [selectLabel release];
    [descriptLabel release];
  }
 return cell;
}
```

Here's the logic behind all that code:

1. **Determine whether there are any cells lying around that you can use.**

   Although a Table view may be displaying only a few rows at a time, the table itself can conceivably hold a lot more. A large table would chew up a lot of memory if you were to create cells for every row. Fortunately, Table views are designed to *reuse* cells. As a Table view's cells scroll off the screen, they're placed in a queue of cells available to be reused.

2. **Create a *cell identifier* that indicates what cell type you're using. Add this to the `Constants.h` file:**

   ```
   #define kCellIdentifier  @"Cell"
   ```

   Table views support multiple cell types, which makes the identifier necessary. In this case, you need only one cell type, but sometimes you may want more than one.

   If the system runs low on memory, the Table view gets rid of the cells in the queue, but as long as it has some available memory for them, it will hold on to them in case you want to use them again.

   You can ask the Table view for a specific reusable cell object by sending it a `dequeueReusableCellWithIdentifier:` message:

   ```
   UITableViewCell *cell = [tableView
      dequeueReusableCellWithIdentifier:kCellIdentifier];
   ```

   This asks whether any cells of the type you want are available.

3. **If there aren't any cells lying around, you'll have to create a cell by using the cell identifier you just created.**

   ```
   if (cell == nil) {
     cell = [[[UITableViewCell alloc]
         initWithStyle:UITableViewCellStyleDefault
         reuseIdentifier:kCellIdentifier] autorelease];
   ```

   You now have a Table view cell that you can return to the Table view.

UITableViewCellStyleDefault gives you a simple cell with a text label (black and left-aligned) and an optional Image view. There are also several other styles:

- UITableViewCellStyleValue1 gives you a cell with a left-aligned black text label on the left side of the cell and smaller blue text and right-aligned label on the right side. (The Settings application uses this style cell.)

- UITableViewCellStyleValue2 gives you a cell with a right-aligned blue text label on the left side of the cell and a left-aligned black label on the right side of the cell.

- UITableViewCellStyleSubtitle gives you a cell with a left-aligned label across the top and a left-aligned label below it in smaller gray text. (The iPod application uses cells in this style.)

4. **Define the accessory type for the cell.**

```
cell.accessoryType =
      UITableViewCellAccessoryDisclosureIndicator;
```

As I mention earlier in during the brief tour of a cell, its layout includes a place for an accessory — usually something like a disclosure indicator.

In this case, use UITableViewCellAccessoryDisclosureIndicator (the one shaped like a regular chevron). It lets the user know that tapping this entry will result in something (hopefully wonderful) happening — the display of the current weather conditions, for example.

If you're using a Table view and you want to display more detailed information about the entry itself, you might use a Detail Disclosure button. This button allows you to then use a tap on the row for something else. In the Favorites view in the iPhone application, for example, selecting the Detail Disclosure button gives you a view of the contact information; if you just tap the row, it places the call for you.

You're not limited to these kinds of indicators; you also have the option of creating your own view — you can put in any kind of control. (That's what you see in the Settings application, for example.)

5. **Create the subviews.**

Here I show you just one example. (The other is the same except for the font size and text color.) I get the contentView frame and base the subview on it. The inset from the left (kInset) and the width of the subview (kLabelWidth) are defined in the Constants.h file. It looks like this:

```
#define kInset               10
#define kSelectLabelWidth     100
#define kDescriptLabelWidth   160
```

To hold the text, the subview I'm creating is a UILabelView, which meets my needs exactly:

```
CGRect subViewFrame = cell.contentView.frame;
subViewFrame.origin.x += kInset;
subViewFrame.size.width = kInset+kSelectLabelWidth;
UILabel *selectLabel = [[UILabel alloc]

        initWithFrame:subViewFrame];
```

You then set the label properties that you are interested in, just as when you created the labels in the DeepThoughts application. This time, however, you'll do it by manually writing code rather than using Interface Builder. Just set the font color and size — the highlighted font color when an item is selected, and the background color of the label (as indicated in the code that follows). Setting the background color to transparent allows me to see the bottom line of the last cell in the group.

```
selectLabel.textColor = [UIColor blackColor];
selectLabel.highlightedTextColor = [UIColor
                                    whiteColor];
selectLabel.font = [UIFont boldSystemFontOfSize:18];
selectLabel.backgroundColor = [UIColor clearColor];
[cell.contentView addSubview:selectLabel];
```

I could have inset the view one pixel up from the bottom, made the label opaque, and given it a white (not clear) background — which would be more efficient to draw. But with such a small number of rows, making that effort really has no appreciable performance impact — and the way I've set it up here requires less code for you to go through. Feel free to do it the "right way" on your own.

After you have your label, you just set its text to one of the values you get from the dictionary created in awakeFromNib representing this row.

The trouble is that you won't get the absolute row passed to you. You get only the row within a particular section — and you need the absolute row to get the right dictionary from the array. Fortunately, one of the arguments used when this method is called is the indexPath, which contains the section and row information in a single object. To get the row or the section out of an NSIndexPath, you just have to invoke its section method (indexPath.section) or its row method (index Path.row), each of which returns an int. This neat trick enables you to compute the offset for the row in the array you created in awakeFrom Nib. This is also why it's so handy to have the number of rows in a section as a constant.

So the first thing you do in the following code is compute the offset. You can then use that dictionary to assign the text to the label.

```
int menuOffset = (indexPath.section*kSection1Rows)+
                                       indexPath.row;
NSDictionary *cellText = [menuList
                        objectAtIndex:menuOffset];
selectLabel.text = [cellText objectForKey:kSelectKey];
descriptLabel.text = [cellText
                        objectForKey:kDescriptKey];
```

If you think about it, the `menuOffset` algorithm will work only if you have two sections. That's why earlier I suggested you create a `sectionsArray`. If you do, the algorithm becomes:

```
int menuOffset = 0;
for (int i =0 ; i < indexPath.section; i++)  {
    menuOffset += [[sectionsArray objectAtIndex:i]
                                       intValue];
}
menuOffset += indexPath.row;
```

Finally, because I no longer need the labels I created because I have added them to the `cell contentView`, I release them

```
[selectLabel release];
[descriptLabel release];
```

and return the cell — formatted and with the text it needs to display in that row.

```
return cell;
```

Responding to a selection

At some point, you have to make sure that something actually happens when a user makes a selection. To do that, all you really need to do is implement the `tableview:didSelectRowAtIndexPath:` method to set up a response to a user tap in the Main view. This method, too, is already in the `MasterViewController.m` file, courtesy of the template.

When the user taps a Table view entry, what happens next depends on what you want your Table view to do for you.

If this application were using the Table view to display data (as the Albums view in the iPod application does, for example), you'd show the next level in the hierarchy — such as the list of songs, to stick with the iPod application — or a Detail view of an item, such as information about a song.

You could also display some new content in the Detail view, as you can see in Figure 15-7.

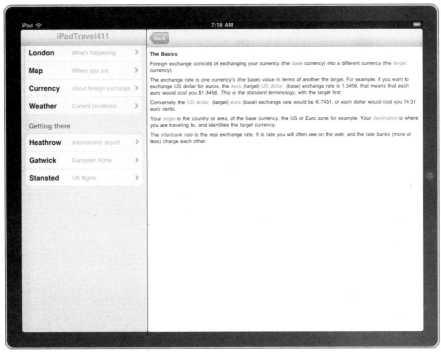

Alternatively, you could display content in the Master view, as you can see in Figure 15-8. I explain how to do that in Chapter 17.

You can actually do a lot of other things — play a movie, play a song, or do anything else the device is capable of — but I don't go into that here.

To move from one view to another view, first you need to create a new view controller for that view; then you launch it so it creates and installs the view on the screen.

This is all done in the final Table view method you'll need to work with: `tableView:didSelectRowAtIndexPath:`. In Listing 15-13, you can see some real code in bold which you should use to replace the `tableView:did SelectRowAtIndexPath:` stub, as well as some "pseudo" code that shows you what you'll be filling in later on in Chapter 17.

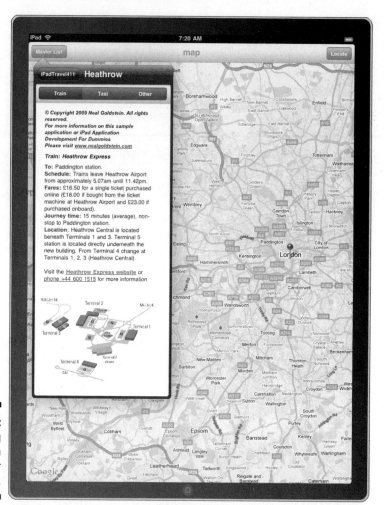

Figure 15-8:
Displaying
content in
the Master
view.

Listing 15-13:   Selecting a Row

```
- (void)tableView:(UITableView *)tableView
      didSelectRowAtIndexPath:(NSIndexPath *)indexPath {

  [tableView deselectRowAtIndexPath:indexPath
                                         animated:YES];

  int menuOffset =
        (indexPath.section*kSection1Rows)+ indexPath.row;
  switch (menuOffset) {
```

```
        case 0:
        //do something
          break;
        case 1:
        //do something
          break;
        case 2:
        //do something
          break;
        case 3:
        //do something
          break;
        case 4:
        //do something
          break;
        case 5:
        //do something
          break;
        case 6:
        //do something
          break;
    }
}
```

Here's what happens when a user makes a selection in the Main view:

1. **You deselect the row the user selected.**

   ```
   [tableView deselectRowAtIndexPath:indexPath
                                      animated:YES];
   ```

   It stands to reason that if you want your app to move on to a new view, you have to deselect the row where you currently are.

2. **You compute the offset (based on section and row) into the menu array.**

   ```
   int menuOffset =
       (indexPath.section*kSection1Rows)+ indexPath.row;
   ```

   You need to figure out where you want your app to land, right?

3. **You do something based on the row selected.**

But before I show you exactly what you need to do, I need to point out a few things:

1. There may be some user preferences that influence what you will do when a user selects a row. I cover that in the next chapter.

2. You need to understand all about navigation controllers. I cover them in Chapter 17.

3. I do things somewhat differently depending on whether I am going to replace content in the Detail view, or display content in the Master view. I cover the differences in Chapter 17.

4. If the selection was made in a Popover view, as is show in Figure 15-7, there will be some additional things I need to do. I cover that in Chapter 17 as well.

And Now . . .

You're off to a good start — and you only had to use five methods to create the table and handle user selections. You still have to implement creating Content views in the Master view controller, and create more Content views as well (you already have one, the map view), but before I do that, I want to show you how to improve the user experience by saving state and allowing the user to set preferences.

Chapter 16

Enhancing the User Experience

In This Chapter
▶ Getting back to where you once belonged
▶ Avoiding bankruptcy because of exorbitant roaming charges

"**K**eep the customer satisfied" is my mantra. If that means constantly refining an application design, so be it. In thinking about my iPadTravel411 design, two things struck me as essential if I really wanted to make this an application that really focuses on the user. The first is part of the Human Interface Guidelines, so it's not really something I can claim credit for; the second is something that flowed straight out of the nature of my design.

In this chapter, I show how I incorporated elements into my design that directly addressed issues relating to an enhanced user experience.

Saving and Restoring State

When the user taps the Home button, the iPad OS terminates your application and returns to the Home screen. The `applicationWillTerminate:` method is called, and your application is terminated — no ifs, ands, or buts. That means you have to save any unsaved data — as well as the current state of your application — if you want to restore the application to its previous state the next time the user launches it. Now, in situations like this one, you have to use common sense to decide what *state* really means. Generally, you wouldn't need to restore the application to where the user last stopped in a scrollable list, for example. For purposes of explanation, I chose to save the last category view that the user selected in the main Table view in the Master view controller — either in the Master view in the landscape mode, or in the popover in portrait mode. (This last category view would correspond to a row in a section in the Table view.) You, the reader, might also consider saving that last view that was selected in that category.

Saving state information

Here's the sequence of events that go into saving the state:

1. **Add a new instance variable (`lastView`) and declare the `@property` in the `iPadTravel411AppDelegate.h` file.**

   I explain properties in Chapter 8.

   This is shown in Listing 16-1. (Again, the new stuff is bold.)

   As you can see, `lastView` is a mutable array. You'll save the section as the first element in the array and the row as the second element. (Because it's mutable, it'll be easier to update when the user selects a new row in a section.)

2. **Add the `@synthesize` statement to the `iPadTravel411AppDelegate.m` file to tell the compiler to create the accessors for you.**

   This is shown in Listing 16-2. (You guessed it — new stuff is bold.)

3. **Define the filename you'll use when saving the state information in the `Constants.h` file.**

   ```
   #define kState  @"LastState"
   ```

4. **Add the code in Listing 16-3 to the beginning of the `tableview:did SelectRowAtIndexPath:` method in the `MasterViewController.m` file to save the section and row that the user last tapped in the `iPadTravel411AppDelegate`'s `lastView` instance variable.**

   The `tableview:didSelectRowAtIndexPath:` method is called when the user taps a row in a section. The section and row information are in the `indexPath` argument of the `tableview:didSelectRowAtIndex Path:` method. All you have to do to save that information is to save the `indexPath.section` as the first array entry, and the `indexPath.row` as the second. (The reason I do it this way will become obvious when I show you how to write this to a file.)

   "Great," you may be thinking, "but how do I get to the `iPadTravel411 AppDelegate` object where the `lastView` instance variable is declared?"

   Easy. You find the `iPadTravel411AppDelegate` by asking the `UIApplication` object where it is. The `UIApplication` is a singleton and is globally accessible, and all you have to do is send it the `shared Application` message.

   ```
   iPadTravel411AppDelegate *appDelegate =
       (iPadTravel411AppDelegate *)
       [[UIApplication sharedApplication] delegate];
   ```

When you use this (and you will a lot) make sure to add the following to any file you use it in::

```
#import "iPadTravel411AppDelegate.h"
```

5. **When the user goes back to the Main view, save that Main view location in the `viewWillAppear:` method. You'll need to add this method to the `MasterViewController.m` file, as shown in Listing 16-4. (It's already there; all you have to do is uncomment it out.)**

The last step is to deal with the case when the user moves back to the Main view and then quits the application. To indicate that the user is at the Main view, I use –1 to represent the section and –1 to represent the row. I use minus ones in this case because, as you recall, the first section and row in a table are both 0, which requires me to represent the Table (Main) view itself in this (clever) way.

6. **Save the section and row in the `applicationWillTerminate:` method. To do that, add the code in Listing 16-5.**

In `applicationWillTerminate:`, I'm saving the `lastView` instance variable (which contains the last section and row the user tapped) to the file `kState`, which is the constant I defined in Step 3 to represent the filename `LastState`.

As you can see, reading or writing to the file system on the iPad is pretty simple: You tell the system which directory to put the file in, specify the file's name — and then pass that information to the `writeToFile` method. Let me take you through what I just did in Step 6:

- *Got the path to the `Documents` directory.*

```
NSArray *paths = NSSearchPathForDirectoriesInDomains
        (NSDocumentDirectory, NSUserDomainMask, YES);
NSString *documentsDirectory =[paths objectAtIndex:0];
```

On the iPad, you really don't have much choice about where the file goes. Although there's a /tmp directory, I'm going to place this file in the `Documents` directory — because (as I explain in Chapter 2), this is part of my application's sandbox, so it's the natural home for all the app's files.

`NSSearchPathForDirectoriesInDomains:` returns an array of directories; because I'm only interested in the `Documents` directory, I use the constant `NSDocumentDirectory` — and because I'm restricted to my home directory, /sandbox, the constant `NSUserDomainMask` limits the search to that *domain*. There will be only one directory in the domain, so the one I want will be the first one returned.

- *Created the complete path by appending the path filename to the directory.*

```
NSString *filePath = [documentsDirectory
            stringByAppendingPathComponent:fileName];
```

`stringByAppendingPathComponent;` precedes the filename with a path separator (/) if necessary.

Unfortunately, this does not work if you are trying to create a string representation of a URL.

• *Wrote the data to the file.*

```
[lastView writeToFile:filePath atomically:YES];
```

`writeToFile:` is an `NSData` method and does what it implies. I am actually telling the array here to write itself to a file, which is why I decided to save the location in this way in the first place. There are a number of other classes that implement that method, including `NSData`, `NSDate`, `NSNumber`, `NSString`, and `NSDictionary`. You can also add this behavior to your own objects, and they could save themselves — but I won't get into that here. The `atomically` parameter first writes the data to an auxiliary file, and once that is successful, it's renamed to the path you've specified. This guarantees that the file won't be corrupted even if the system crashed during the write operation.

Listing 16-1: Adding the Instance Variable to the Interface

```
#import <UIKit/UIKit.h>
@class Destination;
@class MasterViewController;
@class MapController;

@interface iPadTravel411AppDelegate :
                    NSObject <UIApplicationDelegate> {

    UIWindow              *window;
    MapController          *viewController;
    Destination            *destination;
    UISplitViewController  *splitViewController;
    MasterViewController   *masterViewController;
    UIViewController       *detailViewController;
    UINavigationController *initialController;
    UIPopoverController    *popoverController;
    NSMutableArray         *lastView;
}

@property (nonatomic, retain) IBOutlet UIWindow *window;
@property (nonatomic, retain) IBOutlet
                    MapController *viewController;
@property (nonatomic, retain) Destination  *destination;
@property (nonatomic, retain)
        UISplitViewController *splitViewController;
@property (nonatomic, retain)
```

```
                  MasterViewController *masterViewController;
@property (nonatomic, retain)
                  UIViewController *detailViewController;
@property (nonatomic, retain)
                UINavigationController  *initialController;
@property (nonatomic, retain)
                  UIPopoverController *popoverController;
@property (nonatomic, retain) NSMutableArray *lastView;

@end
```

Listing 16-2:   Adding the Synthesize to the Implementation

```
#import "iPadTravel411AppDelegate.h"
#import "MapController.h"
#import "Destination.h";
#import "MasterViewController.h"
#import "Constants.h"

@implementation iPadTravel411AppDelegate

@synthesize window;
@synthesize viewController;
@synthesize destination;
@synthesize splitViewController, masterViewController,
        detailViewController, initialController;
@synthesize popoverController;
@synthesize lastView;
```

Listing 16-3:   Saving indexPath

```
- (void)tableView:(UITableView *)tableView
      didSelectRowAtIndexPath:(NSIndexPath *)indexPath {

  [tableView
          deselectRowAtIndexPath:indexPath animated:YES];
  int menuOffset =
        (indexPath.section*kSection1Rows)+ indexPath.row;

  iPadTravel411AppDelegate *appDelegate =
            (iPadTravel411AppDelegate *)
            [[UIApplication sharedApplication] delegate];
  [appDelegate.lastView
        replaceObjectAtIndex:0 withObject:
        [NSNumber numberWithInteger:indexPath.section]];
  [appDelegate.lastView
            replaceObjectAtIndex:1 withObject:
            [NSNumber numberWithInteger:indexPath.row]];
  ...

}
```

Don't forget to add the following in `MasterViewController.h`

```
#import "iPadTravel411AppDelegate.h"
```

Listing 16-4: Adding viewWillAppear:

```
- (void)viewWillAppear:(BOOL)animated {

  iPadTravel411AppDelegate *appDelegate =
          (iPadTravel411AppDelegate *)
          [[UIApplication sharedApplication] delegate];

  [appDelegate.lastView replaceObjectAtIndex:0
          withObject:[NSNumber numberWithInteger:-1]];
  [appDelegate.lastView replaceObjectAtIndex:1
          withObject:[NSNumber numberWithInteger:-1]];
}
```

Listing 16-5: Adding applicationWillTerminate:

```
- (void)applicationWillTerminate:
                        (UIApplication *)application {

  NSArray *paths = NSSearchPathForDirectoriesInDomains
          (NSDocumentDirectory, NSUserDomainMask, YES);
  NSString *documentsDirectory = [paths objectAtIndex:0];
  NSString *filePath = [documentsDirectory
                  stringByAppendingPathComponent:kState];
  [lastView writeToFile:filePath atomically:YES];
}
```

Restoring the state

Now that I've saved the state, I need to restore it when the application is launched. I use our old friend `didFinishLaunchingWithOptions:` to carry out that task (as shown in Listing 16-6). `didFinishLaunchingWith Options:` is a method you can find in the `iPadTravel411AppDelegate.m` file. The code you need to add is in bold.

Listing 16-6: Adding to applicationDidFinishLaunching:

```
- (BOOL)application:(UIApplication *)
        application didFinishLaunchingWithOptions:
                        (NSDictionary *)launchOptions {
```

```
NSArray *paths = NSSearchPathForDirectoriesInDomains
            (NSDocumentDirectory, NSUserDomainMask, YES);
  NSString *documentsDirectory = [paths objectAtIndex:0];
  NSString *filePath = [documentsDirectory
                    stringByAppendingPathComponent:kState];
  lastView =[[NSMutableArray alloc]
                          initWithContentsOfFile:filePath];
  if (lastView == nil) {
    lastView = [[NSMutableArray arrayWithObjects:
                [NSNumber numberWithInteger:-1],
                [NSNumber numberWithInteger:-1],
                nil] retain];
}
  ...
}
```

Reading is the mirror image of writing. I create the complete path, including the filename, just as I did when I saved the file. This time I send the `init WithContentsOfFile:` message instead of `writeToFile:`, which allocates the `lastView` array and initializes it with the file. If the result is `nil`, there's no file, meaning that this is the first time the application is being used. In that case, I create the array with the value of section and row set to –1 and –1. (As I said earlier, in Step 5, I use –1 –1 to indicate the Main view because 0 0 is actually the first row in the first section.)

`initWithContentsOfFile:` is an `NSData` method similar to `writeTo File:`. The classes that implement `writeToFile:` and those that implement `initWithContentsOfFile:` are the same.

Fortunately, restoring the current state is actually straightforward, given the program architecture. The `MasterViewController`'s `viewDidLoad` method is called at application launch — after the first view is in place but not yet visible. At that point, you're getting ready to display the (Table) view. But instead of just doing that, you see if the saved view was something other than the Table view, and if it was, you take advantage of the same mechanisms that are used when the user taps a row in the Table view. You invoke the `didSelectRowAtIndexPath:` method, which already knows how to display a particular view represented by the `indexPath`, that is, a particular section and row. This is shown in Listing 16-7.

A `viewDidLoad` is already in the `MasterViewController.m` file. Add the code in bold in Listing 16-7 after `[super viewDidLoad]`.

Listing 16-7: Specifying the View to Be Displayed at Launch

```
- (void)viewDidLoad {

    iPadTravel411AppDelegate *appDelegate =
      (iPadTravel411AppDelegate *)
            [[UIApplication sharedApplication] delegate];

    if ([((NSNumber*) [appDelegate.lastView
                        objectAtIndex:0]) intValue] != -1) {
    NSIndexPath* indexPath =
      [NSIndexPath indexPathForRow:
      [[appDelegate.lastView objectAtIndex:1]intValue]
      inSection:
        [[appDelegate.lastView objectAtIndex:0] intValue]];
    [self tableView:((UITableView*) self.tableView)
                        didSelectRowAtIndexPath:indexPath];
    }
  ...
}
```

Here's what you're up to in Listing 16-7:

1. **Check to see whether the last view was the Table view.**

   ```
   if ([((NSNumber*) [appDelegate.lastView
                     objectAtIndex:0]) intValue] != -1) {
   ```

2. **If the last view wasn't the Table view, create the index path using the last section and row information that was loaded into the `lastView` instance variable by `applicationDidFinishLaunching:`.**

   ```
   NSIndexPath* indexPath = [NSIndexPath indexPathForRow:
           [[appDelegate.lastView objectAtIndex:1]
           intValue] inSection:
       [[appDelegate.lastView objectAtIndex:0] intValue]];
   ```

3. **Send the `tableview:didSelectRowAtIndexPath:` message to display the right view.**

   ```
   [self tableView:((UITableView*) self.tableView)
                       didSelectRowAtIndexPath:indexPath];
   ```

The reason I created an index path was to be able to take advantage of the `didSelectRowAtIndexPath:` method to replay the last user tap in the Main view.

Because you'll be working with a Split view controller, as it stands now this saves the last view in the pane in which the user made the last selection. It's up to you to modify it at your leisure to save the last view in each pane.

Respecting User Preferences

Figure 16-1 shows you the Settings screen for my iPadTravel411 application. There you can see that I've added only preference for iPadTravel411 and in this chapter, I show you how to implement it. Any other preferences you might come up with I leave up to you.

The Use Stored Data preference tells the application to use the last version of the data that it accessed, rather than going out on the Internet for the latest information. Even though this does violate my I Want The Most Up To Date Information principle, it can save the user from excessive roaming charges, depending on his or her cell provider's data plan.

No doubt it's way cool to put user preferences in Settings. Some programmers abuse this trick, though; they make you go into Settings when it's just as easy to give the user a preference-setting capability within the app itself. You should only put something in Settings if the user changes it infrequently. In this case, stored data doesn't change often; Use Stored Data mode definitely belongs in Settings.

Figure 16-1:
The
required
prefer-
ences.

In this part of the chapter, I show you how to put a toggle switch in Settings that lets you specify whether to use only stored data — and then show you how to retrieve the setting. In this and in the next chapter, I show you how to actually use the Toggle Switch setting in your code.

The Settings application uses a property list called `Root.plist`, found in the Settings bundle inside your application. The Settings application takes what you put in the property list and builds a Settings section for your application in its list of application settings as well as building the views that display (and enable the user to change) those settings. The next sections spell out how to put that Settings section to work for you.

Adding a Settings bundle to your project

For openers, you have to add a Settings bundle to your application. Here are the moves:

1. **In the Groups & Files list (at left in the Xcode Project window), select the iPadTravel411 folder and then chose File⇨New File from the main menu, or press ⌘+N.**

   The New File dialog appears.

2. **Choose Resource under the iPhone OS heading in the left pane and then select the Settings Bundle icon, as shown in Figure 16-2.**

3. **Click the Next button.**

Figure 16-2:
Creating the application bundle.

4. **Choose the default name of `Settings.bundle`, then press Return (Enter) or click Finish.**

   You should now see a new item called Settings.bundle in the iPadTravel411 folder, in the Groups & Files list.

5. **Click the triangle to expand the `Settings.bundle` subfolder.**

   You see the `Root.plist` file as well as an `en.lproj` folder — the latter is used for dealing with localization issues, as discussed in Chapter 14.

Setting up the property list

Property lists are widely used in iPad applications because they provide an easy way to create structured data using named values for a number of object types.

In my own applications, I use property lists extensively as a way to "parameterize" view controllers and models.

Property lists all have a single root node — a dictionary, which means it stores items using a key-value pair, just as an `NSDictionary` does: All dictionary entries must have both a key and a value. In this dictionary, there are two keys:

- ✔ `StringsTable`
- ✔ `PreferenceSpecifiers`

The value for the first entries is a string — the name of a Strings table used for localization, which I won't get into here. The second entry is an array of dictionaries — one dictionary for each preference. You'll probably need some time to wrap your head around that one. It'll become clearer as I take you through it.

`PreferenceSpecifiers` is where you put a toggle switch so the user can choose to use (or not use, since it's a toggle) only stored data — I'll refer to that choice later as *stored data mode*. Here's how it's done:

1. **In the Groups & Files list of the Project window, select the triangle next to the `Settings.bundle` file to reveal the `Root.plist` file. Then double-click the `Root.plist` file to open it in a separate window, as shown in Figure 16-3.**

   Okay, you don't *really* have to do this, but I find it easier to work with this file when it's sitting in its own window.

2. **In the `Root.plist` window you just opened, expand the triangles next to all the nodes by clicking all those triangles, as shown in Figure 16-3.**

3. **Under the `PreferenceSpecifiers` heading in the `Root.plist` window, move to Item 0.**

PreferenceSpecifiers is an array designed to hold a set of diction-ary nodes, each of which represents a single preference. For each item listed in the array, the first row under it has a key of Type; every prop-erty list node in the PreferenceSpecifiers array must have an entry with this key, which identifies what kind of entry this is. The Type value for the current Item 0 — PSGroupSpecifier — is used to indicate that a new group should be started. The value for this key actually acts like a section heading for a Table view (like you created in Chapter 14). Double-click the value next to Title and delete the default Name, as I have in Figure 16-4 (or you can put in IPadTravel411 Preferences, or be creative if you like).

4. **Seeing that Item 2 is already defined as a toggle switch, you can just modify it by changing the `Title` value from `Enabled` to `Use stored data` and the key from `enabled_preference` to `useStoredData Preference`. This is the key you will use in your application to access the preference.**

5. **Continue your modifications by deselecting the Boolean check box next to `DefaultValue`.**

   I want the Use Stored Data preference initially to be set to Off because I expect most people will still want to go out on the Internet for the latest information, despite the high roaming charges involved.

   When you're done, the `Root.plist` window should look like Figure 16-4.

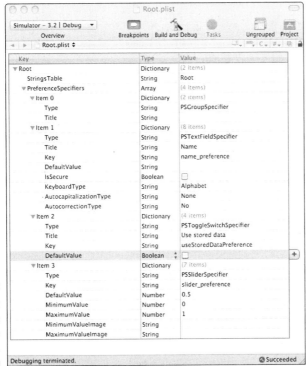

Figure 16-4:
Preferences for IPad-Travel411.

6. **Collapse the little triangles next to items 1 and 3 (as shown in Figure 16-5), and then select those items one by one and delete them.**

   The item numbers do change as you delete them, so be careful. That's why you need to leave the preference item you care about open, so you can see not to delete it. Fortunately, Undo is supported here; if you make a mistake, press ⌘+Z to undo the delete.

7. **Save the property file by pressing ⌘+S.**

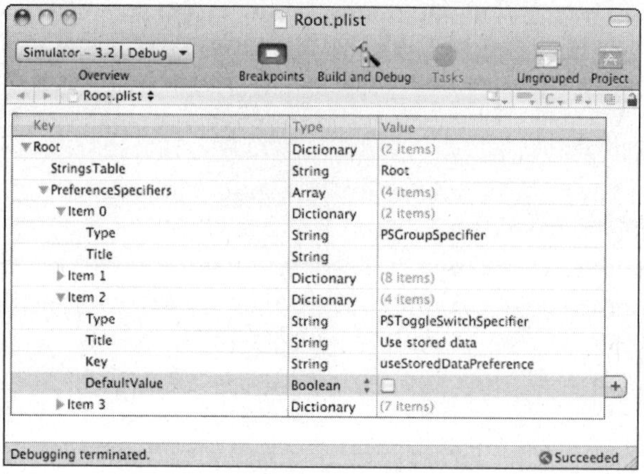

Figure 16-5:
Delete these
items.

Reading Settings in the Application

After you've set it up so your users can let their preferences be known in Settings, you'll need to read those preferences back into the application. You do that in the `applicationDidFinishLaunching:` method of `iPadTravel411AppDelegate`. But first, a little housekeeping:

1. **Add the new instance variable `useStoredData` and declare the @ property in the `iPadTravel411AppDelegate.h` file.**

   This is shown in Listing 16-8. (Again, the new stuff is bold.)

   Notice that the `@property` declaration is a little different than what you've been using so far. Up to now, all your properties have been declared (`nonatomic, retain`) — as was explained back in Chapter 7. What's this `readonly` stuff? Because `useStoredData:` isn't an object (it's a Boolean value), `retain` isn't applicable. In addition, you'll enable it to be read only. If you wanted it to be updatable, you could make it `readwrite`.

2. **Add the `@synthesize` statement to the `iPadTravel411App Delegate.m` file to tell the compiler to create the accessors for you.**

   This is shown in Listing 16-9. (You guessed it — new is bold.)

Listing 16-8: Adding the Instance Variable to the Interface

```
@interface iPadTravel411AppDelegate :
                        NSObject <UIApplicationDelegate> {

  UIWindow                  *window;
  MapController             *viewController;
  Destination               *destination;
  UISplitViewController     *splitViewController;
  MasterViewController      *masterViewController;
  UIViewController          *detailViewController;
  UINavigationController    *initialController;
  NSMutableArray            *lastView;
  BOOL                      useStoredData;
}
@property (nonatomic, retain) IBOutlet UIWindow *window;
@property (nonatomic, retain) IBOutlet MapController
        *viewController;
@property (nonatomic, retain) IBOutlet Destination    *
        destination;
@property (nonatomic, retain) IBOutlet
        UISplitViewController *splitViewController;
@property (nonatomic, retain) IBOutlet
        MasterViewController *masterViewController;
@property (nonatomic, retain) UIViewController
        *detailViewController;
@property (nonatomic, retain) UINavigationController
        *initialController;
@property (nonatomic, retain) NSMutableArray *lastView;
@property (nonatomic, readonly) BOOL useStoredData;

@end
```

Listing 16-9: Adding the Synthesize to the Implementation

```
#import "iPadTravel411AppDelegate.h"
#import "MapController.h"
#import "Destination.h";
#import "MasterViewController.h"

@implementation iPadTravel411AppDelegate

@synthesize window;
@synthesize viewController;
@synthesize destination;
@synthesize splitViewController, masterViewController,
        detailViewController, initialController;
@synthesize lastView;
@synthesize useStoredData;
```

With your housekeeping done, it's time to add the necessary code to the beginning of the `didFinishLaunchingWithOptions:` method. Listing 16-10 shows the code you need:

Listing 16-10:   Adding to didFinishLaunchingWithOptions

```
- (BOOL)application:(UIApplication *)
        application didFinishLaunchingWithOptions:
                        (NSDictionary *)launchOptions {

if (![[NSUserDefaults standardUserDefaults]
              objectForKey:kUseStoredDataPreference]) {
   [[NSUserDefaults standardUserDefaults]setBool:NO
                      forKey:kUseStoredDataPreference];
   useStoredData = NO;
 }
 else
   useStoredData = [[NSUserDefaults standardUserDefaults]
              boolForKey:kUseStoredDataPreference];
...

}
```

Here's what you want all that code to do for you:

1. **Check to see whether the settings have been moved into `NSUserDefaults`.**

   ```
   if (![[NSUserDefaults standardUserDefaults]
           objectForKey:kUseStoredDataPreference]){
   ```

   I explain `NSUserDefaults` back in Chapter 9. The Settings application moves the user's preferences from Settings into `NSUserDefaults` only *after* the application runs for the first time; Settings will, however, update them in `NSUserDefaults` if the user makes any changes.

2. **If the settings have not been moved into `NSUserDefaults` yet, then use the default of `NO` (which corresponds to the default you used for the initial preference value).**

   ```
   [[NSUserDefaults standardUserDefaults]setBool:NO
                   forKey:kUseStoredDataPreference];
   useStoredData = NO;
   ```

3. **If the settings *have* been moved into `NSUserDefaults`, read them in, and then set the `useStoredData` instance variable to whatever the user's preference is.**

   ```
   else
      useStoredData =
               [[NSUserDefaults  standardUserDefaults]
               boolForKey:kUseStoredDataPreference];
   ```

You'll also have to add the following line to `Constants.h`:

```
#define kUseStoredDataPreference
          @"useStoredDataPreference"
```

Using Preferences in Your Application

I said back in Chapter 15 that before you could implement the `tableview:didSelectRowAtIndexPath:` method that makes something happen when a user selects a row in the Table view, you need to have some other things in place. Well, part of it is now done.

Although you won't be able to test restoring state, you can test your `useStoredData` preference.

To do that, first add the code in Listing 16-11 to `MasterViewController.m`.

Listing 16-11:   Try This Out

```
-  (void)tableView:(UITableView *)tableView
        didSelectRowAtIndexPath:(NSIndexPath *)indexPath {

[tableView deselectRowAtIndexPath:indexPath
                                        animated:YES];

int menuOffset =
        (indexPath.section*kSection1Rows)+ indexPath.row;

iPadTravel411AppDelegate *appDelegate =
        (iPadTravel411AppDelegate *)
            [[UIApplication sharedApplication] delegate];
[appDelegate.lastView replaceObjectAtIndex:0 withObject:
        [NSNumber numberWithInteger:indexPath.section]];
[appDelegate.lastView replaceObjectAtIndex:1 withObject:
            [NSNumber numberWithInteger:indexPath.row]];
BOOL realtime = !appDelegate.useStoredData;

if (!realtime) [self displayOfflineAlert:
        [[menuList objectAtIndex:menuOffset]
                            objectForKey:kSelectKey]];
...
}
```

Here's what happens when a user makes a selection in the Main view:

1. Deselect the row the user selected.

```
[tableView deselectRowAtIndexPath:indexPath
                                    animated:YES];
```

It stands to reason that if you want your app to move on to a new view, you have to deselect the row where you currently are.

2. Compute the offset (based on section and row) into the menu array.

```
int menuOffset =
      (indexPath.section*kSection1Rows)+ indexPath.row;
```

You need to figure out where you want your app to land, right?

3. Save the section and row that the user last tapped.

I cover that in Step 4 in the section "Saving state information."

4. Check to see whether you're offline.

```
BOOL realtime = !appDelegate.useStoredData;
```

5. If you are in fact offline, you pose the standard alert dialogue and pass in the offending selection so you can display it to the user.

```
if (!realtime) [self displayOfflineAlert:
[[menuList objectAtIndex:menuOffset]
                         objectForKey:kSelectKey]];
```

The code for displaying an alert is shown in Listing 16-12. You need to add this to `MasterViewController.m` as well.

Listing 16-12:   Displaying an Alert

```
- (void) displayOfflineAlert: (NSString*) selection {

  UIAlertView *alert = [[UIAlertView alloc]
          initWithTitle:selection
          message:@"is not available offline"
          delegate:self cancelButtonTitle: @"Thanks"
          otherButtonTitles:nil];
  [alert show];
  [alert release];
}
```

You also need to add the following to `MainViewController.h`:

```
- (void) displayOfflineAlert: (NSString*) selection;
```

Delete iPhoneTravel411 from your iPad and then compile your project. Then go to Settings, toggle on the Use Stored Data option, and then select a row in the Master view. You should see what's shown in Figure 16-6.

Figure 16-6:
Choosing
a row in
stored data
mode.

You'll actually be using all of the code in Listing 16-11, with the exception of the last line, when you add the rest of the app's functionality in Chapter 17.

Of course, what you see in Figure 16-6 is what you'll always see if you select a row. To see anything more interesting, you need to create a few more view controllers, and you do that in the next chapter.

Chapter 17

Adding the Stuff

. . . .

. . . .

*N*ow that you've done a stellar job of creating the structure necessary to display the content of your app, you probably want to be able to see something happen when you press one of those buttons, so it's time to add more content.

In this chapter, I show you how to use the rest of the view controllers and views I explain in Chapter 13 in order to display content — and even how to get that content. I show you how to display content stored as a resource (part of your application), stored on a Web server, and even how to display a Web page.

This being London, the first thing to do is check the weather.

How's the Weather Over There?

If the user selects Weather from the Main view, what the user sees *does* depend on whether the device is online or in stored data mode. If the device is online, the user sees a Web page from a Web site with the weather information, as illustrated in Figure 17-1. When in stored data mode, the user gets a message stating that weather data is unavailable when offline, as explained in Chapter 16.

Figure 17-1:
Glad I'm in
California
today.

To begin this process, you need to create a view controller that will display a Web site in its view. In this chapter, I finally give you the lowdown on controllers and stacks as they apply to the iPadTravel411 application. To make it happen, you need to code your view controller interface, your implementation files, and your nib files.

Adding the controller and nib file

So many files, so little time. Actually, after you get a rhythm going, cranking out the various view controller, nib, and model files necessary to fill your application architecture with content isn't *that* much work. And even though I want to start with what happens when the user taps Weather (because it allows me to also explain a bit about navigating between views in your program), now is as good a time as any to create all those files you'll need to create.

Okay, check out how easy it is to come up with the view controller and nib files:

1. **Choose File⇨New File from the main menu (or press ⌘+N) to get the New File dialog.**

2. **In the leftmost pane of the dialog, first select Cocoa Touch Classes under the iPhone OS heading, then select the** *UIViewController subclass* **template in the topmost pane, and then make sure that the following are all selected:**

   • With XIB for user interface

   • Targeted for iPad

3. **Click Next.**

   You see a new dialog asking for some more information.

4. **Enter** WeatherController **in the File Name field and then click Finish.**

   Of course, if you look at the choices in the Master view controller, you see there's more to life than complaining about the weather. So, to get it out of the way, you should add the remaining controllers you'll be using.

5. **Repeat Steps 1 through 4 for** `CityController`, `CurrencyController`, **and** `AirportController`.

   When you're done, in your Groups & Files list, you should see `AirportController.h`, `AirportController.m`, `CityController.h`, `CityController.m`, `CurrencyController.h`, `CurrencyController.m`, `WeatherController.h`, and `WeatherController.m` in addition to what you already have there.

I'm having you set up the `CityController` and nib file and the `City` model object, even though I won't be explaining them in this chapter; however, the code is implemented in the listing on my Web site.

Now, you need to do it all over again (and get it out of the way) for the model classes your controllers will use.

Setting up the nib file

For the iPadTravel411 application, you want to use a `UIWebView` to display the Web site you're after. (For the reasoning behind that choice, check out Chapter 13.) You'll set up the `UIWebView` by using Interface Builder, but you'll also need a reference to it from the `WeatherController` so it can load the Web site you want. To do that, you need to create an *outlet* (a special kind of instance that can refer to objects in the nib) in the view controller, just as you did back in Chapter 14 when you were working on the `MapController`. The outlet reference will be filled in automatically when your application is initialized.

Here's how you should deal with this outlet business (it's the same thing you did in Chapter 14 to set up the MapController, so if you're a little hazy, you might want to go back and review what you did there):

1. **Within Xcode, add a `webView` (`UIWebView`) outlet to the `WeatherController.h` interface file.**

   You declare an outlet by using the keyword `IBOutlet` in the `WeatherController` interface file.

   ```
   IBOutlet UIWebView   *webView;
   ```

2. **While you're at it, make the `WeatherController` a `UIWebView` delegate as well. (You'll need that later.)**

   Here's what it should look like when you're done; changes are in bold.

   ```
   @interface WeatherController : UIViewController
                                 <UIWebViewDelegate> {

      IBOutlet UIWebView* webView;
   }
   ```

3. **Do the File⇨Save thing to save the file.**

   After it's saved — and only then — Interface Builder can find the new outlet.

4. **While you're at it, do the same thing for `CityController`, `CurrencyController`, and `AirportController`.**

5. **Use the Groups & Files list on the left in the Project window to drill down to the `WeatherController.xib` file; then double-click the file to launch it in Interface Builder.**

   If the Attributes Inspector window isn't open, choose Tools⇨Inspector or press ⌘+Shift+1. If the View window isn't visible, double-click the View icon in the `WeatherController.xib` window.

   If you can't find the `WeatherController.xib` window (you may have minimized it — accidentally, on purpose, whatever), you can get it back by choosing Window⇨WeatherController.xib or whichever nib file you're working on.

6. **Click in the View window and then choose `UIWebView` from the Class drop-down menu in the Identity Inspector.**

   This step will change the title of the View window to Web view in the `WeatherController.xib` window and in the View window the next time you open it.

7. **Back in the `WeatherController.xib` window, right-click File's Owner to call up a contextual menu with a list of connections.**

   You can get the same list using the Connections tab in the Attributes Inspector.

8. **Drag from the little circle next to the `webView` outlet in the list onto the Web view window.**

   Doing so connects the `webView` outlet in `WeatherController` to the Web view.

   When you're done, the contextual menu should look like Figure 17-2.

9. **And as you may have guessed, repeat Steps 5 to 8 for `CityController.xib`, `CurrencyController.xib`, but this time don't do it for `AirportController.xib`.**

You'll also want to make the `WeatherController` a `UIWebviewDelegate`, but I show you an easier way shortly.

Of course even though it's nice that you have all these controllers, you still need to have them add some actual content. At this point, I have you focus on doing that in `WeatherController`.

The place to start is in the method `viewDidLoad`. As I mention in Chapter 14, this method was included for you in `WebViewController.m` by the `UIViewController` subclass template (albeit, commented out). Simply uncomment out this method and add the code in Listing 17-1 to `WeatherController.m`.

Figure 17-2: Weather Controller connections all in place.

Listing 17-1:   viewDidLoad

```
- (void)viewDidLoad {

    [super viewDidLoad];
    webView.delegate = self;
    webView.scalesPageToFit = YES;
    iPadTravel411AppDelegate *appDelegate =
        (iPadTravel411AppDelegate *)
            [[UIApplication sharedApplication] delegate];
    [webView loadRequest:[NSURLRequest
        requestWithURL: [appDelegate.destination weather]]];
}
```

All this code does is send a message to the `Destination` object to find out where the data the Web view needs is located. (In this case, it goes to grab the URL of the Web site with the weather information, just as the `MapController` did.) Listing 17-1 also sets the Web view delegate to `self` (easier I think then all that dragging in Interface Builder) and tells the Web view to scale the page to fit the view (so you don't have to scroll all over the place). But how does the `WeatherController` know about the `Destination`?

When you implemented the `MapController` you created an initialization method in which you passed a reference to the `Destination` object an argument. In this case, you're going to do it a bit differently — you'll have the `WebController` access the `destination` property of the `iPadTravel411AppDelegate`.

"Great," you may be thinking, "out of the frying pan and into the fire. How do I get to the `iPadTravel411AppDelegate` object?"

Easy. In Listing 17-1, you did what you did in Chapter 16 to access the `iPad411AppDelegate` `lastView` instance variable when you were saving state. You ask the `UIApplication` object where it is. The `UIApplication` is a singleton, and globally accessible and all you have to do is send it the `sharedApplication` message.

```
iPadTravel411AppDelegate *appDelegate =
    (iPadTravel411AppDelegate *)
            [[UIApplication sharedApplication] delegate];
```

Although in general I think you need to be careful of properties, because the indiscriminate use of them does reduce the encapsulation you really want in your classes, this does simplify the code a bit.

You also need to import `iPadTravel411AppDelegate` and `Destination`.

This small task is all it takes to access the Web site — with the exception of the code in `Destination` that returns the URL. To do that bit of business, add the method in Listing 17-2 to `Destination.m` (and do all that other stuff you need to in `Destination.h` as well).

Listing 17-2:   weather

```
- (NSURL*) weather {

  NSURL *url = [NSURL URLWithString:@"http://www.weather.
          com/outlook/travel/businesstraveler/local/
          UKXX0085?lswe=London,%20UNITED%20KINGDOM&l
          wsa=WeatherLocalUndeclared&from=searchbox_
          typeahead"];
  return url;
}
```

This is the same mechanism you used in the `MapController` where the `Destination` object returns back the data (or the address of the data) the view controller needs.

That big long URL you see is one I use for weather for London from www. weather.com. Of course, these things change from time to time, and it may or may not work when you try it. If not, check my Web site (www.neal goldstein.com) for what I'm currently using.

Cruising the Web

Although the Web page I've chosen for my Weather view (refer to Figure 17-1) does have a lot of weather-y information, there's also quite a bit more information available using the links on the page. (Flight Delays comes to mind.) So, in my design I wanted to be able to tap a link on the page to get that additional information. It's actually easy to do in a Web view (in fact, the Web view does it for you), but I need to add a Back button after I go someplace in case I ever want to get back in one piece to my iPadTravel411 app. I created another button and labeled it Back so the user knows he or she can use it to get back to the previous view.

Of course you don't want to display a Back button if there's nothing to go back to — you'll want to display the button only after the user has clicked a link and then remove it when the user is back to the original Web page you first displayed.

All this is accomplished in the WebView:shouldStartLoadWithRequest: navigationType: method. This message is sent to the Web view's delegate at the right time. Add the code in Listing 17-3 to WeatherController.m.

Listing 17-3:   When the User Touches a Link

```
- (BOOL)webView:(UIWebView *)webView
  shouldStartLoadWithRequest:(NSURLRequest *)request
  navigationType:(UIWebViewNavigationType)navigationType {

  if (navigationType ==
        UIWebViewNavigationTypeLinkClicked) {
    UIBarButtonItem *backButton =
        [[UIBarButtonItem alloc] initWithTitle: @"Back"
        style:UIBarButtonItemStylePlain
              target:self action:@selector(goBack:)];
    self.navigationItem.rightBarButtonItem = backButton;
    [backButton release];
  }
  return YES;
}
```

Point-for-point, here's what you're doing with this code:

1. **First, check to see whether the user has touched an embedded link.**

```
if ((navigationType ==
        UIWebViewNavigationTypeLinkClicked) &&
    ([[NSUserDefaults standardUserDefaults]
            boolForKey:kUseStoredDataPreference])) {
```

2. **If he or she has, create and add the Back button.**

```
UIBarButtonItem *backButton =
                    [[UIBarButtonItem alloc]
                    initWithTitle:@"Back"
                    style:UIBarButtonItemStylePlain
                    target:self
                    action:@selector(goBack:)];
self.navigationItem.rightBarButtonItem = backButton;
[backButton release];
```

In this method, you allocate the button and then assign it to an instance variable (`self.navigationItem.rightBarButtonItem`) that the `UINavigationController` will later use to set up the Navigation bar. The `action:@selector(goBack:)` argument is the standard way to specify Target-Action. It says when the button is tapped, send the `goBack:` message to the `target: self`, which is the `AirportController`. I show you how to implement this shortly.

3. **Return YES to tell the Web view to load from the Internet.**

Next, add the delegate method `goBack:`, which you specified as the selector when you created the Back button. Listing 17-4 has the details. Add this to WeatherController.m.

Listing 17-4:   goBack to Where You Once Belonged

```
- (IBAction) goBack:(id)sender{

  if ([webView  canGoBack] == NO ) {
    self.navigationItem.rightBarButtonItem = nil;
  }
  else {
    [webView goBack];
  }
}
```

The `UIWebView` actually implements much of the behavior you need here. When the user touches the Back button and this message is sent, you first check with the Web view to see whether there's someplace to go back *to*. (It keeps a backward *and* forward list.) If there's an appropriate retreat, you send the UIWebView message (goBack:) that will reload the previous page. If not, it means that you're at the first Web page you displayed and you remove the Back button by setting the property (self.navigationItem. rightBarButtonItem) to nil.

Finally, you want to get rid of the Back button when you're in the original view. The code to do that is in Listing 17-5.

Listing 17-5: You Don't Need the Back Button Any Longer

```
- (void)webViewDidFinishLoad:(UIWebView *) webView {
    if ([webView canGoBack] == NO ) {
        self.navigationItem.rightBarButtonItem = nil;
    }
}
```

After the Web page the user has linked to has finished loading, you check to see whether you can go back; if not, you remove the Back button.

When you compile this, you get a compiler warning that says

```
Local declaration of 'webView' hides instance variable
```

This warning is referring to your instance variable and the argument name in webViewDidFinishLoad:. Although this makes no difference because both webView variables refer to the same object, you should get rid of the warning. You can do one of two things. You can change your instance variable name, or you can simply change the name in the method:

```
- (void)webViewDidFinishLoad:(UIWebView *) aWebView
```

That being said, the Apple Human Interface Guidelines say, "In addition to displaying Web content, a Web view provides elements that support navigation through open Web pages. Although you can choose to provide Web page navigation functionality, it's best to avoid creating an application that looks and behaves like a mini Web browser." As far as I am concerned, making it possible to select links in a Web view doesn't do that, but if you really didn't want to enable the user to follow links, Listing 17-6 shows you how to disable links. (As you'll see, there will be other times you'll want to disable links, like when you're in stored data mode, and I explain that more in the "Navigating the Navigation controller" section, later in this chapter).

If you've decided to follow Apple's suggestion and aren't making your app act as a mini browser, you have to disable the links that are available in the content. You can do that in the shouldStartLoadWithRequest: method in the WeatherController.m file by coding it as shown in Listing 17-6.

Listing 17-6: **Disabling Links**

```
- (BOOL)webView:(UIWebView *) webView
       shouldStartLoadWithRequest:(NSURLRequest *) request
       navigationType:
               (UIWebViewNavigationType)navigationType {

    if (navigationType ==
                      UIWebViewNavigationTypeLinkClicked)
      return NO;

    else return YES;
}
```

Responding to a selection

Now that you have the `WeatherController` set up, you can allow the user
to select it in the Master view controller.

When the user taps on a table-view entry, what happens next depends on
what you want your Table view to do for you.

If this application were using the Table view to display data (as the Albums
view in the iPod application does, for example), you'd show the next level in
the hierarchy — such as the list of songs, to stick with the iPod application —
or a Detail view of an item, such as information about a song.

In this case, you're using the Table view as a table of contents, so tapping a
table-view entry transfers the user to the view that presents the desired
information — the weather, for example.

To move from one content view to a new (content) view, first you need to
create a new view controller for that view; then you launch it so it creates
and installs the view on the screen. But you also have to give the user a way
to get back to the Main view!

Brass-tacks time: What kind of code-writing gymnastics do you have to do to
get all this stuff to happen?

Actually, not much. Table views are usually paired with *Navigation bars,*
whose job it is to implement the back stuff. And to get a Navigation bar, all
you have to do is include a *Navigation controller* in your application. You
did that bit of business back in Chapter 15 in the "Creating a Split View
Controller" section. There, you did the following in `didFinishLaunching`
`WithOptions:`.

```
masterViewController = [[MasterViewController alloc]
                initWithDestination: destination];
UINavigationController *navigationController =
  [[UINavigationController alloc]
         initWithRootViewController:masterViewController];

}
```

Navigating the Navigation controller

As the previous section made clear, to give users the option of returning to a view higher up in the hierarchy (in this case, the Master view), Table views are paired with Navigation bars that enable a user to navigate the hierarchy. Here's what you need to know in order to make Navigation bars work for you:

- ✔ The view below the Navigation bar presents the current level of data.

- ✔ A Navigation bar includes a title for the current view.

- ✔ If the current view is lower in the hierarchy than the top level, a Back button appears on the left side of the bar; the user can tap it to return to the previous level. The text in the Back button tells the user what the previous level was. In this case, it's the application's Map view, so you will see the previous view controller's title — map.

- ✔ A Navigation bar may also have an Edit button (on the right side) — used to enter editing mode for the current view — or even custom buttons such a button to launch a popover.

This Navigation bar Back button is of course different from the Back button you created in the Web view. You created that one to get back from a Web page to a previous Web page. This one takes you back from one view controller to a previous view controller.

The Navigation bar for each level is managed by a Navigation controller. The Navigation controller maintains a stack of view controllers, one for each of the views displayed, starting with the Master view controller. The only thing that makes the Master view controller special is that it is the very first view controller that the Navigation controller pushes onto its stack when a user launches the application; it remains active until the user selects the next view to look at.

Time for a concrete example. When the user taps a row of the Table view to get the Weather information, the Root view controller pushes the next view controller onto the stack. The new controller's view (the Weather information) slides into place, and the Navigation bar items are updated appropriately.

When the user taps the Back button in the Navigation bar, the current view controller pops off the stack, the Weather view slides off the screen, and the user lands (so to speak) back in the Map view.

As you will see however, you can also change view controllers in the Master view as well, and I show that when I explain the `AirportController`.

A *stack* is a commonly used data structure that works on the principle of last in, first out. Imagine an "ideal" boarding scenario for an airplane: You would start with the last seat in the last row and board the plane in back-to-front order until you got to the first seat in the first row — that would be the seat for the last person to board. When you got to your destination you'd deplane (is that really a word?) in the reverse order. That last person on — the person in row one seat one — would be the first person off.

A computer stack is pretty much the same. Adding an object is called a *push* — in this case, when you select Weather, the view controller for the Weather view is pushed onto the stack. Removing an object is called a *pop* — touching the Back button pops the view controller for the Heathrow view. When you pop an object off the stack, it's always the last one you pushed onto it. The controller that was there before the push is still there and now becomes the active one — in this case, it's the Root view controller.

Now you're in a position to extend the `tableView:didSelectRowAtInd exPath` method that you coded at the end of Chapter 16. Make the changes in Listing 17-7. (I've commented out the following selections because you haven't implemented them yet.)

```
// targetController = [[CityController alloc] init];
// targetController = [[CurrencyController alloc] init];
// targetController = [[AirportController alloc]
          initWithDestination: destination airportID:1];
// targetController = [[AirportController alloc]
          initWithDestination: destination airportID:1];
// targetController = [[AirportController alloc]
          initWithDestination: destination airportID:1];
```

And there's some code I won't get to explain until you implement the AirportController, so for the time being ignore it.

```
if ([targetController isKindOfClass:
                          [AirportController class]])
    [[self navigationController]
        pushViewController:targetController animated:YES];
```

Listing 17-7: Selecting a Row

```
- (void)tableView:(UITableView *)tableView didSelectRowAtI
        ndexPath:(NSIndexPath *)indexPath {
  [tableView deselectRowAtIndexPath:indexPath
        animated:YES];

  int menuOffset = (indexPath.section*kSection1Rows)+
        indexPath.row;

  iPadTravel411AppDelegate *appDelegate =
        (iPadTravel411AppDelegate *)[[UIApplication
        sharedApplication] delegate];
  [appDelegate.lastView replaceObjectAtIndex:0
        withObject:[NSNumber
        numberWithInteger:indexPath.section]];
  [appDelegate.lastView replaceObjectAtIndex:1
        withObject:[NSNumber
        numberWithInteger:indexPath.row]];
  BOOL realtime = !appDelegate.useStoredData;
// if (!realtime) [self displayOfflineAlert:
//        [[menuList objectAtIndex:menuOffset]
//        objectForKey:kSelectKey]];
  UIViewController *targetController = nil;

  switch (menuOffset) {
    case 0:
      // targetController = [[CityController alloc] init];
      break;
    case 1:
      if (realtime) targetController = [[MapController
          alloc] initWithDestination:destination];
      else [self displayOfflineAlert:[[menuList
          objectAtIndex:menuOffset]
          objectForKey:kSelectKey]];
      break;
    case 2:
      //targetController = [[CurrencyController alloc]
          init];
      break;
    case 3:
      if (realtime) targetController = [[WeatherController
          alloc] init];
      else [self displayOfflineAlert:[[menuList
          objectAtIndex:menuOffset]
          objectForKey:kSelectKey]];
      break;
```

(continued)

Listing 17-7 *(continued)*

```
    case 4:
      //targetController = [[AirportController alloc]
           initWithDestination: destination airportID:1];
      break;
    case 5:
      //targetController = [[AirportController alloc]
           initWithDestination: destination airportID:1];
      break;
    case 6:
      //targetController = [[AirportController alloc]
           initWithDestination: destination airportID:1];
      break;
  }

  if ([targetController isKindOfClass:[AirportController
         class]])
    [[self navigationController] pushViewController:target
         Controller animated:YES];
  else {
    if (targetController) [[appDelegate.
         detailViewController navigationController] push
         ViewController:targetController animated:YES];

    if (appDelegate.popoverController)
     [appDelegate.popoverController
                              dismissPopoverAnimated:YES];
  }
}
```

Here's what happens when a user makes a selection in the Main view:

1. **Deselect the row the user selected.**

   ```
   [tableView deselectRowAtIndexPath:indexPath
                                  animated:YES];
   ```

   It stands to reason that if you want your app to move on to a new view, you have to deselect the row where you currently are.

2. **Compute the offset (based on section and row) into the menu array.**

   ```
   int menuOffset =
       (indexPath.section*kSection1Rows)+ indexPath.row;
   ```

   You need to figure out where you want your app to land, right?

3. **Save the section and row that the user last tapped.**

   I covered that in the section on saving state information in Chapter 16.

4. Create and initialize a new controller if you should.

I explain the mechanics of creating and initializing a new controller in Chapter 16. As you can see, you're going to use another `switch` statement to get to the right controller:

```
switch (menuOffset) {
```

For many of the selections, you'll always create a new controller. For example:

```
case 4:
    targetController = [[AirportController alloc]
        initWithDestination:destination airportID:1];
    break;
```

But for some selections, like Weather, you have decided that if you're not online, you can't deliver the quality of the information a user needs (saved "current" weather conditions is an oxymoron). For other selections, Map for example, a network connection is required. (Right now no caching is available.) In that case, you send an alert to the user (see Listing 17-7) informing him or her that the selection is unavailable.

```
if (realtime) targetController =
                [[MapController alloc]
                initWithDestination:destination];
else [self displayOfflineAlert:
            [[menuList objectAtIndex:menuOffset]
            objectForKey:kSelectKey]];
```

5. If you created a new view controller, push the controller onto the stack and let the Navigation controller do the rest.

```
[[appDelegate.detailViewController
                            navigationController]
    pushViewController:targetController animated:YES];
```

6. If there's a Popover controller, dismiss it.

```
if (appDelegate.popoverController)
    [appDelegate.popoverController
                        dismissPopoverAnimated:YES];
```

Notice I create a new copy of the map if the user selects one from the Table view. This is a temporary one with the original map staying where it is.

Although you won't be creating the remaining view controllers yet, now's a good time to add all the imports you'll need for them.

```
#import "WeatherController.h"
#import "MapController.h"
#import "CityController.h"
#import "CurrencyController.h"
#import "AirportController.h"
```

Navigating in the Master View

So far you've seen how to use the Master view controller to add to the detail view. But you can also push new controllers in the master view. Figure 17-3 shows you how you can be getting information about transportation into London while looking at currency information about what it takes to turn dollars into pounds so you can pay for your Heathrow Express ticket.

The airport controller

The `AirportController` will display the transportation options open to you, and you'll start by adding some stuff to that controller.

Right off the bat, you're going to have to add the initialization method in Listing 17-8 to `AirportController.m`.

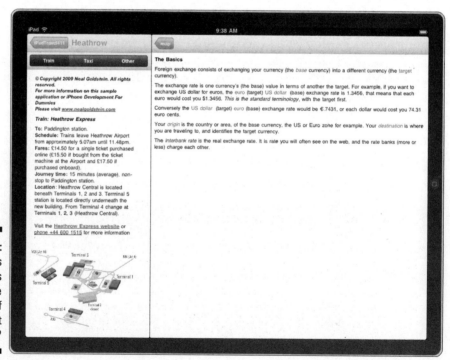

Figure 17-3:
What is all this exchange rate stuff about anyway?

Listing 17-8:   initWithDestination:airportID:

```
- (id)initWithDestination:(Destination*)aDestination
                airportID:(int) theAirport {

  if (self = [super initWithNibName:@"AirportController"
                            bundle:nil]) {
    destination = aDestination;
    self.title = [destination
                returnAirportName:theAirport];   }
  return self;
}
```

As you can see from the Master view controller, I'm planning to provide information for all three of London's airports. Because the kind of information is basically the same, I'd like to have to create only one view controller class that can provide the information for any airport — that's the reason for the airportID. Although I won't be showing you how to implement that in this book, it does provide the beginnings of the framework you need to do it on your own.

You also need to make the changes to AirportController.h you see in Listing 17-9.

Listing 17-9:   AirportController.h

```
#import <UIKit/UIKit.h>
@class Destination;

@interface AirportController : UIViewController
                                   <UIWebViewDelegate> {

  IBOutlet UIWebView *webView;
  Destination        *destination;
  IBOutlet UIToolbar *theToolbar;
  UISegmentedControl *segmentedControl;
}
- (id)initWithDestination:(Destination*)aDestination
                          airportID:(int) theAirport;

@end
```

If you look at the left pane in Figure 17-3, you can see that you're going to be adding a toolbar with a segmented control — the Train-Taxi-Other business — as well as an image. In Listing 17-9, you create some outlets to take care of this.

Now, you can start by taking care of the image. To do that, you'll add the image as a resource in your program bundle. The one I'm showing is a map of Heathrow Airport, and you can download that from my Web site or use any other image you want.

To make it available to the application, I need to include the image in the application bundle itself, although I could have downloaded it the first time the application ran. (But there's method in my madness. Including it in the bundle *does* give me the opportunity to show you how to handle this kind of data.)

Now, you can add it to your bundle one of two ways:

✔ Open the Project window and drag the .png file into the Project folder, like you did with the icon in Chapter 5.

 It's a good idea to create a new folder within your Project folder as a snug little home for the file. (I named my new folder "Static Data.")

 Or

✔ Select Project➪Add to Project and then use the dialog that appears to navigate to and select the file you want. You can see that in Figure 17-4.

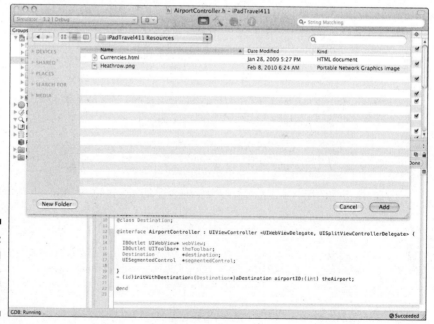

Figure 17-4:
Adding
Heathrow.
png to the
project.

The only thing interesting here is that you're going to use some data that you have included with your application as a *resource* (which you can think about as an included file, although it doesn't live in the iPad file system but rather is embedded in the application itself).

Next, hook thinks up in Interface Builder:

1. **Open Interface Builder by double-clicking `AirportController.xib`.**

2. **After making sure that the Library window and View window are open, drag in a toolbar from the Objects list and place it at the top of the view, as I have in Figure 17-5.**

   Although toolbars should only be on the bottom on an iPhone, on the iPad they can also be on the top.

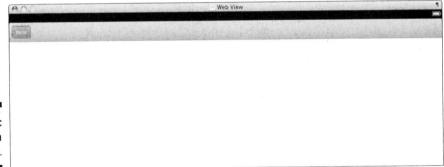

Figure 17-5:
Adding a
toolbar.

3. **Next drag in a Web view from the Objects list.**

   The size of the left (or Master) view controller is fixed at 320 pixels, so you want to be sure to resize the Web view so that it is narrower than that.

   You can set the size in the Size inspector

4. **Drag in an Image View from the Objects list and place it below the Web view.**

   You can see the results in Figure 17-6.

   You can set the size of the various objects in the Size inspector, as you can see in Figure 17-7.

Figure 17-6:
Views in
place.

Finally you need to tell Interface Builder what image to use in the Image View.

5. **Select the Image View element in the View window.**

   Doing so changes what you see in the Attribute inspector. It now displays the attributes for an Image view.

6. **Using the Attribute inspector's Image drop-down menu, choose the image you want to use for the Image View, as shown in Figure 17-8.**

   That inspector's a handy little critter, isn't it?

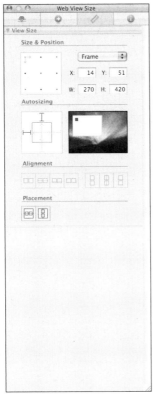

Figure 17-7:
The Size
inspector.

When you're done, your view should look like Figure 17-9.

Of course, you're not done yet.

7. **Back in the `AirportController` window, right-click File's Owner to call up a contextual menu with a list of connections.**

You can get the same list using the Connections tab in the Attributes Inspector.

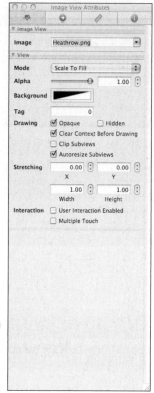

Figure 17-8:
Selecting
the Image.

8. **Drag from the little circle next to the `webView` outlet in the list onto the Web view.**

   Doing so connects the `webView` outlet of `AirportController` to the Web view.

9. **Drag from the little circle next to `toolbar` outlet in the list onto the toolbar you just added**

   When you're done, the contextual menu should look like Figure 17-10.

10. **Finally click in the view and deselect the Autoresize Subviews check box in the Attributes inspector, as I have in Figure 17-11.**

    Although you want to be able to support any orientation, because the width of the Master view and popover are fixed, you don't want the view to try and resize its subviews based on the orientation. (It will try to make them shorter and wider in landscape mode and taller and narrower in portrait mode.)

Figure 17-9:
The final
layout.

Figure 17-10:
All nicely
connected.

Setting up the view

Your `AirportController` is going to be getting the content for any view you've set up from the `Destination` object — content which it then passes on to the view itself. You use the `viewDidLoad` method to get your view nice and prepped for its big day. As I mention in Chapter 14, this method was included for you in `AirportController.m` by the `UIViewController` subclass template (albeit, commented out). The easiest thing to do is to delete this method and add the code in Listing 17-10.

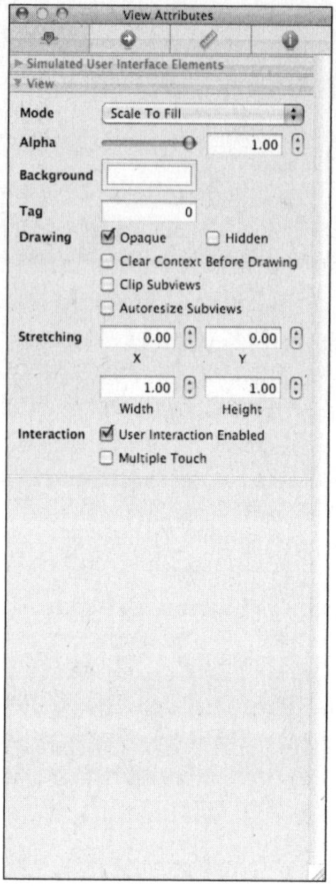

Figure 17-11:
Keeping
my views
exactly the
way they
are.

Listing 17-10: Setting Things Up in viewDidLoad

```
- (void)viewDidLoad {

  [super viewDidLoad];

  webView.delegate = self;

  segmentedControl = [[UISegmentedControl alloc]
          initWithItems: [NSArray arrayWithObjects:
          @"Train", @"Taxi", @"Other", nil]];
  [segmentedControl addTarget:self action:@
          selector(selectTransportation:) forControlEvent
          s:UIControlEventValueChanged];
  segmentedControl.segmentedControlStyle =
                          UISegmentedControlStyleBar;
  segmentedControl.tintColor = [UIColor darkGrayColor];
```

```
iPadTravel411AppDelegate *appDelegate =
        (iPadTravel411AppDelegate *) [[UIApplication
        sharedApplication] delegate];
CGRect segmentedControlFrame = ((UIViewController *)
        appDelegate.masterViewController).view.frame;
segmentedControlFrame.size.width =
                            kPopoverWidth - kLeftMargin;
segmentedControlFrame.size.height =  kSegControlHeight;
segmentedControl.frame =  segmentedControlFrame;
segmentedControl.selectedSegmentIndex = 0;

UIBarButtonItem *choiceItem = [[UIBarButtonItem alloc]
                initWithCustomView:segmentedControl];
theToolbar.items = [NSArray arrayWithObject:choiceItem];
[segmentedControl release];
[choiceItem release];
}
```

This is what you just did in viewDidLoad:.

1. **Make the `AirportController` the Web view's delegate.**

   ```
   webView.delegate = self;
   ```

2. **Create the segmented control that will go inside the toolbar**

   ```
   segmentedControl = [[UISegmentedControl alloc]
           initWithItems: [NSArray arrayWithObjects:
           @"Train", @"Taxi", @"Other", nil]];

    [segmentedControl addTarget:self action:@
           selector(selectTransportation:) forControlEven
           ts:UIControlEventValueChanged];
   segmentedControl.segmentedControlStyle =
                           UISegmentedControlStyleBar;
   segmentedControl.tintColor = [UIColor darkGrayColor];
   iPadTravel411AppDelegate *appDelegate =
           (iPadTravel411AppDelegate *)
             [[UIApplication sharedApplication] delegate];
   CGRect segmentedControlFrame = ((UIViewController *)
           appDelegate.masterViewController).view.frame;
   segmentedControlFrame.size.width =
                           kPopoverWidth - kLeftMargin;
   segmentedControlFrame.size.height = kSegControlHeight;
   segmentedControl.frame =  segmentedControlFrame;
   segmentedControl.selectedSegmentIndex = 0;
   ```

   In the first line of code, you're creating a segmented control and
   an array that specifies the text for each segment. You then set the
   Target-Action parameters saying that if a segment is tapped by
   the user (UIControlEventValueChanged), then the select
   Transportation: message is sent to self — in this case, self is the
   AirportController. You then compute the size of the segmented

control as you would for any other subview. The last line specifies the
initial segment (0) selected when the view is created; before the view
is displayed, the `selectTransportation::` message is sent to display the content associated with segment 0. (You can see the code for
`selectTransportation:` in all its glory in Listing 17-11.)

You also need to add the following constants to `Constants.h`.

```
#define kLeftMargin        16.0
#define kSegControlHeight  30.0
```

3. **Add the segmented control to the toolbar.**

```
UIBarButtonItem *choiceItem = [[UIBarButtonItem alloc]
initWithCustomView:segmentedControl];
theToolbar.items =
              [NSArray arrayWithObject:choiceItem];
[segmentedControl release];
[choiceItem release];
```

You get the `choiceBar` (`UIToolbar`) to display controls by creating an
array of instances of `UIBarButtonItem` and assigning the array to the
`items` property of the `UIToolbar` object (our `choiceBar`). In this case,
you create a `UIBarButtonItem` and initialize it with the segmented control you just created. You then create the array and assign it to `items`.

You then can release `choiceItem` because the `NSArray` has a reference to it.

At this point, you have the view set up, waiting for data, and the segmented
control across the top that will allow the user to select `@"Train"`, `@"Taxi"`,
`@"Other"`.

Responding to the user selection

You've set things up so that when the view is first created — or when
the user taps a control — the `selectTransportation:` method in
`AirportController` is called, allowing the `AirportController` to
hook up what the view needs to display with what the model has to offer.
Listing 17-11 shows the necessary code in all its elegance. Add this to
`AirportController.m`.

Listing 17-11:   selectTransportation

```
- (void)selectTransportation:(id) sender {

  [webView loadRequest:[NSURLRequest requestWithURL:
  [destination returnTransportation:
    (((UISegmentedControl*)
                        sender).selectedSegmentIndex)]]];
}
```

This is the code that gets executed when the user selects one of the segmented controls (Train, Taxi, Other) that you added to the view — (((UISegmentedControl*) sender).selectedSegmentIndex) gives you the segment number. If you'll notice, the controller has no idea — nor should it care — what was selected. It just passes what was selected on to the Destination object. That kind of logic should be (and, as you will soon see, *is*) in the model.

All this does is send a message to the Destination object to find out where the data the Web view needs is located, [destination return Transportation: (((UISegmentedControl*) sender).selected SegmentIndex)], and then send a message to the Web view to load it. This is more or less what you did in Chapter 11, but I explain more about the mechanics of this shortly. You also have to import Destination in AirportController.m.

Before I show you the code in the model that implements return Transportation:, I want to show you one other thing, and that's the implementation of the Back button. You'll be doing this in the same way you did when you implemented it in WeatherController in the "Cruising the Web" section, earlier in this chapter.

Start by adding the methods goBack: and webViewDidFinishLoad: in Listings 17-12 and 17-13 to AirportController.m — these methods are identical to the ones you added in the section "Cruising the Web."

Listing 17-12: goBack to Where You Once Belonged

```
- (IBAction) goBack:(id)sender{

  if ([webView  canGoBack] == NO ) {
    self.navigationItem.rightBarButtonItem = nil;
  }
  else {
    [webView goBack];
  }
}
```

Listing 17-13: You Don't Need the Back Button Any Longer

```
- (void)webViewDidFinishLoad:(UIWebView *) webView {
  if ([webView  canGoBack] == NO ) {
    self.navigationItem.rightBarButtonItem = nil;
  }
}
```

You also need to add the webView:shouldStartLoadWithRequest:nav
igationType: method as you did for the WeatherController. This time
it will be a little different. You'll be adding the method in Listing 17-14, but
you'll notice that this time there is some additional code.

That's because while you won't create the WeatherController if the app is
in stored data mode, you will create the AirportController. In this case,
though, because there are selectable links in the view, if the app is in shared
data model you'll want to disable them and inform the user about why you've
done so.

Listing 17-14: Adding and Implementing Back

```
- (BOOL)webView:(UIWebView *)webView
  shouldStartLoadWithRequest:(NSURLRequest *)request
  navigationType:(UIWebViewNavigationType)navigationType {

  if ((navigationType ==
          UIWebViewNavigationTypeLinkClicked) &&    (
          [[NSUserDefaults standardUserDefaults] boolForK
          ey:kUseStoredDataPreference]) ) {
    UIAlertView *alert = [[UIAlertView
          alloc] initWithTitle:@"" message:
          NSLocalizedString(@"Link not available
                            offline", @"stored data mode")
          delegate:self
          cancelButtonTitle:NSLocalizedString
          (@"Thanks", @"Thanks") otherButtonTitles: nil];
    [alert show];
    [alert release];
    return NO;
  }
  else
    if (navigationType ==
                    UIWebViewNavigationTypeLinkClicked) {
      UIBarButtonItem *backButton =
          [[UIBarButtonItem alloc] initWithTitle: @"Back"
          style:UIBarButtonItemStylePlain
          target:self action:@selector(goBack:)] ;
      self.navigationItem.rightBarButtonItem = backButton;
      [backButton release];
    }
  return YES;
}
```

Here's the process the code uses to get the job done for you:

1. **Check to see whether the user has touched an embedded link while in stored data mode.**

```
if ((navigationType ==
        UIWebViewNavigationTypeLinkClicked) &&
    ([[NSUserDefaults standardUserDefaults]
        boolForKey:kUseStoredDataPreference])) {
```

2. **If the user is in stored data mode, alert him or her to the fact that the link is unavailable, and return NO from the method.**

   This informs the Web view not to load the link. This isn't necessary here because you won't load the Web view, but it is the general way to handle things and you'll use it when you display your own view with external Web links.

```
UIAlertView *alert = [[UIAlertView alloc]
    initWithTitle:@""
    message: NSLocalizedString (@"Link not available
                        offline", @"stored data mode")
    delegate:self
    cancelButtonTitle:NSLocalizedString
        (@"Thanks", @"Thanks") otherButtonTitles: nil];
[alert show];
[alert release];
return NO;
```

   You create an alert here with a message telling the user that the link is not available in stored data mode. The Cancel button's text will be `@"Thanks"`.

3. **If you're not in stored data mode, add and enable the Back button.**

```
UIBarButtonItem *backButton =
                [[UIBarButtonItem alloc]
                initWithTitle:@"Back"
                style:UIBarButtonItemStylePlain
                target:self
                action:@selector(goBack:)];
self.navigationItem.rightBarButtonItem = backButton;
[backButton release];
```

   In this method, you allocate the button and then assign it to an instance variable that the `UINavigationController` will later use to set up the Navigation bar. This is what you also did previously in `WeatherController.m` back in the "Cruising the Web" section, earlier in this chapter.

4. **Return YES to tell the Web view to load from the Internet.**

Resetting the popover size

In Chapter 15, I show you how to override `contentSizeForViewIn PopoverView` method to set the popover size:

```
- (CGSize)contentSizeForViewInPopoverView {

    return CGSizeMake(kPopoverWidth, 400.0);
}
```

Of course, now that you'll be displaying a Content view in the Popover controller when the device is in portrait mode, you'll want to adjust the popover size appropriately. You need to do that in two places.

In the `AirportController viewWillAppear:` method, you set the new popover size to be 750 pixels. To do that, add the code in Listing 17-15 to `AirportController.m`.

Listing 17-15:   Setting the Popover Size for the Content

```
- (void)viewWillAppear:(BOOL)animated {
[super viewWillAppear:animated];

    iPadTravel411AppDelegate *appDelegate =
    (iPadTravel411AppDelegate *) [[UIApplication
                                sharedApplication] delegate];
    appDelegate.popoverController.popoverContentSize =
                        CGSizeMake(kPopoverWidth, 750.0);
}
```

Then, when the user hits the Back button, you want to reset the size to what's appropriate for the Table view. You'll do that in `viewWill Disappear:`, which is invoked right before you return to the Table view. Adding the code in Listing 17-16 to `AirportController.m` takes care of that.

Listing 17-16:   Resetting the Popover Height

```
- (void)viewWillDisappear:(BOOL)animated {

    [super viewWillDisappear:animated];

    iPadTravel411AppDelegate *appDelegate =
        (iPadTravel411AppDelegate *) [[UIApplication
                                sharedApplication] delegate];
appDelegate.popoverController.popoverContentSize =
                        CGSizeMake(kPopoverWidth, 400.00;
}
```

The Destination Model

You're starting to get all your pieces lined up. Now it's time to take a look at what happens when the controller sends messages to the model.

The well-defined `Destination` interface, which I spoke about in Chapter 13 and is seen in Listing 17-17, shows us what you will have to add to support the `AirportController`.

Listing 17-17: Destination.h

```
#import <Foundation/Foundation.h>
#import <MapKit/MapKit.h>
@class Airport;

@interface Destination : NSObject {

  NSString   *destinationName;
  Airport    *airport;
}
- (id) initWithName: (NSString*) theDestination;
- (CLLocationCoordinate2D) initialCoordinate;
- (NSString*)mapTitle;
- (NSMutableArray*) createAnnotations;
- (NSURL*) weather;
- (NSString*) returnAirportName: (int) theAirportID;
- (NSURL*) returnTransportation: (int) aType;

@end
```

The first method here should look familiar to you because you used it when you initialized the `AirportController` object in the "Adding the Destination Model" section, in Chapter 14. The next method is invoked from the `selectTransportation:` method in `AirportController`.

Take a look at how `returnTransportation:` works. Start by adding the code in Listing 17-18 to `Destination.m`.

Listing 17-18: Returning the Transportation Link

```
- (NSURL*) returnTransportation: (int) aType {
  return [airport returnTransportation: aType];
}
```

Hmm. All this does is turn around and send a message to another model object, `Airport`. I explain all this indirection in the next section, but for now, take a look at what goes on in the `Airport` object.

First you have to declare the `Airport` class, which defines the `Airport` object you are going to create:

1. **Choose File⇨New File from the main menu (or press ⌘+N) to get the New File dialog.**

2. **In the leftmost column of the dialog, first select Cocoa Touch Classes under the iPhone OS heading and then select the *Objective-C class* template in the topmost pane, making sure that `NSObject` is selected in the Subclass Of drop-down menu. Then click Next.**

   You see a new dialog asking for some more information.

3. **Enter** Airport **in the File Name field and then click Finish.**

Now you can create the `Airport` object. Add the code in Listing 17-19 to the `initWithName:` method in `Destination.m`.

Listing 17-19:   Creating the Airport Object

```
- (id) initWithName: (NSString*) theDestination {
  if ((self = [super init])) {
    destinationName = theDestination;
    airport = [[Airport alloc] initWithName:
           NSLocalizedString(@"Heathrow", @"Heathrow")
                                              airportID:1];

  }
  return self;
}
```

You also have to add `returnAirportName:` method to `Destination` as well. Add the code in Listing 17-20.

Listing 17-20:   returnAirportName

```
- (NSString*)returnAirportName:(int) theAirportID {

    return airport.airportName;
}
```

In this case, there's only one airport, but when you implement multiple airports, `Destination` would send the `airportName` message to the `Airport` that corresponded to the `AirportID`.

Now that you've seen all the things the `Airport` object is responsible for, you're going to have to "build" one.

Building the Airport

To start work on the `Airport` object, take a look at the methods you'll need to implement. Add the code in Listing 17-21 to `Airport.h`. You also need to add an `@synthesize airportName` to generate the accessors for the `airportName`.

Listing 17-21: Airport.h

```
#import <Foundation/Foundation.h>
#import <MapKit/MapKit.h>
@interface Airport : NSObject {

  NSString *airportName;
}

- (id) initWithName: (NSString*) name airportID: (int)
          theAirport;
- (NSURL*) returnTransportation: (int) transportationType;
- (NSURL*) getAirportData: (NSString*) fileName;
- (void) saveAirportData: (NSString*) fileName
                              withDataURL: (NSURL*) url;
@property (nonatomic, retain)    NSString *airportName;


@end
```

The first method in Listing 17-21 is your run-of-the-mill initialization method. To get the method to work, add the code in Listing 17-22 to `Airport.m`.

Listing 17-22: Initializing the Airport

```
- (id) initWithName: (NSString*) name
                         airportID: (int) theAirport {

  if ((self = [super init])) {
    self.AirportName = name;

  }
  return self;
}
```

The second method in Listing 17-21 should look familiar to you because it was just used in the `Destination` method `returnTransportation:`. The last two are internal methods that are used only by the model itself.

If you're coming from C++, you probably want these last two methods to be private, but there's no private construct in Objective-C. To hide them, you could have moved their declarations to the implementation file and created an Objective-C category. Here's what that would look like:

```
@interface Airport  ()
- (NSURL*) getAirportData: (NSString*) fileName;
- (void) saveAirportData: (NSString*) fileName
                                withDataURL: (NSURL*) url;
@end
```

In Listing 17-23, you can see the `returnTransportation:` method. Add this code to `Airport.m`.

Listing 17-23: Airport Model Method Used by Destination

```
- (NSURL*)returnTransportation:(int) transportationType  {

  NSURL *url = [[NSURL alloc] autorelease];
  iPadTravel411AppDelegate *appDelegate =
          (iPadTravel411AppDelegate *) [[UIApplication
          sharedApplication] delegate];
  BOOL realtime = !appDelegate.useStoredData;
  if (realtime) {
    switch (transportationType) {
      case 0: {
        url = [NSURL URLWithString:
            @"http://nealgoldstein.com/ToFromiPad100.html"];
          [self saveAirportData:
                        @"ToFromiPad100" withDataURL:url];
        break;
      }
      case 1: {
        url = [NSURL URLWithString:
            @"http://nealgoldstein.com/ToFromiPad101.html"];
          [self saveAirportData:
                        @"ToFromiPad101" withDataURL:url];
        break;
      }
      case 2: {
        url = [NSURL URLWithString:
            @"http://nealgoldstein.com/ToFromiPad102.html"];
          [self saveAirportData:
                        @"ToFromiPad102" withDataURL:url];
        break;
      }
    }
  }
  else  {
```

```
    switch (transportationType) {
      case 0:    {
        url = [self getAirportData:@"ToFromiPad100"];
        break;
      }
      case 1: {
        url =   [self getAirportData:@"ToFromiPad101"];
        break;
      }
      case 2: {
        url = [self getAirportData:@"ToFromiPad102"];
        break;
      }
    }
  }
  return url;
}
```

When a message is sent to the model to return the data the view needs to display, it's passed the number of the segmented control that was touched (Train, Taxi, Other). It's the model's responsibility to decide what data is required here.

The data for each of the choices in the segmented control is on a Web site — www.nealgoldstein.com, to be precise. First, the method checks to see whether the user is online or wants to use stored data.

```
BOOL realtime = !appDelegate.useStoredData;
  if (realtime) {
```

If the user is online, the method constructs the NSURL object that the Web view uses to load the data. (The NSURL object is nothing fancy. To refresh your memory, it's simply an object that includes the utilities necessary for downloading files or other resources from Web and FTP servers or accessing local files.)

```
NSURL *url = [NSURL URLWithString:
         @"http://nealgoldstein.com/ToFromiPad100.html"];
```

Then the saveAirportData: message is sent:

```
[self saveAirportData:@"ToFromiPad100" withDataURL: url ];
return url;
```

The saveAirportData method in Listing 17-24 downloads and saves the file containing the latest data for whatever transportation (Taxi, for example) the user selected. It's what will be displayed in the current view, and it'll be used later if the user specifies stored data mode. Add that to `Airport.m`.

Listing 17-24:   Saving Airport Data

```
- (void)saveAirportData:(NSString*) fileName withDataURL:
                                               (NSURL*) url {

  NSData *dataLoaded = [NSData
                               dataWithContentsOfURL:url];
  if (dataLoaded == NULL)
                         NSLog(@"Data not found %@", url);
  NSArray *paths = NSSearchPathForDirectoriesInDomains
            (NSDocumentDirectory, NSUserDomainMask, YES);
  NSString *documentsDirectory = [paths objectAtIndex:0];
  NSString *filePath = [documentsDirectory
                stringByAppendingPathComponent:fileName];
  [dataLoaded writeToFile:filePath atomically:YES];
}
```

You did the exact same thing in Chapter 16 when you saved the current state of the application. If you need a refresher here, go back and work through that part of Chapter 16 again.

I've added an `NSLog` message if the data can't be found. This is a placeholder for error-handling that I've left as an exercise for the reader.

This is definitely not the most efficient way to implement saving files for later use, but given the relatively small amount of data involved, the impact is not noticeable. You would want to give the user a specific option to download all the data for any city, eliminating going to the Internet twice — once to download and save the data and then again to display the page.

If the user wants stored data to be used, the method returns the stored data as opposed to loading the data for its URL on the Internet. It gets the data by calling the `getAirportData:` method, which reads the data that was stored in `saveAirportData:`.

```
return  [self getAirportData:@"ToFromiPad100"];
```

`getAirportData:` also constructs a `NSURL` object that the Web view uses to load the data. Remember that the `NSURL` is more than an object that includes the utilities necessary for downloading files from Web and FTP servers. It also works for local files, and in fact, `NSURL` objects are the preferred way to load the files you'll be interested in.

So you find the path and construct the NSURL object using that path. This is shown in Listing 17-25.

Listing 17-25:   Getting the Saved Airport Data

```
-  (NSURL*)getAirportData:(NSString*) fileName{

  NSArray *paths = NSSearchPathForDirectoriesInDomains
           (NSDocumentDirectory, NSUserDomainMask, YES);
  NSString *documentsDirectory = [paths objectAtIndex:0];
  NSString *filePath = [documentsDirectory
              stringByAppendingPathComponent:fileName];
  NSURL* theNSURL= [NSURL fileURLWithPath: filePath];
  if (theNSURL == NULL) NSLog (@"Data not there");
  return  theNSURL;
}
```

When all is said and done, you will get what you see in Figure 17-12 when
the user selects Heathrow in the Master view and keeps a map visible in the
Detail view.

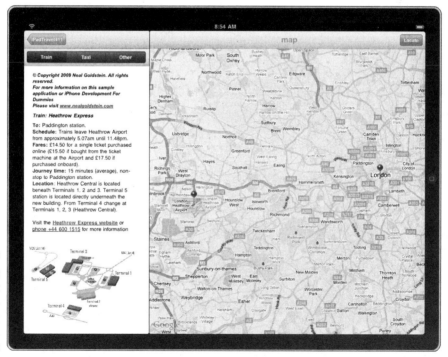

Figure 17-12:
Airport
transporta-
tion inform
and a map.

Selecting the airport

In the "Navigating the Navigation controller" section, earlier in this chapter, I
explained that the logic for handling the selection of a row by the user was in

`tableView:didSelectRowAtIndexPath`. I also had you comment out the airport selection. You can now uncomment out that line.

```
targetController = [[AirportController alloc]
            initWithDestination: destination airportID:1];
```

I also said I'd explain this code:

```
if ([targetController isKindOfClass:
                            [AirportController class]])
  [[self navigationController]
      pushViewController:targetController animated:YES];
else
if (targetController)
  [[appDelegate.detailViewController navigationController]
```

Because the Airport controller will display its view in the Master view, you need to be able to determine if the target controller you created is an Airport controller. If it is, you push it on the Master view controller's Navigation controller stack.

```
[[self navigationController]
      pushViewController:targetController animated:YES];
```

You do this instead of what you did in the case of the Weather controller — pushing it on the Detail view controller stack.

```
[[appDelegate.detailViewController navigationController]
      pushViewController:targetController animated:YES];
```

The way you decide which controller's stack to push things on is simply by asking the object what kind of class it is:

```
if ([targetController isKindOfClass:
                            [AirportController class]])
```

`isKindOfClass` is an `NSObject` protocol method that `NSObject` implements. It returns a Boolean value that indicates whether the object is an instance of a given class (in this case, the AirportController class) or an instance of any class that inherits from that class.

Putting the Airport on the Map

One of the reasons I had you create an `Airport` object is not simply to annoy you with yet another class; it's because (besides the fact it does a good job of encapsulating the logic) `Airport` also allows you to use it as an annotation on a map.

As I explained in Chapter 14, the best kind of annotations are the objects found in your program. In this case, that means the Airport(s) and the City objects (although I'll leave you to implement City on your own).

Annotation objects are any object that conform to the MKAnnotation protocol and are typically existing classes in your application's model. The job of an annotation object is to know its location (coordinate) on the map along with the text to be displayed in the callout. The MKAnnotation protocol requires a class that adopts that protocol to implement the coordinate property. In this case, it will make sense for the Airport and City model objects to add the responsibilities of an annotation object to their bag of tricks. After all, the Airport and City model objects already know what airport or city they represent, respectively. It makes sense for these objects to have the coordinate and title and subtitle data as well.

Airport will be adopting the MKAnnotation protocol. There are three elements to this protocol:

1. A required property coordinate.

2. An optional title method.

3. An optional subtitle method.

Add the code in Listing 17-26 to Airport.h.

Listing 17-26: Making Airport an Annotation

```
#import <Foundation/Foundation.h>
#import <MapKit/MapKit.h>


@interface Airport : NSObject <MKAnnotation> {

  NSString *airportName;
  CLLocationCoordinate2D  coordinate;
}
- (id) initWithName: (NSString*) name airportID: (int)
          theAirport;
- (NSURL*) returnTransportation: (int) transportationType;
- (NSURL*) getAirportData: (NSString*) fileName;
- (void) saveAirportData: (NSString*) fileName
          withDataURL: (NSURL*) url;
@property (nonatomic, retain)   NSString *airportName;
@property (nonatomic) CLLocationCoordinate2D coordinate;

@end
```

Next add the code in Listing 17-27 to `Airport.m`.

Listing 17-27:   Adding the Annotation Implementation

```
@implementation Airport
@synthesize airportName;
@synthesize coordinate;

- (id) initWithName: (NSString*) name airportID: (int)
        theAirport {

  if ((self = [super init])) {
    airportName = name;
    coordinate.latitude = 51.471184;
    coordinate.longitude= -0.452542;
  }
  return self;
}
- (NSString*)title {

  return airportName;
}
```

You're having `Airport` initialize the coordinate property and implementing the (optional) `title` method. Next you'll have to change the code in
`Destination` that creates the array of annotation objects.

Make the changes in Listing 17-28 to do that.

Listing 17-28:   Adding Airport to the Annotations Arrays

```
- (NSMutableArray*) createAnnotations {

  CLLocationCoordinate2D theCoordinate;
// theCoordinate.latitude = 51.471184;
// theCoordinate.longitude = -0.452542;
// MapAnnotation* sampleAnnotation =   [[MapAnnotation
        alloc] initWithTitle: @"Heathrow" subTitle:
        @"International Airport" coordinate:
        theCoordinate];
  NSMutableArray* mapAnnotations = [[NSMutableArray alloc]
        initWithCapacity:1];
// [mapAnnotations addObject:sampleAnnotation];
// [sampleAnnotation release];
  [mapAnnotations addObject:airport];
  MapAnnotation* sampleAnnotation;
  theCoordinate.latitude = 51.500153;
  theCoordinate.longitude= -0.126236;
```

```
sampleAnnotation =    [[MapAnnotation  alloc]
        initWithTitle: @"London"  subTitle:
        @"Your destination" coordinate: theCoordinate];
[mapAnnotations addObject:sampleAnnotation];
[sampleAnnotation release];
return mapAnnotations;
}
```

All you have to do is add the `Airport` object to the `mapAnnotations` array that `Destination` creates for the map controller. You would do something similar to add a `City` object, or even something like an `Attraction` object like the Tower of London (something to explore on your own).

The Currency Implementation Model

If the user selects Currency from the Main view in the iPadTravel411 application, he or she will see some very basic information about exchange rates, as illustrated in Figure 17-13. Because this information changes rarely (if ever), I'm going to include this information in the application. The way to do this is to include it as a resource.

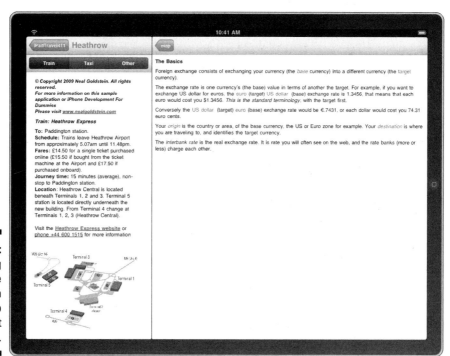

Figure 17-13:
Reading about the pound on your way to buy a ticket on the train.

The Currency view controller, view, and model follow the same pattern laid down by the Airport and Weather implementations. Again, the complete code is on my Web site at www.nealgoldstein.com. There are only a few differences I need to point out.

Currency is always offline, which means it's a great way to show you how to implement static data. Since this information about foreign exchange will hardly ever change, it works to include the information in the application itself.

The content for the Currency view is in a file I created called Currencies. html. To make it available to the application, I need to include it in the application bundle itself,

Now, you can add it to your bundle one of two ways:

✔ Open the Project window and drag an .html file into the Project folder, like you did the icon in Chapter 5.

It's a good idea to create a new folder within your project folder as a snug little home for the file. (I named my new folder Static Data.)

Or

✔ Select Project⇨Add to Project and then use the dialog that appears to navigate to and select the file you want

The only thing interesting here is that you're going to use some data that you've included with your application as a *resource* (which you can think of as an included file, although it doesn't live in the iPad file system but rather is embedded in the application itself).

In Listing 17-29, you can see that, just as with the WeatherController, the CurrencyController tells its Web view to load a URL that it requests from the Destination object.

Listing 17-29: viewDidLoad

```
- (void)viewDidLoad {

  [super viewDidLoad];
  [webView loadRequest:[NSURLRequest requestWithURL:
                        [destination currencyBasics]]];

}
```

In Listing 17-30 you can see the `returnCurrencyBasics` method that you would need to add to `Destination`. You can see how the `returnCurrency Basics` method in the `Destination.m` file constructs the `NSURL`.

Listing 17-30:   returnCurrencyBasics Method

```
-  (NSURL*)currencyBasics {

   NSString *filePath = [[NSBundle mainBundle]
          pathForResource:@"Currencies" ofType:@"html"];
   NSURL* currencyData= [NSURL fileURLWithPath: filePath];
   return currencyData;
}
```

In this case, you're using `pathForResource::`, which is an `NSBundle` method to construct the `NSURL`. (You used an `NSBundle` method when you got the application name in the `RootViewController` to set the title on the main window back in Chapter 14.) Just give `pathForResource::` the name and the file type.

Be sure you provide the right file type; otherwise, this technique won't work.

What's Next?

If I were to actually implement this application on the iPad (which I am), there are some things I would do differently.

Instead of pushing a view controller in the Detail view, I would simply replace the view (and sometimes the view controller itself). Web view would allow me to replace the view, but switching from, say, a map to a Weather view with different view controllers would require that the view controllers replace themselves instead. This would remove some of the linearity from the applications. So, instead of using the right button on the Navigation bar to get back to the previous view and view controller, I would display the Master view button to enable the user to select a new view to appear in the Detail view. I'm sorry to say that is beyond the scope of this book, so I leave it up to you to explore on your own.

The second thing you should be aware of is the issue of content. Most of the views I showed you have limited content, and frankly they look really skimpy. I'll leave it up to you to add your own rich content because that's what makes the iPad really shine.

Although this point marks the end of your guided tour of iPad Software Development, it should also be the start — if you haven't started already — of your own development work.

Developing for the iPad is one of the most exciting opportunities I've come across in a long time. I'm hoping it ends up being as exciting — and perhaps less stressful — an opportunity for you. Keep in touch, check out my Web site at www.nealgoldstein.com for updates and what's new, and keep having fun. I hope I have the opportunity to download one of your applications from the App Store someday.

Part VI
The Part of Tens

"Hold on Barbara. I'm pretty sure there's an app for this."

In this part . . .

You've reached the last part, the part you've come to expect in every *For Dummies* book that neatly encapsulates just about all the interesting aspects of this book's topic. Like the compilers of other important lists — David Letterman's Top Ten, the FBI's Ten Most Wanted, the Seven Steps to Heaven, the 12 Gates to the City, the 12 Steps to Recovery, The 13 Question Method, and the Billboard Hot 100 — we take seriously this ritual of putting together the *For Dummies* Part of Tens.

- In Chapter 18, we offer ten important iPad app design tips that can help you create a more successful app. Included are tips on when your app should save data, how your app should handle starting and stopping, how to support all display orientations, and even how to submit a potent app icon.

- Chapter 19 presents ten techniques for attaining iPad developer enlightenment (or just ways to be happy). Included are tips on following memory management rules, planning ahead to extend your code, and creating code that's easy to understand.

Chapter 18

Ten Tips on iPad App Design

*W*hen John Reed wrote *Ten Days that Shook the World* in 1919, he was writing about a different kind of revolution than the one Steve Jobs referred to in his announcement of the iPad. For this revolution, I put together ten tips that will shake up your thoughts about application design, especially if you're familiar with iPhone app design. There are important differences to know about, and these tips will help you make your iPad app more successful.

You can find more details about each and every one of these tips in the *iPad Human Interface Guidelines* inside the iPhone OS Reference Library. Chapter 4 shows you how to register as a developer and gain access to this library and other resources in Apple's iPhone Dev Center.

Making an App Icon for the Masses

With over 150,000 apps in the App Store, it's a challenge to come up with an icon for your app that would make it stand out in the App Store and look unique and inviting to touch on an iPad display.

Don't even think about using an Apple image, such as an iPad (or iPhone or iPod) in your icon, or you'll most likely receive a polite, but firm, e-mail rejecting the application.

Chapter 9 shows you how to add your icon to your app, and Chapter 6 spells out the details of what form your icon should take — including the fact that you need to use the same (or very similar) graphic image for the small app icon on the iPad display (at 72 x 72 pixels) you'll use for the larger App Store icon (at 512 x 512 pixels). You also need to supply an approximately 48 x 48-pixel version of this icon for display in Spotlight search results and in the Settings application (if you provide settings).

As with iPhone application icons, the iPhone OS on the iPad automatically adds rounded corners, a reflective shine, and a drop shadow, so you shouldn't add those effects to your icon. Create an icon with 90-degree corners and without any shine or gloss (or alpha transparency), and save it in the `.png` format to submit to Apple.

Make sure you fill the entire 72 x 72-pixel area — if your image boundaries are smaller, or you use transparency to create see-through areas within it, your icon will appear to float on a black background with rounded corners. Although this may seem fine at first, remember that users can display custom pictures on their Home screens, and an icon with a visible black background looks bad.

Launching Your App Into View

I go into considerable detail in Chapter 8 about how an app starts up and displays a view. Although the chapter is long and takes a while to read, the iPhone OS on the iPad performs these functions instantaneously — so fast that the view appears instantly.

You should take advantage of the speed of the app launch to display an image that represents the heart of your app's functionality — such as one that resembles the most common view of the app's user interface — in the iPad's current orientation. (See "Supporting All Display Orientations," later in this chapter.) You may think you want to use an About window (with your brand image) or a splash screen, but that slows app startup, and your users will see it every time they start your app. Better to use a simple, stripped-down screen shot of your app's initial user interface or a similar image with only the constant, unvarying elements of the user interface. Avoid all text because you don't want to go through the nightmare of providing different images for different countries.

Your goal during startup should be to present your app's user interface as quickly as possible. Don't load large data structures that your app won't use right away. If your app requires time to load data from the network (or perform other tasks that take a noticeable amount of time), get your interface up and running first and then launch the slow task on a background thread. Then you can display a progress indicator or other feedback to the user to indicate that your app is loading the necessary data or otherwise doing something important.

Stopping Your App on a Dime

When the user presses the Home button, your app comes to an immediate stop, but it shouldn't crumble as if it hit a brick wall. You need to provide a good stopping experience — or more to the point, a good restarting experience for the user who quits and then returns to your app.

If you save data in your app frequently, your app will quit more gracefully without requiring the user to tap a Save button. (See "Saving Grace with Your App's Data," later in this chapter.) Your app needs to save user data while it's running, and as often as reasonable, because an exit or terminate notification — like Immigration or the Spanish Inquisition — can arrive at any time. And be sure to save the current state when stopping, at the finest level of detail possible, because users expect to return to their earlier context when they restart your app. For example, if you use a Split view in your app, store the current selection in the master pane and be sure to display that selection again when the user restarts your app.

For example, in Chapter 10 and 11 you add code to the DeepThoughts app that saves the user's preference settings as they're set (the text for the flowing words, and the animation speed). When the user restarts DeepThoughts, it uses the user's settings for the falling words and speed.

Saving Grace with Your App's Data

Don't force your users to tap a Save button. iPad apps should take responsibility for saving the user's input, not only periodically but also when a user opens a different document or quits the app.

This design goal addresses the very essence of the iPad experience: that users should feel comfortable consuming information and have complete confidence that their work is always preserved (unless they explicitly delete the work or cancel). If your app lets users create and edit documents, design it so that users don't have to explicitly perform saves. If your app doesn't create content but lets users switch between viewing information and editing it (such as Contacts), your app can offer an Edit button that turns into a Save button when users tap it, and the app can include a Cancel button when that happens. By doing both, your app reminds the users that they're in edit mode and that they can either save the edits or cancel.

If your app uses popovers, you should always save information that users enter in a popover (unless they explicitly cancel) because users may dismiss the popover inadvertently.

Supporting All Display Orientations

As you probably know (or read in Chapter 2), when you rotate the iPad from a vertical view (portrait) to a horizontal view (landscape), the accelerometer detects the movement and changes the display accordingly. Motion detection happens so quickly that you can control a game with these movements.

This is important: iPad users expect apps to run well in the device orientation they're currently using. As much as possible, your app should enable users to interact with it from any side by providing a great experience in all orientations.

For example, the iPad app's launch image should be ready to launch in any of the four orientations — so you need to provide four unique launch images. Each launch image should be in the .png format and should match the size of the iPad display in either portrait orientation (1,024 x 768 pixels) or landscape orientation (768 x 1,024 pixels).

Flattening Information Levels

If you've developed for the iPhone, you want to rethink your app design goals for the iPad. One technique in particular is the one-level-per-screen structure of iPhone apps, which forces your information into a hierarchy of screens resembling an upside-down tree (with the first screen acting as the root). As you tap an option on a screen, you go deeper into the upside-down tree into more detailed or more specific screens.

Although this structure makes sense for the iPhone's smaller display that can hold only one screen at a time, for your iPad app you need to flatten this structure — spread the information out horizontally rather than in a vertically-oriented tree structure — so that it doesn't force iPad users to visit many different screens of information to find what they want. They have one large display, so use it. Focus the app's Main view on the primary content and provide additional information or tools in an auxiliary view, such as a popover. (See "Popping Up All Over," later in this chapter.)

Your app needs to provide easy access to the functionality users need, without requiring them to leave the context of the main task. For example, in Chapter 15 you take a Table view for the iPadTravel411 sample app, which is appropriate for an iPhone app, and implement it as one of the views of a *Split view* (two views on the display at once), which is more appropriate for an iPad app. Use a Split view to persistently display the top level of a hierarchy in the left pane and content that changes in the right pane, as shown in Figure 18-1. This flattens your information hierarchy by at least one level, because two levels are always onscreen at the same time.

Figure 18-1:
The split screen design for iPad Travel411 in landscape orientation.

Popping Up All Over

A popover appears, or pops up on top of, the Main view when a user taps a control or an area of the display. You can use a popover to enable actions or provide tools that affect objects in the Main view. A popover can display these actions and tools temporarily on top of the current view, which means people don't have to move on to another view to perform the actions or use the tools.

You can put almost anything in a popover, from tables, images, maps, text, or Web views to Navigation bars, toolbars, and controls. A popover can be useful for displaying the contents of the landscape orientation's left pane when a Split view–based application is in portrait orientation. For example, in Chapter 15 you find out how to display the Master view that you see in landscape orientation in a Popover view in portrait orientation, as shown in Figure 18-2.

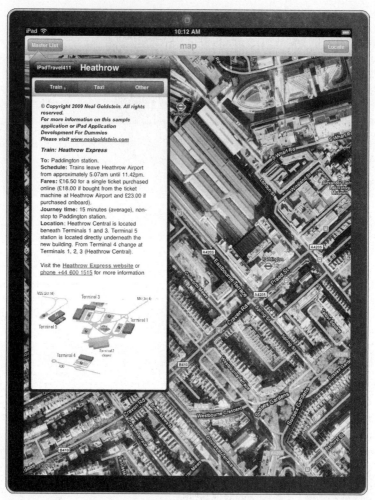

Figure 18-2:
A popover shows the Master view for iPad Travel411 in portrait orientation.

Minimizing Modality to Maximize Simplicity

Yo! Keep it simple! Keep those Modal views to a minimum. A Modal view is a child window, like a dialog in Mac OS X, that appears on top of the parent window (the Main view) and requires the user to interact with it before returning to the parent window. I know, I showed you how to add a Modal view in DeepThoughts in Chapter 11, but that one is for one purpose only — to change the preference settings — and users can choose whether or not to tap the display (or the Info button) to bring it up.

You don't want to annoy users with modal dialogs that force them to perform a task or supply a response. iPad apps should react to taps in flexible, nonlinear ways. Remember that modality prevents freedom of movement through your app by interrupting the user's workflow and forcing the user to choose a particular path. In general, you should use modality only when it's critical to get the user's attention, or a task must be completed (or explicitly abandoned) to avoid leaving the user's data in an ambiguous state, such as unsaved. Got that?

And if you must use a Modal view, keep the modal tasks fairly short and narrowly focused. You don't want your users to experience a Modal view as a mini application within your application.

Turning the Map into the Territory

As you discover in Chapter 14, working with maps is one of the most fun things you can do on the iPad because Apple makes it so easy — you can display a map that supports the standard panning and zooming gestures by simply creating a view controller and a nib file. You can also center the map on a given coordinate, specify the size of the area you want to display, and annotate the map with custom information.

You can also specify the map type — regular, satellite, or hybrid — by changing a single property. For many apps one type may work better than another, but consider using hybrid so that your app displays streets and highways superimposed over the satellite image. What you should do is provide a control for the user to make the choice between all three types.

Making Smaller Transitions (Don't Flip the View)

The iPad's display is inherently immersive; many things can be going on inside a single view. It's far better to change or update only the areas of the view that need it, rather than swapping in a whole new full-page view when some embedded information changes (as you would probably do in an iPhone app).

Don't flip the entire view if something needs to change. Do transitions with smaller views and objects. Associate any visual transitions with the content that's changing. Use a Split view so that only one part of the view changes (see "Flattening Information Levels," earlier in this chapter), or use a popover for information that changes, to lessen the need for a full-screen transition. (See "Popping Up All Over," earlier in this chapter.) As a result, your app will appear to be more visually stable, and users will feel confident that they know where they are in a given task.

Chapter 19

Ten Ways to Be a Happy Developer

In This Chapter
▶ Finding out how not to paint yourself into a corner
▶ Avoiding "There's no way to get there from here."

There are lots of things you know you're supposed to do, but you don't because you think they'll never catch up with you. (After all, not flossing won't cause you problems until your teeth fall out years from now, right?)

But in iPad (and iPhone) application development, those things catch up with you early and often, so I want to tell you about the things I've learned to pay attention to from the very start in app development, as well as a few tips and tricks that lead to happy and healthy users.

It's Never Too Early to Start Speaking a Foreign Language

With the world growing even flatter, and with the iPad available in more than 80 countries, the potential market for your app is considerably larger than just the people who happen to speak English. *Localizing* an application — getting your app to speak the lingo of its user, whether that be Portuguese or Polish — isn't difficult, just tedious. Some of it you can get away with doing late in the project, but when it comes to the strings you use in your application, you'd better build them right — and build them in from the start. The painless way: Use the `NSLocalizedString` macro (refer to Chapter 16) from the very start, and you'll still be a happy camper at the end.

Remember Memory

The iPad OS doesn't store changeable memory (such as object data) on the disk as a way to free up space and then read it back in later when needed. It also doesn't have garbage collection — which means there is a real potential for memory leaks unless you tidy up after your app. Review and follow the memory rules in Chapter 8 — in particular, these:

- ✔ Memory management is really creating *pairs* of messages. Balance every `alloc`, `new`, and `retain` with a `release`.
- ✔ When you assign an instance variable using an accessor with a property attribute of `retain`, you now own the object. When you're done with it, release it in a `dealloc` method.

Constantly Use Constants

In the iPadTravel411 application, I put all my constants in one file. When I develop my own applications, I do the same. The why of it is simple: As I change things during the development process, having *one* place to find my constants makes life much easier.

Don't Fall Off the Cutting Edge

The iPad is cutting edge enough that there are still plenty of opportunities to expand its capabilities — and many of them are (relatively) easy to implement. You're also working with a very mature framework. So if you think something you want your app to do is going to be *really* difficult, check the framework; somewhere in there you may find an easy way to do what you have in mind. If there isn't a ready-made fix, consider the iPad's limited resources — and at least question whether that nifty task you had in mind is something your app should be doing at all. Then again, if you really *need* to track orbital debris with an iPad app, go for it — someone needs to lead the way. Why shouldn't it be you?

Start by Initializing the Right Way

A lot of my really messy code that I found myself re-doing ended up that way because I didn't think through initialization. (For example, adding on initialization-like methods after objects are already initialized is a little late in the game, and so on.)

Keep the Order Straight

One of the things that can really foul up your day as a developer is the order in which methods in objects are called. If you expect an object to be there (and it isn't) or to have been initialized (and it wasn't), you may be in the wrong method. Type up a copy Table 19-1 in a file and/or make a photocopy of it and tack it up where you can easily find it. It shows you in crisp, tabular form the order in which objects are called — from soup (View Controller) to nuts (Delegate).

Table 19-1	The Natural Order of Things
Object	**Method**
View Controller	`awakeFromNib`
Application Delegate	`application:didFinishLaunchingWithOptions:`
View Controller	`viewDidLoad`
View Controller	`viewWillAppear:`
View Controller	`viewWillDisappear:`
Delegate	`applicationWillTerminate:`

What trips up many developers is that the `awakeFromNib` message for the initial view controller (the one you see when the application starts) is sent *before* the `applicationDidFinishLaunching:` message. If you have a problem with that, do what you need to do in `ViewDidLoad`.

Avoid Mistakes in Error Handling

A lot of opportunities for errors are out there; use common sense in figuring out which ones you should spend work time on.

There are, however, some potential pitfalls you do have to pay attention to, such as these two big ones:

- ✔ Your app goes out to load something off the Internet, and (for a variety of reasons) the item isn't there or the app can't get to it.
- ✔ An object can't initialize itself (for a similar range of perverse reasons).

When, not if, those things happen, your code and your user interface must be able to deal with the error.

Remember the User

I've been singing this song since Chapter 2, and I'm still singing it now: Keep your app simple and easy to use. Don't build long pages that take lots of scrolling to get through, and don't create really deep hierarchies. Focus on what the user wants to accomplish and be mindful of the device limitations, especially battery life. And don't forget international roaming charges.

In other words, try to follow the Apple's iPad Human Interface Guidelines, found with all the other documentation in the iPhone Dev Center Web site at `http://developer.apple.com/iphone` under the iPhone Reference Library section — Required Reading. Don't even *think* about bending those rules until you really, *really* understand them.

Keep in Mind that the Software Isn't Finished Until the Last User Is Dead

If there's one thing I can guarantee about app development, it's that Nobody Gets It Right the First Time. The design for all of my apps evolved over time, as I learned the capabilities and intricacies of the platform and the impact of my design changes. Object-orientation makes extending your application (not to mention fixing bugs) easier, so pay attention to the principles.

Keep It Fun

When I started programming the iPhone and then the iPad, it was the most fun I'd had in years. Keep things in perspective: Except for a few tedious tasks (such as provisioning and getting your application into the Apple Store), lo, I prophesy: Developing iPad apps will be fun for you, too. So don't take it *too* seriously.

Especially remember the *fun* part at 4 a.m., when you've spent the last five hours looking for a bug. Here's a handy way to do that: check out what Douglas Adams says about the *Hitchhiker's Guide to the Galaxy* entry for surviving in space: "It says that if you hold a lungful of air you can survive in a total vacuum of space for about thirty seconds. However, it does go on to say that what with space being the mind-boggling size it is the chances of getting picked up by another ship within those thirty seconds are two to the power of two hundred and seventy-six thousand, seven hundred and nine to one against." Now, get back to work!

Index